DATE

OCT 0

PEACE MOVEMENTS OF THE WORLD

PEACE MOVEMENTS
OF THE WORLD

Edited by

ALAN J. DAY

A KEESING'S REFERENCE PUBLICATION

Longman

PEACE MOVEMENTS OF THE WORLD

Published by Longman Group UK Limited, Longman House,
Burnt Mill, Harlow, Essex, CM20 2JE, United Kingdom

Distributed exclusively in the United States and Canada
by The Oryx Press, Suite 103, 2214 North Central at Encanto,
Phoenix, Arizona 85004, United States of America

ISBN 0–582–90268–1 (Longman)
      0–89774–438–1 (Oryx)

British Library Cataloguing in Publication Data
Peace movements of the world.——(A Keesing's
  reference publication)
    1. Peace——Societies, etc.——Directories
    I. Day, Alan J.   II. Series
    327.1'72'025   JX1905.5

    ISBN 0–582–90268–1

Printed in the United Kingdom by
The Eastern Press, London and Reading

CONTENTS

KEESING'S REFERENCE PUBLICATIONS

The Keesing's Reference Publications (KRP) series of books has been developed as an adjunct to *Keesing's Contemporary Archives* (retitled *Keesing's Record of World Events* from January 1987), the monthly news reference service which over the past 56 years has achieved an unrivalled reputation for the accuracy and impartiality of its coverage of current affairs worldwide. Other titles currently available in the KRP series (all published by Longman Group UK Limited) are as follows:—

Border and Territorial Disputes, edited by Alan J. Day (1982)

Political Dissent: An International Guide to Dissident, Extra-Parliamentary, Guerrilla and Illegal Political Movements, compiled by Henry W. Degenhardt (1983)

Political Parties of the World (2nd edition), edited by Alan J. Day & Henry W. Degenhardt (1984)

State Economic Agencies of the Word, edited by Alan J. Day (1985)

Maritime Affairs: A World Handbook, compiled by Henry W. Degenhardt (1985)

Latin American Political Movements, compiled by Ciarán Ó Maoláin (1985)

Communist and Marxist Parties of the World, compiled by Charles Hobday (1986)

OPEC, Its Member States and the World Energy Market, compiled by John Evans (1986)

Treaties and Alliances of the World (4th edition), compiled by Henry W. Degenhardt (1986)

INTRODUCTION

The aim of this reference book is to present factual data on movements and groups involved in campaigning for peace and disarmament broadly defined, set in the context of introductory data on the military position and defence policies of each country covered. Such movements are to be found in substantial numbers in Western Europe and North America, where adherence to peace-orientated groups has been described as the fastest-growing social movement of the 1980s. However, the scope of the volume is global in that relevant organizations in other continents are also covered, notably those of the Pacific region.

The movements described range from the major international and national organizations seeking the peaceful resolution of human conflict and nuclear and/or general disarmament to smaller groups concerned with particular or local issues (although local branches of national movements have not as a rule been listed). Some of the groups covered have a long history, being rooted in the pacifist and conscientious objection traditions dating from the early part of this century; but most are post-1945 movements focusing in particular on the threat posed by the nuclear arms race.

The key criterion for inclusion has been that an organization should be wholly or mainly concerned with peace and disarmament issues, either as a campaigning movement or as a research or documentation centre. In the interests of keeping the book to manageable proportions, movements whose primary focus is on other issues—e.g. environmentalist and development groups or those opposed to civil nuclear power—have not normally been included, even though they may share the same basic aims as the peace movement proper.

Information sources for the book have included data provided by many of the movements themselves, although the editor is entirely responsible for the way and the extent to which such material has been used. This information has been supplemented by substantial additional research into published sources of various kinds, notably the wide range of journals, newsletters and tracts emanating from the peace movement worldwide. Among these, particular acknowledgment should be made to (i) *Disarmament Campaigns*, originally published in its own right from the Netherlands and since January 1986 from London as a supplement to *END Journal* (of the European Nuclear Disarmament movement), itself a prime source for the "new" peace movement of the 1980s; (ii) *WRI Newsletter*, the well-informed and informative bulletin of War Resisters' International; (iii) *Peace News*, the senior British peace-orientated publication; (iv) the well-produced US journal *Nuclear Times*; and (v) the New Zealand periodical *Peacelink*, useful for its coverage of Pacific region issues. There is also the estimable *Housmans Peace Diary*, which each year includes a full listing of peace and other "alternative" movements around the globe.*

---

* The addresses of the sources referred to are: (i) *END Journal/Disarmament Campaigns*, 11 Goodwin Street, London, N4 3HQ, UK; (ii) *WRI Newsletter*, 55 Dawes Street, London, SE17 1EL, UK; (iii) *Peace News*, 8 Elm Avenue, Nottingham, NG3 4GF, UK; (iv) *Nuclear Times*, Room 512, 298 Fifth Avenue, New York, NY 10001, USA; (v) *Peacelink*, Old Chemistry Building, Arts Centre, Hereford Street, P.O. Box 2828, Christchurch, New Zealand; (vi) *Housmans Peace Diary*, 5 Caledonian Road, London, N1 9DX, UK.

Extensive use has also been made of the editorial resources of *Keesing's Contemporary Archives* (see page vi) and every effort has been made to achieve *Keesing's*-style objectivity and balance in the book's coverage and presentation. The contributors are mostly present or past members of the *Keesing's* editorial team, among whom the editor wishes to extend thanks to Martin Wright for his initial work on the project, to Roger East for his comments on the introductions to the NATO countries, to Henry Degenhardt for his guidance on current military alliances and treaties,[†] and to Ciarán Ó Maoláin and Judith Bell for compiling some of the entries. Thanks are also due to Indijana Hidović Harper, Rosemary Hill and Miriam Bianco for compilation assistance and to Nicola Rudland for preparing the indexes. Any errors or omissions in the present work are entirely the responsibility of the editor, who would welcome communication from readers on such shortcomings.

London, October 1986   *AJD*

[†] As covered in his *Treaties and Alliances of the World*, 4th edition (Longman 1986).

1. INTERNATIONAL MOVEMENTS

International Movements

Alps-Adria Peace Network

Address. c/o ARGE-UFI, Völkendorferstrasse 20, A-9500 Villach/Beljak, Austria

Aims and objectives. The Alps-Adria Peace Network links Austrian, Italian and Yugoslav peace groups seeking the demilitarization of the Alps-Adria region. (The latter encompasses the Veneto and Friuli-Venezia Giulia regions of Italy, the Austrian provinces of Carinthia, Styria and Upper Austria, and Croatia and Slovenia in Yugoslavia.)

Formation. The Network was established in November 1984 at the first Alps-Adria peace camp held in north-western Yugoslavia.

Activities. The first Alps-Adria peace camp was organized on the basis of co-operation between Austria, Italian and Yugoslav peace groups dating from the third European Nuclear Disarmament (END) convention held in Perugia in June 1984. At the camp itself (Nov. 1–4, 1984), which was attended by representatives from Hungary, West Germany and Switzerland as well as from Austria, Italy and Yugoslavia, discussion centred on the demand for nuclear-free zones in the Alps-Adria region and in the Balkans generally. Also considered was the "Villach proposal" (put forward by the Austrian peace movement in December 1983) calling for the withdrawal of nuclear weapons and offensive troops from the areas of West Germany, Italy, Hungary and Czechoslovakia which adjoin Austrian territory.

Subsequent activities of the Network have included the exchange of speakers for demonstrations, peace actions at meetings and festivals in border regions, the promotion of town-twinning and the signing of personal peace treaties. The participating groups have also sought to utilize existing local government and trade union structures to promote peace and disarmament initiatives and to develop "peace education" in schools. The second Alps-Adria peace camp was held in Rechberg/Reberca (Austria) in November 1985 and focused on (i) the role of ethnic minorities as a bridge between nations, (ii) East–West dialogue, (iii) detente from below, (iv) the Central European identity, (v) alternative conceptions of military security and (vi) the launching of an Alps-Adria peace manifesto.

Membership. The core groups of the Network are the relevant local organizations of the Working Group of Independent Peace Initiatives of Austria (ARGE-UFI), the Friuli-Venezia Giulia Peace Groups Co-ordination of Italy and the Working Group for Peace of Yugoslavia. As indicated above, however, groups from countries adjoining the Alps-Adria region are also associated with the Network.

Asian Buddhists' Conference for Peace (ABCP)

Address. c/o Gangdantekchenling Monastery, Ulan Bator, Mongolia

Aims and objectives. The ABCP seeks to mobilize the influence of the Buddhist faith in Asia in the cause of regional and world peace, in accordance with fundamental Buddhist tenets.

Membership. The ABCP has particularly strong centres in Kampuchea, Mongolia and Vietnam (enjoying the backing of the communist regimes of each of these countries).

Publication. Buddhists for Peace, quarterly.

Christian Movement for Peace (CMP)
Mouvement Chrétien pour la Paix (MCP)

Address. 46 rue de Vaugirard, 75006 Paris, France

Aims and objectives. Basing itself on the teachings of the Christian gospels, the CMP seeks to build an international movement of Christians and others aspiring to a world order based on peace and justice.

Formation. The CMP was founded in 1923 as a means of bringing together peoples of different nationalities following the First World War.

Membership. The CMP's member organizations are concentrated in the countries of the developed world.

Publication. Flash Info, quarterly.

Christian Peace Conference (CPC)

Address. General Secretariat, Jungmannova 9, 111 21, Prague 1, Czechoslovakia

Aims and objectives. The CPC defines its role as that of "an ecumenical movement which gives expression to the Christian responsibility for peace, social justice and a life worthy of man to be enjoyed by all". It stands for "the peaceful resolution of international disputes without recourse to violence" and for "general and complete disarmament".

Formation. Founded in 1958 by a group of religious leaders from East and West, the CPC was established with the aim of convening an "All Christian Peace Assembly".

Activities. Since its formation, six such Assemblies have been held, with varying themes, in 1961, 1964, 1968 (March), 1971, 1978 and 1985. The most recent was held under the slogan of "God Calls: Choose Life—The Hour is Late!", and was attended by 700 individuals from 100 countries.

A number of subsidiary bodies, including the Working Committee, International Secretariat and Study Commission, hold regular follow-up meetings related to the resolutions of the previous Assembly.

Membership. Churches, ecumenical councils, regional committees and individuals are all represented in the CPC.

Publications. The *CPC Bulletin* is produced twice a month in English and German (and monthly in Spanish), and the *CPC Magazine* appears quarterly. The Conference also publishes study papers as well as "occasional books on specific issues with regard to the struggle for peace and justice in a religious context".

Affiliations. The CPC has consultative status with the UN Economic and Social Council and is a member of CONGO (the conference of non-governmental organizations).

Council on Christian Approaches to Defence and Disarmament (CCADD)—see entry under United Kingdom

Doctors Against Nuclear War—see entry for **International Physicians for the Prevention of Nuclear War (IPPNW)**

EIRENE
International Christian Service for Peace
Internationaler Christlicher Friedensdienst
Service Chrétien International pour la Paix
Servicio Cristiano Internacional por la Paz

Address. Engerser Str. 74 b, D-5450 Neuwied 1, Federal Republic of Germany

Aims and objectives. EIRENE (the Greek word for peace) is a Christian organization which offers long-term voluntary service in the southern and northern hemispheres and regards itself as part of the peace movement. Believing that states in the north and south of the globe "are bound together by economic, political and cultural ties", EIRENE takes the view that "peace work cannot be limited to the southern hemisphere" since "many of the roots of the conflicts, the injustice and the misery of the southern countries lie in the industrial countries of the north". Accordingly, EIRENE participates "here in the north in the process of non-violent change in the direction of a world in which everybody has the opportunity of developing all his potentialities in an atmosphere of justice, humanity and freedom".

EIRENE believes that there is a "close connection between development and peace work", in that "while the misery in the Third World is patently increasing, on the other side some 1,000 million US dollars are being spent each day for armaments". As a service for peace, the organization seeks to work within a larger movement "which gathers together those who question unjust structures and suggest credible, non-violent alternatives".

Formation. EIRENE was founded in 1957 by the traditionally pacifist Mennonite and Brethren churches of the United States together with the International Fellowship of Reconciliation and concerned European Christians.

Activities. In the southern hemisphere EIRENE has sought partnership with groups "which practise just ways of using material resources . . . and are trying to free themselves from economic, political or cultural repression or isolation". These groups co-operate in the planning and execution of projects, which do not replace indigenous labour, do not require high financial investment and can be carried on later independently. Having started in 1957 by giving assistance to refugees from the Algerian liberation struggle, the organization, through its volunteer workers, is currently co-operating in programmes in Niger (agricultural assistance to Tuaregs), Chad (advising a weavers' co-operative), Morocco (training lepers) and Nicaragua (supporting an agricultural school). It is also working with "alternative development" groups in Sri Lanka, Senegambia, Peru, Ecuador and Bangladesh.

In the northern hemisphere EIRENE volunteers are currently active in France (work with handicapped and marginal groups), Spain (work with conscientious objectors), Switzerland (peace work), Ireland (work for reconciliation), Great Britain (work with marginal groups), Belgium (peace work) and the United

States (in the anti-nuclear movement). Volunteers are expected to work with a group which will support their service financially.

Since 1978 EIRENE has organized regular exchanges of volunteers between Europe and the United States.

Membership. EIRENE has as its member organizations the Mennonite Central Committee, the Brethren Church, the International Fellowship of Reconciliation and branches in France, West Germany, the Netherlands and Switzerland. These member bodies meet twice a year in a general assembly to determine the policy of the organization.

Publication. EIRENE publishes a circular letter four times a year.

Esperantist Movement for World Peace
Mondpaca Esperantista Movado (MEM)

Address. c/o Imre Perthes, H-1144, Budapest, Füredi ut.11/A, Hungary

Aims and objectives. MEM is a peace movement based on the use of the Esperanto language (which was invented in 1887 and which has speakers in approximately 90 countries). MEM believes that international co-operation between peace movements and "all progressive individuals" will be rendered more effective if conducted in Esperanto. MEM supports a range of peace and disarmament efforts, and also "fights against militarism and neo-fascism, against racism and neo-colonialism, and for all the oppressed".

Formation. MEM was established in 1935.

Activities. The group organizes a number of conferences as well as seminars and lectures for the Esperanto-speaking community. It also encourages letter-writing and petition campaigns.

Membership. MEM has between 10,000 and 12,000 members worldwide, organized by country in 33 sections.

Publications. MEM's journal, *Paco* (Peace), is published six times a year. It also produces brochures and information sheets.

Affiliations. MEM has particularly strong links with the World Peace Council, in which it has two representatives.

European Bureau for Conscientious Objection (EBCO)
Bureau Européen de l'Objection de Conscience (BEOC)

Address. 35 rue van Elewyck, 1050 Bruxelles, Belgium

Aims and objectives. EBCO is principally concerned with (i) promoting the right to conscientious objection world-wide but with special emphasis on the member states of the Council of Europe; (ii) pushing for recognition of conscientious objection as a human right by means of an additional protocol to the European Human Rights Convention; and (iii) lobbying European and national politicians with the aim of securing improvements to legislation on conscientious objection.

Formation. EBCO held its official founding meeting on June 1, 1985, although it had been informally in active existence for some time before that.

Activities. Before its official formation EBCO was informally involved in organizing a symposium on "Conscientious Objection as a Human Right" held in the European Youth Centre in Strasbourg in October 1984; upwards of 100 participants from most Council of Europe member states attended and approved a draft protocol on conscientious objection for addition to the European Convention. In addition to its information and lobbying work, EBCO has also established working groups on internationalization of alternative service, conscientious objection in Eastern Europe and the social situation on conscientious objectors.

Membership. EBCO has individual members in Belgium, France, the Federal Republic of Germany, Italy, the Netherlands, Spain, the United Kingdom and the United States. Its membership includes socialists, Christians and environmentalists.

Publication. EBCO has published *The Right to Refuse to Kill* (a survey of conscientious objection and related issues in Europe).

Affiliations. EBCO is not affiliated as such to any group or party, but as a consequence of its pluralist set-up it has close links with War Resisters' International, the International Fellowship of Reconciliation, the Quakers and other church organizations and with various national groups concerned with conscientious objection.

European Network for East–West Dialogue

Address. c/o Dieter Esche, Niebuhrstr. 61, D-1000 Berlin 12, Federal Republic of Germany

Aims and objectives. The Network seeks to deepen and broaden East–West dialogue from below, aiming to promote such dialogue "as an integral part of the discussion and practice of the Western peace movements". Its two main functions are (i) bringing together the various threads of the dialogue between groups from the Western peace movement, independent peace initiatives and also the democratic opposition in Eastern Europe, and (ii) organizing "a political-strategic debate on central themes of East–West relations especially directed towards the aim of a peaceful European order beyond the blocs".

Formation. The Network was founded in mid-1984 during a conference of European Nuclear Disarmament (END) in Perugia (Italy).

Activities. The Network's first major event was an international discussion forum on the theme "Peace in Divided Europe—40 Years after Yalta" held in West Berlin in February 1985; apart from the groups involved in the Network, peace researchers, politicians and numerous East Europeans living in the West took part in the forum, which also received written submissions from independent peace movements and democratic opposition groups in Poland, East Germany, Czechoslovakia, Hungary and the Soviet Union. A second discussion forum was held in February 1986 on the theme "The Meaning of the Helsinki Final Act and the Helsinki Process for Bloc-Overcoming Peace Politics". The second forum marked the launching of a political initiative for the drafting of an East–West joint declaration for submission to the CSCE follow-up conference in Vienna in November 1986.

Membership. The Network regards itself less as a group with its own programme and fixed organizational structure and more as an open, informal communication

7

and discussion association seeking co-operation with all groups and initiatives interested in East–West dialogue. Active members of the Network include the Committee for Nuclear Disarmament in Europe (CODENE) of France, Lega per l'Ambiente of Italy, ARGE-UFI of Austria, Independent Peace Movement (AKE) of Greece, Flemish Action Committee Against Nuclear Weapons (VAKA), No to Nuclear Weapons of Denmark and the Swiss Peace Council; also involved are exiled groups of the East European democratic opposition and some West European political parties (including the West German Greens and the Unified Socialist Party, PSU, of France). Members of other West European peace movements have participated in Network activities on an individual basis.

Publication. The proceedings of the Network's February 1985 discussion forum (see above) have been published (in German) by Initiative Ost–West–Dialog of West Berlin.

European Network of Scientists for Nuclear Disarmament

Address. c/o CERN, EP Division, 1221 Geneva 23, Switzerland

Aims and objectives. The Network seeks to promote and co-ordinate research by European scientists on the potential effects of nuclear war, thus enabling scientists to provide expert support for nuclear disarmament campaigns.

Formation. The Network was created as a result of an initiative taken at the European Nuclear Disarmament (END) Convention held in Brussels in 1982.

Membership. Groups of scientists in 18 European countries are involved in the Network's activities.

Publications. The Network publishes regular reports on the research activities of its participating groups.

European Nuclear Disarmament (END)—see under United Kingdom

European Ports Peace Conference (EPPC)

Address. Willem Smalthof 95, 3031 NM Rotterdam, Netherlands

Aims and objectives. EPPC takes as its basic proposition that "due to their vital military and economic positions, ports in Europe will be among the first targets of a nuclear exchange". Thus the ports of Europe, both Western and Eastern, are able to make "a direct contribution towards a nuclear-free Europe", particularly by influencing public opinion and national and international decision-making. Both seaports and airports are covered by this proposition (although EPPC activities have to date been largely concentrated on the former).

The central aims of the EPPC are (i) to exchange information between ports concerning making cities, regions and countries nuclear-free zones; (ii) to develop and discuss relevant strategies for the denuclearization of ports; (iii) to formulate new suggestions and proposals which can be translated into specific political, cultural and social goals for each port; and (iv) to provide an international framework in which ports can co-ordinate their policies and activities in the campaign for peace and nuclear disarmament.

Formation. EPPC was created in 1981 with a first conference held in the port of Hull (north-east England), attended by a delegation from the Dutch port of

Rotterdam made up of trade unionists, church representatives, peace movement activists and representatives of women's organizations, the Dutch Labour Party (PvdA) and the Radical Political Party (PPR).

Activities. Since its inaugural meeting in Hull in 1981, the EPPC has held a succession of major conferences, most recently in Antwerp in 1984. Between conferences member ports are encouraged to participate in peace and anti-nuclear demonstrations in each other's cities. Declarations issued by EPPC conferences have been sent to relevant governmental authorities and the organization has sought to promote and co-ordinate publicity and information work in participating port cities.

Membership. The ports of Hull, Rotterdam, Hamburg, Antwerp, Liverpool, Teesside and Southampton have sent delegations to EPPC conferences, while Stavanger, Aarhus, Bremen, Amsterdam and Newcastle have expressed interest. Delegations consist of a mix of trade unionists, local political representatives, peace campaigners and religious denominations.

Publications. In addition to a newsletter (2–4 times a year), the EPPC has published conference documents.

Five Continents Peace Initiative

Address. c/o PGA, 304 East 45th Street, 12th floor, New York, NY 10017, USA

Aims and objectives. Concerned at the lack of progress in disarmament negotiations, five government leaders (later six), independent of either Moscow or Washington, launched the Initiative in the hope that they would be able to break the political impasse by using their combined influence to appeal directly to the United States and the Soviet Union (as well as to Britain, France and China as the other three nuclear-weapons states) to halt what they described as "the rush towards global genocide".

Formation. The Initiative was launched on May 22, 1984, by the Prime Ministers Andreas Papandreou of Greece, Indira Gandhi of India (subsequently assassinated in October 1984) and Olof Palme of Sweden (also later assassinated, in February 1986) and Presidents Miguel de la Madrid Hurtado of Mexico and Julius Nyerere of Tanzania. It resulted in part from an initiative by Parliamentarians for World Order (PWO), which later became Parliamentarians Global Action (see separate entry).
Mrs Gandhi's son Rajiv, her successor as Indian premier, subsequently became associated with the Initiative, which was also joined by President Raúl Alfonsín of Argentina.

Activities. In simultaneous press conferences given in their respective capitals on May 22, 1984, the five leaders issued the following statement:
"(1) Today, the survival of humankind is in jeopardy. The escalating arms race, the rise in international tensions and the lack of constructive dialogue among the nuclear weapons states has increased the risk of nuclear war. Such a war, even using part of the present stockpiles, would bring death and destruction to all peoples.
"(2) As leaders of nations, member states of the United Nations, we have a commitment to take constructive action towards halting and reversing the nuclear arms race. The people we represent are no less threatened by nuclear war than the citizens of the nuclear weapons states. It is primarily the responsibility of the

nuclear weapons states to prevent a nuclear catastrophe, but this problem is too important to be left to those states alone.

"(3) We come from different parts of the globe, with differences in religion, culture and political systems. But we are united in the conviction that there must not be another world war. On this, the most crucial of all issues, we have resolved to make a common effort in the interests of peace.

"(4) Agreements which merely regulate an arms build-up are clearly insufficient. The probability of nuclear holocaust increases as warning time decreases and the weapons become swifter, more accurate and more deadly. The rush towards global suicide must be stopped and then reversed. We urge, as a necessary first step, the United States and the Soviet Union, as well as the United Kingdom, France and China, to halt all testing, production and deployment of nuclear weapons and their delivery systems, to be immediately followed by substantial reductions in nuclear forces.

We are convinced that it is possible to work out the details of an arrangement along these lines that takes into account the interests and concerns of all, and contains adequate measures for verification. This first step must be followed by a continuing programme of arms reductions leading to general and complete disarmament, accompanied by measures to strengthen the United Nations system and to ensure an urgently needed transfer of substantial resources from the arms race into social and economic development. The essential goal must be to reduce and then eliminate the risk of war between nations.

"(5) We will do everything in our power to facilitate agreement among the nuclear weapons states. We will continue to keep in touch with one another about the best ways and means of achieving this objective. We will be consulting with the leaders of the nuclear weapons states and with other world leaders as well as pursuing discussions through United Nations channels.

"(6) We affirm our belief in detente and mutual understanding, with broad international co-operation and respect for the right of each state to a peaceful, secure and independent existence and of the right of each people to organise its life according to its own aspirations. There can be no assurance of safety for one side only. That is why we attach such importance to a halt in the nuclear arms race that allows for renewed talks on nuclear disarmament.

"(7) All people have an overriding interest in common security and the avoidance of a nuclear war which threatens human survival. Citizens throughout the world are expressing, as never before, their concern for the future—this public discussion of peace and disarmament must continue and increase. The support and encouragement of an informed public will greatly strengthen governmental action to reverse the nuclear arms race.

"(8) We have faith in the capacity of human beings to rise above the current divisions and create a world free from the shadow of nuclear war. The power and ingenuity of the human race must be used not to perfect weapons of annihilation, but to harness the resources of the earth so that all people may enjoy a life of security and dignity in an international system free of war and based on peace and justice.

"(9) Today, the world hangs in the balance between war and peace. We hope that our combined efforts will help to influence the outcome."

Following their initial announcement the five leaders began a process of contact and consultation with their counterparts in the five nuclear-weapons states, exploring possibilities for progress in disarmament negotiations with a view to drawing up detailed recommendations. The assassination of two of the original leaders had the effect of delaying the programme of the Initiative. It was resumed in March 1986, however, with the publication of an appeal to President Reagan of the United States and General Secretary Gorbachev of the Soviet Union to forego nuclear testing until their next summit meeting. In their letter the six Initiative leaders offered to verify such test bans through on-site inspections and "monitoring activities", including the use of seismological equipment next test sites. (The letter was signed by Olof Palme on Feb. 28 shortly before his assassination.)

Friends World Committee for Consultation

Address. Drayton House, Gordon Street, London, WC1H 0AX, United Kingdom

Aims and objectives. The Friends World Committee is the principal liaison organization of Quaker groups around the world, seeking to provide an international focus for activities in furtherance of Quaker precepts of peace and universal brotherhood.

Formation. The Friends World Committee was established in 1937.

Activities. The World Committee meets every three years, most recently near Mexico City in the summer of 1985, with the 1988 meeting being scheduled to be held in Tokyo (Japan). An interim (executive) committee meets annually.

Membership. There are Quaker communities in 56 countries; about half the world's 250,000 Quakers are in the United States and Canada.

Publications. *Quaker Information Network* (every two months); *Friends World News* (twice a year); *Finding Friends Around the World* (last edition 1979).

Generals for Peace and Disarmament

Address. c/o London Centre for International Peacebuilding, Southbank House, Black Prince Road, London, SE1 7SJ, United Kingdom

Aims and objectives. Generals for Peace and Disarmament comprises a small group of retired NATO senior officers who question the wisdom of the current NATO strategy in so far as it depends upon the nuclear deterrent. Certain members of the group retired early from the armed forces in preference to finding themselves in a position where they could be called upon to initiate the use of nuclear weapons. The group are committed to the belief that "nuclear arms have no relevance to military strategy or tactics".

Formation. Generals for Peace and Disarmament was formed after the publication of Generale fur den Frieden (Generals for Peace) in 1981, principally on an initiative by a prominent member of the Helsinki-based World Peace Council.

Activities. The Generals meet together regularly to analyse current military and political decisions that affect arms control and disarmament efforts. Since their formation, the group has submitted a series of memoranda dealing with European security and East–West relations, with military confidence-building, and with NATO's nuclear deterrent policy and the deployment of cruise and Pershing missiles. These have been circulated to the European Security and Co-operation conferences, to NATO foreign and defence ministers meetings and to all delegations at the second UN special session on disarmament (UNSSOD II) in 1982.

In May 1984 the group held a three-day meeting in Vienna, Austria, with retired generals from all the Warsaw Pact countries participating. The meeting was aimed at establishing a working relationship based on common professional experience and understanding of the military issues which affect European security. Due to the success of the meeting, similar encounters are planned for the future.

Membership. The membership of the group includes the following: Generalmajor Gert Bastian (West Germany); General Johan Christie (Norway); Marshal Francisco da Costa Gomes (Portugal); Brigadier Michael Harbottle, OBE (UK—Administrator); Major General Leonard V. Johnston (Canada); General Georgios Koumanakos (Greece); General Rangel de Lima (Portugal); Admiral Miltiades Papathanassiou (Greece); Generaal-majoor Michiel H. von Meyenfeldt (Netherlands—Chairman); General Nino Pasti (Italy); Admiral Antoine Sanguinetti (France); Brigadier Michalis Tombopoulos (Greece); and Generalmajor Gunter Vollmer (West Germany).

Publications. The group has published three books—*Generale für den Frieden*; *Generale gegen Nachrüstung* (published in English as *The Arms Race to Armageddon*); and *Generals for Peace and Disarmament—10 Questions Answered*. It also produces a regular annual *Bulletin*.

Affiliations. While the group has no formal affiliations, its members are all to some extent involved with national peace campaigns in their respective countries.

Global Education Associates (GEA)

Address. 552 Park Avenue, East Orange, New Jersey, NJ 07017, USA

Aims and objectives. GEA seeks to promote international collaborative research, writing and teaching on peace, disarmament and other issues. It seeks a new world order "based on the values of peace, social and economic justice, ecological balance and participation".

Membership. The GEA network extends to some 50 countries.

Publications. The Whole Earth Papers (series).

International Association of Educators for World Peace (IAEWP)

Address. P.O. Box 705, Clarksville, Maryland, MD 21209, USA

Aims and objectives. As its name implies, the IAEWP is an international organization seeking to promote co-operation and exchange between teachers and educationalists concerned for world peace.

Activities. The Association held its third European convention in August 1983 at the Hesbjerg Peace Research College in Denmark (see entry under that country).

International Confederation for Disarmament and Peace—see under entry for International Peace Bureau

International Fellowship of Reconciliation (IFOR)

Address. Hof von Sonoy 17, 1811 LD, Alkmaar, Netherlands

Aims and objectives. IFOR is a religious movement committed to "active non-violence" as the basis principle for a world community of peace and freedom.

Formation. IFOR had its origins in the First World War and was formally established at a conference in the Netherlands in 1919.

Activities. IFOR co-ordinates the activities of its many branches all over the world through its international secretariat, which organizes conferences and carries out a number of international projects, including ones dealing with East–West contacts, theological work on peace issues and non-violence education in several countries, including the Philippines and South Africa.

Membership. IFOR has 125,000 members worldwide, most of whom are affiliated to national branches in some 30 countries. Members sign a statement of purpose committing themselves to help realize the movement's aims. Members have included Mahatma Gandhi, Martin Luther King, Adolfo Perez Esquivel and Joan Baez. Seven IFOR members have received the Nobel Peace Prize.

Publications. *IFOR Report* (five issues per year).

Affiliations. IFOR works with the following peace groups: Pax Christi International, War Resisters' International, the Christian Peace Conference, Church and Peace and the Inter-Church Peace Council. It also has a role within the UN as a non-governmental organization with consultative status; it also works with Amnesty International and the World Council of Churches.

International Institute for Peace (IIP)

Address. Mollwaldplatz 5, A-1040, Vienna, Austria

Aims and objectives. The IIP is the research arm of the Helsinki-based World Peace Council (see separate entry), which had been located in Vienna until being banned by the Austrian Government in 1957.

Publication. *Peace and Science* (quarterly).

International Mobilization for Survival—see entry for Mobilization for Survival under United States of America

International Nuclear-Free Zone Network

Address. P.O. Box 532, Town Hall, Manchester, M60 2LA, United Kingdom (*for elected officials*); c/o Nuclear Free America, 2521 Guilford Avenue, Baltimore, Maryland 21218, USA (*for local activists*)

Aims and objectives. The Network provides an international link between local authorities and activists throughout the world who have established, or seek to establish, nuclear-free zones in their localities.

Formation. Following the first declaration of a local nuclear-free zone in Japan in 1958, the grassroots NFZ movement grew rapidly in the 1960s and 1970s, leading to the establishment of formal international links in the spring of 1984.

Activities. The first two international NFZ conferences were held in the English cities of Huddersfield and Manchester respectively in the spring of 1984, the latter attended by over 200 mayors, councillors and others representing NFZs in 10 countries. Two parallel networks were established as a result of these conferences, one with an "international secretariat" in Manchester to serve local authorities and the other with a clearing-house provided by Nuclear Free America in Baltimore to serve individual activists. The two centres have co-operated on major projects such as the second international conference of NFZ local authorities held in Cordoba (Spain) in March 1985, with a third due to be held in Perugia (Italy) in October 1986.

Membership. According to the tally kept by the Network, there were nearly 3,000 NFZ communities in 17 countries as at the end of 1985, with Japan having the greatest number, followed by the Netherlands, Spain, Belgium, Italy and Great Britain.

International Peace Bureau (IPB)

Address. 41 rue de Zurich, CH-1201, Geneva, Switzerland

Aims and objectives. The IPB's twin aims as laid down in its constitution are (i) "to serve the cause of peace by the promotion of international co-operation and non-violent solutions of international problems", and (ii) "to serve the independent peace movements of the world. It seeks to further communication between peace groups and to assist in co-ordinating their activities, as well as facilitating contact between governments and the peace movement, although it emphasizes the importance of the peace movement remaining independent of governmental or ideological pressure.

The IPB supports the "legal and procedural" structures of international co-operation, such as the UN, World Health Organization and UNESCO, and it seeks to represent the interests of peace groups affiliated to it in international forums such as these.

The Bureau also recognizes the need for political, social and economic changes as a condition of peace, although it stresses that the achievement of such changes should be through peaceful means. It "seeks to spread the conviction that a life of dignity and justice is the inalienable right of all men and women, and that it is capable of realization on the basis that peace is not only the goal, but the means towards it as well".

Formation. The IPB was formed in 1892, taking as its inspiration the International Union of Peace Societies, which had its roots in the London Peace Society, founded on a Quaker initiative in 1816.

Activities. After initially establishing itself in Berne, Switzerland, the IPB transferred its headquarters to Geneva in 1924, in order to be closer to the League of Nations, the establishment of which had been one of the Bureau's principal goals following the First World War, during which its activities were necessarily restricted. During the Second World War, the IPB was closed and its assets taken into the custody of the Swiss government. In 1946, several Scandinavian and British peace groups established the International Liaison Committee of Organizations for Peace (ILCOP), which was subsequently recognized by the Swiss government as the legal successor to the IPB, the assets of which were handed over to the new organization. The IPB's extensive library was placed in the care of the UN Librarian. The title of "International Peace Bureau" was revived following the Swiss government's decision and ILCOP became a trust fund charged with the administration of IPB finances.

Throughout its history, the IPB has organized regular conferences on peace and disarmament. In the years preceding and immediately following the First World War, these took the form of annual "World Peace Congresses", which undertook thorough surveys of world issues. In the years since the Second World War, however, they have taken the form of smaller, seminar-style discussions of specific issues, preliminary research for which is carried out by a number of working groups. The seminars' findings are transmitted to government and inter-government bodies.

Subjects covered in such seminars have included the following: Aspects of Non-Violence; Requirements of a World at Peace; UN Peace-Keeping; Alternatives to Military Defence; The Right to Refuse Military Service and Orders (the report on this seminar was adopted by members of the UN Human Rights Commission and was used as part of the effort to have such a refusal established as a universal human right); The Call for a World Disarmament Conference with Non-Governmental Participation; and The After-Effects of the Atomic Bomb on Hiroshima and Nagasaki.

The IPB was actively involved in promoting negotiations between the United States and the Soviet Union which resulted in the Joint Statement of Agreed Principles of 1961, this being approved by the UN General Assembly at the end of the same year. In June 1984, Sean MacBride, the president of the IPB, wrote to the Presidents of the United States and the Soviet Union proposing that they should meet in order to reaffirm that the aim of all future disarmament negotiations should be the achievement of general and complete disarmament, as laid down in the Agreed Principles.

In 1974 the IPB convened an international conference at Bradford University (UK), which was attended by representatives of all the non-governmental organizations involved in peace work. The conference adopted a set of proposals calling for the holding of a world conference on disarmament. The proposals have since been endorsed by a large number of national and international non-governmental organizations.

The Bureau's 1981 conference was devoted to drawing up proposals for a comprehensive treaty on world disarmament (again based on the 1961 principles). The proposals were presented to the second special session of the UN General Assembly on Disarmament (UNSSOD II) in 1982. In September 1983 the IPB merged with the International Confederation for Disarmament and Peace, the unified organization retaining the name International Peace Bureau. Currently the IPB is investigating the question of the illegality of nuclear weapons and other weapons of mass destruction.

A total of 13 officials of the IPB have been awarded the Nobel Peace Prize, including Sean MacBride (in 1974). The Bureau itself was awarded the prize in 1910.

Membership. The IPB has affiliated peace organizations in Belgium, Denmark, Finland, France, West Germany, Ireland, Italy, Japan, Norway, Spain, Sweden, Switzerland, the United Kingdom, the United States and Yugoslavia. IPB policy is decided at regular annual meetings, while an elected executive meets at least twice per year.

Publications. The Bureau issues press releases and news-sheets, as well as booklets and papers emanating from their various conferences. These have included *The Right to Refuse to Kill, Call for a World Disarmament Conference* and *Children and War.*

Affiliations. The IPB is an international non-governmental organization which has consultative status with UNESCO.

International Peace Communication and Co-ordination Network (IPCC)

Address. c/o IKV, P.O. Box 18747, 2502 ES The Hague, Netherlands

Aims and objectives. The IPCC provides a co-ordinating focus for the main peace movements in a number of countries, notably those of Western Europe and

North America. A statement drafted for the IPCC in late 1984 by representatives of European Nuclear Disarmament of the UK, the US Nuclear Weapons Freeze Campaign and No to Nuclear Weapons of Norway said that the goal of freeing the world of nuclear weapons was "to be achieved in a stepwise process", the first step being "to halt the nuclear arms build-up".

The statement continued: "This is the idea behind a nuclear weapons *freeze*. Such a freeze includes a complete stop of all production, testing and deployment of nuclear weapons. The purpose of a freeze is not merely to preserve the status quo, but to pave the way for real disarmament. A ban on new nuclear weapons does not mean an acceptance of old ones. On the contrary, it is an incitement to go on and have them removed. We demand freeze and *withdrawal*." It concluded: "Freeze and withdrawal is a political proposal which could contribute to achieving [the goal of a world completely free from the threat of nuclear annihilation]. In a European context where so many American and Soviet weapons are based, it would loosen the nuclear ties of the two military blocs and create space between the superpowers, and so help to overcome the global East–West confrontation. Combined with other political and economic initiatives to alleviate the tensions between East and West, North and South, and especially if combined with efforts to stop interventionism, it may help to create an international climate where disputes can be settled without use of military force."

Formation. The IPCC was established at a meeting held in Copenhagen in September 1981, in light of the perceived need of the "new" peace movements which had developed in Western Europe and North America in the late 1970s for an independent forum in which political strategy and common actions could be discussed. The Inter-Church Peace Council (IKV) of the Netherlands agreed to serve as the secretariat for the Network.

Activities. Whereas the IPCC was initially a campaign forum for efforts to prevent the deployment of cruise and Pershing II missiles in Western Europe, as deployment has gone ahead the Network has broadened the range of issues with which it is concerned (East-West relations, nuclear-free zones, new weapons system research etc.) and has sought to focus on one of these at its regular conferences. An IPCC conference held in Solingen (West Germany) in September 1985 took as its theme the political and military integration of Europe and focused on the concept of "Europeanization" and on East-West co-operation.

In mid-1986 the IPCC released an international appeal against the US Strategic Defence Initiative (SDI) signed by over 80 prominent persons from 11 countries, maintaining that "all existing or proposed space weapons are ill-conceived and dangerous, more apt to lead to nuclear war than prevent it" and urging all governments "to abandon and actively oppose any space or ground-based programmes for weapons in outer space."

International Peace Research Association (IPRA)

Address. c/o Chadwick F. Alger, Mershon Center, Ohio State University, 199 West Tenth Avenue, Columbus, Ohio 43201, USA

Aims and objectives. To advance interdisciplinary research into the causes of war and the preconditions for peace and to promote peace through contacts and co-operation between scholars and educators from different countries.

Formation. IPRA developed from a Quaker-inspired conference held in Clarens, Switzerland, in August 1963, when the participants decided to hold international conferences on research into international peace and security to be modelled on the Pugwash conferences.

Activities. IPRA has held (usually biennial) conferences since 1965, with venues in both Western and Eastern bloc countries.

Membership. 446 individual members from 55 countries; 64 corporate members from 25 countries; 181 newsletter subscribers in 24 countries. IPRA Council members come from both Western and Soviet bloc countries, and also from the Third World.

Publications. International Peace Research Newsletter, quarterly; proceedings of the biennial general conferences.

Affiliations. IPRA holds consultative status with UNESCO and receives an annual subvention from it. Other affiliations are the Asian Peace Research Association, the Latin American Council for Peace Research and the Consortium on Peace Research, Education and Development (COPRED).

International Philosophers for the Prevention of Nuclear Omnicide (IPPNO)

Address. c/o Prof. John Somerville, 1426 Merritt Drive, El Cajon, California 92020, USA

Aims and objectives. IPPNO has as its central purpose the promotion of international co-operation between all philosophers, irrespective of their political viewpoint, in the areas of theoretical discussion and practical action directed towards the prevention of nuclear war.

Formation. IPPNO was formed in August 1983 at an organizing meeting during the 17th World Congress of Philosophy (WCP) held in Montreal (Canada).

Activities. The first IPPNO international conference was held in St Louis (USA) in May 1986 under the general theme "Philosophy and the new problem of nuclear omnicide: analysis, education, action". The conference was attended by delegates from Western, Eastern bloc and third world countries. The next IPPNO meeting is scheduled to be held at Sussex University (England) in August 1988 during a WCP gathering; a further IPPNO international conference will be held in the Soviet Union, probably in 1989.

Membership. Membership of IPPNO is open to individual philosophers or can be achieved through membership of national organizations of philosophers for peace. Under the IPPNO constitution, the organization's international presidency (currently held by Prof. John Somerville of the USA) "shall not be selected twice in succession from countries strongly identified with either NATO or the Warsaw Pact".

International Physicians for the Prevention of Nuclear War (IPPNW)

Address. 225 Longwood Avenue, Boston, MA 02115, USA (central office); Southbank House, Black Prince Road, London, SE1 7SJ, United Kingdom (European office)

Aims and objectives. IPPNW is a federation of national groups which is dedicated to mobilizing the influence of the medical profession against the threat of nuclear weapons. Its activities are based on the "four-point consensus" laid down at its foundation. This states (i) that IPPNW would restrict its area of concern to nuclear war; (ii) that its members would work to prevent nuclear war in the light of their professional commitments to preserve life; (iii) that it would seek to involve doctors from both East and West and would disseminate identical information about nuclear war throughout the world; and (iv) that, while advocating certain measures to prevent war, it would not adopt a position on any specific government policies. IPPNW is sometimes referred to as Doctors Against Nuclear War.

Formation. The IPPNW was founded in December 1980 as a result of a meeting in Geneva between six Soviet and US doctors. The meeting itself arose out of a long-standing professional contact between Dr Bernard Lown of the Harvard School of Public Health and Dr Evgueni Chazov of the Soviet Cardiological Institute (and Deputy Health Minister), who became co-presidents of the IPPNW.

Activities. Since its foundation, IPPNW has held five annual international congresses (in the USA, UK, Netherlands, Finland and Hungary). The fifth congress, held in Budapest on June 28–July 1, 1985, attracted over 800 participants and had as its slogan "Co-operation not Confrontation". It adopted an appeal to the Soviet Union and the USA to freeze the production, testing and deployment of all nuclear weapons. It also urged international co-operation for the vaccination of all children against infectious diseases and pointed out that a fraction of the sums spent on armaments could save the lives of millions of children. The sixth IPPNW congress took place in Cologne (West Germany) on May 29–June 1, 1986.

In 1982 IPPNW organized a televised discussion on Soviet TV between three US and three Soviet doctors on the likely medical consequences of nuclear war. The programme was subsequently broadcast in the USA, Netherlands, Scandinavia and elsewhere.

Members of IPPNW have drawn up study programmes on nuclear war for leading medical schools in many countries. Research currently being undertaken by the organization includes the study of the atmospheric effects of nuclear war, and of the possibility of such a war breaking out by accident.

IPPNW is particularly concerned with the psychological effects of the nuclear arms race on children. It has recently worked with the Center for Nuclear Psychology at Harvard University on an examination of the responses of US and Soviet children to the threat of nuclear war. This project, which received considerable press coverage, included videotaped interviews with children in America and in the Soviet Union. National affiliates of the IPPNW are assisted by the supply of written and audiovisual material, by the organization of co-operative programmes and by exchange visits.

In 1984 the IPPNW received the UNESCO Peace Education Prize and the following year it was awarded the Nobel Peace Prize. The latter award (by the Nobel Committee of the Norwegian Parliament) generated considerable controversy, notably in that 11 West European Christian Democratic parties publicly alleged that Dr Chazov (IPPNW co-chairman) had been involved in the official campaign against the dissident Soviet scientist Dr Andrei Sakharov in the early 1970s.

Membership. IPPNW is a federation linking separate groups in over 40 countries. Total membership of all groups combined is some 145,000, all of whom are doctors or workers in other fields of the health care profession. Several additional groups currently under formation. Full-time staff are based at IPPNW headquarters in London and Boston (USA). Recent emphasis has been placed upon the need to establish affiliates in the Middle East, Latin America and the Indian sub-continent.

Publications. An explanatory IPPNW brochure is available in English, French and Spanish. Other publications (available only in English) are *IPPNW Update*, a bi-monthly news-sheet, and *IPPNW Report*, a journal of news and opinion published twice a year. IPPNW produces summary proceedings of each annual congress, and working papers presented by delegates to the first (1981) congress have been published collectively as *Last Aid: The Medical Dimensions of Nuclear Winter*.

International Seminars on Training for Non-Violent Action (ISTNA)

Address. PO Box 515, Waltham, Massachusetts, MA 02254, USA

Aims and objectives. ISTNA organizes international study and discussion meetings for those committed to peace and non-violence, aimed at increasing knowledge of and skills in the techniques of non-violent action in furtherance of the aims of the peace movement.

Affiliations. ISTNA is an associated organization of War Resisters' International (see separate entry).

International Students' Peace Network

Address. PO Box 282, Kingston, New Jersey, NJ 08528, USA

Aims and objectives. The Network seeks to build an international alliance of students' peace movements and to foster co-operation between them.

International Trade Union Committee for Peace and Disarmament

Address. PO Box 514, 1121 Prague 1, Czechoslovakia

Aims and objectives. To bring together trade unions on an international basis, irrespective of their ideological or other differences, to work for peace and détente.

Formation. The Committee was formed as a consequence of the International Trade Union Conference on the Social and Economic Consequences of Disarmament held in Paris in December 1981 (on a recommendation by the "World Parliament of the Peoples for Peace" held in Sofia the previous year).

Activities. Organizes regular meetings, held in both East and West. The second International Conference on the Social and Economic Consequences of Disarmament was held in Dublin in May 1986. During 1986 a regional conference was scheduled to be held in Sofia, Bulgaria, on the subject of the Balkan region as a nuclear-free zone.

Membership. Claims to represent 20 million trade unionists in affiliated organizations.

Publications. Produces a quarterly bulletin and posters to mark September 1, the international trade union day for peace and disarmament.

Affiliations. The Committee is an associate member of the Geneva-based UN Committee of Non-Governmental Organizations on Disarmament, and a member of the Brussels-based International Committee for European Security and Co-operation.

Neutral and Non-Aligned Peace Network (CONNPI)

Address. Nestroyplatz 1/20A, 1020 Vienna, Austria

Aims and objectives. CONNPI co-ordinates action and exchange of information between independent peace movements in the neutral and non-aligned (N + N) countries. It seeks to use N + N status as a third force to break through "bloc thinking".

Formation. After preliminary discussions dating from 1983, CONNPI came formally into being early in 1986.

Activities. The "theoretical, scientific and organizational" framework for the Network is provided by the Society for the Promotion of the Theory of Neutrality, Research in Neutrality and an Active Neutrality Policy in Vienna. The latter body concerns itself with (i) developing forms of active neutrality in the sense of responding to conflict in a peaceful manner, more justice in economic relations with the Third World, and breaking up the military blocs; (ii) ending the arms trade between neutral and "bloc-free" countries and arms production within these countries; (iii) investigating whether or not neutral and bloc-free countries can be more successful in creating an active peace policy than the bloc-aligned countries; (iv) investigating whether or not N + N countries can play a special role in building contacts between independent peace movements in East and West; and (v) using neutrality to support nuclear-free-zone initiatives and international disarmament.

CONNPI has issued joint resolutions on arms exports, on the creation of nuclear-free zones and against the SDI/Eureka programmes.

North Atlantic Network (NAN)

Address. c/o Nei til Atomvapen, Youngstørget 7, 0181 Oslo 1, Norway.

Aims and objectives. NAN seeks to co-ordinate opposition to the militarization of the North Atlantic Ocean and to link such opposition with the broader aims of the international peace movement. The Network's symbol is the puffin and its slogan "Disarming the Seas".

Formation. NAN came into being in April 1983 as an offshoot of the European Nuclear Disarmament (END) movement formed in 1980 (see entry under United Kingdom).

Activities. After an inaugural conference in Glasgow in April 1983, the second NAN conference, held in August 1984 in Reykjavik (Iceland) and attended for the first time by representatives of US peace movements, declared its opposition to the upgrading of NATO military installations in the Faroe Islands and to the building of extensive new US/NATO communications facilities in Iceland.

On June 15, 1985, NAN participated in an international day of action against sea-launched cruise missiles (both the US Tomahawk and the Soviet SS-NX-21), together with the Nuclear-Free and Independent Pacific (NFIP) movement and Mediterranean peace groups. Actions organized by NAN took place in Denmark, England, Iceland, Ireland, Norway and the United States.

The third NAN conference was held in Bergen (Norway) on Aug. 22–25, 1985, and attended by 100 activists from Northern Europe, the United States and Canada as well as representatives from Australia and Japan.

Membership. NAN has some 40 active participating groups in 14 Atlantic seaboard countries, especially those belonging to NATO.

Publication. A NAN newsletter is published from Oslo.

Nuclear-Free and Independent Pacific (NFIP)

Address. c/o P.O. Box A243, Sydney South, New South Wales 2000, Australia

Aims and objectives. The NFIP network of movements opposes the testing, deployment and transit of nuclear weapons and nuclear-powered ships in the Pacific. It also opposes the dumping of nuclear waste in the Pacific and backs the moves to create a nuclear-free zone in that ocean.

Activities. The NFIP network has been prominent in many protest and other actions in the Pacific region, notably the international day of action against sea-launched cruise missiles held on June 15, 1985, in co-operation with the North Atlantic Network and other movements.

Membership. The NFIP network embraces groups in Australia, Fiji, Hawaii, Japan, New Zealand, the Philippines and the west coast of the United States.

Nuclear-Free Ports Network (NFPN)

Address. c/o Alf Harbitz, Auroral Observatory, PO Box 952, Tromsö 9001, Norway

Aims and objectives. As an offshoot of the North Atlantic Network (see separate entry), the NFPN seeks to co-ordinate local campaigns and actions to secure the banning of nuclear-armed or nuclear-powered ships from the ports of the North Atlantic seaboard.

Pacific Trade Union Forum

Address. c/o Australian Council of Trade Unions, 393–397 Swanston Street, Melbourne, Victoria 3000, Australia

Aims and objectives. As a body for maintaining and strengthening links between the trade union federations of the Pacific states, the Forum has as a central policy aim the establishment of a nuclear-free zone in the Pacific.

Formation. The Forum was established in 1980.

Activities. The Forum has held conferences in Vanuatu (1981), New Caledonia (1982), Fiji (1984) and Auckland (May 1986). Its co-ordinating committee (executive) meets once or twice a year.

Membership. Trade union centres in 14 countries.

Parliamentarians Global Action (PGA)

Address. 304 East 45th Street, 12th floor, New York, NY 10017, USA

Aims and objectives. PGA seeks to provide an international focus for parliamentarians and other citizens who are working for world peace and disarmament.

Formation. The organization came into existence in 1979 (originally as Parliamentarians for World Order).

Activities. PGA acts as a channel of communication for members of national parliaments seeking to exert pressure on governments to bring about progress in disarmament negotiations. It has been particularly involved in the Five Continents Peace Initiative (see separate entry), which came about directly as a result of preparatory work by its members, notably the two co-presidents, John Silkin (UK) and Douglas Roche (Canada).

Pax Christi International (PCI)

Address. Kerkstraat 150, B-2000 Antwerp, Belgium

Aims and objectives. As the "international Catholic movement for peace", Pax Christi International seeks to educate Catholics throughout the world to work for peace and co-operation in accordance with the teachings of the Church of Rome. While emphasizing its essential concern for peace on earth, the organization and its constituent sections urge disarmament, and particularly the abolition of nuclear weapons, as prerequisites for a just world order. Although not an official arm of the Roman Catholic Church, PCI is officially recognized by the Vatican.

Formation. Pax Christi International was established in 1945 at Agen in France, as a vehicle for post-war Franco-German reconciliation.

Activities. Over the past 40 years Pax Christi International has acted as the international focus for Catholic peace work throughout the world, enabling the numerous national sections to achieve greater awareness of each other and to co-operate in various activities. Through annual meetings of its International Council (which elects an international executive committee) and the work of specialist commissions, the organization contributes to the development and propagation of a Catholic response to peace and disarmament questions.

In February 1986 PCI's security and disarmament commission issued a declaration (i) urging the United States, Britain and France to join the moratorium on nuclear testing then being observed by the Soviet Union; (ii) calling for the elimination of Soviet SS20 and US cruise and Pershing II missiles, starting with a moratorium on any further deployment; and (iii) stressing the importance of progress on a comprehensive nuclear test-ban treaty and an agreement on intermediate forces in Europe.

Membership. Pax Christi International has 16 national sections, mostly in developed countries, although it has recently promoted the creation of new sections in Latin America, the Caribbean and South-East Asia.

Publication. International Bulletin, quarterly.

Peace and Justice Service
Servicio Paz y Justicia (Serpaj)

Address. Av. Ipiranga 1273, 01039 São Paulo, Brazil; Serpaj-Europa: Bohemen 25, 3831 EP Leuden, Netherlands

Aims and objectives. The Serpaj network of groups in Latin America is committed to non-violent action to promote regional peace in the broad sense, involving not only resistance to US interventionism but also active participation in human rights campaigns and developmental work.

Activities. Serpaj branches have been established in most Central and South American countries, where the movement's activists work in villages, schools and churches on humanitarian and developmental projects, and human rights initiatives based on the principle of non-violence. The movement has been closely involved in promoting the "pledge of resistance", which commits signatories to take action if the United States invades or otherwise escalates its intervention in Central America. At the Serpaj "continental meeting" held in Lima (Peru) in February 1986 Adolfo Pérez Esquivel of Argentina (winner of the Nobel Peace Prize in 1980) stood down after 12 years as co-ordinator of the movement and was succeeded by Creuza Maciel of Brazil.

With support from War Resisters' International, the International Fellowship of Reconciliation and Pax Christi International, a Serpaj presence has been established in Western Europe (with an office in the Netherlands) for the channelling of financial and moral support to the movement in Latin America.

Peace Brigades International (PBI)

Address. 4722 Baltimore Avenue, suite 2, Philadelphia, PA 19143, USA

Aims and objectives. PBI acts as a central agency for the sending of groups of voluntary workers overseas to participate in community and developmental projects, especially in developing countries, with a view to promoting international understanding and peace.

Activities. PBI has in recent years been particularly active in arranging for "peace brigades" to serve in the Central American region. It has also worked with War Resisters' International on a number of projects.

Publication. Peace Brigades (quarterly).

Pensioners for Peace International (PPI)

Address. c/o Jack Sheppard, No. 1, Viewfield, Como Road, Great Malvern, WR14 2TH, United Kingdom

Aims and objectives. PPI seeks to promote the formation of groups of retired people to enable them to participate in the peace movement. It has a single policy statement—"The only true road to peace and world disarmament lies through love, friendship and understanding"—and calls upon its supporters to work to achieve that end. It believes that the vote of pensioners "is vital if peace is to be achieved through the ballot box". PPI declares itself to be "non-party, non-sectarian, non-racial".

Formation. The organization was started (by Jack Sheppard, a Quaker) in Britain in May 1981 as Pensioners for Peace; the designation International was added the following year when overseas groups began to be formed.

Activities. PPI has built up a network of groups of retired people in many countries who meet regularly to discuss the issues of peace and disarmament; such groups have complete autonomy, with the PPI itself acting as a clearing house for information and establishment of contacts. In 1983 PPI initiated Peace and Friendship Tours to Eastern Bloc Countries with the aim of facilitating visits to communist-ruled states by pensioners and others. The PPI has undertaken promotion tours to Australia, New Zealand and South Africa.

Membership. PPI links groups in Andorra, Australia, Bulgaria, Canada, Czechoslovakia, France, East and West Germany, India, Ireland, Italy, Japan, Mauritius, the Netherlands, New Zealand, Norway, Portugal, Romania, South Africa, the Soviet Union, Spain, Sweden, the United Kingdom, the United

States and Yugoslavia. It claims to be "one of the most dynamic and fastest growing peace movements in the world".

Publications. In addition to a regular newsletter, PPI has published three pamphlets: *Russian Threat* (by Richard Tolhurst). *To Begin at the Beginning* (by Phil Braithwaite) and *The Truth about the Allied Intervention in Soviet Russia* (by M. Philips Price).

Quaker Council for European Affairs

Address. 50 Square Ambiorix, 1040 Brussels, Belgium

Aims and objectives. To give voice in the European political context to the Quaker precept to "speak truth to power", and foster "the ideals of love, peace and justice in the social, economic and political life of Europe today."

Formation. The Council was established in 1979.

Activities. The Council has joined Christian and peace organizations in various actions and events in Brussels (Churches Committee for Migrant Workers in Europe, European Nuclear Disarmament, Committee for Security and Co-operation in Europe etc.). It organizes seminars and conferences, actively supports conscientious objection, works for an East-West reconciliation and against poverty.

Membership. There is no official membership; mailing list of monthly periodical is around 3,500.

Publications. Around Europe (monthly magazine); various pamphlets: *Conscientious Objection to Military Service in Europe* (1981/84), *Paying for Peace* (1982/85), *Europe and the Third World* (1985), *Crowd Control* (1985), *Prisoners on Remand in Europe* (1985).

Affiliations. European yearly meetings of Society of Friends; Quaker peace groups; Quaker United Nations Office; church organizations in Brussels; peace organizations in Belgium; European Nuclear Disarmament (END); conscientious objection movements in Europe.

Science for Peace International Network (SPIN)

Address. c/o Science for Peace, University College, Toronto University, Toronto, Ontario, M5S 1A1, Canada

Aims and objectives. SPIN seeks to facilitate co-operation between scientists in various national movements dedicated to the prevention of nuclear war. It is a loose organization whose principal objective is the exchange of literature between its member groups. It also aims to assist in convening peace symposia of scientists at relevant international gatherings.

Membership. SPIN has member organizations in Argentina, Canada, Iceland, New Zealand, Japan, the Soviet Union and the United States.

Servas International

Address. 11 John Street, room 406, New York, NY 10038, USA

Aims and objectives. Servas International is an international co-operative network of hosts and travellers seeking to help build world peace, goodwill and understanding by providing opportunities for deeper, more personal contacts among people of diverse cultures and backgrounds. It is a non-profit, non-governmental, inter-racial and inter-faith organization.

Formation. Servas was first conceived by an international youth group studying in Askov (Denmark) in 1948 and was originally called the "Open-door System of Work, Study and Travel". The name Servas (the Esperanto word for "serve") was later adopted to denote the spirit of international mutual service to which the movement aspires.

Activities. The Servas International network around the world is basically concerned with the organization of international visits during which the traveller shares in the life of the home and the community of the host. He or she also shares the hosts' concerns for social and international problems, their interest in creative activity and mutual responsibility for their fellow beings.

Membership. Servas International has hosts in every region of the United States and hosts or contacts in the following countries and territories: Antigua, Argentina, Australia, Austria, Bahrain, Bangladesh, Barbados, Belgium, Belize, Bolivia, Botswana, Brazil, Britain, Bulgaria, Burkina Faso, Burundu, Canada, Chile, Colombia, Costa Rica, Denmark, Dominica, Ecuador, Egypt, Fiji, Finland, France, Germany, Ghana, Greece, Guadeloupe, Guam, Guatemala, Honduras, Hong Kong, Hungary, Iceland, India, Indonesia, Ireland, Israel, Italy, Jamaica, Japan, Kenya, Korea, Kuwait, Lesotho, Luxembourg, Madagascar, Malaysia, Mali, Malta, Martinique, Mauritius, Mexico, Morocco, Nepal, Netherlands, Netherlands Antilles, New Zealand, Nicaragua, Nigeria, Norway, Pakistan, Panama, Papua New Guinea, Peru, Philippines, Poland, Portugal, Puerto Rico, Réunion, Romania, St Kitts, Samoa, Saudi Arabia, Sierra Leone, Singapore, South Africa, Spain, Sri Lanka, Sudan, Sweden, Switzerland, Taiwan, Tahiti, Tanzania, Thailand, Trinidad, Tunisia, Turkey, Uganda, Uruguay, USSR, Venezuela, Virgin Islands, Yugoslavia, Zaïre, Zambia and Zimbabwe.

Publication. International News.

Affiliations. Servas International has consultative status with the United Nations.

Service Civil International (SCI)

Address. 13 Wincheap, Canterbury, Kent, CT1 3TB, United Kingdom (international secretariat); Venusstraat 28, 2000 Antwerp, Belgium (European secretariat)

Aims and objectives. SCI is an international non-governmental organization committed to the promotion of peace and international understanding through voluntary service activities.

Formation. SCI was originally established in 1920.

Activities. SCI acts as the international co-ordinating body for national SCI groups, identifying and organizing projects in which voluntary workers are able to assist countries other than their own. It co-operates with independent organizations in over 30 countries.

Membership. There are over 20 national SCI groups and branches in Western Europe, Asia and North America.

Publication. Action (bi-monthly).

Affiliations. SCI has consultative status with UNESCO and the Council of Europe and is a member of the Co-ordinating Committee for International Voluntary Service and the Youth Forum of the European Communities.

United Nations Department for Disarmament Affairs

Address. Department for Disarmament Affairs, UN, New York, NY 10017, USA

Aims and objectives. The Department functions as the organizational unit of the UN Secretariat dealing with matters related to disarmament. The Secretariat's duties in this field derive from both the founding charter of the UN and subsequent resolutions passed by the General Assembly and Security Council.

In the Charter, founding member states of the UN committed themselves to "maintain international peace and security . . . with the least diversion for armaments of the world's human and economic resources". Subsequent resolutions and decisions of the Security Council and General Assembly have confirmed and expanded these aims, particularly in the context of the General Assembly's special sessions on disarmament in 1978 and 1982.

Formation. The Department was formed as a result of decisions taken in resolution 37/99 K (adopted in 1982), which covered efforts to strengthen the role of the UN in disarmament matters. The resolution provided specifically for the transformation of the Centre for Disarmament within the Department of Political and Security Council Affairs into the Department of Disarmament Affairs, to be headed by an under-secretary general reporting direct to the UN Secretary-General. The transformation took place with effect from January 1, 1983.

Activities. The Department consists of the Office of the Under-Secretary-General, which includes a Co-ordination and World Disarmament Campaigns Section, together with a Committee and Conference Services Branch, an Information and Studies Branch and a Geneva Branch.

The Office of the Under-Secretary-General deals with policy formulation and decision-making, as well as assessing "disarmament-related developments" within and outside the UN. The Co-ordination and World Disarmament Campaign Section deals with the Department's relations with other UN agencies. It co-ordinates the work of the World Disarmament Campaign within the UN and maintains links with related non-governmental organizations (NGOs) and with groups affiliated to the World Disarmament Campaign. (For Disarmament Committee of NGOs recognized by the United Nations, see next entry.)

The Committee and Conference Services branch fulfils secretariat and administrative "support services" for the First Committee of the General Assembly (which deals specifically with questions related to disarmament and international security) to the Disarmament Commission, and to relevant ad hoc committees, working groups and conferences to review disarmament agreements, treaties and conventions. It follows up and reports on resolutions and decisions of the General Assembly.

The Department's Information and Studies Branch prepares UN publications on disarmament and provides support to meetings of expert groups on disarmament. It maintains a library of documents and literature on armaments and disarmament.

The Geneva branch fulfils broadly similar duties to those outlined above, as well as providing "support services" to the Conference on Disarmament, which is based at Geneva.

Publications. Among the publications prepared by the Information and Studies Branch of the Department are the *UN Disarmament Yearbook,* the *Fact Sheet* series and the *Disarmament Studies* series. It also produces the periodical *Disarmament.*

United Nations Non-Governmental Organizations' Committee on Disarmament

Address. 777 UN Plaza, New York, NY 10017, USA

Aims and objectives. The Committee seeks to promote international peace and disarmament in terms of the recommendations of the two special sessions of the UN General Assembly on disarmament (held in 1978 and 1982). It operates within the framework of the UN Conference of Non-Governmental Organizations (CONGO), i.e. those NGOs which have consultative status at the United Nations.

Universal House of Justice—Baha'i World Centre

Address. P.O. Box 155, 31 001 Haifa, Israel

Aims and objectives. The Universal House of Justice is the international governing council of the world-wide Baha'i community. On the basis of the teachings of its founder, Baha'u'llah, the Baha'i faith teaches universal peace and human brotherhood. In a tract called *The Promise of World Peace* published to mark 1986 as International Year of Peace, the Universal House of Justice asserts that "the current world confusion and calamitous condition in human affairs" should be seen as "a natural phase in an organic process leading ultimately and irresistibly to the unification of the human race in a single social order whose boundaries are those of the planet". "The human race", it continues, "has passed through evolutionary stages analogous to the stages of infancy and childhood in the lives of its individual members, and is now in the culminating period of its turbulent adolescence approaching its long-awaited coming of age".

University Days for Peace, International Association
Association Internationale des Journées Universitaires de la Paix

Address. Avenue Jeanne 44, B-1050 Brussels, Belgium

Aims and objectives. This Association seeks to persuade all universities and further education colleges throughout the world, without distinction as to nationality or philosophical affiliation, to dedicate one day a year to the study of peace. It also seeks to promote discussion, dialogue and research within the university community on the means and modalities of realizing and maintaining world peace.

Activities. Pursuant to its basic objectives, the Association has organized annual university weeks for the study of peace issues as well as international colloquia on such topics as the (US) Strategic Defence Initiative.

Publications. The Arms Race and University Opinion (report of the Association's 1981 colloquium); *The American Strategic Defence Initiative* (1985).

Affiliations. The Association does not affiliate to other peace groups in order to ensure optimal co-operation with all groups.

War Resisters' International (WRI)
Internationale des Résistants à la Guerre

Address. 55 Dawes Street, London, SE17 1EL, United Kingdom

Aims and objectives. WRI is a non-aligned peace group with sections in 17 countries. It is opposed to all forms of militarism and to the use of war as a means to an end, and it works for non-violent means of solving conflicts. Members accept a basic statement which runs as follows: "War is a crime against humanity. I am therefore determined not to support any kind of war and to strive for the removal of all causes of war."

Formation. WRI was founded in 1921.

Activities. The recognition of conscientious objection to military service as a basic human right has remained the principal goal of WRI's activities over the years. The group presented its first petition on this subject to the UN General Assembly in 1949, and it has subsequently lobbied the UN Commission on Human Rights, the European Parliament and the Council of Europe, as well as national governments, in an effort to achieve this goal.

WRI provides advice and support for conscientious objectors and army deserters. In recent years it has assisted objectors in the USA and Europe, and also in Israel, Egypt, Iraq, Thailand and South Africa. It publishes surveys on conscription and conscientious objection, and, on Prisoners for Peace Day (December 1), it issues a list of objectors currently serving terms of imprisonment. WRI holds regular conferences and meetings on the subject.

The group also provide support for various "peace tax" initiatives and for individuals who refuse to work in military industries or to take part in military ceremonies or instruction.

WRI sections have taken part in national demonstrations on disarmament and the arms trade and also racism, apartheid and other economic and social issues. WRI has also helped organize several international demonstrations, including the San Francisco to Moscow march against nuclear weapons in 1960–61, the Helsinki to Belgrade disarmament relay in 1978 and the Brussels to Warsaw Peace Caravan of 1979. The group helped establish the International Non-Violent March for Demilitarization. It also participated in protests against the French nuclear tests programme in the Sahara in the early 1960s.

In response to the Soviet-led intervention in Czechoslovakia in 1968, WRI sent international teams to convey messages of protest to the Soviet, Hungarian, Bulgarian, East German and Polish governments.

Regular conferences are held every three years, and the group also participates in meetings organized by other bodies, such as the European Antimilitarist Congress (held in Brussels in 1974) and the International Womens' Gatherings, held every four years. It was also represented at the UN General Assembly's Second Special Session on Disarmament (UNSSOD II) in 1982.

WRI co-operates with other organizations in research on such issues as non-violent civilian defence policy, conversion of military industries to socially useful production and peace education. A number of national WRI sections are involved in non-violent action training programmes, these experiences being brought together in the International Seminars on Training for Non-Violent Action.

WRI works actively with human rights groups and individuals in Latin America, Eastern Europe and South Africa. It also seeks to provide support to minority groups, including the Samis of Norway, the Tamils of Sri Lanka and the North American Indians. It has also given assistance to refugees and victims of war, notably in the Spanish Civil War and the Second World War. In the early

1970s WRI members helped organize the transport of medicines across the Indian-Bangladesh border. WRI formed a World Peace Brigade in the early 1950s, and recently it has become involved with the work of the Peace Brigades International, some members of which travelled to Central America in 1983.

WRI held its 18th triennial conference in India in January 1986 under the slogan "Resistance and Reconstruction".

Membership. WRI has sections in Belgium, Canada, Denmark, France, West Germany, India, Israel, Italy, Japan, the Netherlands, New Zealand, Norway, Spain, Sri Lanka, Sweden, the United Kingdom and the United States, as well as associated organizations in Austria, Belgium, Finland, France, West Germany, Italy, Japan, the Netherlands, Spain, Sweden, the United Kingdom and the United States (International Seminars on Training for Non-Violent Action and the Scandinavian-wide Campaign Against Conscription also being associated with WRI). The activities of affiliates are co-ordinated and linked through the London headquarters and through regular meetings of an elected International Council. The group is attempting to extend its membership in Eastern Europe and the Third World in particular.

Publications. *WRI Newsletter* is published six times per year; in the months between, a news-sheet (*The Broken Rifle* in English, *Le Fusil Brise* in French and *Das Zerbrochene Gewehr* in German) carries urgent information. The group has also published a number of booklets, including *Towards Liberation* (an analysis of non-violent revolution) and *Polish Summer* (on the rise of Solidarity). National sections produce their own publications, while *Peace News* (UK) and *Dawn* (Ireland) are associated with the WRI.

Affiliations. WRI has consultative status with UNESCO as a non-governmental organization.

Women's International League for Peace and Freedom (WILPF)

Address. 1 rue de Varembé, C.P. 28, 1211 Geneva 20, Switzerland

Aims and objectives. WILPF's main aim is to bring together women from different political and philosophical backgrounds who are "united in their determination to study, make known and help abolish the political, social, economic and psychological causes of war, and to work for a constructive peace". It seeks complete and universal disarmament and the abolition of violent or coercive means of settling conflicts. It supports the strengthening of the UN and its specialized agencies as institutions for the prevention of war and engendering of international political, social and economic co-operation.

WILPF supports non-violent political change to secure the elimination of racial and sexual discrimination, respect for basic human rights and the achievement of economic and political equality within and between states. Its "ultimate goal" is stated as "the establishment of an international economic order founded on meeting the needs of all peoples and not on privilege and profit".

Formation. WILPF arose out of a decision taken in April 1915 at an international congress of women meeting at The Hague, Netherlands, which had been called as a protest against the war and to discuss ways of peacefully resolving it. The congress, organized by members of the international suffrage alliance, brought together over 1,000 women from both neutral and belligerent countries. It established an International Committee of Women for Permanent Peace, which sent delegations to heads of 13 states in Europe and to the USA. In 1919 the

International Committee was reconstituted as the Women's International League for Peace and Freedom.

Activities. WILPF has held numerous conferences through its history, commencing with the inaugural Zürich congress in 1919, which passed resolutions denouncing the Versailles treaty as likely to create the conditions for a future world war. In 1922 it held a Conference for a New Peace, which demanded the establishment of a new economic order as a means of removing grievances which could become seeds for future conflict.

WILPF held a conference on chemical and biological weapons in London in 1969. The following year, an Inter-American Women's Congress took place in Bogota, Colombia. In 1975, WILPF convened the Women's Disarmament Conference at the UN in New York, and a conference on Women and the World Disarmament Campaign took place in March 1984, also at the UN.

WILPF has organized a series of campaigns on various issues, of which the first, launched in 1924, aimed to mobilize scientists to refuse to engage in research for military purposes. A campaign against traffic in opium followed in 1929, and in 1932 WILPF succeeded in collecting over 6,000,000 signatures for a World Disarmament Petition, which was subsequently delivered to the World Disarmament Conference held in Geneva in that year. During the Second World War, the League's activities were concentrated on providing relief and assistance to victims of fascism.

WILPF was actively involved in the campaign against US involvement in the Vietnam war from 1965 onwards, and it sent missions to both North and South Vietnam in 1971. In 1982 it launched its Stop The Arms Race (STAR) signature campaign, and in March of the following year held a conference and mass rally in Brussels (Belgium) to protest against the NATO decision to deploy Cruise and Pershing missiles in Europe.

WILPF has sent several missions to areas of conflict. Following its call for the pursuance by the US government of a "good neighbour" policy towards Latin American countries, WILPF in 1962 dispatched a mission to Haiti to investigate the effects of the stationing of US marines in that country. The following year WILPF members visited China and Indo-China to establish and strengthen links with women there. In 1967, a mission visited the Middle East to investigate prospects for peace following the Six Day Arab-Israeli war. A further visit to this area was made in 1975. In 1982, a WILPF mission travelled to Central America.

Jane Addams, then WILPF's international president, received the Nobel Peace Prize in 1931, while Emily Greene Balch, WILPF's first international secretary, was awarded the prize in 1946. The recipient of the 1982 Nobel Peace Prize, Alva Myrdal of Sweden, was a longstanding WILPF member.

WILPF maintains close contact with the UN (with which it has consultative status—see below), and offers two one-year internships to young women to learn about the work of the UN in the fields of disarmament and human rights.

Regular WILPF congresses are held every three years to formulate policies and elect officers. Each national section is represented by its own delegation. An executive committee meets annually to review the organization's work and plan activities for the following year in the light of congress decisions.

Membership. WILPF has 30 national sections in 26 countries and over 50,000 individual members. It operates on the local, national and international level.

Publications. WILPF's journal, *Pax et Libertas*, is published quarterly; it also produces an *International Newsletter* and *United Nations Action Alerts*, as well as brochures, leaflets and reports.

Affiliations. WILPF has consultative status with the Economic and Social Council of the UN (ECOSOC), the UN Educational, Scientific and Cultural Organization (UNESCO), and the UN Conference on Trade and Development (UNCTAD). It has established special relations with the UN Children's Fund (UNICEF), the International Labour Office (ILO) and the Food and Agriculture Organization (FAO).

World Association for the School as an Instrument of Peace
Association Mondiale pour l'Ecole Instrument de Paix (EIP)

Address. 5 rue du Simplon, 1207 Geneva, Switzerland

Aims and objectives. EIP promotes peace and human rights education in primary and secondary schools and in "professional training centres". It is committed in particular to the introduction of school classes on the UN's Declaration of Human Rights, so that "children and young people will have the opportunity to learn and understand the principles of this declaration, which form a real basis for peace in the world".

Formation. EIP was formed in Geneva in 1967 by Jacques Mühlethaler.

Activities. During 1980–82, the EIP organized a series of seminars on human rights education for teachers in primary and secondary schools. These seminars were subsequently expanded to take the form of international human rights teacher training sessions, intended for teachers in primary and secondary schools and also in colleges of education. They were held in 1983–85 in Strasbourg and in Geneva.

EIP is currently planning to establish an international human rights teacher training centre, which will organize regular teaching sessions, as well as providing information about human rights.

EIP runs the *Cahiers de l'Amitié* (Friendship Exercise Books) project, which is designed to provide a link between children in Europe and the developing world.

Membership. EIP has a total of 5,000 members, both individuals and organizations. Among its patrons are Sean MacBride, Alfred Kastler, Linus Pauling and Jean Piaget.

Publications. EIP publishes a quarterly newspaper, *Ecole et Paix*, as well as an explanatory pamphlet. It has also produced *Pour mieux comprendre la Declaration universelle des droits de l'homme* (For a Better Understanding of the Universal Declaration of Human Rights), which is available in French, English, Spanish, German and Esperanto, and *Dessine-moi un droit de l'homme* (Draw me a Human Right), a version of the Declaration with illustrations by 53 artists.

EIP is working with the University of Geneva on the production of a simplified version of the Declaration of Human Rights, to be used for educational purposes, written in basic French.

Affiliations. Recognized as a non-governmental organization with consultative status B at UNESCO, EIP is accredited to the UN and to the Council of Europe. It maintains informal links with other peace and human rights groups.

World Conference on Religion and Peace (WCRP)

Address. Apt. 12, 777 UN Plaza, New York, NY 10017, USA; 14 chemin Auguste-Vilbert, 1218 GD Saconnex, Geneva, Switzerland (European office)

Aims and objectives. WCRP seeks to promote co-operation between the world's religions in the cause of peace and justice. It also undertakes humanitarian work on a multi-religious basis.

Formation. The first WCRP world assembly was held in Kyoto (Japan) in 1970.

Activities. The second world assembly was held in Louvain (Belgium) in 1974, the third in Princeton (USA) in 1979 and the fourth in Nairobi (Kenya) in 1984. Humanitarian projects have been carried out with the Vietnamese boat people, Kampuchean refugees and the victims of drought in Africa (to whom $400,000 in "multi-religious aid" was donated in 1985). In 1985 the WCRP organized eight youth camps in Asia, Africa and Europe and also undertook a "reconciliation visit" to all religious communities in South Africa in September 1985.

Membership. WCRP has approximately 1,500 formal subscription-paying members but a much wider network based on the religions of the world (its assemblies being attended by fraternal delegates from a variety of religious and peace organizations). It has national chapters in some 30 countries and regional organizations in Asia, Africa and Europe.

Publications. The newsletter *Religion and Peace* is published three times a year; the proceedings of the four WCRP world assemblies have also been published.

Affiliations. Consultative status (category 2) at UNESCO; working relationships with a wide range of religious and peace movements throughout the world.

World Disarmament Campaign—see under United Kingdom

World Peace Council (WPC)

Address. Lönnrotinkatu 25A/VI, SF 00180 Helsinki 18, Finland

Aims and objectives. The WPC seeks to build an international alliance of democratic forces to campaign for the prevention of nuclear war, peaceful co-existence and general disarmament. Its basic principles advocate the settlement of inter-state disputes by negotiation and respect for the right of all peoples to sovereignty and independence. It also calls for the abolition of colonialism and racial discrimination, seeing these phenomena as threats to international peace.

Formation. The WPC was created in 1950 at the Second World Peace Congress held in Warsaw in 1950; it succeeded the World Committee of Partisans of Peace established the previous year.

Activities. Originally based in Paris, the WPC was expelled from that capital in 1952 (the French government claiming that it was engaging in "fifth column" activities) and moved its headquarters first to Prague and then to Vienna. In 1957, however, it was banned by the Austrian government, whereupon it changed its name and continued to function in the Austrian capital until 1968, when its headquarters were transferred to Helsinki and its original title resumed.

The WPC has engaged in a wide range of activities in furtherance of its principles, notably a series of major world peace congresses and other international gatherings (usually held in Soviet-bloc countries). It can claim to be the world's premier peace organization in terms of the numbers of participating bodies (see below). However, the WPC is regarded by most Western governments as a "communist front" organization; moreover, many non-communist parties and groups have expressed reservations over the extent to which WPC declarations tend to echo official Soviet policy theses.

Membership. The WPC claims over 2,000 participating parties and movements from some 140 countries, as well as over 30 international organizations.

Publications. Peace Courier (monthly); *New Perspectives* (six a year).

Affiliations. NGO status at the United Nations, UNESCO, UNCTAD, UNIDO and ILO.

2. WESTERN EUROPE

Austria

capital: Vienna   **population: 7,579,000**

The Austrian State Treaty, ending more than 10 years of Allied occupation preceded by seven years of political and military union with Nazi Germany, was signed in Vienna on May 15, 1955, by the Foreign Ministers and ambassadors of the four occupying powers (the Soviet Union, the United States, the United Kingdom and France) and by the Austrian Foreign Minister. Under its terms the Allied and associated powers recognized the re-establishment of Austria as a "sovereign, independent and democratic state" and declared their respect for Austria's territorial integrity within the frontiers of Jan. 1, 1938. The treaty specifically banned any future political or economic union with Germany and also provided that Austria "shall not possess, construct or experiment with" certain categories of weapons, including nuclear weapons, other weapons of mass destruction, and chemical or biological weapons.

Following the signature of the State Treaty a resolution on Austria's permanent neutrality was adopted as a constitutional law on Oct. 26, 1955, and came into force on Nov. 5, 1955. It stated (i) that with the object of the lasting and perpetual maintenance of her independence and the inviolability of her territory, as well as in the interest of maintaining internal law and order, "Austria declares of her own free will her perpetual neutrality, and is resolved to maintain and defend it with all means at her disposal"; and (ii) that Austria, in order to secure these objectives, "will join no military alliances and will not permit the establishment of military bases of foreign states on her territory".

As at end-1985 the total strength of the Austrian armed forces was about 55,000 personnel (including some 5,000 in the air force), of which about half were conscripts and half professional soldiers. There is compulsory military service in Austria, currently of six months' initial training for conscripts (reduced from nine months in 1971) followed by up to 60 days of refresher training for reservists (who number about 170,000). A special form of service is available for conscientious objectors. Defence expenditure rose from 16,484 million schillings in 1984 to 17,875 million schillings in 1985, the latter figure representing about 4 per cent of the total federal budget.

Austrian Peace Research Institute
Österreichisches Institut für Friedensforschung

Address. 7461 Stadschlaining, Burg, Austria

Aims and objectives. This Institute has as its main objectives the promotion, co-ordination and funding of peace research, particular emphasis being placed on educative and informational work.

Formation. The Institute was established as a non-profit-making body and as a joint undertaking of the federal Government, the Burgenland provincial administration and the Austrian Academy of Sciences.

37

Activities. Research sponsored by the Institute has focused on such topics as the nature of confidence-building measures between East and West, human rights and the North-South conflict. The Institute has sought to promote East-West dialogue on scientific and political questions and also to assist the teaching of peace studies at school and university levels.

Citizens' Initiative Against Nuclear Weapons
Bürgerinitiative gegen Atomgefahren

Address. Postfach 14, A-1123 Vienna, Austria

Aims and objectives. This movement seeks to mobilize public opinion against the use of nuclear power, for military and civil purposes.

Activities. Through regular conferences and other initiatives, the movement has emphasized the threat posed by the nuclear arms race to Austria notwithstanding its non-nuclear-weapons and neutral status.

Publication. Information des Zentralverbandes (newsletter).

International Voluntary Service—Austrian Group of SCI (SCI-Austria)
Internationale Freiwilligendienste—Österreichische Gruppe Des Service Civil International

Address. Schottengasse 3A/1/4/59, A-1010 Vienna, Austria

Aims and objectives. SCI aims to promote peace and international understanding through voluntary service.

Formation. There were Austrian SCI branches in the 1950s and 1960s but the group was re-formed in 1982.

Activities. SCI-Austria runs five or six international work camps a year and participates in the Austrian peace movement. The organization has also organized an ecology cycle tour and participated in grassroots initiatives.

Membership. SCI-Austria has 50 members; around 80 volunteers take part in work camps of SCI branches and other partner organizations every year.

Affiliations. Service Civil International (SCI).

Meeting Centre for Active Non-Violence
Begegnungs Zentrum für Active Gewaltlösigkeit

Address. St Wolfgangerstrasse 26, A-4820 Bad Ischl, Austria

Aims and objectives. This Centre seeks to provide a focus for the development and furtherance of the principles of non-violence and conscientious objection.

Publication. Rundbrief (quarterly).

Affiliations. War Resisters' International; International Fellowship of Reconciliation.

Paxclub

Address. Postfach 488, A-4021 Linz, Austria

Aims and objectives. Paxclub defines its objectives as "the collection and distribution of information about peace".

Activities. Its members hold what it describes as "semi-private" discussions concerning the "real mechanisms of war" and the consequent strategy to be adopted for the achievement of peace.

The organization is currently taking part in work leading towards the proposed worldwide referendum on nuclear weapons, as initiated by Matt Sherman of the USA.

Membership. Paxclub has a limited membership which is, by intention, "small and selective".

Publications. While having no publications of its own, several members have produced their own material independently.

Respect for Life (REST)

Address. Studio International, Postfach 488, A-4021 Linz, Austria

Aims and objectives. The achievement of peace through respect for life.

Formation. REST was originally founded in Huntsville, Alabama, USA, in 1970.

Activities. REST moved to Linz in December 1971 and established the *World Peace Press* in 1975. Emphasis in the future will be on peace research "with applicable results".

Publications. World Peace Press (quarterly); and three books (*The Principle of Natural Borders, Bericht über Jesus Christus* and *Jesus Spricht*).

Vienna Peace Club
Friedensgesellschaft Wien

Address. Steinergasse 15/9, A-1170 Vienna, Austria

Working Group for Civilian Service, Non-Violence and Social Defence
Arbeitsgemeinschaft für Zivildienst, Gewaltfreiheit und Soziale Verteidigung

Address. Schottengasse 3A/1/59, A-1010 Vienna, Austria

Aims and objectives. The Group aims to develop alternative forms of war resistance and to promote non-violence, unilateral disarmament and basic democracy.

Formation. The Group was formed in 1977, two years after it became possible to do civilian service as an alternative to military service in Austria.

Activities. As part of its overall resistance to the militarization of society the Working Group began by opposing the concept of "comprehensive defence", i.e. the involvement of all civilians in the defence of the country and preparation for war. It subsequently widened its resistance to exclude even civilian service as an acceptable alternative. The Group opposes the deployment in Austria of a new generation of military aircraft purchased from Sweden (due in 1987) and it plans to carry out public relations exercises in anti-militarism. The Group also organizes direct actions against military parades and exercises.

Publications. Non-violent Resistance (published every two months); *Civilian Service* (an information bulletin published from time to time).

Affiliations. The Working Group is affiliated to War Resisters' International and regards itself as part of the Austrian peace movement.

Working Group of Independent Peace Initiatives of Austria
Arbeitsgemeinschaft Unabhängiger Friedensinitiativen Österreichs
(ARGE-UFI)

Address. Seilerstätte 30, A-1010 Vienna, Austria

Aims and objectives. ARGE-UFI is the principal umbrella organization for Austrian peace and anti-nuclear movements that are independent of political parties, as well as for other "alternative" groups. Its particular aims include the dissolution of the NATO and Warsaw Pact blocs and the establishment of a nuclear-free zone around Austria.

Formation. ARGE-UFI came into being at a meeting held in Innsbruck in April 1982, when a number of loosely linked peace and anti-nuclear groups met to consider future strategy. The new organization arose out of a major peace march held in June 1981, described as the first manifestation of the "new" Austrian peace movement.

Activities. ARGE-UFI participated in a 70,000-strong Austrian peace demonstration on May 15, 1982, and in August of that year organized an "East-West dialogue" in Vienna with participation by East European civil rights activists. In subsequent activities it has campaigned against Austrian arms manufacture and exports and in favour of non-violent alternatives, including the conversion of the arms manufacturing industry to socially useful purposes. It has also strongly advocated measures to reduce East-West tensions arising from military confrontation in sensitive Central European areas adjoining Austrian territory.

ARGE-UFI worked closely with Italian peace activists in a successful campaign to secure the withdrawal (in mid-1983) of Lance nuclear missiles from NATO bases in South Tirol. In December 1983 it put forward the "Villach proposal" (drawn up by the peace committee of that Austrian city in co-operation with the Italian peace movement) calling for a nuclear-free and partially demilitarized zone around Austria and envisaging the withdrawal of nuclear weapons and offensive troops from adjoining areas of West Germany, Italy, Hungary and Czechoslovakia. ARGE-UFI has also worked closely with the Italian and independent Yugoslav peace movements in campaigns for the demilitarization of the Alps-Adria region, to which end the Alps-Adria Peace Network was established in November 1984 (see entry under International Organizations).

Publication. Friedensinfo (quarterly).

Affiliations. ARGE-UFI has represented the Austrian peace movement at successive conventions of European Nuclear Disarmament (END).

Belgium

capital: Brussels   **population: 9,920,000**

Belgium was an original signatory on April 4, 1949, of the treaty creating the North Atlantic Treaty Organization (NATO), together with Canada, Denmark, France, Iceland, Italy, Luxembourg, the Netherlands, Norway, Portugal, the United Kingdom and the United States (later adherents being Greece and Turkey in 1952, the Federal Republic of Germany in 1955 and Spain in 1982). Following the withdrawal of France from NATO's integrated military organization in 1966, NATO's Supreme Headquarters Allied Powers in Europe (SHAPE) were transferred from Paris to Mons in Belgium and the seat of the NATO Council from the French capital to Brussels. Within the framework of Belgium's full participation in NATO's structures, some 28,000 Belgian troops are currently stationed in West Germany and a small US military contingent is stationed in Belgium.

Belgium is also a member (together with France, the Federal Republic of Germany, Italy, Luxembourg, the Netherlands and the United Kingdom) of the Western European Union (WEU). The WEU was established as such in 1955 on the basis of the Brussels Treaty Organization, which had been created in 1948 (by Belgium, France, Luxembourg, the Netherlands and the United Kingdom) but had been largely subsumed as an alliance for military defence into the NATO structure. In October 1984 Belgium endorsed a French-initiated proposal to reactivate the WEU in order to increase security policy co-operation between the seven member states (prospectively to increase to nine with the accession of Portugal and Spain).

As at end-1985 the Belgian armed forces totalled some 92,000 personnel, including about 20,000 in the air force and 4,500 in the navy. About a third of the total were conscripts, there being compulsory military service of 10 months (or eight for conscripts stationed in West Germany). The defence budget in 1985 was 107,000 million Belgian francs, representing about 5.7 per cent of total government expenditure.

On March 15, 1985, Belgium's centre-right coalition Government announced its unanimous agreement on the immediate deployment according to schedule of 16 of the 48 US cruise missiles due to be stationed in Belgium under the 1979 NATO "twin-track" decision. Within three hours of the announcement the first such missile was in place at the Florennes base 67 kilometres south of Brussels. As regards the remaining 32 missiles the Cabinet agreed (i) that if by the end of 1987 East-West agreement had been reached on the so-called "zero option" (involving no further missiles being stationed in Europe) no deployment would take place in Belgium; (ii) that if there were agreement on a reduced number of weapons Belgium would expect to station fewer weapons on its territory; and (iii) that if no agreement had been reached by the end of 1987 deployment of the remaining missiles in Belgium would only follow after a further six-month period had elapsed.

A parliamentary debate on March 20, 1985, ended with a vote in the Chamber of Representatives endorsing the Government's deployment decision by 116 votes to 93 with one abstention. Following the centre-right coalition's victory in the October 1985 general elections, Prime Minister Wilfried Martens reaffirmed the March 1985 deployment decision but added that it could be modified if US–Soviet negotiations at Geneva resulted in an agreement on intermediate-range nuclear weapons.

Flemish Movements

Civilian Service for Youth
Burgerdienst voor de Jeugd (BDJ)

Address. Van Elewyckstraat 35, B-1050 Brussels, Belgium

Aims and objectives. BDJ is a support organization for actual and prospective conscientious objectors, seeking to defend their interests both in general public terms and through representations to the Interior Ministry.

Formation. After five years of embryonic existence, BDJ was formally established in 1969 as an offshoot of the Flemish organization War Resisters' International (IOT).

Doctors Against Nuclear Weapons
Medici Tegen Atoomwapens

Address. Woestijnenstraat 18, B-9300 Aalst, Belgium

Aims and objectives. To provide information on the risks, the consequences and the prevention of nuclear war.

Formation. The group was formed in 1981.

Activities. Active in the (northern) Dutch-speaking part of Belgium, this movement organizes meetings, debates and interviews and publishes articles and books. It organized the first European Regional IPPNW meeting in Brussels.

Membership. 1,700 doctors and health workers.

Publications. *De Nieuwsbrief* (bi-monthly newsletter); *En Niemand Hoort Je Huilen (And Nobody Will Hear You Crying)*, by Jef & Mieke De Loof; and *Artsen Tegen Oorlog* (Physicians Against War), by Jef De Loof.

Affiliations. The group is the Flemish Belgian affiliate of International Physicians for the Prevention of Nuclear War.

Flemish Action Committee Against Nuclear Weapons
Vlaams Aktiekomitee Tegen Atoomwapens (VAKA)

Address. Muntstraat 8, B-2000 Antwerp, Belgium

Aims and objectives. VAKA's principal recent objective has been to prevent the deployment of cruise missiles in Belgium. In more general terms, it sees itself as the main organization in Flanders working against the nuclear arms race. Its concerns extend to the broader issues of the arms race and problems associated with it, such as relations between the Eastern and Western blocs, between the

North and South, and human rights. VAKA also carries out research on current military policies and alternative defence policies.

While not demanding unilateral disarmament by Belgium, VAKA favours the adoption of limited unilateral steps towards disarmament within the NATO framework, as a means of building confidence between East and West and thereby encouraging substantial disarmament negotiations.

Formation. VAKA was first established in 1979 as an umbrella organization of various peace movements, political, youth and education groups and third-world development organizations.

Activities. VAKA took part in the peace demonstrations in Brussels in December 1979, October 1981 and October 1983. It also participated in lower-level local and regional actions, including demonstrations near the Florennes base in April 1983 and April 1984, and organized a number of activities during "peace weeks" in late 1983 and 1984.

VAKA took part in campaigning activities during the run-up to the October 1985 Belgian parliamentary elections, opposing the government decision of March 1985 to proceed with the deployment of cruise missiles in Belgium. Following that decision it participated in a major protest demonstration in Brussels on March 20, 1985, which was followed by a further demonstration in October.

Membership. VAKA has no formal membership structure, but is based on a network of over 100 local groups.

Publications. *De Vlaamse Vredeskrant* (Flemish Peace Journal) is published four times a year, and the *Intern Bulletin* appears every other month. VAKA has also published three booklets as follows: *Raketten? In geen geval* (1982); *Raketten in geen geval—Informatie-brochure over de kernwapenproblematiek* (1983); and *Aktiebrochure—Vrede zonder Raketten* (1984).

Affiliations. VAKA is a member of the European Nuclear Disarmament (END) liaison committee and of the International Peace Communication and Co-ordination Network. Although it has no formal affiliations with any other political, social or religious bodies, VAKA holds regular consultations with sympathetic political parties, with labour organizations and with Catholic bodies.

Initiative Committee for the Defence of Peace in Europe
Initiatiefkomitee voor de Verdedicing van de Vrede in Europa (IKoVE)

Address. Moretusstraat 21, B-1070 Brussels, Belgium

Aims and objectives. IKoVE seeks to raise public awareness of peace issues by means of information and documentation, as well as by participation in specific actions.

Formation. IKoVE came into being in 1976.

Activities. The Committee has organized a series of annual study days on various topics of concern to the peace movement, most recently on the US Strategic Defence Initiative (SDI) and the European Eureka project.

Membership. About 400.

Publications. *IKoVE Dossier*, quarterly; *IKoVE Nieuws*, bi-monthly.

Affiliations. IKoVE is a member of the Flemish Action Committee Against Nuclear Weapons (VAKA) and of the Peace Co-ordination Centre (OCV).

Pax Christi Flanders
Pax Christi Vlaanderen (PCV)

Address. Kerkstraat 150, B-2000 Antwerp, Belgium

Aims and objectives. Like other national sections of Pax Christi International, this Catholic organization seeks to influence public opinion to achieve peace between nations; it is also concerned with human rights issues and the problems of the Third World. PCV operates in the Flemish-speaking part of Belgium.

Formation. A Flemish Belgium section was set up soon after the foundation of Pax Christi in 1945.

Activities. Pax Christi Flanders has participated with other Belgian peace movements in various demonstrations and actions, notably those relating to the campaign against the deployment of cruise missiles in Belgium. It has organized conferences and seminars on peace issues and has working groups and commissions studying particular themes, such as disarmament and non-violent options. It has made a special study of the Belgian arms trade and is particularly active in the propagation of peace studies in schools and churches.

Publications. PCV-Koerier, bi-monthly newsletter; *Kommentar*, monthly.

Affiliations. Pax Christi International.

Peace Co-ordination Centre
Overlegcentrum voor de Vrede (OCV)

Address. Nieuw Achturenhuis, Fonttainaplein 9-11, B-1000 Brussels, Belgium

Aims and objectives. The OCV seeks to co-ordinate the actions of the various branches of the peace movement in Flemish-speaking Belgium, seeking common ground on which groups of different political and philosophical persuasions can co-operate to achieve greater effectiveness.

Formation. The OCV came into being in 1979.

Activities. In terms of its basic declaration of principles the OCV has campaigned for (i) the abolition of all threats to peace, military or political or personal; (ii) the furtherance of security and co-operation within Europe; (iii) recognition by government of public opinion on peace issues; and (iv) the equal right of all peoples to sovereignty and political/economic independence. Although operating as the umbrella organization for Flanders, the OCV has co-operated with French-speaking peace movements in demonstrations and other actions, notably the campaign against the deployment of cruise missiles in Belgium.

Membership. Some 30 separate peace groups are members of the OCV, which operates essentially as a co-ordinating body rather than a central directing authority.

Research and Information Centre for Problems of Peace and Development

Address. Knokkestraat 44, B-9000 Ghent, Belgium

Aims and objectives. To contribute to peaceful coexistence and respect for human rights.

Formation. The Centre was established on June 3, 1973, when it took over the work of the Belgian Union for the Defence of Peace (founded in 1949).

Activities. In addition to its publishing programme, the Centre organizes educational evenings and special courses and has a documentation and information facility.

Membership. The Centre's activities are open to people of all social, religious and political groups.

Publications. *Vrede* (Peace), monthly; various other publications on peace issues.

Affiliations. Internationally the Centre is affiliated to the World Peace Council; within Belgium it is a member (and co-founder) of the Flemish Action Committee Against Nuclear Weapons (VAKA) and also of the Peace Co-ordination Centre (OCV).

Service Civil International (SCI)
Vrywillige Internationalle Aktie

Address. Venusstraat 28, B-2000 Antwerp, Belgium

Aims and objectives. This organization is the Flemish Belgian section of the international organization of the same name, working for peace and international understanding through voluntary service activities.

Affiliations. Service Civil International.

War Resisters' International
Internationale van Oorlogtegenstanders (IOT)

Address. Van Elewyckstraat 35, B-1050 Brussels, Belgium

Aims and objectives. IOT is an independent and pluralist pacifist movement (operating in Flanders) opposed to the arms race and militarism, and particularly to nuclear weapons and military conscription. It advocates the conversion of the arms industry to socially useful production and regards social defence as an alternative to present arrangements. It seeks the transformation of the militarized culture by means of general peace education, working mainly through parliamentary and democratic procedures but also espousing direct non-violent action.

Formation. IOT was founded in 1968 as the Flemish Belgian section of War Resisters' International.

Activities. IOT operates by means of "personal dedication" (e.g. refusal of conscription), symbolic acts such as demonstrations (in which it has participated with other Belgian peace movements), information campaigns, political lobbying and acts of civil disobedience (such as holding picnics at the NATO base at Florennes south of Brussels). It has participated in campaigns with other Belgian peace movements, notably with the Flemish Action Committee Against Nuclear Weapons (VAKA) against the deployment of cruise missiles in Belgium. IOT has also given particular attention to peace education. Its activities for 1986 as the UN's International Year of Peace include the elaboration of a social defence project, peace education initiatives and a "Belgian-US peace action tour" involving the sending of a delegation of Belgian peace activists on a speaking tour of the United States.

IOT has spawned two specialist offshoots, namely (i) Civilian Service for Youth and (ii) Youth and Peace (see separate entries).

Membership. IOT has about 1,000 members, for the most part in the 20-35 age bracket and of leftist political persuasion.

Publications. Protest, bi-monthly; *De Vredesgazet.*

Affiliations. At the international level IOT is affiliated to War Resisters' International, the International Peace Bureau and European Nuclear Disarmament (END). Within Belgium it is affiliated to the Peace Co-ordination Centre (OCV), the Flemish Action Committee Against Nuclear Weapons (VAKA), the Action Committee Against the Arms Trade/Conversion of the Arms Industry and Doctors Against Nuclear Weapons.

Youth and Peace
Jeugd en Vrede

Address. Van Elewyckstraat 35, B-1050 Brussels, Belgium

Aims and objectives. Youth and Peace specializes in promoting peace education.

Formation. It was created in 1982 as an offshoot of the Flemish organization War Resisters' International (IOT).

Activities. Youth and Peace has concerned itself with the technical co-ordination of peace education initiatives in Flanders, being particularly active in developing an "alternative defence" strategy based on non-violence. In addition to studying and propagating techniques of non-violent action such as civil disobedience, it has also been closely involved in campaigns for the conversion of the arms industry to social purposes.

French-speaking Movements

Belgian Union for the Defence of Peace
Union Belge pour la Défense de la Paix

Address. Rue de la Tulipe 29, B-1050 Brussels, Belgium

Publication. Le Monde et la Paix, bi-monthly.

Christian Peace Movement
Mouvement Chrétien pour la Paix

Address. Rue du Trône 102, B-1050 Brussels, Belgium

Affiliations. This Movement is affiliated to the Christian Movement for Peace and has links with War Resisters' International.

Gandhi Centre at the Service of Man and Life
Centre Gandhi au Service de l'Homme et de la Vie

Address. Rue de l'Aqueduc 36, B-1050 Brussels, Belgium

Aims and objectives. The Gandhi Centre promotes non-violence through teaching and aims to achieve harmony in individual lives and between people. The Centre also aims to raise the level of awareness in the general public in favour of general disarmament with strict international controls in accordance with United Nations formulations.

The Centre also teaches natural health care to enable people to achieve a harmony of mind and body without resorting to modern medicines.

Formation. The Centre was founded in 1974 by the Friends of the Arc.

Activities. The Centre has been actively involved in various campaigns and has made interventions in public meetings. Non-violence meetings, initiation weekends, seminars and conferences are organized regularly. The Centre also publishes and distributes material and has participated in demonstrations and marches.

Among the Centre's recent activities have been: participation in the CSCE meeting in Ottawa (Canada); celebration of the 10th anniversary of the signing of the Helsinki agreement; meeting to examine the non-proliferation treaty in Geneva; commemoration of the bombing of Hiroshima and Nagasaki; and participation in the 4th international demonstration for nuclear disarmament in Amsterdam.

Membership. The Centre has around 200 members from a variety of social and political backgrounds.

Publications. Mutations (every two months).

Affiliations. The Centre is affiliated to the Communauté de l'Arche de Lanza del Vasto (France).

International Movement of Reconciliation/War Resisters' International Mouvement International de la Réconciliation/Internationale des Résistants à la Guerre (MIR/IRG)

Address. Rue van Elewyck 35, B-1050 Brussels, Belgium

Aims and objectives. As the francophone Belgian section of both the International Fellowship of Reconciliation (IFOR) and War Resisters' International (WRI), the MIR/IRG is a radical pacifist movement seeking to propagate non-violent alternatives, to oppose militarism and to support conscientious objection to military service. As part of the Belgian peace movement, the organization advocates unilateral disarmament and in particular the abandonment of nuclear weapons.

Formation. The MIR/IRG became established in French-speaking Belgium after the Second World War (combining the Christian orientation of IFOR with the humanist/ libertarian tendency of the WRI).

Activities. In addition to direct participation in peace campaigns, the MIR/IRG undertakes research, information and educational work on peace and disarmament issues.

Publication. Non-Violence et Société (Non-Violence and Society), bi-monthly.

Affiliations. International Fellowship of Reconciliation; War Resisters' International.

Medical Association for the Prevention of Nuclear War
Association Médicale pour la Prévention de la Guerre Nucléaire (AMPGN)

Address. 2 Place des Nations, B-1050 Brussels, Belgium

Aims and objectives. AMPGN aims to inform doctors, medical students and the general public of the medical consequences of nuclear war.

Formation. AMPGN was set up by five Belgian doctors in October 1981.

Activities. The group arranges lectures and debates in universities, secondary schools and public meetings. Members also participate in radio and television discussions, and contribute articles on the medical effects of nuclear war to newspapers and specialist journals.
AMPGN working groups are currently undertaking studies of Belgian civil defence policy, of the environmental consequences of nuclear war (in the light of the recent "nuclear winter" predictions) and of the effects of chemical and bacteriological weapons. They plan to publish papers on all three subjects.

Membership. There are approximately 350 members, 90 cent of whom are doctors, with the remainder including university teachers, nurses and chemists.

Publications. A quarterly newsletter, *AMPGN Nouvelles*, is sent to all members and circulated in an effort to recruit new supporters. The group has also published a small book, *Armes Nucléaires: Les Médecins Désarmés* (Nuclear Weapons: Disarmed Doctors).

Affiliations. AMPGN is the French-speaking Belgian section of International Physicians for the Prevention of Nuclear War.

National Action Committee for Peace and Development
Comité National d'Action pour la Paix et le Développement (CNAPD)

Address. Rue de la Tulipe 34, B-1050 Brussels, Belgium

Aims and objectives. CNAPD works for peace, détente and the dissolution of military pacts. Its main objective is to achieve bilateral disarmament of the two military blocs, a withdrawal of all nuclear weapons from Europe and to see a dialogue develop between East and West.
The Committee also works for third-world development and the realization of democratic liberties.

Formation. CNAPD was founded in 1970 and has led the anti-cruise campaign in the French-speaking part of Belgium.

Activities. Together with the Flemish Action Committee Against Nuclear Weapons (VAKA), CNAPD has organized several mass demonstrations against cruise which have attracted up to 400,000 participants. (In March 1985 a demonstration in Brussels two days after the deployment of 16 cruise missiles at the Florennes airbase was said by the organizers to have been attended by 100,000 people.)
CNAPD tries to influence political and social life in Belgium for peace by providing information to the media, political parties, trade unions and other social groups. It organizes meetings, debates in schools and local group discussions, and tries to promote peace education.

Membership. As an umbrella organization for 33 peace, youth and other groups, CNAPD has no membership as such. It also co-ordinates a network of 100 independent committees.

Publications. CNAPD produces a monthly newsletter (*La Feuille de Liaison*) as well as leaflets, posters and booklets.

Affiliations. CNAPD participates in the International Peace Communication and Co-ordination Network and in the European Nuclear Disarmament (END) network.

Pax Christi Wallonia-Brussels
Pax Christi Wallonie-Bruxelles

Address. Rue du Marteau 19, B-1040 Brussels, Belgium

Aims and objectives. Like other national sections of Pax Christi International, this Catholic organization seeks to influence public opinion in the cause of international peace, and is also concerned with human rights issues and the problems of the Third World. Pax Christi Wallonia-Brussels operates in the French-speaking parts of Belgium.

Formation. A francophone Belgian section was established soon after the foundation of Pax Christi in 1945.

Activities. Pax Christi Wallonia-Brussels has participated with other Belgian peace movements in demonstrations against nuclear weapons and militarism and in favour of international peace and disarmament. It has a programme of conferences and seminars on relevant themes and also a number of working groups and commissions studying such issues as East-West and North-South relations, peace theology, European security and co-operation and human rights.

Membership. About 1,200 people (lay and clergy) belong to the organization, operating in regional and local groups.

Publications. *Pax Christi*, quarterly bulletin; *Trait d'Union*, bi-monthly; various dossiers and documents.

Affiliations. Pax Christi International.

Peace University
Université de la Paix

Address. 4 Boulevard du Nord, B-5000 Namur, Belgium

Aims and objectives. The University of Peace aims to promote peace by increasing public awareness of the issues involved. It operates an information centre and produces numerous publications to this end.

Formation. The University was founded in 1960.

Activities. The University holds an international session every year as well as regular peace workshops. It has also produced a record for children and distributed videos on human rights issues, T-shirts, post cards, posters and badges.

Publications. UP Information is published every three months; various books and leaflets dealing with human rights, peace and disarmament have also been published.

Affiliations. International Peace Research Association (IPRA).

Service Civil International (SCI)

Address. Avenue de Stalingrad 24, B-1000 Brussels, Belgium

Aims and objectives. As the francophone Belgian section of the international organization of the same name, SCI works for peace and international understanding through voluntary service activities.

Affiliations. Service Civil International.

Women for Peace
Femmes pour la Paix

Address. Chausée de Wavre 1540, B-1160 Brussels, Belgium

Aims and objectives. This group seeks to act as a channel for the particular contribution which it believes that women can make to the peace movement. It derives its inspiration from Greenham Common Women's Peace Camp in the United Kingdom.

Formation. The Belgian group came into being soon after the formation of the original Women for Peace movement in Switzerland in 1976.

Activities. The group holds regular meetings and also participates in demonstrations and educational work.

Denmark

capital: Copenhagen   **population: 5,100,000**

Denmark abandoned its longstanding neutrality after the Second World War and was an original signatory on April 4, 1949, of the treaty creating the North Atlantic Treaty Organization (NATO), together with Belgium, Canada, France, Iceland, Italy, Luxembourg, the Netherlands, Norway, Portugal, the United Kingdom and the United States (later adherents being Greece and Turkey in 1952, the Federal Republic of Germany in 1955 and Spain in 1982). Denmark participates in NATO's integrated military structure and the Alliance has naval bases at Frederikshavn and Copenhagen as well as at Tórshavn in the Faroes and at Grönnedal and Thule in Greenland. There are, however, no non-Danish NATO land forces stationed in Denmark and no nuclear missiles may be deployed in Danish territory in peacetime (although non-nuclear NATO weapons are stockpiled in Denmark for use in an emergency).

As at end-1985 the Danish armed forces totalled about 30,000 personnel, including 7,000 in the air force and 6,000 in the navy; there were also some 130,000 reservists. Military service of nine months is compulsory. Under an agreement between the major political parties announced on June 29, 1984, the annual defence budget for the period 1986–89 was fixed at its existing level in real terms, defence spending in 1985 being budgeted at 12,578 million kroner, representing 6.7 per cent of total government expenditure.

Although Denmark's NATO membership has commanded broad support among the country's major political parties, there is a significant anti-NATO minority centred on the smaller formations to the left of the Social Democratic Party (SDP). Moreover, since the SDP went into opposition in September 1982 its own anti-NATO minority has become increasingly visible, while the party as a whole has mounted a series of parliamentary challenges to the pro-NATO defence policies of the ruling centre-right coalition. Underlying this revival of the "NATO issue" in Danish politics has been widespread concern in the country over NATO's 1979 "twin-track" decision—to which the then SDP minority government was a party—to deploy new intermediate-range missiles in Western Europe (although not in Denmark itself) unless a satisfactory agreement could be reached with the Soviet Union on a reduction of missile levels.

Recent parliamentary decisions on NATO and other defence-related matters have included (i) the adoption on Dec. 7, 1982, of an SDP motion that "future Danish allocations [to NATO] for the deployment of medium-range missiles . . . should be suspended until further notice"; (ii) the passage on May 26, 1983, of an SDP proposal that British and French missiles should be included in the US–Soviet INF negotiations at Geneva (as advocated by the Soviet Union); (iii) the adoption on Nov. 3, 1983, of an SDP motion enjoining the Government to work "actively" to halt the arms race and to persuade NATO to re-evaluate the situation in Europe before cruise and Pershing II missiles were deployed; (iv) the passage on Dec. 1, 1983, of an SDP-proposed instruction to the Government that it should refuse to take any responsibility for new missile deployment and should enter reservations to this effect in NATO communiqués; (v) a decision, also on

Dec. 1, 1983, that the Danish delegation to the UN General Assembly should be instructed to vote in favour of a Swedish–Mexican resolution calling for a nuclear weapons freeze; (vi) the approval on May 3, 1984, of an SDP motion instructing the Government to work towards banning nuclear weapons in times of peace and of war, in the context of a Nordic nuclear-weapons-free zone recognized by the United States and the Soviet Union; (vii) the adoption on May 10, 1984, of a further SDP motion blocking payment of Denmark's agreed contribution to the cost of cruise and Pershing II deployment, with the funds being switched to the domestic defence programme; (viii) a decision in November 1984 calling for a public renunciation of any first use of nuclear weapons by NATO; and (ix) approval in May 1985 of a motion opposing any Danish involvement in the US Strategic Defence Initiative (SDI).

Campaign Against Conscription
Kampanjen Mot Verneplikt

Address. Holbergsgade 13/4, DK-1057 Copenhagen K, Denmark

Aims and objectives. This organization seeks the abolition of conscription and military service in Denmark.

Formation. The Danish group was established soon after the formation of the Norwegian movement of the same name in November 1981.

Affiliations. The Scandinavian-wide Kampanjen Mot Verneplikt is an associated member of War Resisters' International.

Christians for Disarmament
Kristne for Nedrustning (KFN)

Address. Eriksholmvej 11, DK-2720 Vensøse, Denmark

Aims and objectives. KFN aims to raise the consciousness of Christians in Denmark about the issues of disarmament and improved East–West relations. To this end they encourage Christians to work actively for peace, by organizing rallies and peace marches, and try to achieve co-operation between churches and church groups of all nations.

Formation. KFN was formed in 1979 on the basis of an appeal for disarmament, particularly nuclear, and for alternative security. The petition was signed by many prominent representatives of the Church and was delivered to the Danish Government.

Activities. KFN has organized meetings between church representatives from East and West. They have also worked in co-operation with other peace organizations in Denmark to promote national rallies and disseminate information.

Membership. KFN has around 300 members.

Affiliations. Christian Movement for Peace.

Danish Institute for Critical Peace Research

Address. P.O. Box 7516, DK-9210 Aalborg SØ, Denmark

Aims and objectives. The Institute is primarily concerned with research into the causes of war and researching peace research itself. Its work aims to be independent of political bias.

Formation. The Institute was established in 1981.

Activities. The Institute is involved in research work and the publication of information.

Membership. There are around 20 members of the Institute who all have academic qualifications equivalent to a masters degree.

Fellowship of Reconciliation
Forsoningsforbundet (DK-FOR)

Address. c/o Palludan Windfeldt, Åvendingen 6A, DK-2700 Brønshøj, Denmark

Aims and objectives. DK-FOR aims to further good will between countries and races through non-violent work in information, debate and action. It actively supports peace and justice and works for fundamental changes in unjust social, political and economic structures.

Formation. DK-FOR was founded as a pacifist group in 1913. Other peace groups have grown out of the DK-FOR, such as an anti-militaristic working group and an organization which exists to publicize the dangers of nuclear power.

Activities. DK-FOR has presented several statements to the Danish Government and Parliament asking that the authorities should say no to nuclear weapons in Europe.
DK-FOR has also worked actively on behalf of oppressed people in Latin America. It made a statement to the US Senate and President Reagan with a request that the USA abstain from intervening in Nicaragua, and supported the Danish Witness for Peace initiatives in Nicaragua.
DK-FOR supports peace marches and demonstrations and provides information on peace issues on request.

Membership. DK-FOR has 130 members.

Publications. A newsletter is produced 3–4 times a year. DK-FOR has also published a history of the organization over the last 70 years and produces information pamphlets.

Affiliations. DK-FOR is affiliated to the International Fellowship of Reconciliation and, in Denmark, Christians for Disarmament.

Hesbjerg Peace Research College

Address. Karma Nalanda Buddhist-Christian Peace Centre, Hesbjergvej 50, DK-5491 Blommenslyst, Denmark

Aims and objectives. The College is dedicated to promoting the view that war is obsolete as a method of solving international problems, with the ultimate objective of a viable world government.

Activities. As a rural residential community of peace workers and researchers, the College engages in cultural and artistic activities as well as participating in international peace work with various organizations. The College has a library for peace research, Buddhism and humanities. In August 1983 the third European convention of the International Association of Educators for World Peace was held at Hesbjerg.

International League for Peace and Freedom
International Lige for Fred og Frihed (ILFF)

Address. Købmagergade 69/I, DK-1150 Copenhagen, Denmark

Aims and objectives. As the Danish section of the Women's International League for Peace and Freedom, the ILLF works to eradicate the political, social, economic and psychological causes of war and to create the conditions for peace. It seeks complete and universal disarmament and the abolition of violent or coercive means for settling conflicts.

Activities. The ILFF participates with other peace movements in campaigns against the further deployment of nuclear missiles in Europe and also against the stockpiling of NATO weapons on Danish soil. It also undertakes educational and information work, particularly among women.

Publication. Fred og Frihed (Peace and Freedom), quarterly.

Affiliations. Women's International League for Peace and Freedom.

Never Again War
Aldrig Mere Krig

Address. Thørsgade 79, DK-2200 Copenhagen N, Denmark

Aims and objectives. This movement campaigns for the elimination of the possibility of war through complete disarmament, the renunciation of force as a means of settling disputes and the general espousal of the principle of non-violence.

Publication. Ikkevold (Non-Violence), nine times a year.

Affiliations. War Resisters' International; International Peace Bureau.

No to Nuclear Weapons
Nej til Atomvaben

Address. Dronningensgade 14, DK-1420 Copenhagen K, Denmark

Aims and objectives. Nej til Atomvaben favours unilateral disarmament by Denmark, the country's withdrawal from NATO's nuclear planning group and the cancellation of an agreement to receive US warplanes during times of crisis. It campaigns for the creation of a Nordic nuclear-free zone and for the development of a neutral Europe. Regarding the level of money spent on armaments as a burden on the world's economy, the group also favours the transfer of resources from military industries in the richer countries to development projects in the Third World.

Activities. Nej til Atomvaben was founded in January 1980 after a national advertising campaign against the NATO decision to deploy cruise and Pershing missiles in November 1979. In addition to campaigning against the missile deployment, Nej til Atomvaben represented the Danish peace movement in meetings on the Nordic nuclear-free zone proposals. The group takes part in the North Atlantic Network of peace movements and it is also establishing contacts with independent peace groups in the Eastern bloc.
Future plans include intensifying educational work and formulating an alternative defence plan for Denmark.

Membership. Nej til Atomvaben has no formal membership structure.

Publications. Nej til Atomvaben, a quarterly newsletter. The group also publishes an occasional newsletter in English.

Affiliations. The group works informally with other peace organizations and with church and development groups.

Peace and Security Liaison Committee
Samarbejdskomiteen for Fred og Sikkerhed (SAK)

Address. Gothersgade 8C, DK–1123 Copenhagen K, Denmark

Aims and objectives. SAK "promotes proposals and measures, at the national and international level, which are designed to decrease tensions, to stop and reverse the arms race on earth and to prevent the militarization of outer space", while working towards the goal of "general and complete disarmament" as proposed by the UN. In the immediate term, it supports the establishment of a Nordic nuclear-weapons-free zone.

Formation. The Committee was set up in 1974.

Activities. SAK has assisted with the formation of several Danish peace groups, including Trade Unions for Peace, Youth for Peace and the "No to Nuclear Weapons" (Nej til Atomvaben) campaign. In collaboration with other peace groups, it produced the 14-point Programme of the Danish Peace Movement in 1982, parts of which were subsequently endorsed by Parliament. The Programme is currently being updated.

SAK holds regular seminars and meetings devoted to the formulation of an alternative Danish policy on security and defence. It holds annual conferences, normally attended by around 400 people. Participants at the 1985 conference included Knud Damgard, the Social Democrat spokesman on defence, Gert Petersen, the secretary of the People's Socialist Party, Jørgen Jensen, secretary of the Danish Communist Party, and Col. G.K. Kristensen. Resolutions passed at the conference included a condemnation of the US Strategic Defence Initiative (SDI), a decision to place more emphasis on the "bread not bombs" side of the campaign, and a denunciation of all "violent actions committed against people and property in the name of peace".

Recent actions mounted by the SAK have included a march into Copenhagen at Easter 1985, participation with trade unions and local councils in celebrations marking the 40th anniversary of the end of the Second World War, and involvement in the Nordic cycling peace tours, culminating in Oslo on Aug. 6, 1985, the anniversary of the Hiroshima bombing.

Membership. SAK itself has 1,600 members, 58 of whom are on its council, which includes clergy, academics, politicians, trade unionists and journalists. A number of local peace groups and of professional, women's and youth peace movements are affiliated to SAK.

Publications. Fredsavisen (Peace Journal), has a circulation of about 8,000. SAK also publishes (i) *International Bulletin*, a quarterly containing a selection of articles and studies from a number of foreign publications; (ii) *Information Bulletin*; and (iii) the English-language *Peace Newsletter*. It has published several reports and booklets.

Affiliations. Danish UN Association; Danish Organization for International Co-operation.

Teachers for Peace

Address. Fredscentret, Gothersgade 8C, DK-1123 Copenhagen K, Denmark

Aims and objectives. To encourage the discussion of peace issues in Danish schools.

Formation. The group was established in 1982.

Activities. The group is seeking to establish an annual "disarmament week" in Danish schools. Many Danish schools now devote one day or week each year to the discussion of peace and Third World issues. In August 1986 the group held an International Peace Congress of Pedagogues in Copenhagen to discuss peace and disarmament education.

Membership. There are about 600 members.

Publications. Teachers for Peace News.

Affiliations. The group co-operates with other Danish peace groups.

Union of Conscientious Objectors/Association of Anti-Militarist Socialists Militaer og Naegterforeningen/Foreningen af Socialistiske Antimilitarister (MNF/FASA)

Address. Noerregade 28C, DK-1165 Copenhagen K, Denmark

Aims and objectives. MNF/FASA's declared aim is to "expose and combat the bourgeois military power system and the military-industrial complex, both national and international".

Formation. The organization was originally formed in 1967 as the Union of Conscientious Objectors. From 1976 onwards it began to be involved in wider political issues, and this trend culminated in the adoption of the additional title "Association of Anti-Militarist Socialists" in 1983.

Activities. Currently MNF/FASA is campaigning against compulsory military service and Denmark's membership of NATO and in favour of voluntary peace work.

Membership. The group has between 200 and 300 individual members.

Publications. NB Tidsskrift for Socialistisk Antimilitarisme, the group's own journal, appears six times a year. It has also produced two publications dealing specifically with conscientious objection—*Militaernaegtervilkoer* and *Special issues of Militaernaegtervilkoer*, the latter including a list of placements on which conscripts are liable to be sent.

Affiliations. MNF/FASA is a member of the Peace and Security Liaison Committee, the umbrella organization of Danish peace groups.

Women for Peace
Kvinder for Fred

Address. Dronningensgade 42, DK-1420 Copenhagen-K, Denmark

Aims and objectives. This organization aims to raise public consciousness about the dangers of the arms race, principally through discussion in locally-based groups, and thereby to influence the Danish debate on disarmament.

Activities. Women for Peace takes part in local and national marches and demonstrations, and has also established peace camps outside military installations, including one formed in June 1984 outside a new NATO command centre in Viborg, Jutland. They claim to be the inspiration for much of the women's peace movement in Britain, including the Greenham Common Women's Peace Camp.

The group has also participated in several international demonstrations, including the 1981 Copenhagen to Paris march and the 1982 Stockholm-Moscow-Minsk march. They also hold regular lectures and discussion seminars.

Membership. Women for Peace is not a membership organization as such, but rather operates as a co-ordinating body for numerous local groups, holding regular regional meetings and annual national conferences. There is no central body, and each component group takes turns to act as co-ordinator.

Publications. The group's membership journal, *Kokkenrullen* (The Kitchen Roll), has a circulation of 1,000 copies and is produced between 10 and 12 times a year, with member groups taking on the editorial and production tasks in rotation.

Affiliations. Women for Peace maintains close links with women's peace groups in Norway, Sweden and Finland. Beyond this, it has a deliberate policy of remaining free of any political or other affiliations, in line with its aim to have as broad a membership base as possible.

Finland

capital: Helsinki   **population: 4,873,000**

The peace treaty signed between Finland and the Allied and associated powers on Feb. 10, 1947 (and in force from Sept. 10, 1947), contained provisions for the payment of war reparations (Finland having joined with Nazi Germany in attacking the Soviet Union in 1941) and also imposed limitations on the Finnish armed forces, prohibiting in particular the possession or construction of nuclear weapons. The treaty confirmed the cession to the Soviet Union of the northern province of Petsamo (thus depriving Finland of direct access to the Arctic Ocean and giving the Soviet Union a common frontier with Norway). It also endorsed the frontier changes specified under the 1940 Finno–Soviet peace treaty (ending the brief "winter war" between the two countries), namely that the Soviet Union acquired the Karelian Isthmus, Viborg and other territories west of Lake Ladoga and obtained a 50-year lease on the Porkkala-Udd area (south-west of Helsinki) for the establishment of a Soviet naval base.

The Porkkala base was, however, evacuated by the Soviet Union in 1955 after the two countries had agreed a 20-year extension of their Treaty of Friendship, Co-operation and Mutual Assistance originally signed on April 6, 1948. Article 1 of this treaty—which was renewed for further 20-year periods in 1970 and 1983—provides that Finland will fight "with all the forces at her disposal" to repel any attack on the Soviet Union launched through Finnish territory by Germany "or any state allied to the latter". In such an eventuality "the Soviet Union will render Finland the necessary assistance, in regard to the granting of which the parties will agree between themselves".

The Finnish armed forces (which are limited by treaty to 41,900) currently number some 36,500 personnel, including 3,000 in the air force and 2,700 in the navy. About two-thirds of the total are conscripts, there being compulsory military service for men of a basic eight months (11 months for officers and NCOs). There are some 700,000 reservists (of which 200,000 would form a "fast deployment force" in an emergency) and 3,500 paramilitary border guards. The defence budget amounted to 5,106 million markka in 1985, representing about 5 per cent of total government expenditure.

Under a revised law adopted in 1985 to come into effect on Jan. 1, 1987, the duration of alternative service for conscientious objectors was extended from 12 to 16 months and such alternative service was required to contribute to the country's "total defence" capabilities (e.g. civil defence, the fire and rescue services etc.). Such alternative service became available to all applicants without the previous requirement of scrutiny by an examination board, but total resisters (with the specific exemption of Jehovah's Witnesses) became liable to an increased maximum penalty of 16 months' imprisonment.

Successive post-war Finnish governments have maintained a stance of neutrality in foreign affairs, balancing the country's particular relationship with its super-power neighbour with participation in the economic structures of the free-market West (becoming, for example, a full member of the European Free Trade Association in January 1986 after a quarter-century of associate status). Finland has also attached particular importance to Nordic co-operation—i.e. with Denmark, Iceland, Norway and Sweden—and in this context has consistently promoted the concept of a nuclear-weapons-free zone in the Nordic area. Originally proposed by the Soviet Union in 1957, this concept was subsequently taken up by President Kekkonen of Finland with the principal aim of isolating the Nordic countries from the ramifications of East-West nuclear strategy and weapons development. Although the other Nordic states, particularly Denmark, Iceland and Norway as NATO members, have expressed reservations over the proposal, it has gained increasing support in recent years (notably within the dominant Scandinavian social democratic parties) and is a central objective of the Finnish and other Nordic peace movements.

Aalands Peace Association
Ålands Fredsforening

Address. Norragatan 6 A, SF-22100 Marieham, Aaland Islands, Finland

Aims and objectives. The Aalands Peace Association seeks in particular to propagate to the wider world the example provided by the demilitarized status of these strategically important islands located at the entrance to the Gulf of Bothnia between Finland and Sweden. (Inhabited by ethnic Swedes, the Aaland Islands were part of Sweden until 1809, when they were seized by Russia and joined with the partially autonomous Grand-Duchy of Finland within the Russian Empire. Following Finland's proclamation of independence in 1917 the Aaland islanders sought reunion with Sweden but the League of Nations ruled in April 1921 that the islands should remain part of Finland subject to guarantees being given to protect their national identity and culture. This decision was embodied in the London convention of October 1921, whose signatories included both Finland and Sweden and which provided for the islands' regional autonomy within the Finnish Republic, their demilitarization and neutralization and the exemption of their inhabitants from Finnish military service. The islands were temporarily remilitarized by Finland during its 1939–40 war with the Soviet Union, whose victory obliged Finland inter alia to ensure their immediate demilitarization. At the end of the Second World War the islanders again demanded reunion with Sweden, but the 1947 peace treaty between Finland and the Allied powers, including the Soviet Union, laid down in Article 5 that the Aaland Islands would remain demilitarized as part of Finland.)

Publication. The Association has recently published a booklet called *The Aaland Islands: Autonomous, Demilitarized Region*, in Finnish and English (with French and German translations planned).

Affiliations. International Peace Bureau.

Campaign Against Conscription
Kampanja Asevelvollisuus Pois
Kampanjen Mot Verneplikt

Address. Vanha-Hämeentie 18 as 4, SF-20540 Turku 54, Finland

Aims and objectives. This organization seeks the abolition of conscription and military service in Finland.

Formation. The Finnish group was established soon after the formation of the Norwegian movement of the same name in November 1981.

Activities. Together with the Finnish Union of Conscientious Objectors, the Campaign has vigorously opposed the revised law on conscientious objection effective from Jan. 1, 1987 (see introductory section above).

Affiliations. The Scandinavian-wide Kampanjen Mot Verneplikt is an associated member of War Resisters' International.

Committee of 100 in Finland
Suomen Sadankomitealiitto

Address. Veturitori, Itä-Pasila, SF-00520 Helsinki, Finland

Aims and objectives. The Committee is "a radical and pacifist organization", which works for Finnish unilateralism and for an alternative to military service.

Formation. The Committee of 100 was founded in 1963, taking its title from the organization of the same name in the United Kingdom.

Activities. The Committee's principal campaign focus has been the effort to establish the right of conscientious objection. It has also concerned itself with producing plans for an alternative defence and security policy. The Committee issues periodic appeals on these subjects and organizes mass rallies and demonstrations.

The Committee has converted a disused railway station building for use as a "peace station", which houses the Committee's headquarters and provides a permanent base for other Finnish peace groups.

Membership. Members number approximately 4,000, of whom the majority are young people and students.

Publications. The Committee's journal, *Ydin* (Nucleus), is published eight times a year. A newspaper, *Pax*, is published jointly with the Peace Union of Finland, and is available free to members of both organizations.

Affiliations. In Finland the Committee is formally affiliated to the Peace Union of Finland, and it maintains informal contacts with left-wing and green parties; internationally it is a member of the International Peace Bureau, the International Peace Communication and Co-ordination Network and the European Nuclear Disarmament (END) movement.

Fellowship of Reconciliation
Sovinnonliitto Försoningsförbundet

Address. Lahteenk 7–9 G 50, SF-33500 Tampere, Finland

Aims and objectives. The Finnish section of the International Fellowship of Reconciliation (IFOR), the group draws together religious pacifists from the Christian, Jewish, Buddhist and agnostic traditions for the study and furtherance of pacifist issues.

Formation. The organization was set up in Helsinki in 1919 by Mathilda Wrede, a Finnish woman who had participated in the inaugural conference of IFOR in the Netherlands earlier the same year. Among its early supporters were Quakers, Methodists, Lutherans and Congregationalists.

Activities. In its early years the group concentrated on providing assistance to Armenian immigrants and to conscientious objectors, on whose behalf it lobbied the Finnish Parliament. Currently, it takes part in peace demonstrations and co-operates with other movements and religious bodies in such actions as "peace-worship" church services. It conducts courses on non-violent tactics and strategy and on pacifist theological traditions of different denominations.

Membership. There were 98 individual members in mid-1985.

Publications. The group has produced a number of booklets and pamphlets, including a series covering pacifist thinking in the Russian Orthodox, Buddhist, Islamic, Bahai, Sikh and Jehovah's Witness communities.

Affiliations. As well as belonging to the International Fellowship of Reconciliation, the group plays an active role in the Peace Union of Finland (a national umbrella organization). It also works closely with the Finnish Peace Committee and with Finnish ecologists, as well as the Christian Peace Conference at international level.

Finnish Christian Peace Movement
Suomen Kristillinen Rauhanliike
Finlands Kristliga Fredsrörelse

Address. P.O. Box 59, SF-00521 Helsinki 2, Finland

Aims and objectives. This Movement seeks to encourage action for peace in churches and Christian communities on the basis of the gospel and Christian faith.

Formation. The Movement was established in 1976.

Activities. Seminars are held on peace themes twice a year; there are also regional meetings. In addition to its publishing activities, the Movement also awards an annual peace prize.

Membership. About 250, mainly active members of Christian communities. Pax Christi Finlandiae is affiliated to the Movement.

Publications. Rauhantie, members' newsletter.

Affiliations. The Movement is a member of the Peace Union of Finland and the Finnish UN Association; internationally it is affiliated to the International Peace Bureau and has contacts with the Christian Peace Conference.

Finnish Peace Committee
Suomen Rauhanpuolustajat

Address. Bulevardi 13 A 9, SF-00120 Helsinki 12, Finland

Aims and objectives. As the largest peace organization in the country, the Finnish Peace Committee aims to consolidate different forces in society in working for peace. The Committee is concerned about international peace and more specific questions related to the security of Finland. On this basis action has been concentrated to achieve a nuclear-free zone in Northern Europe. This has meant working against doctrines of limited nuclear war, Euro-strategic missiles and the neutron bomb. The Committee also supports negotiations with the objective of limiting existing nuclear armaments in East and West.

Activities. The Finnish Peace Committee has organized several peace marches, and in 1981 it was behind the largest mass event for peace in the history of Finland, when over 120,000 people marched for peace. It has also prepared petitions for peace, including an appeal for a nuclear-free zone in Northern Europe, which collected over 300,000 signatures. The Committee gives active support to other groups working for peace.

Membership. The Finnish Peace Committee has over 30,000 individual members from all over the country. Around 100 different national organizations are affiliated, including trade unions, friendly societies, solidarity committees, political youth and student organizations and two political parties, namely the Centre Party and the Communist Party. Representatives from all the influential political parties are included on the board and national council of the Committee.

Publications. *Rauhan Puolesta* is published eight times a year in Finnish and annually in English. The Committee also produces various books and booklets on peace and solidarity.

Affiliations. The Committee is affiliated to many organizations within Finland and on an international level it has links with the World Peace Council and the European Nuclear Disarmament (END) movement.

Finnish Peace Research Association (FPRA)

Address. P.O. Box 447, SF-33101 Tampere 10, Finland

Aims and objectives. The FPRA seeks to promote and encourage peace research by students and others with the aim of assisting in the creation of a permanent and just peace in the world.

Publications. *Rauhan Tutkien*, quarterly newsletter in Finnish; *Rauhantutkimus Tänään* (Peace Research Today), series of books.

Finnish Physicians for Social Responsibility (FPSR)

Address. c/o Duodecim Service Office, Kalevankatu 11, SF-00100 Helsinki, Finland

Aims and objectives. The main objective of FPSR is the prevention of nuclear war. They also work for the protection of the environment, support co-operation in third-world development and stand for ethical responsibility of physicians.

Formation. The organization was founded on Feb. 27, 1982.

Activities. FPSR hosted the fourth international congress of International Physicians for the Prevention of Nuclear War in 1984 and arranges national congresses on the prevention of nuclear war.

In the area of development co-operation the group has worked in Bangladesh, where it built a factory to produce vaccines and provided basic information on medicine. FPSR is also funding a school project in Tanzania.

Membership. FPSR has 1,300 members in local groups in 12 Finnish cities; 65 per cent of members are physicians, 30 per cent students of medicine and the rest are dentists and veterinarians. No other professions are accepted.

Publications. FPSR produces a newsletter four times a year. They have translated various books on nuclear warfare and development issues and produced books about development co-operation, medicine in the Third World and aspects of nuclear war.

Affiliations. International Physicians for the Prevention of Nuclear War.

Finnish Union of Conscientious Objectors
Suomen Siviilipalvelusliitto

Address. Sähköttäjänkatu 6, SF-00520 Helsinki 52, Finland

Aims and objectives. This group works to strengthen peace by combating militarism in Finland. It aims to increase the number of conscientious objectors in the country and supports objectors to military service.

Formation. The need for an organization representing conscientious objectors was felt after the Second World War, when the number of objectors began to rise steadily.

Activities. The Union has organized protests, petitions and provides information in its own radio broadcast which goes out once a month. The organization supports conscientious objectors who are imprisoned for their beliefs. The Union is currently campaigning strongly against the revision of the law on conscientious objection (effective from Jan. 1, 1987—see introductory section above) increasing the length of alternative service from 12 to 16 months (i.e. double the period of military service) and stipulating that such alternative service must contribute to overall defensive capacity.

Membership. The Union has 2,500 members, including past and current conscientious objectors.

Publications. The Union produces a paper six times a year and has published several books covering conscientious objection and peace.

Affiliations. The Union is in contact with all Finnish peace groups and is an associated member of War Resisters' International.

Pax Christi Finlandiae

Address. Asemapaallikonkatu 3 A 22, SF-00520 Helsinki 52/06, Finland

Aims and objectives. As the Finnish section of Pax Christi International, this organization seeks to involve Catholics in peace and co-operation work.

Affiliations. Pax Christi International; Finnish Christian Peace Movement.

Peace Union of Finland
Suomen Rauhanliitto

Address. Sähköttäjänkatu 6, SF-00520 Helsinki 52, Finland

Aims and objectives. The Peace Union is a national umbrella organization seeking to provide support for non-violent solutions to international crises, to assist in scientific peace research and peace education, and to further adherence to the principles of the United Nations.

Formation. The organization dates from 1920 and is therefore the oldest peace movement in Finland.

Activities. The Peace Union campaigns for a nuclear-weapons-free zone in Scandinavia and has recently participated in building a new centre for the peace movement in Finland, known as the "peace station".

Membership. The Union embraces more than a dozen separate peace groups with a total membership of about 9,000 people.

Publications. *PAX*, bi-monthly in Finnish; *Fredsposten*, bi-monthly in Swedish.

Affiliations. International Peace Bureau.

Women's International League for Peace and Freedom (WILPF)

Address. Hietalahdenkatu 8 A 21, SF-00180 Helsinki 18, Finland

Aims and objectives. As the Finnish section of the international movement of the same name, the WILPF in Finland seeks to eradicate the political, social, economic and psychological causes of war and to create the conditions for peace, including complete and universal disarmament and the renunciation of violent or coercive methods of settling disputes.

Affiliations. Women's International League for Peace and Freedom.

Other Movements

Architects' Peace Committee
Arkkitehtien Rauhantoimikunta

Address. Esplanadi 22 A, SF-00130 Helsinki, Finland

Association for the Promotion of Peace Literature
Rauhankirjallisuuden Edistamisseura

Address. Sähköttäjänkatu 6, SF-00520 Helsinki 52, Finland

Journalists' Peace Committee
Journalistien Rauhantoimikunta

Address. Yrjonk 11 A 2, SF-00120 Helsinki, Finland

Performers and Artists for Nuclear Disarmament

Address. Lintukallionrinne 7 E, SF-01620 Vantaa, Finland

Physicians Against Nuclear War
Laakarit Ydiensotaa Vastaan

Address. Stenbackinkatu 11, SF-00290 Helsinki, Finland

Psychologists' Peace Committee
Psykologien Rauhantoimikunta

Address. Laajaniittyntie 1, SF-00162 Vantaa, Finland

Teachers' Peace Association of Finland
Suomen Opettajien Rauhanliitto

Address. Riitankuja 1/3 C, SF-00840 Helsinki, Finland

Trade Union Peace Committee
SAK Rauhanvaliokunta

Address. Siltasaarenkatu 3-5 A, SF-00530 Helsinki, Finland

Women for Peace
Naiset Rauhan Puolesta

Address. Unioni Bulevardi 11 A, SF-00120 Helsinki, Finland

France

capital: Paris   **population: 55,200,000**

France was an original signatory on April 4, 1949, of the treaty creating the North Atlantic Treaty Organization (NATO), together with Belgium, Canada, Denmark, Iceland, Italy, Luxembourg, the Netherlands, Norway, Portugal, the United Kingdom and the United States (later adherents being Greece and Turkey in 1952, the Federal Republic of Germany in 1955 and Spain in 1982). With the return to power of Gen. de Gaulle in 1958, however, France began a gradual withdrawal from NATO's integrated military organization, on the grounds that it deprived France of sovereignty over its own military forces. This process culminated in the removal of all NATO installations from French soil in 1966–67, although France remained a member of NATO as such. This situation has remained basically unchanged under successive French governments, although in recent years the classic "Gaullist" stance of independence from all potential European conflicts has evolved into a desire for closer West European co-operation on defence, particularly between France and the Federal Republic of Germany.

France is also a member (together with Belgium, the Federal Republic of Germany, Italy, Luxembourg, the Netherlands and the United Kingdom) of the Western European Union (WEU), established in 1955 on the basis of the former Brussels Treaty Organization. The latter had been created in 1948 (by Belgium, France, Luxembourg, the Netherlands and the United Kingdom) but had been largely subsumed as an alliance for military defence into the NATO structure. On the initiative of France, the WEU was reactivated in 1984 with the aim of increasing security policy co-operation among the seven current member states (Portugal and Spain being prospective adherents).

Outside the European theatre France maintains a significant military presence (about 8,000 personnel in total) in a number of French-speaking African countries and also has a major base at Djibouti (at the western end of the Gulf of Aden). In addition, some 18,000 French military personnel are stationed in the French overseas departments and territories in the Caribbean, the Indian Ocean and the South Pacific.

As at end-1985 the French armed forces totalled 476,500 men and women, including 300,000 army, 96,500 air force and 67,700 navy personnel, in addition to which the para-military Gendarmerie numbered some 90,000. About half of the total armed forces are conscripts, there being compulsory military service for men of 12 months; there are a total of 395,000 reserves. The defence budget for 1985 was set at F 150,200 million, representing about 15 per cent of overall government expenditure.

France has the world's third largest nuclear-weapons arsenal (after the USA and the USSR), its "strategic nuclear forces" being equipped with missile-launching nuclear submarines, land-based strategic missiles and nuclear bomber aircraft. Successive governments have believed in the necessity for France to maintain an independent nuclear capability (the *force de frappe*), in which connection France conducts an annual series of nuclear tests at the Mururoa Atoll site in the South

Pacific. These tests—in the atmosphere until 1974 but underground since 1975—have continued despite unanimous condemnation by the countries of the region. France has not signed the 1963 partial test-ban treaty nor the 1970 nuclear non-proliferation treaty (NPT), although it has undertaken to abide by the latter's provisions.

Association for the Support of Conscientious Objectors
Association de Soutien aux Objecteurs de Conscience (ASOC)

Address. B.P.176, F-57104 Thionville Cédex, France

Aims and objectives. The Association's aim is to develop conscientious objection as a means of combating national and international militarism.

Formation. ASOC was formed in 1982.

Activities. The Association consists mainly of potential and existing conscientious objectors. It functions at local level but has contacts with all other national groups and with War Resisters' International. It distributes information on conscientious objection and militarism in schools; organizes demonstrations on anniversaries marking the end of wars; and stages an annual rally in conjunction with other local associations opposing nuclear weapons, racism etc. In future it hopes to participate more actively in meetings at European and international level.

Membership. The number of members of ASOC varies from year to year.

Publications. ASOC publishes a practical guide to conscientious objection.

Affiliations. ASOC is an associated member of War Resisters' International and a member of the National Anti-Militarist Commission (*Commission Nationale Antimilitariste*).

Committee for European Nuclear Disarmament
Comité pour le Désarmement Nucléaire en Europe (CODENE)

Address. 23 rue Nôtre Dame de Lorette, F-75009 Paris, France

Aims and objectives. As part of the European Nuclear Disarmament (END) network of groups (see entry under United Kingdom), CODENE is the French umbrella organization for the END initiative. It stresses three principal objectives, as set out in its appeal of December 1981: (i) to prevent further deployment of US and Soviet nuclear missiles in Europe (defined as stretching from Poland to Portugal) and to secure the withdrawal of existing missiles; (ii) to persuade the French Government to abandon the *force de frappe*; and (iii) to work with other European peace movements to secure nuclear disarmament.

Formation. CODENE launched its appeal in December 1981, following the publication of the original END Appeal in early 1980.

Activities. CODENE has been in the forefront of recent campaigns and actions by the French peace movement calling for the dismantling of the French nuclear deterrent and the withdrawal of all nuclear missiles from Europe, East and West. It has represented the French peace movement at successive END conventions and has been particularly active in promoting the twinning of nuclear-free zones in France with those declared in other countries. Through its member groups it has also undertaken extensive peace education work at local level.

Publications. Codene, monthly bulletin.

Affiliations. CODENE is the French umbrella organization for the European Nuclear Disarmament (END) movement.

The Community of the Ark
La Communauté de l'Arche

Address. F-34260 Le Bousquet D'Orb, France

Aims and objectives. The Community is a lay order, founded on Gandhian principles, which aims to put active non-violence into practice in daily life. The members share the objective of simplifying their needs and becoming aware of the needs of others near and far and working together without exploiting others.

Formation. The order was founded by Lanza del Vasto in 1948 but the first community was unsuccessful and was re-formed in the 1950s.

Activities. In the 1950s the Community was actively involved in non-violent actions in France, particularly against the war in Algeria. More recently efforts have been made to expand membership in France and Spain and in 1980 the Abbey of Bounecombe was leased and is developing into a conference centre. Introductory sessions are held in various languages and in 1984 the International Movement of Reconciliation held its annual meeting at the Abbey. Plans are now being made to start a community in Italy.

Members are involved in the daily running of the Community, where they run a farm. They also work with a local village in non-violent actions in protest against uranium mining.

Membership. The Community of the Ark embraces three communities: La Borie has around 70 members, Nogaret 25 and Laftaysserie 20. Members range in age from newborn babies to the oldest inhabitant, who is 63.

Publications. The Community publishes *Les Nouvelles de l'Arche* (News of the Ark).

Affiliations. Internationally the Community of the Ark is affiliated to Church and Peace (of West Germany). It also collaborates with other non-violent movements, including International Fellowship of Reconciliation, Paz y Justicia in Latin America and Peace Brigades International; within France the Community has links with the Movement for a Non-Violent Alternative and the Committee for European Nuclear Disarmament (CODENE).

Conscientious Objectors Movement
Mouvement des Objecteurs de Conscience

Address. 24 rue Cremieux, F-75012 Paris, France

Aims and objectives. The Movement is actively opposed to militarism and advocates conscientious objection as a means to achieve a peaceful society. Through research and promoting the aims of conscientious objectors, it aims to defend peace.

Formation. The Movement was formed in 1983.

Activities. The Movement has organized strike action by conscientious objectors who are completing civilian service and provides support for objectors and deserters. It also distributes information and aims to increase awareness among conscientious objectors.

Membership. The Movement has 200 members.

Publications. Journal des Objecteurs.

Affiliations. Associated member of War Resisters' International; affiliation to the (French) Co-ordination Committee for Civilian Service.

Co-ordination Committee for Civilian Service
Comité Coordination Service Civil

Address. 129 rue du Faubourg Poissonnière, F-75009 Paris, France.

Aims and objectives. As the French section of Service Civil International (SCI), this group seeks to promote peace and international understanding through voluntary service activities. It also works with other French organizations providing support for conscientious objectors and advocating alternatives to military service for conscripts.

Affiliations. Service Civil International.

Le Cun de Larzac

Address. Route de St Martin à Pierrefiche, F-12100 Millau, France

Aims and objectives. Having arisen out of the countrywide support generated by local peasants' opposition to the extension of a military camp at Larzac in southern France, Le Cun de Larzac has become a research and documentation centre for peace campaigners.

Activities. The campaign against the military camp extension lasted 10 years and was eventually successful when the plans were abandoned following the election of a Socialist Government in 1981. Since then Le Cun de Larzac has sought to promote research on peace and disarmament questions and on non-violent alternatives, establishing a library and documentation centre for this purpose and also conducting peace education activities.

Publication. Le Cun de Larzac, bi-monthly bulletin.

Documentation and Research Centre on Peace and Conflict
Centre de Documentation et de Recherche sur la Paix et les Conflits

Address. B.P. 1027, F-69201 Lyons, Cédex 01, France

Aims and objectives. The Centre aims to make accessible to ordinary peace movement activists information on defence and strategic questions often regarded as the preserve of specialists or academics.

Formation. The Centre was established in May 1984 (its status as an association being recorded in the *Journal Officiel* of May 24, 1984).

Activities. The Centre collects, processes and disseminates information on the problems of strategy, war and peace, militarization and defence. It runs a specialist library for peace research and makes its facilities available to peace movements.

Publications. Since April 1985 the Centre has published a monthly documentation bulletin called *Damocles*, which contains a broad range of data on relevant matters. It also publishes *Cahiers Damocles* (an irregular series of studies of particular themes), press dossiers and bibliographies.

Affiliations. The Centre is independent of any political, social or religious group.

Education Collective for Peace
Collectif Education à la Paix (CEP)

Address. 47 bis avenue de Clichy, 4 cour St Pierre, F-75017 Paris, France

Aims and objectives. The CEP seeks to promote an education, in schools and elsewhere, that will be a source of peace and justice. As a collective organization it provides support for various individual groups working in this field.

Formation. The Collective came into being as a result of a colloquium held in Paris in October 1982 on the theme "For Peace Teaching in Our School System".

Activities. Through its participating groups, the CEP works with teachers, parents, administrators, researchers and others to promote peace education in schools. A range of methods and media are used, including role-playing games, stories and novels, exhibitions, pictures and audio-visual aids. The Collective operates on the premise that "to understand peace is not to indoctrinate but to create an opening, a positive and voluntary attitude, whatever the age of the child, in the family, at school and in the street".

Membership. Participating organizations of the CEP include the Movement for Disarmament, Peace and Freedom, the Movement for a Non-Violent Alternative, Women's International Resistance to War and Le Cun de Larzac. In all over 20 peace educational groups are associated with the Collective.

Publication. La Colombe et l'Encrier, containing the proceedings of the 1982 colloquium (published by Editions Syros).

French Association for Universal Peace
Association Français pour la Paix Universelle

Address. 50 rue du Dammartin, F-59100 Roubaix, France

Aims and objectives. The Association aims to propagate the founding principles of the United Nations, seeking "to save succeeding generations from the scourge of war" while stressing "the indissoluble link which unites respect for human rights with the survival of humanity". Its headquarters in Roubaix are a House of Peace, the only one of its kind in France.

Activities. The Association's activities are concentrated on the dissemination, in poster and leaflet form, of the Universal Declaration of Human Rights. The House of Peace is at the disposal of all French organizations working for peace.

The impetus for the establishment of the House of Peace had arisen from contacts with Sean MacBride (former chief of staff of the Irish Republican Army, Irish Foreign Minister in 1948–51 and joint recipient of the Nobel Peace Prize in 1974) during his visit to Lille in 1975. The house in Roubaix had subsequently been purchased on the initiative of Paul Carette, who had played a leading part in the establishment of similar premises in Belgium. The French Peace House had been inaugurated by Sean MacBride in December 1976 and had been designated "Sean MacBride House" in December 1978 on the occasion of the 30th anniversary of the adoption of the Universal Declaration of Human Rights.

House of Peace/Sean MacBride House—see under French Association for Universal Peace

Interdisciplinary Centre for Peace Research and Strategic Studies
Centre Interdisciplinaire de Recherches sur la Paix et d'Etudes Stratégiques (CIRPES)

Address. 71 boulevard Raspail, F-75006 Paris, France

Aims and objectives. The objective of CIRPES is "to create a centre of research, documentation and publications on war and peace and to co-ordinate different disciplinary approaches around a defined programme in order to produce a more global and more efficacious analysis of the problems of security and disarmament".

Formation. CIRPES was established in 1982 on the initiative of a group of academics of various disciplines and from assorted institutions. It received initial financial support from the Ministry of Industry and Research and has also obtained subventions from other ministries (including Defence and Foreign Affairs) and a number of other bodies (notably UNESCO).

Activities. CIRPES has established itself as a specialized documentation centre linking French and overseas researchers in an active publications policy based on individual or collective research. It also organizes colloquia on theoretical or practical questions, with particular reference to the issues thrown up by new missile deployment in Europe by the United States and the Soviet Union.

Publications. The Centre publishes monograph studies with the series title *Cahiers d'Etudes Stratégiques*.

International Movement of Reconciliation
Mouvement International de la Réconciliation (MIR)

Address. B.P. 369, F-75625 Paris, Cédex 13, France

Aims and objectives. As the French section of the International Fellowship of Reconciliation (IFOR), the MIR campaigns for justice, liberation, peace and disarmament, basing itself on non-violence in accordance with the Christian gospel. It fights against "all forms of violence and oppression (national, military, ideological, racial, economic, sexist, ecological etc.) and for the implementing of a non-violent popular civilian defence requiring a new examination of our security criteria, a reconversion of the arms industries and a more equitable distribution of the world's riches and responsibilities taking the Third World particularly into account". In addition, the MIR "fights for the right to dignity and effective existence of all ethnic, social and cultural minorities and all the misfits of our society of consumption and waste" and "supports conscientious objectors whose commitment constitutes an important contribution to the resistance against the growing militarization of our societies". In summary, the MIR "unites in a pluralistic prospect all those who refuse to conform . . . to a military order, open or disguised" and calls upon believers "to live their faith with more coherence" and upon activists "to lead their struggle with greater pertinence as regards military and security problems".

Formation. IFOR itself was founded in 1919.

Activities. The MIR has engaged in (i) the struggle for an effective acknowledgement of conscientious objection in France and in other countries; (ii) the struggle for disarmament in unison with other peace movements; (iii) support for French peasants opposing the extension of the military camp at Larzac; (iv) support for the Kanak liberation struggle in French New Caledonia; (v) support for peace and reconciliation initiatives in Central America; (vi) support for the South African people in their struggle against apartheid; (vii) support for all peoples subjected to dictatorial regimes; (viii) actions to stimulate Christians of the Catholic and Protestant churches to awareness of the evangelical message of non-violence; and (ix) lectures, seminars and publicity on the themes of reconciliation and non-violence.

Membership. The MIR has about 300 members.

Publications. *Les Cahiers de la Réconciliation*, monthly review with 900 subscribers; *Les Monographies de la Défense Civile*.

Affiliations. International Fellowship of Reconciliation; Co-ordination Committee for Civilian Service; Committee for European Nuclear Disarmament (CODENE); International Emergency Action; War Resisters' International (associated member).

Justice and Peace, French Commission
Justice et Paix, Commission Française

Address. 71 rue Notre-Dame des Champs, F-75006 Paris, France

Aims and objectives. This Commission seeks to increase awareness among the Catholic community of the questions of peace, the rights of man and the development of peoples. It co-operates with the French episcopal conference in these areas.

Formation. The Commission was founded in 1967 in the context of the papal encyclical *Populorum Progressio*, against which background it has concentrated its interest on development questions in accordance with the maxim that "development is the new name of peace".

Activities. The Commission has been concerned with civil and political rights in such countries as Vietnam, Brazil, Uruguay and Chile and has also given particular attention to the arms trade. Since 1981 it has studied defence and peace questions, leading to the publication of an ecumenical document *Pour Construire la Paix* (To Construct Peace) in February 1985. The Commission participates in peace initiatives (e.g. for the Middle East) and has also investigated how human rights are covered in Catholic religious training.

Publications. The Commission publishes a quarterly information bulletin and has issued a number of brochures on specific issues.

Local Information and Co-ordination Centre for Non-Violent Action
Centre Local d'Information et de Coordination pour l'Action Non-Violente (CLICAN)

Address. B.P. 624, F-83053 Toulon Cédex, France

Aims and objectives. CLICAN aims to stimulate awareness of peace issues and non-violent alternatives by means of grass-roots information and educational work.

Formation. CLICAN was originally founded in 1969.

Activities. CLICAN has organized conferences and seminars on various themes for local activists. It also has an extensive publishing programme and acts as a clearing-house for information on non-violence, the arms trade, civilian defence and nuclear issues.

Affiliations. CLICAN is part of the network of groups associated with the Movement for a Non-Violent Alternative (MAN).

Movement for a Non-Violent Alternative
Mouvement pour une Alternative Non-Violente (MAN)

Address. 20 rue du Dévidet, F-45200 Montargis, France

Aims and objectives. The MAN has as its basic objectives (i) to combat institutional violence by a non-violent strategy and to promote a society founded on the principle of socialist self-management (*autogestion*); (ii) to replace armed national defence by popular non-violent defence (*défense populaire non-violente*, DPNV) inspired by the historical examples of Gandhi and Martin Luther King; (iii) cultural revolution to prevent the domination of man by man; and (iv) to inform and influence public opinion on non-violent alternatives.

Formation. The MAN was founded at Poitiers in 1974.

Activities. The MAN presented its political orientation in 1976 in a tract entitled *Pour le socialisme autogestionnaire, une non-violence politique.* For the March 1978 French Assembly elections it combined with the Unified Socialist Party (PSU) and various ecological, feminist and regional groupings to form the *Front Autogestionnaire*, a local-level alliance which put up 228 candidates (in some cases in alliance with the Communist Party). After the elections the *Front Autogestionnaire* was transformed into the *Convergence pour l'Autogestion.*

The MAN has participated in collective actions of civil disobedience, notably in the resistance to the extension of the Larzac military camp, and in the campaign of refusal to pay taxes for the seventh nuclear submarine for the French navy. It is also active in campaigns in support of conscientious objection and immigrant rights and against civil nuclear power. It participated in the European peace convention held in Berlin in 1983 and also supports the "civil resistance" of the Polish people.

Membership. The MAN is a federation of 45 local groups with an aggregate membership of 630. It holds an annual congress which elects a co-ordination committee.

Publication. Non-Violence Actualité (monthly).

Affiliations. The MAN is a member of the Committee for European Nuclear Disarmament (CODENE) and the Co-ordination Committee for Civilian Service.

Movement for Disarmament, Peace and Freedom
Mouvement pour le Désarmement, la Paix et la Liberté (MDPL)

Address. B.P. 2135, F-34026 Montpellier, France

Aims and objectives. The Movement for Disarmament, Peace and Freedom is opposed to all forms of oppression, repression and aggression in the spheres of economic, political and social life. It condemns all weapons of mass destruction and all forms of imperialism. The MDPL supports all movements which fight against oppression in the belief that all such struggles are inseparable from the struggle for peace and the establishment of a socialist society.

Formation. The MDPL was founded in 1963 as the *Mouvement Contre l'Armement Atomique.* By 1968 the movement was concerning itself with a wider range of issues arising from militarism and world aggression and so the name was changed.

Activities. The MDPF has been active in its support for oppressed people throughout the world. Opposing the Vietnam war, it helped found the *Front de Solidarité Indochine*; launched the Anti-Outspan Campaign against South Africa and was active in the formation of the *Comité de Défense des Prisonnières Politiques Chiliennes.*

The MDPL has opposed French militarism by organizing demonstrations against nuclear testing in French Polynesia in the South Pacific. It successfully campaigned against the extension of the military camp at Larzac and supports conscientious objectors, being active in the creation of the Committee for the Support of Conscripts. The MDPL also works for the re-allocation of funds at present spent in the armaments industry. It is particularly active in trying to prevent the exportation of French weapons to oppressive regimes.

Since 1978 the movement has developed a research programme in the field of peace education. It produces peace material for teachers, parents and educators.

Membership. The MDPL has 1,000 members.

Publications. The MDPL produces a periodical review *Alerte*, which covers a variety of themes, including nuclear issues, peace education, liberation struggles and arms sales. It also produces audio-visual material and has published two books: *La Colombe et l'Encrier* and *Le Poker Nucléaire.*

Affiliations. The MDPL is affiliated to the (French) Committee for European Nuclear Disarmament (CODENE) and the International Peace Bureau.

National Co-ordinating Body for Conscientious Objector Reservists
Coordination Nationale des Objecteurs-Réservistes

Address. c/o P. Coulon & B. Bayada, 10 rue Clotilde Morisseau, F-45200 Montargis, France

Aims and objectives. This group represents men who, having completed compulsory military service, object on grounds of conscience to being placed in the military reserve, and to military means of defence in general. It sees itself as part of the wider peace movement in France.

Formation. The group developed out of the Conscientious Objectors Movement, and in particular from organizations advocating the refusal of call-up papers, some of which were active soon after the First World War.

Activities. Since 1970 some 3,000 people have refused call-up papers, leading to a large number of trials. In 1981 the group began to campaign for a law recognizing the right of reservists to object to call-up, and in 1983 it achieved that end, albeit with some restrictions.

The group continues to work for the elimination of restrictions on reservist conscientious objection, and encourages women and others exempt from military service to make a "declaration of conscientious objection". It took part in activities to mark European Conscientious Objection Day on May 15, 1986.

Membership. The group has 20 regional co-ordinators, as well as departmental and local organizers.

Publications. Les Luttes des Réservistes (Reservists' Struggles); occasional tracts and papers.

Affiliations. Although it has no formal affiliations, the group co-operates with other pacifist organizations.

Pacifist Union of France
Union Pacifiste de France (UPF)

Address. 4 rue Lazare-Hoche, F-92100 Boulogne-sur-Seine, France

Aims and objectives. The UPF is the French section of War Resisters' International. It claims to be the sole French peace group which is wholly independent of any political or religious organization. The group is opposed to all forms of armaments, warfare and militarism, and is concerned with their social, psychological and economic causes. It supports French unilateral disarmament, in order to create a nation of conscientious objectors and thereby to set an example to other states.

Formation. The UPF was formed during the 1960s, in the wake of a hunger strike by Louis Lecoin which in part led to the passage of a law recognizing the right to conscientious objection. Certain members of the group were prosecuted for their part in the campaign leading to the law change.

Activities. The UPF has taken part in all the major peace demonstrations in France, and offers support and advice to army deserters. It has also presented petitions to the Government calling for unilateral disarmament. It recently launched a campaign against government directives dating from 1959 which provide for the conscription of the entire civilian population in peacetime. It supports peace education, and opposes visits to schools by members of the armed forces.

Membership. The UPF currently has approximately 2,000 members, of varying backgrounds and professions.

Publications. Journal Mensuel l'Union Pacifiste, a monthly publication which has some 3,000 subscribers.

Affiliations. War Resisters' International.

Pax Christi France

Address. 44 rue de la Santé, F-75014 Paris, France

Aims and objectives. As the French section of "the international Catholic movement for peace", Pax Christi in France seeks to educate Catholics and others on peace and reconciliation between nations. It forms part of the French peace movement in that it advocates disarmament, particularly the abolition of nuclear weapons, and pursuance of non-violent alternatives.

Formation. The Pax Christi movement was originally established in France (at Agen) in 1945, its initial priority being to promote *Franco*-German reconciliation in the aftermath of the Second World War.

Activities. The French section has given particular attention to conflicts in Indochina and Lebanon and also to peace work in francophone Africa. In addition to an annual conference, it organizes peace exhibitions, peace weeks and special seminars. It is also active in peace education work and in developing international contacts between Catholic peace activists.

Publications. Le Journal de la Paix (Journal of Peace), monthly; *Les Dossiers de la Paix*, occasional.

Affiliations. Pax Christi International.

Peace Book Association in France
Association du Livre de la Paix, France

Address. Haut Maubisson, F-33121 Carcans, France

Aims and objectives. The Peace Book Association seeks to bring about genuine world peace by non-violent means, based on the principles of the Peace Book by Bernard Benson.

Formation. The Association was formed in France in October 1981 upon the publication of the Peace Book. Its patrons are the Nobel laureates Sean MacBride, Alfred Kastler and Philip Noel-Baker.

Activities. In August 1982, following the publication in the international press of a "peace network" advertisement, 20,000,000 letters were sent to the US and Soviet Presidents urging them to devote 5 per cent of their military budgets to projects enhancing life and peace. Bernard Benson was invited to the Soviet Union as a consequence. The first congress of the Peace Book Association took place in Paris in May 1983.

Projects have included the distribution of 2,000,000 tapes about Hiroshima to French schoolchildren in May 1983. A current project known as "Espoir" (Hope) involves children in peace activities centred around exhibitions, school discussions and international contacts and exchanges, while under a future "Bird of Peace" project children from different countries will urge heads of state to meet to put a world peace plan into effect.

Membership. The number of members in France is variable, and many participants are not actually members. The Association is organized in local groups and decisions are taken by a collegiate of a dozen elected members.

Publications. A liaison bulletin for Peace Book Association groups in France is issued approximately every two months.

Affiliations. The Association has no formal affiliations and follows no specific political or religious line.

Peace Movement
Mouvement de la Paix

Address. 35 rue de Clichy, F-75009 Paris, France

Aims and objectives. The Movement seeks to inform and mobilize public opinion on questions of peace, disarmament and the achievement of conflict solution through negotiated solutions. It is working progressively to achieve an end to any further missile deployments in Europe and a worldwide freeze on the development of nuclear weapons, to be followed by a negotiated reduction in the nuclear arsenals of both East and West. The Movement supports a complete ban on development of the neutron bomb and on the militarization of space. Longer-term goals include a reduction in the level of world military expenditure and the simultaneous dissolution of NATO and the Warsaw Pact. The Movement is also committed to "development and social progress".

Formation. It was established in 1949 (following a World Peace Congress in Paris) by individuals who had played a leading part in the resistance against Nazi occupation during the Second World War.

Activities. Major campaigns mounted by the Movement since its formation have included ones against nuclear weapons, against the (eventually aborted) European Defence Community concept and against French colonial wars (notably that in Algeria). The Movement has also supported initiatives aimed at securing détente between the super-powers and the implementation of the 1975 Helsinki Final Act of the Conference on Security and Co-operation in Europe (CSCE).

The Movement organized a rally against nuclear escalation in Paris in 1981 which it claimed attracted 100,000 supporters, while a petition campaign on the same subject yielded approximately 1,000,000 signatures. Delegations representing the Movement have been despatched to the Stockholm and Madrid CSCE follow-up meetings, and to disarmament negotiations in Geneva. A series of campaigns for a nuclear freeze and for negotiated disarmament were conducted during 1985 under the slogan "No more Hiroshimas" and the Movement has organized a series of actions and events to mark 1986 an International Year of Peace.

Membership. There are between 300 and 400 locally-based committees, with a 400-member National Council acting as a co-ordinating body. Support comes from broad political, religious and social spectra.

Publications. The Movement publishes *Combat pour la Paix* (Fight for Peace) eight times a year.

Women for Peace, France
Femmes pour la Paix, France

Address. c/o Solange Fernex, F-68480 Biederthal, France

Aims and objectives. Women for Peace is opposed to nuclear armaments and other weapons of mass destruction, from the standpoint that women, constituting half of humanity and having the mission of bearing life, should cease being silent on such issues.

Formation. Women for Peace was established in France in the mid-1970s, as similar groups were being formed in other West European countries.

Activities. The group concentrates its activities in the following fields: (i) study of the nuclear weapons threat (with emphasis on the memory of what happened at Hiroshima and Nagasaki); (ii) exerting pressure on governments by means of petitions and other actions; and (iii) developing contacts with other pacifist and non-violent movements, including those of feminist orientation.

Membership. The French group has about 100 active members.

Affiliations. As well as its association with Women for Peace groups in other West European countries, the French group participates in the (French) Committee for European Nuclear Disarmament (CODENE).

Women's International League for Peace and Freedom
Ligue International des Femmes pour la Paix et la Liberté (LIFPL)

Address. 24 quai Louis Bleriot, F-75016 Paris, France

Aims and objectives. As the French section of the WILPF, the LIFPL seeks to mobilize women to work for the eradication of the political, social, economic and psychological causes of war and the creation of the conditions for peace, including complete and universal disarmament and the renunciation of violent or coercive methods of settling disputes. It regards peace education as of particular importance.

Publication. Paix et Liberté, quarterly.

Affiliations. Women's International League for Peace and Freedom.

Women's International Resistance to War
Résistance Internationale des Femmes à la Guerre (RIFG)

Address. 65 avenue du Bac, F-94210 La Varenne, France

Aims and objectives. This movement seeks (i) to undertake reflexion and action against war in all forms and from all causes; (ii) to persuade women to be aware of their power and to take responsibility on such matters; and (iii) to conceive and promote peace education.

Activities. RIFG has operated as a feminist movement in participating in campaigns against war, stressing that political, economic and technological power has always escaped women in a society organized "according to a patriarchal division of human groups". It has organized demonstrations and seminars on various themes, notably those related to peace education and the role of women in the cause of pacifism.

Membership. RIFG has some 2,000 members.

Publications. RIFG's recent publications include *Féminisme et Pacifisme,* the proceedings of a seminar held in 1984.

Affiliations. RIFG is affiliated to the (French) Committee for European Nuclear Disarmament (CODENE) and is a member of the Education Collective for Peace.

World Citizens' Popular Movement
Mouvement Populaire des Citoyens du Monde (MPCDM)

Address. Centre Social, rue de Pavigny, F-39000 Lons le Saunier, France

Aims and objectives. The MPCDM promotes world citizenship, world government and world peace; the abolition of racism and oppression; universal respect for human rights, and the mobilization of public opinion in support of these objectives.

Formation. The Movement was started in the Jura region in 1976 by adherents of the world citizenship movement.

Activities. The Movement takes part in demonstrations and meetings, produces publicity material and organizes two seminars each year.

Membership. About 1,000.

Publications. Peuples Unis (Peoples United), quarterly; *Flashes-Contacts-Échanges*, international monthly.

Affiliations. No formal affiliations, but numerous national and international contacts.

Other Movements

Christian Movement for Peace
Mouvement Chrétien pour la Paix

Address. 46 rue de Vaugirard, 75006 Paris, France

Committee for the Support of Conscripts
Comité de Soutien aux Insoumis

Address. 145 rue Amelot, Paris 11ème, France

Education for Disarmament and Peace
Education pour le Désarmement et la Paix

Address. 11 avenue Maximilien Robespierre, F-92290 Chatenay-Malabry, France

International Peace Library
Bibliothèque Internationale de la Paix

Address. 9–11 rue du Forst, F-57200 Sarreguémines, France

National Committee for Independence and Peace
Comité National pour l'Indépendance et la Paix (CNIP)

Address. 35 rue de Clichy, F-75009 Paris, France

Federal Republic of Germany

capital: Bonn   **population: 62,000,000**

Germany was effectively partitioned after its defeat in the Second World War, the western zones occupied by US, UK and French forces becoming the Federal Republic of Germany (FRG) from May 1949 and the Soviet-occupied zone in the east becoming the German Democratic Republic (GDR) from October 1949. In a "partition within a partition" the former capital city of Berlin in eastern Germany was divided into a Soviet and three Western sectors, the latter (i.e. West Berlin) becoming linked to the FRG although not a constituent part of it. Under post-war frontier dispositions, former German territory to the east of the Oder-Neisse line was acquired by Poland, while the Soviet Union annexed the northern half of East Prussia (as well as substantial tracts of former Polish and Czechoslovakian territory adjoining the pre-war Soviet border in the west). In the absence of a formal peace treaty between the war-time allies and Germany, these territorial adjustments have been recognized as "inviolable" by the FRG in various bilateral and multilateral treaties signed in the 1970s, as has the border between East and West Germany. However, the FRG does not regard the GDR as a "foreign" country, nor has it abandoned the goal of the peaceful reunification of Germany within borders to be determined by international treaty.

The FRG achieved full sovereignty as from May 5, 1955, under the October 1954 Paris Agreements providing for its accession (from the same date) to two defensive alliances, namely (i) the Brussels Treaty Organization, renamed the Western European Union (WEU) and also embracing Belgium, France, Italy, Luxembourg, the Netherlands and the United Kingdom; and (ii) the North Atlantic Treaty Organization (NATO), the then members of which were the other six WEU countries together with Canada, Denmark, Greece, Iceland, Norway, Portugal, Turkey and the United States (Spain becoming a member in 1982). Under the Paris Agreements the FRG was forbidden to manufacture nuclear, biological or chemical weapons and various restrictions were placed on its possession of conventional armaments. However, the latter restrictions have been progressively relaxed over the years, culminating in the remaining controls being entirely lifted as from Jan. 1, 1986.

In a declaration incorporated into the 1954 Paris Agreements the FRG undertook "never to have recourse to force to achieve the reunification of Germany or the modification of the present boundaries of the FRG, and to resolve by peaceful means any disputes which may arise between the Federal Republic and other states". In a simultaneous declaration the three Western powers recorded their belief (i) that "a peace settlement for the whole of Germany, freely negotiated between Germany and her former enemies, . . . remains an essential aim of their policy"; (ii) that the "final determination of the boundaries of Germany must await such a settlement"; (iii) that "the achievement through peaceful means of a fully free and unified Germany remains a fundamental goal of their policy"; and (iv) that "the security and welfare of Berlin and the maintenance of the position of the three powers there are regarded by the three powers as essential elements of the peace of the free world" and that "they will treat any attack against Berlin from any quarter as an attack upon their forces and themselves".

As at end-1985 the West German armed forces totalled 478,000, including 335,600 army, 106,000 air force and 36,200 navy personnel. There were also some 20,000 para-military forces. Just under half the total armed forces complement were conscripts, there being compulsory military service for men of 15 months (to rise to 18 months from 1989). The total number of reserves was about 770,000. The defence budget for 1985 amounted to DM49,014 million, representing about 8 per cent of overall government expenditure.

With the "intra-German" borders marking the most sensitive frontier between NATO and Warsaw Pact Europe, each German state is the location of large concentrations of military forces of their respective alliances. Stationed in the FRG there are, in addition to the NATO-integrated West German forces, some 400,000 military personnel from other NATO countries, namely the United States (205,000 army and 41,000 air force), the United Kingdom (55,000 army and 10,500 air force), France (48,500), Belgium (28,000), the Netherlands (5,500) and Canada (5,000). There is also a NATO naval base at the Baltic port of Kiel. Moreover, the three Western powers have a military presence in West Berlin, consisting of 4,300 US, 3,000 UK and 2,700 French troops.

In view of the substantial numerical superiority of the Warsaw Pact's conventional forces, certain NATO units in West Germany are equipped with tactical and "battle-field" nuclear weapons, the intention being to deter a conventional attack by the threat of rapid escalation to the nuclear threshold. For this reason, the NATO side has consistently refused to enter into a commitment not to resort to "first use" of nuclear weapons. As regards nuclear missiles, NATO's December 1979 "twin-track" decision to modernize its intermediate-range nuclear force (INF) capability in Western Europe provided for the deployment of 96 US cruise and 108 US Pershing II missiles in the FRG.

As in other intended INF deployment countries, the 1979 NATO decision provoked major controversy in the FRG and has been vigorously opposed by the country's peace movement as being a further guarantee of the immediate devastation of West Germany in any future East-West conflict. At the political level, the deployment of the new missiles secured final approval in the *Bundestag* (federal lower house) on Nov. 22, 1983, by 286 votes to 226 with one abstention, following which the first Pershing IIs were in place on West German territory by the end of the year. In the *Bundestag* vote deployment was opposed not only by the Greens but also by the opposition Social Democrats, who had been the senior coalition partner in the FRG government which had been a party to the original NATO decision in 1979.

Having failed in attempts in the *Bundestag* to secure the holding of an official referendum on the missile deployment issue, the Greens (supported by the Social Democrats) organized an unofficial popular consultation on June 17, 1984, to coincide with European Parliament elections. According to the West German peace movement, some 5,200,000 people (out of an electorate of nearly 44,500,000) participated in the unofficial poll, conducted at approximately 18,000 polling stations, and 88 per cent of those voting supported a proposition calling for an end to deployment. The Federal Constitutional Court in Karlsruhe had on Dec. 22, 1983, rejected a number of petitions seeking an injunction on the deployment of the new missiles, ruling that their deployment was not in contravention of the federal constitution.

In other significant defence-related developments under the Christian Democratic-Free Democratic coalition which came to power in October 1982, (i) the FRG in October 1984 endorsed a French-initiated proposal to reactivate the WEU in order to increase security policy co-operation between the seven member states (prospectively to increase to nine with the accession of Portugal and Spain); (ii) the FRG moved to closer bilateral co-operation on defence matters with France, on the basis of the 1963 Franco-German friendship treaty; and (iii) the Government on Dec. 18, 1985, reaffirmed its political support for the US Strategic Defence Initiative (SDI) and agreed that negotiations should be opened with the USA on the mutual transfer of technology, including SDI research, by private concerns.

Anti-Militarist Book Mail Order Firm/Association for the Promotion of Peace Ideas and Initiatives
Antimilitaristischer Buchversand/Verein zur Förderung Friedenspolitischer Ideen und Initiativen

Address. Eichwaldstrasse 75 H, D-6000 Frankfurt 60, Fed. Rep. of Germany

Aims and objectives. The organization seeks to provide and give access to literature of theoretical and practical importance for the peace movement.

Formation. The mail order firm and Association were formed in 1974 by a local group of War Resisters' International.

Activities. The organization originally sold books and compiled annotated lists, but since 1977 it has also published books. It organizes discussions and seminars on peace issues and plans to widen these into regular sessions for youth groups. It hopes to build up a library of relevant literature and to broaden its publishing activities.

Membership. About 15, eight of them active.

Publications. Books and booklists.

Church and Peace
Kirche und Frieden

Address. Kalsmuntstrasse 21, D-6331 Schoeffengrund, Fed. Rep. of Germany

Aims and objectives. Church and Peace is an ecumenical network of Christian communities and congregations, who believe that the Christian church should be primarily a church of peace. The various groups which make up Church and Peace work for peace in different ways: some are active politically, some lead contemplative lives and some aim to live together in peace. One task of Church and Peace is to bring these groups together so they can exchange experiences, challenge each other, and learn together what it means to be a peace church. The organization provides theological assistance in this process.

Members of the Church and Peace network share the following objectives: to understand the gospel and share it with others; to refuse the use of violence; to aid victims of violence; to work for alternatives to violence.

Formation. Church and Peace is the successor organization of the European continuation committee of the Historic Peace Churches (i.e. Quakers and Mennonites). One function of the continuation committee was to maintain a dialogue with the World Council of Churches on Christian participation in warfare. In 1955 the continuation committee sponsored the first in a series of "Puidoux conferences" which involved an exchange between theologians of the Historic Peace Churches and theologians from the mainstream European churches, under the title "The Lordship of Christ over Church and State". In 1957 the continuation committee participated in the formation of the International Christian Service for Peace (EIRENE—see entry under International Organizations).

In 1977 the continuation committee adopted the present name of Church and Peace and its present form.

Activities. Church and Peace organizes conferences, seminars, theological study groups, visits to communities, house churches and congregations. It arranged the "First European Peace Church Gathering", held in June 1986 in Braunfels (West Germany).

Membership. The founding members of the organization were the service agencies of the Historic Peace Churches and the International Fellowship of Reconciliation. There are 14 further corporate members (communities, churches and congregations) and numerous individual members. There are also many groups who form part of the Church and Peace network but are not official members.

Publications. Kirche und Frieden, quarterly, also in English (*Church and Peace*) and French (*Eglise et Paix*).

Affiliations. International Fellowship of Reconciliation.

Civil Disobedience Co-ordination Centre—see under Federal Conference of Independent Peace Groups

Education and Meetings Centre for Non-Violent Action
Bildungs- und Begegnungsstatte für Gewaltfreie Aktion

Address. Kirchstrasse 14, D-3131 Wustrow, Fed. Rep. of Germany

Aims and objectives. This Centre works to support non-violent resistance to the destruction of nature, and against war and social injustice.

Formation. The Centre was established in 1981.

Activities. The Centre has a house close to the planned nuclear waste dumps near Gotleben where it holds seminars on peace, ecological, women's issues etc.

Membership. 250.

Publications. Rundbrief, newsletter; seminar programme, twice a year.

Ecumenical Action Group for Peace and Justice—see entry for Living Without Armaments

Federal Conference of Independent Peace Groups
Bundeskonferenz Unabhängiger Friedensgruppen (BUF)

Address. Am Schwarzen Meer 67, D-2800 Bremen 1, Fed. Rep. of Germany

Aims and objectives. The BUF acts as a central co-ordinating point for West German peace groups which are not connected with larger organizations. It also co-ordinates civil disobedience actions through its *Koordinationsstelle Ziviler Ungehorsam* (Civil Disobedience Co-ordination Centre) based at the same address.

Formation. The BUF came into existence in January 1984, in succession to earlier organizations with the same purpose.

German-American Peace Embassy

Address. c/o Lilo Klug, Kazensteige 40/1, D-7100 Heilbronn, Fed. Rep. of Germany

Aims and objectives. This group seeks to serve as a clearing-house and contact point for the exchange of information between peace activists of West Germany and the United States, with particular emphasis on the grassroots level.

Formation. The group came into being in June 1985.

Activities. Located adjacent to a US/NATO Pershing II missile deployment site, the group is involved in developing exchange visits between West Germany and the United States, supplying contacts to both sides and supplying information (in English) on the West German and European situation to US movements. It has also promoted the establishment of common goals for peace activists of the two countries.

German Peace Society—United War Resisters
Deutsche Friedensgesellschaft—Vereinigte Kriegsdienstgegner (DFG-VK)

Address. Schwanerstrasse 16, D-5620 Velbert 1, Fed. Rep. of Germany

Aims and objectives. The DFG-VK calls for general and complete disarmament and for the peaceful solution of conflicts in a framework of a system of collective security. Members refuse to participate in war preparations and support conscientious objectors. They demand the right to conscientious objection to be recognized as a human right by the United Nations.

The DFG-VK supports the political aims of liberation movements throughout the world. It works by non-violent means to overcome colonialism, racism, suppressive regimes and for the establishment of a new international economic order.

Formation. The DFG-VK was formed in Bonn in 1974 by the merger of three, formerly independent, peace groups: the *Deutsche Friedensgesellschaft* (DFG), the *Internationale der Kriegsdienstgegner* (IdK) and the *Verband der Kriegsdienstverweigerer* (VK).

The DFG was founded in 1892 and opposed the aggressive militarism of imperial Germany. During the First World War it worked for an armistice. After the war the DFG demanded general disarmament and was in the forefront of the struggle against the rise of fascism. After the Second World War both the DFG and the IdK (which was founded in 1947) opposed the cold war and campaigned for mutual understanding and for a peaceful co-existence between East and West. Both organizations opposed German rearmament and the deployment of tactical nuclear weapons in West Germany. Together with the VK (which was founded in 1953) the DFG and the IdK counselled conscientious objectors and opposed all attempts by the Government to restrict the right to conscientious objection.

Activities. In the early 1970s the DFG, IdK and VK supported the policy of détente pursued by the newly established Social Democratic-Liberal Government and called for corresponding disarmament measures. Following their merger, the DFG-VK launched a new campaign for conscientious objection of all military

84

services both inside and outside the army. The organization is especially concerned with the development of alternative non-military defence perspectives, especially for central Europe and to this end held an Information Week for Peace in November 1985. It has also sponsored a Prisoners for Peace solidarity campaign and supported South African conscientious objectors.

The DFG-VK campaigns for the abolition of nuclear and chemical weapons and the reallocation of funds to promoting development.

Membership. The DFG-VK has 17,000 individual members in eight regional districts and over a hundred local groups. The membership is 85 per cent male and 15 per cent female.

Publications. *Zivilcourage*, a bi-monthly publication with a circulation of 20,000; the DFG-VK has also produced several books in German.

Affiliations. War Resisters' International; International Peace Bureau.

German Peace Society—War Resisters' International
Deutsche Friedensgesellschaft—Internationale der Kriegsdienstgegner (DFG-IdK)

Address. Jungfrauenthal 37, D-2000 Hamburg 13, Fed. Rep. of Germany

Aims and objectives. The DFG-IdK operates in Hamburg with essentially the same aims and objectives as the DFG-VK (see previous entry), being one of four separate German affiliates of War Resisters' International.

Publication. *DFG-IdK Info.*

Affiliations. War Resisters' International.

Grassroots Revolution—Federation of Non-Violent Action Groups
Graswurzel-Revolution—Föderation Gewaltfreier Aktionsgruppen (FöGA)

Address. Graswurzel-Werkstaff, Königsallee 28A, D-3400 Göttingen, Fed. Rep. of Germany

Aims and objectives. This group seeks (i) the creation of a non-violent society with decentralized economic and political self-determination; (ii) the abolition of war and all military organizations and the substitution of social non-violent defence; (iii) the establishment of an ecological way of life, with an end to "structures of domination depending on race, sex, belief, age, cultural or social position".

Formation. The group was founded in 1979 to co-ordinate groups and individuals of the German non-violent movement active since the early 1970s.

Activities. These have included demonstrations, leafleting, rallies and non-violent direct action, directed against military installations, conscription, attacks on civil liberties, neo-fascist groups, nuclear power plants and other big industrial projects. The group campaigned in 1985 against civil defence as a form of preparation for war, spread information to assist German and other soldiers to leave the army (legally or illegally), helped to blockade military trains crossing Germany to US bases, and participated in the resistance to the construction of nuclear fuel facilities at Gorleben and Wackersdorf.

Membership. The group has 200 members, mostly co-workers in 72 affiliated groups.

Publications. *Graswurzelrevolution*, monthly; occasional brochures and booklets; a yearbook (from 1984).

Affiliations. War Resisters' International; also a member of the Federal Conference of Independent Peace Groups (BUF).

Information Bureau for Peace Work
Informationsstelle für Friedensarbeit

Address. c/o H. P. Mortier, Messdorfer Strasse 192, D-5300 Bonn 1, Fed. Rep. of Germany

Aims and objectives. The Bureau collects and disseminates information about the aims and methods of peace work, particularly the theory and practice of non-violence, and co-operates with non-violent action groups.

Formation. The Bureau was founded by Hans Peter Mortier in 1978.

Activities. The Bureau has been involved in many non-violent actions since its foundation, working closely with other organizations seeking the creation of a non-violent society.

Information Centre for Total Resisters Against Civil and Military Conscription
Informationsstelle für Totale Kriegsdienstverweigerer (ITK)

Address. Nernstweg 32, D-2000 Hamburg 50, Fed. Rep. of Germany

Aims and objectives. ITK aims to provide support, advice and information to individuals who are conscientiously opposed to any form of conscription by the state.

Activities. ITK offers advice to conscientious objectors on such matters as conscript registration and medical examinations, as well as counselling on broader questions related to civil and military service.

Publications. ITK produce a range of information literature designed to serve the requirements of conscientious objectors.

Affiliations. War Resisters' International.

Information Unit Peace Research Bonn
Arbeitsstelle Friedensforschung Bonn (AFB)

Address. Theaterplatz 28, D-5300 Bonn 2, Fed. Rep. of Germany

Aims and objectives. The AFB performs "information, consultation and mediation functions" in the field of peace and conflict research on both national and international levels.

Formation. The AFB is an independent institution affiliated to the Peace Research Institute Frankfurt (PRIF); it was established in 1984 and is sponsored by the Federal Government and the governments of Hesse and North Rhine-Westphalia.

Activities. The AFB arranges contacts between German and foreign peace researchers, scientists and others; provides online information on the activities of peace and conflict research institutions internationally; offers a reference library; and serves as a contact office for peace research groups.

Publications. The AFB publishes a regular information bulletin.

Living Without Armaments
Ohne Rüstung Leben

Address. Kornbergstrasse 32, D-7000 Stuttgart 1, Fed. Rep. of Germany

Aims and objectives. This "Ecumenical Action Group for Peace and Justice" calls upon Christians to renounce military solutions to internal and international political conflicts and to campaign for peace without armaments.

Formation. The movement was established in February 1978 by a group composed mainly of Protestant clergymen, who were dissatisfied with the reaction of the German churches to the declaration of the Fifth General Assembly of the World Council of Churches in Nairobi in 1975 that "the churches should point out their readiness to live without the protection of arms and to take a significant initiative in pressing for effective disarmament".

Activities. The movement supports campaigns against the arms trade and in resistance to taxation for military purposes; it has also helped to develop a peace-and-education centre at the Pershing II deployment site at Mutlangen (West Germany) and is helping conscientious objectors in prisons. In September 1986 the movement sponsored an International Conference of War Tax Resisters and Peace Tax Campaigns in Stuttgart.

Memberships. 26,000 Germans have individually pledged: "I am prepared to live without the protection of military armaments. I wish to take a stand in our country for the political development of peace without arms."

Publications. The movement publishes a quarterly newsletter in German, various brochures and books on subjects related to peace.

Affiliations. International Fellowship of Reconciliation; also a number of Christian and other non-violent action groups.

Non-Violent Resistance Collective Against Militarism
Kollektiver Gewaltfreier Widerstand Gegen Militarismus

Address. Gasstrasse 22, D-2000 Hamburg 50, Fed. Rep. of Germany

Aims and objectives. The Collective is primarily concerned with presenting total resistance to military conscription.

Formation. The Collective was founded in 1976.

Activities. As part of the Grassroots Revolution network, the Collective has been active in co-ordinating support for conscientious objectors and in campaigns of opposition to military conscription.

Pax Christi

Address. Windmuhlstrasse 2, D-6000 Frankfurt 1, Fed. Rep. of Germany

Aims and objectives. As the West German section of the "international Catholic movement for peace", this organization seeks to involve Catholics in work for peace and co-operation in accordance with the teachings of the Church of Rome. It urges international disarmament, particularly the abolition of nuclear weapons, as prerequisites for a just world order.

Publication. Pax Christi, bi-monthly.

Affiliations. Pax Christi International.

Peace Policy Research Institute
Forschungsinstitut für Friedenspolitik (FF)

Address. Postfach 1529, D-8130 Starnberg, Fed. Rep. of Germany

Aims and objectives. The Institute is a private, non-profit-making body for research into peace issues. It is independent of government, relying on private funding to finance its activities.

Formation. The Institute was established in 1981 by members of the Max Planck Institute.

Publications. Mediatus, monthly.

Peace Research Institute Frankfurt (PRIF)
Hessische Stiftung Friedens- und Konfliktforschung

Address. Leimenrode 29, D-6000 Frankfurt 1, Fed. Rep. of Germany

Aims and objectives. The PRIF examines the causes of conflicts, their manifestations and the possibility of their resolution or management. On the basis of research, it attempts to develop creative concepts for social change and the resolution of conflicts in which decreasing violence, increasing social justice and political freedom in the international system and in individual societies can be interrelated.

The Institute also aims to disseminate the knowledge obtained from its investigations among the general public and see that it is applied in the field of political education.

Formation. Founded by the Hesse state government in 1970, the PRIF is a non-governmental, independent, non-profit-making foundation.

Activities. The PRIF concentrates its efforts on research and providing politicians and peace groups with information about peace-related issues. The scientific activities of the Institute are primarily focused on: (i) research into social and international factors which determine the dynamics of the East-West arms race and the possibilities of influencing the dynamics of such armament; (ii) specific West European interests in the context of East-West conflict; and (iii) the confrontation between the super-powers in the Third World and its consequences for the North-South conflict. Research is also being done on the origins of oppressive behaviour in early childhood, in families and groups. Programmes for peace education are developed.

The PRIF is organized in five research groups which examine the following areas: the international arms race and arms control; the United States of America; the Federal Republic of Germany; the socialist countries; and political psychology and peace education.

Membership. The PRIF is not a membership organization. It is exclusively a research institution working with professional researchers. At present there are about 23 researchers and a technical staff of about 12, including three conscientious objectors serving their civil service for 20 months.

Publications. Friedensanalysen (Peace Analyses), about two a year. The PRIF also produces an annual bulletin, *Mitteilungen* (Notifications), which informs about various PRIF activities and programmes. Reports analyse topics of current interest and include issue-related documents and *Friedensforschung Aktuell* (Current Peace Research) addresses issues of immediate interest and is mainly written for the press, educators and the peace movement.

People's Referendum for Peace
Volksbegehren für den Frieden

Address. Kissingerstrasse 66A, D-7000 Stuttgart 50, Fed. Rep. of Germany

Aims and objectives. This movement has as its objective the holding of a referendum on the deployment of US/NATO cruise and Pershing II missiles in the state of Baden-Württemberg. (While there is no provision in the West German constitution for referenda to be held at national level, they can be called in seven of the 11 states subject to sufficient initial support being mobilized for a particular proposal.) Before the deployment commenced (in December 1983) the aim of the movement was to secure endorsement in a referendum of a draft law committing the state government "to take every measure possible . . . to avoid any deployment of new nuclear, biological and chemical weapons—especially Pershing II and cruise missiles—and to work towards a withdrawal of the weapons of mass destruction that are already deployed in the area". Since the deployment the movement for a referendum to secure their withdrawal has continued.

Membership. The People's Referendum for Peace movement embraces most sections of the West German peace movement.

Reconciliation Action/Service for Peace
Aktion Sühnezeichen/Friedensdienste (ASF)

Address. Jebensstrasse 1, 1000 Berlin 12, Germany

Aims and objectives. ASF is a youth organization dedicated to reconciliation work in the light of Germany's fascist past. It works to maintain peace and prevent the re-emergence of fascist ideology by carrying out voluntary service in countries which suffered under Nazism and by supporting modern pacifist initiatives.

Formation. It was founded in 1958 by a group of leading Christians who during the fascist period took an active role in the "Confessing Church" in opposing the influence of Nazism.

Activities. In its early years, ASF focused its activities on providing voluntary labour, with volunteers helping to build a centre of international reconciliation at

Coventry Cathedral (which had been destroyed by a German air-raid in 1942), a synagogue in France, a home for the blind in Israel and an orphans' home in Norway. Recently emphasis has shifted to involvement in youth and community work in Britain, France, the Netherlands, Israel and the USA.

From 1967 onwards, ASF provided voluntary service and study opportunities for young people at memorial centres in the former Nazi concentration camps of Auschwitz, Majdanek and Stutthof in Poland. It is currently playing a part in the establishment of an international "youth encounter" centre at Auschwitz.

Since 1980 ASF has become involved in the wider concerns of the peace movement, sponsoring an annual national peace week each November and assisting in the organization of several demonstrations.

Membership. There are 300 full members, with several thousand others designated as "donating members", providing financial support.

Publications. ASF produces two quarterly magazines, *Zeichen* and *Pax An*.

Service for Peace Action Committee
Aktionsgemeinschaft Dienst für den Frieden (AGDF)

Address. Blücherstrasse 14, D-5300 Bonn 1, Fed. Rep. of Germany

Aims and objectives. The AGDF serves as a co-ordinating committee for a number of Christian-oriented West German groups campaigning on peace and development issues.

Membership. There are currently 19 groups linked by the Committee, including the Christian Peace Service, Church and Peace, the International Christian Service for Peace (EIRENE), Living Without Armaments and Reconciliation Action/Service for Peace.

Publications. Friedens- und Freiwilligendienste.

Affiliations. Service Civil International.

Study Society of Peace Pedagogy
Arbeitsgemeinschaft Friedenspädagogik (AGFP)

Address. Bavariastrasse 28, D-8000 Munich 2, Fed. Rep. of Germany

Aims and objectives. The AGFP seeks to promote peace and peace education through multi-media presentations.

Formation. The Society was founded by a group of artists and designers in 1974 to create an anti-war exhibition. The original group was joined by a number of educationalists in 1976.

Activities. The AGFP organizes exhibitions on peace issues and produces various booklets, slide shows etc. for use in schools and by peace groups.

Membership. About 50.

Publications. Various booklets on peace related subjects.

Affiliations. The AGFP has working relations with many peace groups but is independent of any political or religious organization.

Teachers Against the Madness of the Arms Race
Pädagogen Gegen Rüstunswahnsinn

Address. c/o Lutz van Dick, Postfach 2841, D-2000 Hamburg 20, Fed. Rep. of Germany

Aims and objectives. The group aims to make the responsibility of teachers for the future welfare of their children a central feature of the peace movement and to bring the goals of the movement into the classroom.

Formation. The group arose as a result of an appeal published by four of the country's leading educational journals in early 1981.

Activities. Its first "peace congress", involving 1,300 teachers from West Germany and Austria, was held in Hamburg in May 1982. The second congress, in Cologne in September 1983, was attended by over 3,000 people, including some from Britain, the USA, India and Australia, while the third was held in Mainz in April 1985 and involved 1,200 participants. The group also organized the "First International Peace Congress of Teachers and Educators," in co-operation with "Scandinavian Teachers for Peace", to mark UN peace year in 1986.

Membership. Statements of support for the group have been signed by 14,000 teachers.

Publications. Lernen in der Friedensbewegung—Verantwortung von Pädagogen (Learning in the Peace Movement—The Responsibility of Teachers) by Lutz van Dick (ed.).

War Resisters' International
Internationale der Kriegsdienstgegner (IdK)

Address. Cranachstrasse, 7, D-1000 Berlin 41, Germany

Aims and objectives. The IdK operates in West Berlin with essentially the same objectives as the other three German affiliates of War Resisters' International, namely the German Peace Society—United War Resisters (DFG-VK) in Velbert, the German Peace Society—War Resisters' International (DFG-IdK) in Hamburg and the Grassroots Revolution network based in Göttingen.

Affiliations. War Resisters' International.

Women Against War and Militarism
Frauen Gegen Krieg und Militarismus

Address. c/o Bernadette Ridard, Lornsenstrasse 27, D-2000 Hamburg 50, Fed. Rep. of Germany

Aims and objectives. The group is opposed to all armaments and preparations for war and in favour of the extension of the right of conscientious objection to all services connected with such preparations. It is particularly concerned with the enrolment of women into the armed forces and with the use of women as nursing personnel for the military during wartime.

Formation. The group was founded in 1981 as a result of a national week of action on "Women Against War and Militarism" in March of that year.

Activities. The group has carried out information work on the role of women in warfare and on the position of West Germany in NATO. It has taken part in national peace campaigns, including the opposition to the siting of cruise and Pershing missiles in the country, and also in women's conferences on militarism and on nuclear power.

Membership. There is no formal structure, and the number of active supporters declined from several thousand in 1981–82 to a few hundred in 1985.

Publications. *Frauen Gegen Kriegsdienste* (Women Against Military Service) and several other leaflets.

Affiliations. Through its supporters, the group has links to various sympathetic church, women's and left-wing organizations.

Work Community for Peace
Arbeitsgemeinschaft Frieden (AGF)

Address. Friedenszentrom, Palast Strasse 3, D-5500 Trier, Fed. Rep. of Germany

Aims and objectives. Also known as the Trier Peace Centre, the AGF takes the view that peace is more than just the absence of war and tries to contribute through its work to justice and freedom for everybody, the reduction of poverty and violence, the realization of human rights (including rights of minorities in Germany) and international reconciliation.

Formation. The AGF was founded in March 1979 and had its origins in the experience shared by a group of social workers and students who participated in the first "peace week", held in Trier in late 1978.

Activities. The AGF has organized lectures on peace issues, annual "peace weeks" in Trier, a peace camp and peace marches; it supports resistance of peace groups in nearby Hasselbach/Hunsrück, where 96 cruise missiles were scheduled to be deployed in 1986. One of its working groups is responsible for the European co-ordination of support work for *Servicio Paz y Justicia* in Latin America.

Membership. About 350, among them five Christian groups.

Publications. Newsletter, bi-monthly.

Affiliations. *Servicio Paz y Justicia*; Peace Brigades International; Peace Research Institute Frankfurt; Living Without Armaments; local peace co-ordination committees.

Other Movements

Albert Schweitzer Peace Centre
Albert Schweitzer Friedenscentrum

Address. Feldmannstrasse 40, D-6600 Saarbrücken 1, Fed. Rep. of Germany

Christian Peace Service
Christlicher Friedensdienst

Address. Rendelstrasse 9–11, D-6000 Frankfurt-Bornheim 60, Fed. Rep. of Germany

Initiative for Peace, International Co-operation and Security
Initiative für Frieden, Internationalen Ausgleich und Sicherheit

Address. Postfach 2280, D-5300 Bonn 1, Fed. Rep. of Germany

Mennonite Peace Committee
Mennonitisches Friedenskomitee

Address. Beuzlen 8, D-7140 Ludwigsburg/Neckarweihingen, Fed. Rep. of Germany

Prolifers for Survival

Address. Alstaterstrasse 36, D-6900 Heidelberg, Fed. Rep. of Germany

Quaker Peace Committee
Quaker Friedenskomitee

Address. Fohrensteg 8, D-2070 Ahrensburg, Fed. Rep. of Germany

Women for Peace
Frauen für den Frieden

Address. Schlüterstrasse 28, D-1000 Berlin 12, Germany

Women's International League for Peace and Freedom

Address. Weseler Weg 2, D-4005 Meerbusch-Buderich, Fed. Rep. of Germany

Working Group for a Nuclear-Free Europe
Arbeits Kreis Atomwaffenfreies Europa

Address. Fidicinistrasse 3, D-1000 Berlin 61, Germany

Working Group for International Community Service
Arbeits Kreis Internationaler Gemeinschaftsdienste

Address. Auf der Kurnerwiese 5, D-6000 Frankfurt 1, Fed. Rep. of Germany

Gibraltar

capital: Gibraltar   population: 31,000

Gibraltar passed from Spanish to British rule under the 1713 Treaty of Utrecht ending the War of Spanish Succession. It remains a British colony today, with internal self-government but with its foreign and defence policy the responsibility of the UK Government. In recent years successive Spanish governments have actively prosecuted a claim for the recovery of sovereignty over the territory, whose population has nevertheless consistently declared its wish to remain British. Having a strategically important location on the northern side of the western entrance to the Mediterranean Sea, Gibraltar serves as a NATO naval base and there is a British military presence on the Rock of some 2,000 army, navy and air force personnel.

The strategic sensitivity of the Strait of Gibraltar was illustrated in September 1984, when an unidentified Soviet nuclear submarine collided in the Strait with a Soviet freighter which was returning from naval exercises in the Atlantic and was reported by Spanish naval intelligence to have multiple nuclear warheads on board. The Spanish Foreign Minister described the incident as "very serious" and requested the Soviet Union to explain why one of its submarines had been cruising at periscope depth in the Strait in contravention of the 1958 Geneva Convention which required all vessels passing through the Strait to do so on the surface.

Gibraltar Campaign for Nuclear Disarmament (CND)

Address. c/o Conchita Triay, Paradise Cottage, Castle Road, Gibraltar

Aims and objectives. Gibraltar CND seeks to publicize the dangers of a nuclear war, with particular reference to the status of the Rock as a NATO/UK military base. Deriving its inspiration from CND in Britain, it campaigns for nuclear disarmament and for the development of Gibraltar's economy so that it is less dependent on the British military presence. It also calls for the demilitarization of the Mediterranean.

Formation. The Campaign was launched in early 1982, its initial founders being mostly women.

Activities. Gibraltar CND has held publicity and recruitment events, including film shows illustrating the nuclear threat. It promotes discussion groups on the particular situation of Gibraltar and seeks to secure more official information on such matters as the number of visits made to the Rock by nuclear-armed submarines and whether there is a NATO stockpile of nuclear weapons in Gibraltar.

Gibraltar CND has sought to establish contacts with Spanish peace movements (facilitated by the reopening of the border with Spain in February 1985) and with other European groups. In April 1986 it held a public meeting to protest against the US air-strike on Libya.

Affiliations. Gibraltar CND is affiliated to CND in Britain.

Greece

capital: Athens   **population: 10,000,000**

Greece became a member of the North Atlantic Treaty Organization (NATO), together with Turkey, on February 18, 1952—some three years after its creation by Belgium, Canada, Denmark, France, Italy, Luxembourg, the Netherlands, Norway, Portugal, the United Kingdom and the United States (later adherents being the Federal Republic of Germany in 1955 and Spain in 1982). Greece's participation in NATO has, however, frequently been overshadowed by its traditional rivalries with fellow member Turkey. Following the Turkish occupation of northern Cyprus in August 1974 Greece withdrew its armed forces from NATO in protest against its "inability to prevent Turkey from creating a state of conflict between two allies". Not until October 1980 did Greece rejoin the military organization of NATO (even though Turkish troops remained in northern Cyprus).

In October 1981 the Pan-Hellenic Socialist Movement (Pasok) came to power on a platform of renegotiating Greece's military participation in NATO, removing US bases from Greece and seeking in the longer term the dissolution of both NATO and the Warsaw Pact. In September 1983, however, Greece signed a new five-year defence and economic co-operation agreement with the United States under which the four US bases (in Athens and Crete) and 20 auxiliary US installations were to remain at least until the end of 1988, while Greece was to receive substantial US financial aid. In accompanying letters the United States undertook to maintain the balance of power in the region (the Greek Government having dropped its earlier demand for a specific US guarantee of its frontiers). Nevertheless, Greece has, principally in the context of its unresolved disputes with Turkey over the Aegean Sea continental shelf and over Cyprus, maintained its boycott of NATO military exercises in the region.

The Pasok Government's commitment to an independent foreign policy was demonstrated by the signature of a 10-year economic co-operation agreement with the Soviet Union in 1983. It has also revived the proposal (first made by Romania in 1957 and publicly supported by the Soviet Union in 1983) for the creation of a nuclear-weapons-free zone in the Balkans, talks on which took place in Athens in January 1984 between officials of Greece, Bulgaria, Romania and Yugoslavia, with Turkey present as an observer. The Government's pursuit of Balkan co-operation was also apparent in its decision in August 1985 to end the state of war with Albania which had technically existed since 1940, this move involving the effective renunciation of any territorial claim by Greece to the Greek-populated region of southern Albania.

As at end-1985 the Greek armed forces totalled 201,500 (including 2,000 women), consisting of an army of 158,000, an air force of 24,000 and a navy of 19,500. The para-military Gendarmerie numbered some 25,000 and there were about 400,000 reserves (including a National Guard of 100,000). Some 1,750 Greek forces are currently deployed in Cyprus. About two-thirds of the armed forces are conscripts, there being compulsory military service for men of 22 months for the army, 24 months for the air force and 26 months for the navy.

Women can volunteer for 30–50 days' basic military service and for more specialized training. Greece currently recognizes no right of conscientious objection, although the Pasok Government is considering the introduction of such legislation. The estimated defence budget for 1985 was 281,713 million drachmae, representing about 4 per cent of aggregate government expenditure.

Committee for International Détente and Peace (EEDYE)

Address. 1 Halcocondyli Street, Athens 141, Greece

Aims and objectives. This movement reflects the aim of the (pro-Moscow) Exterior Communist Party that all NATO (i.e. US) bases should be removed from Greece in the interests of promoting peace and stability in Europe.

Affiliations. World Peace Council.

Conscientious Objection Movement

Address. c/o Stelios Psomas, Arkadiou 49, 51621 Ampelokipi, Thessalonika, Greece

Aims and objectives. This group has as its central objective the enactment of legislation recognizing the right of conscientious objection to military service, without subjection to a military tribunal, and giving the option of non-military alternative service of the same duration as military service and under the administration of a non-governmental body. (Conscientious objectors are classed as "deserters" in Greece and are liable to punishment until they reach the age of 45. According to the Movement, an estimated 300 Jehovah's Witnesses are currently in prison for refusing military service, while the number of draft evaders in exile is put at 16,000.)

Activities. In its biggest action to date, the Movement marked International Conscientious Objection Day on May 15, 1986, by distributing posters and leaflets in 10 Greek towns and staging associated events. Simultaneous actions were held in several European countries and in the United States, with the lack of any conscientious objection legislation in Greece being the principal focus of this international activity.

Affiliations. The Movement has links with War Resisters' International, although it is not formally affiliated.

Independent Peace Movement (AKE)

Address. 39 Panepistimou Street, Athens 105 64, Greece

Aims and objectives. The AKE seeks nuclear disarmament and especially the creation of Mediterranean and Balkan nuclear-free zones. It also works for solidarity against colonialism and discrimination and in support of women's and environmental causes.

Formation. The AKE was established in 1981 by members of the Greek Committee for Nuclear Disarmament and Peace (itself linked to Bertrand Russell's Committee of 100) and others, with the intention of building a peace movement independent of the Greek political parties.

Activities. The AKE's principal activity is the organization of the annual (every May) International Marathon March for Peace, from the ancient battle site to Athens, to demand the removal of US bases from Greece and the creation of a nuclear-free Balkans. (The Marathon marches were started in 1963 by the Greek Committee for Nuclear Disarmament and Peace.) The AKE has also participated in campaigns for the recognition of conscientious objection to military service.

Membership. The AKE has branches throughout Greece. Although originally founded as an independent peace movement, the AKE has among its most active membership adherents of the (Eurocommunist) Interior Communist Party.

Publications. Press bulletin, daily; *Peace*, monthly.

Affiliations. International Peace Bureau; International Peace Communication and Co-ordination Network; European Nuclear Disarmament (END) movement.

Movement for Independence, International Peace and Disarmament (KEADEA)

Address. 1 Valaoritou Street, Athens 134, Greece

Aims and objectives. This Movement advocates the dismantling of the opposing military blocs in Europe, in which context it seeks the removal of foreign military bases and nuclear weapons from Greece and the conversion of the Mediterranean into a sea of peace. In addition, the KEADEA seeks to link its campaign for international peace with the struggle for full Greek national independence.

Activities. The KEADEA has mounted campaigns intended to promote grassroots involvement in the peace movement, carrying out a broad range of education and information work to this end.

Membership. Strongly based in the intellectual and civil service strata, KEADEA also includes workers, scientists and artists within its membership. The movement is close to the ruling Pan-Hellenic Socialist Movement (Pasok).

Iceland

capital: Reykjavik   **population: 240,000**

Iceland was an original signatory on April 4, 1949, of the treaty creating the North Atlantic Treaty Organization (NATO), together with Belgium, Canada, Denmark, France, Italy, Luxembourg, the Netherlands, Norway, Portugal, the United Kingdom and the United States (later adherents being Greece and Turkey in 1952, the Federal Republic of Germany in 1955 and Spain in 1982). Under a defence agreement with the United States pursuant to Iceland's membership of NATO—originally signed in May 1951 and renewed in October 1974—some 3,000 US air force and navy personnel are stationed at the US/NATO base at Keflavik (40 km west of Reykjavik), from which air and submarine surveillance of the North Atlantic is maintained. Iceland has no defence forces of its own.

The existence of the Keflavik base has been a perennial issue in Icelandic politics, in that two of the major parties, the (Communist-dominated) People's Alliance (PA) and the Progressive Party (representing farming and fisheries interests), seek its removal, while the PA also advocates Iceland's withdrawal from NATO. However, when these two parties led a centre-left coalition in 1978–83 these demands were not pressed, the Government concentrating instead on increasing the number of Icelandic civilian workers employed on monitoring operations at the base. Immediately after the formation of a centre-right coalition between the Progressive and Independence parties, the Government in July 1983 agreed to the construction of a new military/civilian air terminal at Keflavik, with the United States undertaking to meet the cost.

A major controversy arose in December 1984 when the then Icelandic Foreign Minister (of the Progressive Party) received a document reported to be a copy of classified US presidential instructions to US armed forces on where to position nuclear weapons in time of war. These included instructions to store 48 anti-submarine nuclear depth charges at the Keflavik base. The Icelandic Government subsequently received a US assurance that the United States would not deploy nuclear weapons in Iceland without Icelandic approval. Nevertheless, the Icelandic Parliament on May 24, 1985, unanimously resolved to declare the whole country a nuclear-free zone, where the deployment of nuclear weapons on land, in territorial waters or in Icelandic airspace was banned.

It was announced on Oct. 1, 1985, that the United States had begun stationing 18 F-15 jet fighters at Keflavik, to replace 12 F-4 Phantom jets. It was also planned to build two new NATO radar stations in Iceland by 1987, while the two existing stations were to be modernized by 1990.

Campaign Against Military Bases

Address. P.O. Box 314, 101 Reykjavik, Iceland

Aims and objectives. This movement seeks the removal of the US/NATO military base at Keflavik, the withdrawal of Iceland from the NATO alliance and the dissolution of the NATO and Warsaw Pacts military blocs.

Activities. In addition to organizing local actions and campaigns demanding the removal of the Keflavik base, this movement also participates actively in the North Atlantic Network (NAN), formed in April 1983 as an offshoot of the European Nuclear Disarmament (END) movement to co-ordinate opposition to the militarization of the North Atlantic (see entry under International Organizations). The second NAN conference was held in Reykjavik in August 1984 (attended by representatives of European and US peace groups) and inter alia declared its opposition to the building of new US/NATO communications facilities in Iceland. The Icelandic movement also took part in an international day of action against sea-launched cruise missiles held on June 15, 1985.

Affiliations. European Nuclear Disarmament (END) movement; North Atlantic Network.

Ireland

capital: Dublin   **population: 3,675,000**

Having remained neutral during the Second World War, the Republic of Ireland reaffirmed a policy of permanent neutrality on leaving the Commonwealth in 1949 (and is the only one of the 12 member states of the European Communities which is not also a member of the North Atlantic Treaty Organization). This attitude reflects in part the Republic's unwillingness to participate in an alliance of which the United Kingdom is a member, which in turn derives from the Republic's non-acceptance of what it regards as the artificial partition of Ireland (dating from 1922).*

As at end-1985 the Irish Republic's armed forces totalled nearly 14,000 men (army 12,000, navy 900 and air force 900), while reserves numbered over 16,000. Military service is voluntary. Defence spending in 1985 was budgeted at IR£277,000,000, representing 4.6 per cent of total government expenditure.

Action From Ireland (AFRI)

Address. 86 Summerhill, Dublin 1, Ireland

Aims and objectives. AFRI is concerned to promote a new world order based on peace and justice.

Formation. The movement originated as Aid from Ireland to raise funds for third-world relief. During 1982 it broadened its scope to engage in a range of peace and justice causes.

Activities. A major AFRI activity has been the "Pound for Peace" Campaign (launched in October 1982) intended to raise the equivalent of one minute's arms expenditure to finance AFRI and development projects in Ireland and the Third World. It has also worked to oppose South African apartheid in co-operation with Bishop Desmond Tutu.

Membership. There are 2,000 associate members, with an executive committee and four full-time staff.

Publications. Peacemaker, quarterly newsletter.

Affiliations. International Peace Bureau; Irish Anti-Apartheid Movement; Irish Campaign Against Reagan's Foreign Policies; Confederation of Non-Governmental Organizations for Overseas Development (COGOOD).

---

* Peace movements operating specifically in Northern Ireland are covered in the section on the United Kingdom (pp. 216–19).

Fellowship of Reconciliation in Ireland—see entry under United Kingdom/Northern Ireland

Glencree Centre for Reconciliation

Address. Glencree, Near Bray, Co. Wicklow, Ireland

Aims and objectives. The Centre seeks to encourage respect, tolerance and understanding between people, demonstrate the moral strength of non-violent action, compile a programme of peace education, and provide opportunities for people to meet and talk in an atmosphere of neutrality and goodwill.

Formation. The Centre was established in 1973, as a response by the people in the south of Ireland to the violence in Northern Ireland.

Activities. The Glencree Centre runs various adult seminars, workshops, six international work camps, school peace studies for secondary pupils including work with disturbed children and a farm education programme for primary school pupils (the Centre has its own 32-acre farm, on which labour is largely voluntary); it also organizes holidays for families and youth groups from Northern Ireland. A Glencree House was opened in Belfast in 1978, and there is a town house in Dublin.

Membership. There are 250 members, 11 resident at the Centre.

Irish Campaign for Nuclear Disarmament (ICND)

Address. 37 Lower Ormond Quay, Dublin 1, Ireland

Aims and objectives. ICND's immediate aim is to secure the amendment of the Irish constitution so as to make it illegal for Ireland to enter into any military alliance or military conflict, thereby securing the country's neutrality. Its ultimate objective is to secure the peaceful destruction of nuclear weapons.

Formation. Having been active briefly in the 1950s, ICND was re-established in 1979.

Activities. As an Ireland-wide body, ICND's activities are centred on campaigning for the constitutional amendment as outlined above. It supports the peace camp at RAF Bishopscourt, Co. Down. ICND also takes part in international activities in co-operation with other European peace movements, notably British CND. It is currently laying stress on public education activities and on an expansion of its youth work.

Membership. There are 5,000 members, organized in 49 branches covering all counties in both parts of Ireland, including clergy and members of Parliament.

Publications. *Disarm*, a bi-monthly paper.

Irish International Peace Movement (IIPM)

Address. 4 New Park Road, Blackrock, Co. Dublin, Ireland

Aims and objectives. The IIPM campaigns within Ireland and elsewhere against war in general and nuclear war in particular. It supports Irish neutrality.

Activities. Formally known as the Irish Peace Group, the IIPM has been represented at numerous European peace conventions.

Affiliations. IIPM is affiliated to the World Peace Council and the International Peace Bureau.

Other Movements

Justice and Peace, Irish Commission

Address. 169 Booterstown Avenue, Blackrock, Co. Dublin, Ireland

Pax Christi

Address. 52 Lower Rathmines Road, Dublin 6, Ireland

Quaker Peace Committee

Address. 6 Eustace Street, Dublin 2, Ireland

Voluntary Service International

Address. 4–5 Eustace Street, Dublin 2, Ireland

Italy

capital: Rome   **population: 57,000,000**

Two years after having signed a peace treaty with the war-time Allies and Associated Powers, Italy was on April 4, 1949, an original signatory of the treaty creating the North Atlantic Treaty Organization (NATO), together with Belgium, Canada, Denmark, France, Iceland, Luxembourg, the Netherlands, Norway, Portugal, the United Kingdom and the United States (later adherents being Greece and Turkey in 1952, the Federal Republic of Germany in 1955 and Spain in 1982). Italy participates fully in NATO's integrated military organization, there being nine NATO naval bases in the country (at Venice, La Spezia, Ancona, Naples, Messina, Cagliari, Augusta, Brindisi and Taranto) as well as US-manned air and missile bases. US forces stationed in Italy number about 10,000, two-thirds being air force personnel. Excluding participation in special UN contingents, Italy has no military forces stationed abroad.

As at end-1985 the Italian armed forces totalled 385,000 men, consisting of 270,000 army, 70,500 air force and 44,500 navy personnel. The *Carabineri* and other para-military forces number some 206,000 and there are 800,000 reserves. About two-thirds of the armed forces are conscripts, there being compulsory military service of 12 months for the army and air force and of 18 months for the navy. The defence budget for 1985 amounted to 16,380,000 million lire, representing about 4.6 per cent of total government expenditure.

NATO's December 1979 "twin-track" decision to upgrade its European nuclear missile capability (envisaging the deployment of 112 US cruise missiles in Italy) has consistently commanded parliamentary majorities in Italy but at the same time has been strenuously opposed both within and outside Parliament. Originally entered into by a coalition led by the Christian Democrats (DC) and including the Democratic Socialists (PSDI) and Liberals (PLI), the NATO plan secured initial approval in the Chamber of Deputies on Dec. 6, 1979, by 328 votes to 230. Following the installation in June 1981 of a coalition led by the Republican Party (PRI) and including the DC, Socialists (PSI), PSDI and PLI, the Government decided on Aug. 7, 1981, that the Italian site for cruise missiles would be the Comiso air base in southern Sicily. The PSI-led coalition which came to power in August 1983 (also including the DC, PSDI, PRI and PLI) reaffirmed Italy's determination to proceed with deployment if no satisfactory US-Soviet agreement was reached at the Geneva INF negotiations. Accordingly, cruise deployment began at Comiso towards the end of 1983 and was endorsed by the Chamber on Nov. 16, 1983, by 351 votes to 219, after the rejection of a Communist motion calling for a postponement pending further INF talks.

With an estimated 16 cruise missiles having already been deployed at Comiso, the Chamber on April 3, 1984, rejected by 290 votes to eight a Proletarian Democracy motion calling for their immediate withdrawal. On this occasion the then Defence Minister (a Republican) said (i) that the Government was ready at any moment to limit, reduce or withdraw completely the installed missiles if an agreement with the Soviet Union intervened; (ii) that the "dual key" system would be respected and that no missiles would therefore be fired without an

Italian government decision; and (iii) that although the final decision to use US weapons was known to lie with the US President, the NATO treaty provided for full sovereignty of the member states and close consultation before any decision was taken which would affect them directly or indirectly. The Government's defence report was approved by the Chamber on April 4, 1984, by 371 votes to 25 (with one abstention), with the Communist and radical left-wing deputies taking no part in the vote.

Italy is also a member, together with Belgium, France, the Federal Republic of Germany, Luxembourg, the Netherlands and the United Kingdom, of the Western European Union (WEU), which was established as such in 1955 on the basis of the five-nation Brussels Treaty Organization created in 1948. In October 1984 Italy was a party to the Rome Declaration which, as initiated by France, envisaged the reactivation of the WEU with a view to increasing security policy co-operation between the seven member states (prospectively to increase to nine with the accession of Portugal and Spain).

Action Group for Peace
Gruppo di Lavoro per la Pace

Address. Via dell'Aquila 2, I-42100 Reggio Emilia, Italy

Aims and objectives. The Group educates and campaigns on behalf of disarmament and pacifist issues.

Formation. It was formed in late 1982.

Activities. The Group has campaigned against the siting of cruise missiles at Comiso (Sicily) and for a nuclear-free zone in Reggio Emilia.

Membership. About 20 people.

Publications. Instead of Missiles (a bulletin).

Affiliations. Provincial, regional and national peace committees.

Anglo-American Peace Group (A-APG)

Address. Casa del Popolo 25 Aprile, Via Bronzino 117, Florence, Italy

Aims and objectives. The A-APG seeks to provide a focus for the participation of English-speaking people in the Italian peace movement.

Formation. The Group was created in 1981.

Activities. The A-APG has participated in campaigns seeking to prevent the deployment of US cruise missiles at the Comiso NATO base in Sicily. It has also developed contacts with other peace groups in Italy and Western Europe in the broader campaign for nuclear and general disarmament.

Membership. Based among English-speaking residents of Florence, the A-APG has members in other parts of Italy.

Publication. Futura, an English-language bulletin which "seeks to inform foreign readers on questions of peace and disarmament in Italy and on the activities of the Italian peace movement".

Civilian Defence Research Centre
Centro Studi Difesa Civile

Address. Via Clementina 7, I-00184 Rome, Italy

Aims and objectives. This organization conducts research on civilian defence and other alternative methods of defence. It provides information on these subjects and maintains a documentation centre for all groups working on civil defence in Italy.

Formation. It was created in 1984.

Membership. About 10 directly-involved members (physicians, teachers, students).

Publications. The Centre has translated H. D. Thoreau's essay on civil resistance.

Affiliations. The Centre has close relations with other Italian groups working on civil defence.

Friuli-Venezia Giulia Peace Groups Co-ordination

Aims and objectives. This umbrella organization co-ordinates the activities of peace groups in the Friuli-Venezia Giulia region (north-eastern Italy), seeking in particular the creation of a nuclear-free zone in the Alps-Adria region (spanning Italian, Austrian and Yugoslav territory).

Activities. The organization has participated in international peace camps with Austrian, Yugoslav and other groups and in November 1984 was one of the founders of the Alps-Adria Peace Network (see entry under International Organizations).

Information and Documentation Centre on Problems of Disarmament and Peace
Ufficio di Collegamento Informazione e Documentazione sui Problemi del Disarmo e della Pace (UCID)

Address. c/o Centro NEF, Via Isidora La Lumia 5–7, I-90139 Palermo, Italy

Aims and objectives. The UCID is a research and documentation centre specializing in issues related to the denuclearization of the Mediterranean region with particular reference to Sicily (the site of the NATO base at Comiso).

Formation. Initially connected with the United Committee for Disarmament and Peace—Comiso (see separate entry), the Centre became an independent organization in 1983.

Interfaith Peace Centre
Centro Interconfessionale per la Pace (CIPax)

Address. Via Acciaioli 7, I-00186 Rome, Italy

Aims and objectives. CIPax works to involve Italian Christian groups, notably the Roman Catholic Church, in the activities of the peace movement.

Formation. CIPax was set up in October 1982 by Fr Gianni Novelli, who had been impressed by the active involvement of the Church in the peace movement in other European countries and the USA.

Activities. The Centre's earliest activities consisted of translating and disseminating articles and documents on the peace movement in other countries. It subsequently organized its own activities in Rome, Comiso (Sicily) and elsewhere. CIPax's first public demonstration occurred when 12,000 nuns and friars marched behind a "Christians for Peace" banner in the national peace march held in Rome in October 1983. It currently organizes a regular peace march in Rome on Jan. 1 each year. In 1983 and 1984 it held a "Way of the Cross" demonstration in Comiso, with the concluding station being celebrated outside the cruise missile base. Regular monthly prayer vigils take place outside churches in central Rome. It also set up an "Ecumenical Week for Peace" with several other pacifist and religious organizations. The Centre has held a number of conferences and study meetings for theological teachers.

Membership. CIPax has four categories of members: (i) founding members, numbering about 50, who make the Centre's policy; (ii) honorary members; (iii) the "scientific committee"; and (iv) ordinary members, who pay an annual subscription and who number about 100.

Publications. CIPax produces its own monthly newsletter, *Strumenti di pace* (*Instrument of Peace*), the title of which is taken from the quotation by St Francis of Assisi "Lord, make me an instrument of your peace".

It has translated and distributed pastoral letters from the USA, Ireland, France, Japan, East and West Germany, as well as documents from the Pontifical Academy of Science and articles on peace and disarmament from various sources in other countries. CIPax includes at least one item on the Church and the peace movement twice weekly in the Catholic press service, ADISTA.

Affiliations. CIPax has worked closely with the following bodies: Pax Christi; the Franciscan Justice and Peace Commission; Italian Bishops' Conference Justice and Peace Commission; Caritas (Catholic Charities) of Rome; and several other religious groups, both Catholic and non-Catholic.

League for Unilateral Disarmament
Lega per il Disarmo Unilaterale

Address. Via Clementina 7, I-00184, Rome, Italy

Aims and objectives. The League works for the achievement of Italian unilateral disarmament "as an example for other countries". It describes itself as "anti-militarist", and is particularly concerned with the transformation of military institutions into civil ones.

Formation. The League was set up in 1979.

Activities. The League has been primarily involved in the campaign against the installation of cruise missiles in Italy. Its members have also demonstrated in Eastern Europe against the deployment of SS-20 missiles. The League has taken part in international peace marches. Other actions in Italy have included a successful campaign leading to the closure of a military prison at Gauta. It stages a demonstration each year against the military parade in Rome on June 2. The League also participates with other Italian movements in the "Peace Tax Campaign" (see under entry for Non-Violent Movement).

Membership. The League has around 1,000 active supporters.

Publications. It produces a regular bulletin.

Affiliations. The League describes itself as "part of the non-violent movement in Italy".

League of Conscientious Objectors
Lega degli Obietiori di Coscienza (LOC)

Address. Via Dante 125, I-30100 Mestre-VE, Italy

Aims and objectives. The League advocates "an alternative concept of life" leading to the establishment of a world with social justice and without arms and violence.

Formation. The inaugural meeting of the LOC was held in Rome in 1972.

Activities. The movement is primarily concerned with defending conscientious objectors, but as part of its effort to change the world it also embraces pacifist, anti-nuclear and vegetarian causes. The League also participates with other Italian movements in the "Peace Tax Campaign" (see under entry for Non-Violent Movement).

Membership. Variable, from five to 20 individuals.

Publications. Gramigna, occasional bulletin.

Affiliations. War Resisters' International (associated member); ecologist and libertarian movements within Italy.

International Movement of Reconciliation
Movimento Internazionale della Riconciliazione (MIR)

Address. Riviera Tito Livio 29, I-35100 Padua, Italy

Aims and objectives. In common with other national sections of the International Fellowship of Reconciliation, the Italian MIR promotes non-violence, conflict resolution and peace.

Formation. The Italian section was formed in Bergamo in 1952.

Activities. The MIR now has branches in Rome, Milan and most other large cities, with a national secretariat in Padua. It has taken part in non-violent demonstrations to further its aims since 1963.

Activities. The Movement maintains a library and an information and documentation centre on peace and non-violence. It works through churches, schools and groups, and in public demonstrations. Conscientious objectors can carry out civilian national service in MIR groups. The Movement is also closely involved in the "Peace Tax Campaign" with other peace groups (see under entry for Non-Violent Movement).

Publications. Quaderni della Riconciliazione (Reconciliation Studies); *Cristiani Nonviolenti* (Christians against Violence).

Affiliations. International Fellowship of Reconciliation.

Non-Violent Information Centre
Centro di Informazione Non-Violenta

Address. C.P. 78, I-47023 Cesena, Forli, Italy

Aims and objectives. The Centre houses a collection of books, articles and other information resources which are freely accessible to the public on such subjects as disarmament, peace education, ecology, conscientious objection and voluntary social service (as an alternative to conscription).

Formation. The Centre was opened in June 1983.

Activities. The Centre is principally concerned with loaning out materials to students and teachers.

Membership. The Centre is maintained and run by approximately 20 supporters.

Publications. The Centre produces a bi-monthly magazine *Per Aire . . . Fra la Gente*; it has also published several papers on topics including militarism and sexism, and the North-South relationship.

Non-Violent Movement
Movimento Nonviolento (MN)

Address. C.P. 201, I-06100 Perugia, Italy

Aims and objectives. The MN seeks unilateral disarmament and the extension of the right of conscientious objection to all forms of military service and to taxes levied for military purposes. The Movement is based on the non-violent principles of Gandhi and of Aldo Capitini; it works for the application of such principles in everyday contacts.

Formation. The Movement was founded after the "March for Peace and Fraternity" from Perugia to Assisi in September 1961. This march had been organized by the Perugia Centre for Non-Violence, which had itself been established by Aldo Capitini in 1952. The MN was the product of a union between the Perugia Centre and similar groups in neighbouring towns.

Activities. Following a "Workshop on the Techniques of Non-Violence" in 1963, a direct action group (the Italian acronym for which was GAN) was set up within the MN, and this co-ordinated actions in a number of towns, including Milan, Florence and Rome.

The MN has campaigned against US involvement in Vietnam and for the closure of US bases in Italy. It also protested against the Soviet invasion of Czechoslovakia in 1968. The group has been involved with other demonstrations concerned with civil rights and nuclear power. It organized the "Perugia-Assisi March for Peace and Disarmament" in 1981, which involved around 70,000 people, and it also helped in the organization of the peace demonstration in Rome on Oct. 20, 1981, in which an estimated 500,000 people took part. As part of the campaign against the stationing of US cruise missiles in Sicily, the MN, in collaboration with the International Peace Camp, promoted the Catania-Comiso marches of December 1982 and January 1983.

The group has also participated in the "Green Vine" project at Comiso, involving the purchase by over 1,000 individuals of small parcels of land directly contiguous to the base, with the intention of hindering any planned extension of the base perimeter.

For the past three years, the MN has campaigned against the "unlimited leave" system, whereby, after completion of the compulsory twelve months military service, each citizen is merely given "unlimited leave" from the armed forces, rather than being formally released from the service. (This leave can be revoked if the military so requires.)

In 1981 the MN joined with other movements to launch a campaign to withhold 5.5 per cent of income tax contributions, equivalent to the proportion of national expenditure allocated to defence. By early 1986 this "Peace Tax Campaign" had nearly 3,000 "registered military tax registers", who have allocated the money withheld to work for non-violent popular defence and third-world development (after first offering it, unsuccessfully, to the Italian President to be used for peaceful purposes).

The MN participated in protests against the US bombing of Libya on April 15, 1986, following which it announced the creation of a transnational "Non-Violent Intervention Force for the Mediterranean".

Membership. Approximately 400, mostly students.

Publications. *Azione Nonviolenta* (Non-Violent Action), a monthly magazine with 10,000 subscribers, founded in 1964 by Aldo Capitini.

Affiliations. War Resisters' International.

Peace and Disarmament Documentation Centre
Archivio Disarmo

Address. Via di Torre Argentina 18, I-00186 Rome, Italy

Aims and objectives. The Archivio Disarmo engages in research on peace issues and in the dissemination of information on disarmament and security questions, with particular emphasis on the Italian situation.

Formation. The Centre was established in 1982 as a private, non-profit-making institution.

Activities. The Centre has undertaken research projects on behalf of government bodies, political parties, private foundations and others. Work in progress includes studies of the constitutional aspects of the deployment of cruise missiles in Italy, the legal and sociological background to conscientious objection in Italy, the relationship between the Italian political and military establishments, the economics of the Italian arms industry and the Italian peace movement's media coverage.

Publications. The Centre regularly publishes papers on its research findings.

Peace Committees' National Co-ordination
Coordinamento Nazionale dei Comitati per la Pace (CNCP)

Address. Via Muzio Clementi 68/A, I-00193 Rome, Italy

Aims and objectives. The CNCP aims to provide national co-ordination of Italian peace groups, with the central objectives of securing the removal of nuclear missiles from the whole of Europe (and Italy in particular) and the dismantling of the contending military blocs. It is independent of political parties and ideologies and subscribes to the principles of non-violence.

Formation. The CNCP came into being in October 1981 on the occasion of a major demonstration in Rome protesting against the decision to deploy US cruise missiles at the NATO base at Comiso in Sicily.

Activities. In the context of its campaigning and co-ordination activities, the CNCP has also demanded that a referendum should be held in Italy on the cruise deployment issue. It has also given particular prominence to the demand for the denuclearization of the whole Mediterranean region.

Membership. The CNCP is an umbrella organization for some 700 local peace groups.

Publications. *Pace in Movimento* (Peace in Motion), monthly.

Peace Documentation and Initiative Centre
Centro di Documentazione e di Iniziative per la Pace (CEDIP)

Address. Via Cantarella 6, I-95125 Catania, Italy

Aims and objectives. CEDIP has as its goals (i) research and information work on the militarization of the Mediterranean region, and (ii) peace education work in schools and the workplace.

Formation. The Centre was launched in 1982 on the initiative of the Protestant Youth Federation of Italy.

Peace Tax Campaign—see entry for Non-Violent Movement

Union of Scientists for Disarmament
Unione Scienziati per il Disarmo (USD)

Address. c/o Istituto di Biofisica, via S. Lorenzo 26, I-56100 Pisa, Italy

Aims and objectives. The USD seeks (i) to promote peace research in Italy; (ii) to provide the public, the media and policy-makers with objective information on the arms race, arms control and security issues; and (iii) to organize lectures, seminars, debates and meetings on these issues.

Formation. The USD was founded in 1982.

Activities. In addition to its informational work (including making Italian translations of relevant works such as the Yearbooks of the Stockholm Peace Research Institute), the USD has organized a series of national and international meetings, the most recent in Castiglioncello in October 1985 on the theme "Nuclear Weapons and Arms Control in Europe" with about 200 participants from both East and West. There are also several working groups actively studying particular themes.

Membership. The USD has about 500 members (mainly scientists and researchers) organized in some 20 local groups. There is a national scientific council of seven members headed by F. Lenci as national secretary.

Publication. The Union publishes a quarterly bulletin.

United Committee for Disarmament and Peace—Comiso
Comitato Unitario per il Disarmo e la Pace (CUDIP-Comiso)

Address. Via della Resistenza 13, Comiso, I-97013 Sicily, Italy

Aims and objectives. CUDIP-Comiso seeks generally to contribute towards a peaceful and more humane culture without nuclear weapons and specifically to stage determined resistance to the Comiso nuclear missile base in Sicily and elsewhere by all possible constitutional means. In doing so it stresses not only the danger posed by nuclear weapons to peace and people's right to freedom but also in particular the need to resist American "colonization" of Sicily because of the dangers this would represent for the Italian constitution and for the culture and development of the Sicilian people.

Formation. The Committee came into being in 1981 immediately after the Italian Government's decision in favour of cruise deployment at Comiso.

Activities. The Committee has staged actions such as demonstrations, blockades of the missile base and hunger strikes.

Membership. CUDIP-Comiso has 180 members from many different walks of life.

Publications. Alternatives to Comiso, published monthly; several booklets including *No to Missiles, No to War; Nine Days of Struggle; Comiso without Limits; Three Years at and for Comiso.*

Affiliations. The Committee is an independent organization but works alongside all those committed to peace, disarmament, the independence of peoples and general wellbeing throughout the world.

Women for Peace and Disarmament
Donne per la Pace e il Disarmo (DPD)

Address. C.P. 713, I-36100 Vicenza, Italy

Aims and objectives. DPD is an all-women peace group which aims to create a non-violent society. It is particularly opposed to military service for women and supports conscientious objectors.

Formation. The group was founded in 1980.

Activities. In 1981 DPD established a women's peace camp in S. Giuiegueno and a further peace camp was set up in Comiso in 1983, using non-violent action to oppose the deployment of cruise missiles. Some DPD peace protestors were brought to trial and jailed for their actions. DPD is planning a national meeting in Rome where issues of militarism, disarmament and non-violent opposition will be discussed.

Publications. For a Non-Violent Future, a book which sets out the ideas of the DPD.

Affiliations. DPD has close ties with the women's peace camp in Comiso.

Other Movements

International Camp for Peace
Campo Internazionale per la Pace

Address. Via San Giuseppe 1, I-97013 Comiso, Sicily, Italy

111

Pax Christi

Address. Piazza Castello 3, I-10015 Ivrea-Turin, Italy

Service Civil International
Servizio Civile Internationale

Address. Via dei Laterani 28, I-00185 Rome, Italy

World Peace Council—Italian Committee
Comitato Italiano del Movimento Mondiale della Pace

Address. Piazza Scavolini 61, I-00186 Rome, Italy

Luxembourg

capital: Luxembourg-Ville   **population: 366,000**

Luxembourg was an original signatory on April 4, 1949, of the treaty creating the North Atlantic Treaty Organization (NATO), together with Belgium, Canada, Denmark, France, Iceland, Italy, the Netherlands, Norway, Portugal, the United Kingdom and the United States (later adherents being Greece and Turkey in 1952, the Federal Republic of Germany in 1955 and Spain in 1982). Luxembourg is also a member (together with Belgium, France, the Federal Republic of Germany, Italy, the Netherlands and the United Kingdom) of the Western European Union (WEU), which was established as such in 1955 when West Germany and Italy joined the five-nation Brussels Treaty Organization dating from 1948. In October 1984 Luxembourg was a party to the Rome Declaration (initiated by France) envisaging a reactivation of the WEU with a view to closer security co-operation between the seven member states (prospectively to increase to nine with the accession of Portugal and Spain).

Compulsory military service having been abolished in 1967, Luxembourg has a volunteer army of 720 men and a para-military Gendarmerie numbering about 500. The country's defence budget in 1985 was some 2,317 million Luxembourg francs, representing about 3 per cent of total government expenditure.

Action for Peace
Aktioun fir den Fridden
Action pour la Paix

Address. c/o V. Hommel, 4 rue P. Federspiel, L-1512 Luxembourg

Aims and objectives. Action for Peace works towards a reduction in armaments and the total elimination of nuclear weapons in both East and West. One of its concerns is to make people more aware and to provide them with better information as regards nuclear weapons and government action in matters of world peace.

Formation. The organizers created the group in 1982 after having been members of an exclusively communist peace group. As a consequence the emphasis is on pluralism and consensus whether members' motivation is political, religious, humane or educative.

Activities. Action for Peace has staged various actions and events including anti-nuclear demonstrations, a "peace weekend", interviews and discussions with political groups and the US and Soviet ambassadors, conferences and discussion sessions, and the creation of a "circle of silence" one Sunday in a pedestrian zone. It plans to hold a peace weekend for young people, to publicize its views through the media, to hold discussion evenings in collaboration with Medical Resistance to Nuclear Arms, to become involved in "parallel courses" in secondary schools, and to prepare an information dossier on peace issues for teachers.

113

Membership. Action for Peace has about 30 honorary members and 20 active members from different walks of life.

Medical Resistance to Nuclear Arms
Résistance Médicale aux Arms Nucléaires

Address. B.P. 1165, L-1011 Luxembourg

Aims and objectives. This group of people working in the medical profession works to increase public consciousness of the potential consequences of a nuclear war.

Activities. The group carries out public information and education work, concentrating on the dissemination of research findings. It works with other sections of the Luxembourg peace movement, notably Action for Peace.

Affiliations. International Physicians for the Prevention of Nuclear War.

Pax Christi Luxembourg

Address. 3 rue du Curé, L-1368 Luxembourg

Aims and objectives. As the Luxembourg section of Pax Christi International (the "international Catholic movement for peace"), this movement seeks to educate and involve Catholics in peace and development issues. As part of the country's peace movement, it urges disarmament, and particularly the abolition of nuclear weapons, as prerequisites for a just world order.

Affiliations. Pax Christi International.

Popular Movement of World Citizens
Mouvement Populaire des Citoyens du Monde (MPCDM)

Address. B.P. 208, L-2012 Luxembourg

Aims and objectives. As a world federalist movement advocating the use of esperanto for international communication, the MPCDM rejects nationalism and the domination of nation-states over people, calling instead for international disarmament as a key step towards a co-operative world order. The Movement supports conscientious objection to military service and urges the elaboration of non-violent forms of civilian defence.

Publications. *Peuples Unis* (United Peoples), quarterly; newsletter for members and sympathizers, bi-monthly.

Malta

capital: Valletta   **population: 330,000**

On achieving independence from Britain in September 1964, Malta entered into a 10-year defence and financial aid agreement with the United Kingdom, but this was declared invalid by the Labour Government which came to power in mid-1971 on a platform of neutrality and non-alignment. A new seven-year agreement, signed in March 1972, provided for greatly increased UK payments for use of military facilities on Malta (principally naval dockyards) by the North Atlantic Treaty Organization (NATO), with other NATO countries also contributing. British troops were finally withdrawn at midnight on March 31, 1979, whereupon the Government reaffirmed Malta's status as a neutral and non-aligned country which aspired to form a "bridge of peace" between Europe and North Africa.

Under an Italian-Maltese agreement concluded in September 1980, (i) Malta formally declared its neutrality and undertook not to allow foreign forces or military bases on its territory and not to make its naval dockyards available to either the US or the Soviet navies; and (ii) Italy called on all countries to respect Malta's neutrality and undertook to enter into immediate consultations in the event of this neutrality being threatened or violated, and to afford Malta military assistance if this was considered necessary by both sides. Countries which have subsequently formally recognized Malta's neutrality include the Soviet Union, France, Algeria and Libya. In January 1981 Malta signed an agreement with the Soviet Union placing former NATO oil storage and refuelling facilities in Malta at the disposal of the Soviet merchant fleet. By mid-1986, however, relations with the United Kingdom had been restored to the extent that Malta received (on Aug. 15) a goodwill visit from a Royal Navy warship.

In November 1984 Malta signed a five-year treaty of economic and security co-operation with Libya under which the latter undertook to assist in the training of the Maltese armed forces and to provide military assistance if Malta were attacked. As at end-1985 the country's armed forces consisted of a regular army of 775 men and a para-military reserve of about 900. Military service is voluntary.

The defence budget for 1986 was 6,722,000 liri, representing 2.8 per cent of total government expenditure.

John XXIII Peace Laboratory
Laboratorju Tal-Paci Gwanni XXIII

Address. Hal-Far, Malta

Aims and objectives. Named after Pope John XXIII (Supreme Pontiff 1958–63) the Peace Laboratory is a Christian-inspired movement which works to combat all theories and practices which propagate the superiority of one group over another. It aims to foster better understanding among all peoples, irrespective of creed, colour or nationality, promote and preserve social justice and nurture positive human values. It also tries to open lines of communication when these are absent or have collapsed.

Formation. The Peace Laboratory was founded in 1971 by Fr Dionysius Mintoff, a Franciscan friar. Its establishment coincided with the coming to power of a Labour Government committed to ending the presence of foreign (i.e. British) armed forces in Malta.

Activities. As a research institute, the Peace Laboratory takes initiatives to be followed by other elements of society, while it concentrates on the continuous development of its philosophy of peace. In its 15 years of existence, the Laboratory has organized many activities on a national level, including the setting up and running of a home for teenagers leaving orphanages and the first protest in Malta against the stationing of nuclear weapons in Comiso, Sicily. It also convened the first International Conference of Peace and Liberation Movements and it tries to bridge the gap between Malta's political parties. The Peace Laboratory also propagates its ideas through a weekly radio programme, seminars and a monthly youth paper. It gives an annual award to kindness, and has recently established a women's peace group which meets under its auspices.

In early July 1986 the Peace Laboratory organized a conference on "Peace and Security in the Mediterranean", jointly with the Libyan-based World Centre Against Imperialism, Zionism, Racism, Reaction and Fascism. Attended by representatives from 12 Mediterranean countries and also from Britain and Ireland, the conference devoted considerable time to condemning the April 15 US airstrike against Libya.

Membership. As a voluntary organization, the Peace Laboratory has no subscribed members, but its activities are always well supported by volunteers and members of the general public.

Publications. The Peace Laboratory produces a monthly magazine for young people entitled *It-Tieqa*. It has also produced various other publications, mainly dealing with international workers for peace.

Affiliations. The Laboratory is a member of the Christian Movement for Peace. It also maintains contact with various peace movements throughout the world and participates in international conferences every year.

The Netherlands

capital: The Hague   population: 14,500,000

The Netherlands abandoned its traditional neutrality after the Second World War, becoming an original signatory on April 4, 1949, of the treaty creating the North Atlantic Treaty Organization (NATO), together with Belgium, Canada, Denmark, France, Iceland, Italy, Luxembourg, Norway, Portugal, the United Kingdom and the United States (later adherents being Greece and Turkey in 1952, the Federal Republic of Germany in 1955 and Spain in 1982). The Dutch armed forces participate fully in NATO's integrated military organization, there being 5,500 Dutch trrops stationed in West Germany and some 3,000 US military personnel (including 2,000 of the US Air Force) stationed in the Netherlands.

The Netherlands is also a member (together with Belgium, France, the Federal Republic of Germany, Italy, Luxembourg and the United Kingdom) of the Western European Union (WEU), which was established as such in 1955 when West Germany and Italy joined the five-nation Brussels Treaty Organization dating from 1948. In October 1984 the Netherlands was a party to the French-initiated Rome Declaration envisaging the reactivation of the WEU with a view to developing security co-operation between the seven member states (prospectively to increase to nine with the accession of Portugal and Spain).

As at end-1985 the Dutch armed forces numbered 106,000 (including 1,500 women), including 67,000 army, 17,000 navy, 17,000 air force and 4,500 Royal Military Constabulary personnel. Nearly half the total were conscripts, there being compulsory military service for men of 14–16 months for the army and 14–17 months for the navy and air force; reserves numbered some 176,000. Under current legislation alternative service lasting 18 months is available to conscientious objectors. The defence budget for 1985 was some 13,550 million guilders, representing about 7.7 per cent of total government expenditure. In addition to the Dutch troops stationed in West Germany (see above), the Netherlands also has a small force in the Netherlands Antilles in the Caribbean.

Although NATO membership commands majority support within the larger Dutch political parties, the deployment with NATO forces of nuclear missiles and other nuclear weapons has generated persistent political controversy, heightened by the multi-party character of politics in the Netherlands and the traditional difficulty of finding stable governmental coalitions. Most controversial in recent years has been NATO's December 1979 "twin-track" decision to deploy a new generation of nuclear missiles in Western Europe, including 48 US cruise missiles in the Netherlands, unless US-Soviet INF negotiations at Geneva produced a satisfactory limitation agreement. Aware of the sensitivity of domestic public opinion on this issue, the Dutch Government which was party to the NATO decision—a coalition of the centrist Christian Democratic Appeal (CDA) and the right-wing liberal People's Party for Freedom and Democracy (VVD)—had entered a statement at the time deferring a decision on cruise deployment in the Netherlands until December 1981, when the crucial criterion would be "whether or not arms control negotiations have by then achieved success in the form of concrete results". The statement had recorded the Government's

117

agreement "that there is a need for a political and military answer to threatening developments in relations to Soviet LRTNF, particularly the SS-20 missile and the *Backfire* bomber", but had stressed "the importance we attach to arms control and to the 'zero option' as the ultimate objective in the long-range theatre nuclear field" and had also warned that the Government "cannot act on such a principal aspect of policy without the support of a parliamentary majority".

Even before the formal NATO decision the Dutch Second Chamber had on Dec. 6, 1979, approved by 76 votes to 69 an opposition motion rejecting both the production and the deployment of the missiles, the Government's defeat arising from the defection of 10 left-wing CDA deputies. Although on Dec. 20, 1979, the opposition failed by 81 votes to 66 to carry a motion dissociating the Netherlands from the NATO decision, opinion polls consistently showed a substantial majority as being against deployment and the issue dominated the May 1981 general elections. These resulted in the CDA-VVD coalition losing its majority and the formation in September 1981 of a centre-left coalition of the CDA together with the Labour Party (PvdA) and the Democrats-66 (D-66), both the latter parties being opposed to cruise deployment. This coalition agreed on a postponement of the deployment decision beyond the December 1981 deadline but it survived only until May 1982, when the PvdA returned to opposition. Further general elections in October 1982 resulted in the re-establishment of a CDA-VVD coalition, which announced that preparations for cruise deployment would continue, although no final decision had yet been taken.

On June 28, 1983, the Government disclosed that the 48 cruise missiles earmarked for the Netherlands would be sited at the US base at Woensdrecht (in south-west Brabant, near the Belgian border) but added that deployment would not commence until the end of 1986 at the earliest. On Jan. 24, 1984, the Council of State advised that deployment was in conformity with the Dutch constitution and therefore required only a simple parliamentary majority (rather than a constitutional amendment which would itself involve general elections and require a two-thirds parliamentary majority); it further advised that any bases must be retained under full Netherlands sovereignty. On June 1, 1984, the Prime Minister announced that the cruise decision had been further postponed until Nov. 1, 1985, and that December 1988 was now the final deadline for actual deployment, although preparatory works were continuing. He added that the final Dutch decision would involve two main considerations (i) if by Nov. 1, 1985, agreement had been reached between the United States and the Soviet Union which included the maintenance of a number of INF systems in Western Europe, the Netherlands would accept a reasonable share of these and authorize deployment, under a treaty to be concluded between the United States and the Netherlands; (ii) if by Nov. 1, 1985, no such US-Soviet agreement had been reached, and if the Soviet Union had increased the number of deployed SS-20s after June 1, 1984, or had not reduced the number of SS-20s to the June 1, 1984, level, the treaty to be concluded between the United States and the Netherlands would cover deployment of the full complement of 48 cruise missiles on Dutch territory.

The Government's approach was implicitly approved on June 13, 1984, when the Second Chamber rejected, by 79 votes to 71, an opposition motion which would have made the number of nuclear weapons to be deployed in the Netherlands dependent on NATO efforts to achieve arms limitation as well as on the attitude of the Soviet Union. At the conclusion of a three-day debate on Oct. 22–24, 1985, the Second Chamber endorsed an outline five-year treaty with the United States on the deployment of cruise missiles in the Netherlands, following which a petition with 3,743,000 signatures opposing deployment was presented to the Government on October 26. On Nov. 1, 1985, the Government agreed that cruise deployment would commence in 1988 and on Nov. 4 signed the treaty with the United States, this latter document securing ratification by the Second Chamber on Feb. 27, 1986, by 79 votes to 69. In the May 1986 general elections both the PvdA and D-66 made significant gains on platforms which included opposition to cruise deployment, but these were negated by equivalent CDA gains enabling the CDA-VVD coalition to remain in power.

Beat the Swords into Ploughshares
Smeed de Zwaarden tot Ploegscharen

Address. Meeuwsstraat 18, N-4005 VV Tiel, The Netherlands

Aims and objectives. This group, centred around the journal *Zwaarden of Ploegscharen?* (Swords or Ploughshares?), is opposed to all forms of armaments. It seeks to promote unity in the peace movement and to disseminate the latter's ideas to the ordinary man in the street.

Activities. The group seeks to influence the general public and decision-makers to bring about progress towards peace. It has concerned itself with peace education and has supported conscientious objectors in the Netherlands.

Membership. The journal has 3,000 subscribers, mainly political or religious activists.

Publication. Zwaarden of Ploegscharen? (Swords or Ploughshares?), bi-monthly.

Affiliations. National Federation of Peace Organizations.

Church and Peace
Kerk en Vrede

Address. Utrechtseweg 159, N-3818 ED Amersfoort, The Netherlands

Aims and objectives. This movement seeks a just world without weapons or wars, to be attained by non-violent action for peace and justice.

Formation. Founded in 1924, Kerk en Vrede is the oldest peace movement in Holland.

Activities. The organization runs courses on non-violent action and has taken an active part in the campaign against the stationing of nuclear weapons in Europe. It has helped initiate a "peace tax" campaign in Holland, and it also runs a counselling service.

Membership. 2,500 members and an additional 1,000 subscribers to *Kerk en Vrede.*

Publications. Kerk en Vrede, monthly.

Affiliations. International Fellowship of Reconciliation.

Committee on South African War Resistance—Netherlands Division
(COSAWR—Netherlands)

Address. P.O. Box 543, N-1000 AM Amsterdam, The Netherlands

Aims and objectives. COSAWR—Netherlands shares the objectives of COSAWR in the United Kingdom (see entry under United Kingdom).

119

Formation. The Committee was established in Amsterdam in 1979.

Activities. COSAWR—Netherlands engages in broadly similar activities to the UK section. It also campaigns for the granting of full refugee rights in the Netherlands to South Africans who have left their country to avoid conscription, and lobbies the Dutch Parliament to enact a law providing for the removal of citizenship from those Dutch nationals who volunteer for service with the South African armed forces.

Membership. The Committee is composed of South Africans in exile.

Publications. COSAWR Nieuws, bi-monthly; several booklets.

Dutch Mennonite Peace Group
Doopsgezinde Vredesgroep

Address. P.O. Box 355, N-3800 AJ Amersfoort, The Netherlands

Aims and objectives. A fellowship of Mennonites and other Christians, the Group works for peace and justice on the basis of biblical teachings, adopting the life of Christ as a model of non-violence.

Formation. The origins of the Group lie in the *Arbeidsgroep tegen den Krijgsdienst* (Working Group Against Military Service), which was formed in the early 1920s as a rallying point for conscientious objectors, many of whom received prison sentences for refusing to perform military service. It was re-named after the Second World War.

Activities. The Group now bases itself on "Anabaptist values", emphasising the "incompatibility of the State and the Kingdom of God" and such principles as "it is better to suffer from injustice than commit injustice". In particular, it seeks to draw the attention of present-day Mennonite congregations to the pacifist traditions of their church.

The group organizes conferences and summer camps and maintains contacts with other peace movements abroad. It has played a part in the resistance against the deployment of cruise missiles in the Netherlands, and is also associated with the peace tax campaign in the country. Through its affiliation to Church and Peace, it contributes to the Ploughshare Fund.

Membership. Approximately 700 full members, although a "broad acceptance" is also claimed among the Dutch Mennonite congregations, who together number around 21,000.

Publications. De Brief (The Letter), monthly, as well as several pamphlets.

Affiliations. International Fellowship of Reconciliation; Church and Peace.

Gandhi Peace Centre
Gandhi Vredescentrum (GVC)

Address. P.O. Box 18, N-5550 AA Valkenswaard, The Netherlands

Aims and objectives. The Gandhi Peace Centre aims to promote and co-ordinate activities about Gandhi and Gandhian projects in Holland and represent foreign Gandhian organizations in the country.

Formation. The GVC was established in September 1983.

Activities. The GVC is trying to establish a Peace Centre to facilitate study, meetings and enable courses to be run. In October 1985 they organized a Gandhi Memorial Day and are publishing a booklet about Gandhi.

Membership. The GVC has around 100 members.

Affiliations. In the Netherlands the GVC is affiliated to the Non-Violent Action Information Foundation and the Centre for Non-Violent Resistance.

Inter-Church Peace Council
Interkerkelijk Vredesberaad (IKV)

Address. P.O. Box 18747, N-2502 ES The Hague, The Netherlands

Aims and objectives. IKV is an inter-church organization in which all major Churches in the Netherlands, including the Roman Catholic Church, are represented. It was created to promote peace work at a local parish level and to take a stance on questions of peace, justice and human rights. Its principal aim today is nuclear disarmament under the slogan "Help rid the world of nuclear weapons—Let it begin in the Netherlands".

IKV is neither pacifist or neutralist. It works with professional soldiers and makes no demand for a unilateral Dutch withdrawal from NATO.

Formation. IKV was formed in 1966.

Activities. IKV's major regular activity has been the annual Peace Week, in which local churches and groups in most cities, towns and villages in the Netherlands take part.

IKV launched its long-term campaign against nuclear weapons in September 1977, since when over 400 local "core" groups committed to the goal of unilateral nuclear disarmament have been formed. From 1979 onwards, the group has been heavily involved in the campaign against the stationing of cruise missiles in the Netherlands.

The group's main campaign methods include door-to-door convassing, letter-writing to politicians, making local political issues out of nuclear war preparations, such as public nuclear shelter programmes, and organizing mass demonstrations.

IKV received major encouragement in November 1980 when the General Synod of the Netherlands Reform Church adopted a resolution demanding the removal of all nuclear weapons from the Netherlands, this decision being communicated to each congregation in the form of a pastoral letter. Further support came in June 1983, when the Dutch Roman Catholic bishops stated in a pastoral letter that they opposed the deployment of the new missiles, that the use of nuclear weapons should never be permitted, and that they considered unilateral moves as an appropriate means of halting the arms race. Several smaller Churches, such as the Remonstrant Brotherhood, the Mennonites, the Lutheran Church and the Quakers, have explicitly endorsed IKV's campaign.

While the Dutch Government continued to delay a final decision on missile deployment, IKV helped organize a series of major public demonstrations against deployment, including one in Amsterdam in November 1981, which was attended by some 400,000 people, and also in The Hague in October 1983, when a crowd of about 500,000—the largest post-war demonstration in the Netherlands—was addressed by, among others, Princess Irene, Queen Beatrix's sister.

IKV organized a visit to Nicaragua by a joint delegation of West European and US peace movements in April 1983. It also initiated an appeal for support for peace groups to the World Council of Churches Assembly in Vancouver, Canada, in mid-1983. The group helped organize a conference on the theme "The Future of Europe: Armed Security or Political Peace?" in December 1984, and it has held several seminars on contacts with Eastern Europe. IKV took part in the fourth annual European Nuclear Disarmament Convention in Amsterdam in mid-1985, and it also carried out lobbying work during the campaign for the May 1986 general elections in the Netherlands.

Membership. IKV has 25 members nominated by the supporting Churches. The 400 local groups together contain approximately 4,000 members, who, together with the 25 "official" members, are represented in the *Campagneraad* (Campaign Council), the decision-making body of the movement.

Publications. IKV publishes a monthly newsletter in Dutch, *Kernblad*, and a quarterly one in English, *IKV Reports*. During the annual peace week it produces *Vredeskrant* (Peace Newspaper), and has also published several books and pamphlets on disarmament.

Affiliations. Within the Netherlands IKV is a member of the *Komite Kruisraketten Nee* (No Cruise Missiles Committee—a national co-ordinating body). It is a member of the liaison committee of the European Nuclear Disarmament (END) movement and of the International Peace Communication and Co-ordination Network. Since 1981 IKV has maintained close ties with the Nuclear Freeze movement in the USA, while contacts have recently been intensified with groups in Canada, Australia, New Zealand, Japan and the Pacific. On a more modest scale, the group strives to maintain contact with a variety of organizations in Eastern Europe.

International Christian Peace Service
Internationale Christen Vredesdienst (ICVD)

Address. P.O. Box 377, N-1000 AJ Amsterdam, The Netherlands

Aims and objectives. As part of the world-wide Christian Movement for Peace (see entry under International Organizations), the ICVD seeks to build an international movement of Christians and others aspiring to a world order based on peace, justice and solidarity.

Activities. The ICVD's activities derive from its opposition to all forms of violence and to any repression of people (for ideological, religious, cultural, political or economic reasons). It participates in international work-camps; local, national and international peace education and information work; organization of seminars on peace and disarmament themes; and the sponsoring of voluntary work projects at home and abroad.

Publication. *ICVD Mededelingenblad*, five times a year.

Affiliations. Christian Movement for Peace.

It Can be Done Differently
'T Kan Anders

Address. Vlamingstraat 82, N-2611 La Delft, The Netherlands

Aims and objectives. *'T Kan Anders* has broad aims which include opposition to any form of warfare, to all forms of pollution and environmental damage and "resistance against oppression, exploitation and discrimination".

Formation. *'T Kan Anders* was founded in 1978 as a result of a merger between United Dutch Peace Action (ANVA—formed in the 1920s) and the WEPS (a splinter group which broke away from the Pacifist Socialist Party in 1976).

Activities. *'T Kan Anders* has played an active part in the nuclear disarmament campaign in the Netherlands, and has been particularly involved with organizing actions on the annual Unilateral Disarmament Day (October 24). It helped found the "Holland Out of NATO" campaign, although it has now ceased to participate in this.

In the international field, *'T Kan Anders* organized a Nicaragua Action Day on November 1, 1984, and has also taken part in fund-raising projects for peace organizations in India and Sri Lanka.

Membership. There are 700 members, most of whom are described as "pacifist socialists".

Publications. *'T Kan Anders*, a 64-page quarterly, is distributed to all members; the group has also produced brochures on subjects such as antimilitarism, arms industry conversion, ecology, civil disobedience and nuclear energy.

Affiliations. *'T Kan Anders* is a member of War Resisters' International. It has links with other Netherlands-based groups through the "Radical Peace" platform, which it helped to establish.

Movement for the Refusal to Pay Taxes for Defence
Beweging Weigering Defensiebelasting (BWD)

Address. Utrechtsweg 159, N-3818 ED Amersfoort, The Netherlands

Aims and objectives. The BWD aims to bring about the passage of legislation extending the right of conscientious objection (which already exists in the Netherlands for military service and social security) to the expenditure of tax money on nuclear weapons, and the establishment by the Government of a Peace Tax Fund to which the defence portions of an individual's taxes could be transferred. The BWD calculates that 10 per cent of the national tax income, or 950 guilders per head, is spent on arms each year, and it recommends refusal to pay 10 per cent of income tax, or 950 guilders, or an amount related to the number of missiles to be stationed in the country.

Formation. The campaign was started in January 1980 by five church organizations and has since been joined by others.

Activities. Cases of tax refusal in the Netherlands date back to the 1920s, when deep pacifist principles moved some citizens to refuse to pay taxes for military purposes. The recent campaign for tax refusal was inspired by the NATO decision of 1979 to station new medium-range nuclear missiles in Western Europe, including cruise missiles in the Netherlands. In protest at the lack of progress on the tax refusal issue since 1981, the BWD launched a nationwide appeal in which it called on each BWD member to persuade five other people to contribute a symbolic amount from the VAT levied on their gas bills. Several court cases resulted. The BWD has also given its support to a civil disobedience initiative called "Don't Pay" (*Betaal Niet Mee*) designed to pressurize the Government over the NATO missile deployment issue, again by urging people to withhold 5.72 guilders from the VAT on their gas bills (this amount to be paid into the movement's Peace Tax Fund or offered later). This protest—which was not universally supported by churches and peace movements because of a fundamental debate over whether civil disobedience was a civic duty or an illegal action—was to reach its climax at the time of the Government's final decision on whether to station nuclear missiles in the Netherlands.

In conjunction with BWD, the Ban the Cruise Missiles Foundation (*Stichting Verbiedt de Kruisraketten*) in November 1984 brought a case against the Dutch State, questioning whether the deployment and use of cruise missiles in the Netherlands contravened international agreements entered into by the Government.

Membership. There are eight groups within the BWD, including Church and Peace, the Dutch Mennonite Peace Group, It Can Be Done Differently and the Union of War Resisters.

Publications. A quarterly newsletter and two handbooks for tax resisters.

Non-Violent Action Information Foundation
Stichting Voorlichting Aktieve Geweldloosheid (SVAG)

Address. P.O. Box 137, N-8000 AC Zwolle, The Netherlands

Aims and objectives. SVAG works for a society based on "active non-violence" as a means of controlling tensions and solving conflicts and developing respect between nations.

Formation. SVAG was founded in 1976.

Activities. SVAG's principal activities focus on publishing and distributing books and pamphlets on non-violent politics. SVAG also translates material on the subject from English and German sources. The group supports non-violent actions of other peace movements.

Future plans include organizing non-violent training and initiating projects on children and non-violence and on non-violence in schools. The group is also hoping to establish a resource bank of literature and videos on non-violence.

Membership. SVAG has no formal membership structure, but is based on a network of supporters who help fund the organization.

Publications. *SVAG-mededelingen*, a twice-yearly newsletter.

Nuclear-Free State
Atoomvrÿstaat

Address. P.O. Box 80159, N-1005 BD Amsterdam, The Netherlands

Aims and objectives. This movement issues passports in the name of the "Nuclear-Free State" which contain the following declaration: "The bearer of this passport is a citizen of the Nuclear-Free State, and declares that he/she no longer accepts being the possession of any state that suppresses the most elementary rights of Mother Earth and her inhabitants."

Activities. With the receipts from sales of the passports, the movement undertakes the purchase of land near nuclear weapons bases in Holland and also near nuclear energy installations, seeking in this way to prevent their expansion. It currently owns three pieces of land near the Woensdrecht base (earmarked for cruise missiles), a house in the local village and land near the Volkel base (the location of nuclear missiles since 1959).

Membership. The movement has some 6,000 members.

Over-50s Against Nuclear Violence
50+ Tegen Kerngeweld

Address. Gasthuislaan 93A, N-3817 EH Amersfoort, The Netherlands

Aims and objectives. The purpose of this group is to work in a non-violent way, independently or together with young people, to make people aware of the "impermissibility of nuclear violence in our society". The group caters for the desire of many over-50s who oppose nuclear weapons and power "to do so in co-operation with contemporaries".

Formation. The group came into being in mid-1981 and was formally established on Nov. 21, 1981.

Activities. The group has participated in demonstrations and actions against nuclear weapons and against civil nuclear installations. It is working with other peace groups in various initiatives to try to prevent the deployment of US cruise missiles in the Netherlands.

Membership. There are about 350 members (in the 50–80 age bracket).

Affiliations. The group works closely with other Dutch peace groups such as the Inter-Church Peace Council, Pax Christi and Women for Peace.

Pacifist Socialist Party
Pacifistisch Socialistische Partij (PSP)

Address. Nieuwe Looierstraat 45–47, N-1017 VB Amsterdam, The Netherlands

Aims and objectives. The PSP is a political party which combines Marxism with pacifism, which it holds to be inseparable from socialism. It advocates disarmament and the development of the United Nations into a world government, as well as socialization of the economy.

Formation. The PSP was founded in January 1957 by about 300 former members of the Dutch Labour Party (PvdA).

Activities. The PSP has contested general elections since 1959, winning two seats in the 150-member Second Chamber in that year, four in 1963 and 1967, two in 1971 and 1972, one in 1977, three in 1981 and 1982, and one in the general elections of May 1986 (when its share of the vote fell from 2.3 to 1.2 per cent). The PSP has not participated in any Dutch government. It has been one of the strongest critics, both in Parliament and in the country, of the decision to deploy US cruise missiles in the Netherlands.

In January 1984 the PSP participated in a congress with the Communist Party of the Netherlands (CPN) and the Radical Political Party (PPR) to investigate the possibilities of political co-operation between the three formations. A contact group was formed called "Left Breakthrough", although the majority in each party remained in favour of preserving an independent identity. In the June 1984 Dutch elections for the European Parliament the PSP presented a joint list with the CPN, the PPR and the Greens, called the Green Progressive Alliance (GPA), which in a low turn-out won 296,516 votes (5.6 per cent) and two of the 25 seats allocated to the Netherlands.

Membership. The PSP has some 10,000 members.

Publications. *Bevrijding* (Liberation), fortnightly; *Socialistisch Perspectief* (Socialist Perspective), quarterly.

Pax Christi Netherlands

Address. P.O. Box 85627, N-2508 CH The Hague, The Netherlands

Aims and objectives. As the Dutch section of Pax Christi International (the "international Catholic movement for peace"), this organization seeks to educate and involve Catholics in peace and development issues, believing that general disarmament is a prerequisite for a just world order.

Activities. Pax Christi in the Netherlands has been particularly involved in campaigns (i) for the abolition of nuclear weapons, starting with those in the Netherlands, (ii) for improvements to the country's law on conscientious objection to military service, (iii) for a halt to the arms export trade and the conversion of the armaments industry to socially useful purposes, and (iv) for action by shareholders against Royal Dutch Shell's business interests in South Africa.

In February 1986 Pax Christi Netherlands organized—in co-operation with the (Dutch) Inter-Church Peace Council, the (French) Committee for European Nuclear Disarmament, the American Friends Service Committee and other religious peace groups—a Middle East Study Conference in Amersfoort, at which invited guests included Palestinian and Israeli representatives. Later in 1986 the organization announced the establishment of a contact and communication office in Managua, Nicaragua, to assist the development of relations between European and Central American peace movements.

Publication. Kommunikatieblad, bi-monthly.

Affiliations. Pax Christi International.

Peace Education Commission (PEC)

Address. P.O. Box 2060, N-1000 CB Amsterdam, The Netherlands

Aims and objectives. The PEC seeks to promote co-operation, in the Netherlands and internationally, between peace researchers and educators in the interests of furthering knowledge of peace and disarmament questions. It is also a research and educational body in its own right.

Activities. In addition to its research, peace education and publications programmes, the PEC is involved in organizing seminars on peace questions and also participates in numerous international conferences concerned with peace education and research.

Publications. The PEC has published a series of books and studies on peace education and related themes.

Affiliations. International Peace Research Association.

Peace Promotion Foundation
Stichting Vredesopbouw

Address. Antwoordnummer 2261, N-3500 ZJ Utrecht, The Netherlands

Aims and objectives. The Foundation works for peace, for abolition of violence, for the establishment of an acceptable standard of living for everyone and equilibrium between man and his environment. It functions as a centre for information and education.

Formation. The Foundation originated "in a growing concern and anxiety about the nuclear deterrent and the increasing militarization of world society". Since 1963 the Foundation has had a professorial chair at Gröningen University.

Activities. Perceiving that "people feel powerless when confronted with political problems", the Foundation sees the essence of its work as being the translation of these problems for a wider public, "to clarify matters of war, peace and development and their relationship to the everyday way of life". In addition to its publications and information work, the Foundation works in co-operation with other organizations in peace education work, in schools and at adult level.

Publications. Vredesopbouw, monthly; many pamphlets and books.

Stop the Neutron Bomb/Stop the Nuclear Arms Race Confederation
Samenwerkingsverband Stop de Neutronen Bom—Stop de
Kernwapenwedloop

Address. Lauriergracht 13, N-1016 RD Amsterdam, The Netherlands

Aims and objectives. The Confederation is in favour of unilateral nuclear disarmament by the Netherlands and of a nuclear-free Europe. Although the group concentrates on the nuclear arms race, it is also concerned with the conventional military build-up.

Formation. Stop de Neutronen Bom was established in August 1977. It joined with *Stop de Kernwapenwedloop* shortly afterwards, at which time it broadened its scope of activity from the neutron bomb to nuclear weapons in general.

Activities. The group was responsible for initiating a prolonged campaign against the neutron bomb, including the collection of over one million signatures for a petition to the Netherlands Government. Since late 1979, the Confederation has concentrated its efforts to prevent the deployment of cruise missiles in the Netherlands and elsewhere in Western Europe. The Confederation has held numerous meetings at local and national level, as well as taking part in several major peace demonstrations in the country.

In the future, the group plans to emphasize its campaign for nuclear-free zones, as well as increasing its opposition to conventional armaments and the rising level of defence expenditure. It is also investigating alternative security policies for Europe and exploring the potential for further dialogue and detente between East and West.

Membership. While there is no formal membership structure, the Confederation's activities across the country take place in the framework of local groups, of which there are currently about 200, with a varying number of activists.

Publications: Kernwapens Weg, a monthly newsletter; *International Newsletter,* published twice a year.

Affiliations. The Confederation is a member of four "umbrella" organizations: the LOVO, composed of eight Dutch peace groups; the KKN, a joint committee of political parties, trade unions and peace groups opposed to the cruise missile deployment; the OtK, a nuclear weapons discussion forum, grouping together trade unions, parties and peace campaigners; and the VtK, an umbrella committee of womens' organizations.

Union of War Resisters
Vereniging Dienstweigersars (VD)

Address. P.O. Box 4802, N-1009 AV Amsterdam, The Netherlands

Aims and objectives. VD's primary objective is to further the interests of conscientious objectors, with the broader aim of working for the creation of a "socialist, democratic society, freed of militarism, violence and repression".

It is working for various reforms in the Netherlands' "civilian service" (available to conscientious objectors as an alternative to compulsory military service), including a reduction in the length of service to the same length as the military equivalent, and the broadening of civilian service's scope to include work with peace groups, peace education and training in non-violent forms of defence.

VD is also opposed to the requirement that conscientious objectors should have to justify their beliefs to the Defence Ministry.

Formation. VD was founded in December 1981.

Activities. VD holds regular information sessions for conscientious objectors in over 20 locations around the country. It runs lecture programmes and other educational activities in schools and local institutes, covering themes such as militarism, conscription and conscientious objection.

Local VD groups take part in demonstrations on many pacifist issues, in some cases involving non-violent direct action, including the disruption of air shows and arms fairs. VD co-operated with other peace groups in blockading trains carrying munitions to US forces in West Germany in January 1982.

VD has also supported a series of (illegal) strikes by conscientious objectors in the civilian service. The strikers were demanding reforms similar to those supported by VD.

Membership. VD has over 1,600 members, most of whom are conscientious objectors. It has a broadly decentralized structure, with two civilian service full-time workers in its Amsterdam national office.

Publications. The group publish three journals: *Veedee*, *Prawda* and *Wapenfeiten*. It also produces an information kit for objectors.

Affiliations. War Resisters' International.

Women for Peace
Vrouwen voor Vrede

Address. P.O. Box 963, N-3800 AZ Amersfoort, The Netherlands

Aims and objectives. This movement seeks to involve women in the campaign for peace and disarmament, seeking in particular the abolition of nuclear weapons generally and the withdrawal of nuclear missiles from the Netherlands in particular.

Formation. Women for Peace was originally founded in Switzerland in 1976, national sections being subsequently established in the Netherlands and other European countries.

Activities. Together with other Dutch peace movements, Women for Peace has participated in a series of major demonstrations and actions against nuclear missile bases in the Netherlands and in particular against the US cruise missile deployment decision. It holds an annual study gathering, that of October 1985 being devoted to "The Arms Race and Development" and involving analysis of the positions of the Dutch political parties on this subject. The gathering ended with a torch-light march to the Parliament building in which 3,000 women took part.

Publications. Women for Peace issues a bulletin two or three times a year.

Affiliations. The Dutch movement has close links with Women for Peace groups in other European countries.

Working Group for Peace
Werkgroep voor de Vrede

Address. c/o Europlaan 791, N-6441 VX Brunssum, The Netherlands

Aims and objectives. This Group believes that war is a crime against humanity; it therefore refuses to support any kind of war and strives to achieve the removal of all causes of war. As an affiliate of War Resisters' International, the Group is part of the Dutch conscientious objection movement.

Formation. The Group dates from 1930, when young Dutch pacifists in Limburg, members of Youth Peace Action (JVA), began holding meetings on the German and Belgian frontiers with counterparts from those countries. Suspended during the period of German occupation, the Group was re-formed after the Second World War.

Activities. Although the frontier meetings stopped after Hitler came to power in 1933, the Group assisted pacifists who were forced to flee from Nazi Germany (others being imprisoned or killed). Suspended from 1940–45 (during which members helped to shelter Jews from the Nazi occupation forces), the Group re-emerged at the end of the war as part of United Dutch Peace Action (ANVA) and since then has continued to work within the Dutch peace movement, concentrating on support for conscientious objectors and dissemination of information on that theme. As a "radical" peace movement, the Group was for some years proscribed by the Roman Catholic Church, a local bishop of which once described its members as "heathens and communists"; however, this proscription was later relaxed, the Group having had a Roman Catholic chairman for a number of years.

Affiliations. War Resisters' International.

Norway

capital: Oslo   **population: 4,145,000**

Norway was an original signatory on April 4, 1949, of the treaty creating the North Atlantic Treaty Organization (NATO), together with Belgium, Canada, Denmark, France, Iceland, Italy, Luxembourg, the Netherlands, Portugal, the United Kingdom and the United States (later adherents being Greece and Turkey in 1952, the Federal Republic of Germany in 1955 and Spain in 1982). Norway participates in NATO's integrated military organization, there being Norwegian/NATO naval bases at Bergen, Harstad, Hörten and Tromsö. Like Denmark, Norway does not allow the stationing or stockpiling of nuclear weapons in its territory in peacetime, although under an established, but increasingly controversial, formula it is neither confirmed nor denied that NATO (principally US) warships entering Norwegian waters and ports are carrying nuclear weapons.

Apart from periodic participation in UN peacekeeping forces, Norway has no troops stationed abroad, and no other NATO forces are permanently stationed in Norway. At the same time, NATO manoeuvres and training exercises are frequently held in the northern county of Finnmark, where Norway has a common frontier with the Soviet Union. Moreover, non-nuclear armaments and military equipment are stockpiled in Norway for use by NATO reinforcements which would arrive in time of crisis, and a number of airfields are maintained as prospective bases for such reinforcements.

As at end-1985 the Norwegian armed forces numbered 37,000, consisting of an army of 20,000, an air force of 9,400 and a navy of 7.600. About two-thirds of the total were conscripts, there being compulsory military service for men of 12 months for the army and 15 months for the air force and navy. Reserves totalled some 220,000, the Home Guard 80,000 and civil defence personnel 112,000. The defence budget for 1985 was 14,327 million kroner, representing 8.7 per cent of total government expenditure and maintaining Norway's position as the third-highest per capita spender in defence in NATO (after the United States and the United Kingdom).

In that NATO's December 1979 "twin-track" decision to modernize its nuclear missile capability in Western Europe did not envisage the deployment of any missiles on Norwegian territory, the issue has generated less political controversy in Norway than in the five countries which were so designated. In November 1983 the Norwegian Parliament rejected by 78 votes to 77 a motion calling on the Government to oppose deployment while the US-Soviet INF negotiations in Geneva were still in progress, those supporting the motion being the opposition Labour, Socialist Left and Liberal parties, as well as three Christian Democratic and two Centre deputies whose parties were then members of a three-party coalition led by the Conservatives. During this period of opposition, the Labour Party (Norway's dominant political formation) gravitated towards the "zero option" concept as the solution to the European missile deployment impasse; the party also became committed to a positive exploration of the Finnish-backed proposal for a nuclear-weapons-free Nordic zone, on which successive Norwegian administrations had hitherto remained cool.

In May 1986 the centre-right coalition was replaced by a minority Labour Government, which reaffirmed Norway's commitment to NATO membership and announced (on June 9, 1986) that specific defence and security policy questions, such as the Nordic zone proposal, would be evaluated in the light of the eventual reports of three parliamentary commissions currently examining such matters.

Campaign Against Conscription
Kampanjen Mot Verneplikt

Address. P.O. Box 8248, Hammersborg, Oslo 1, Norway

Aims and objectives. This group campaigns for the abolition of conscription and military service in Norway, as part of a Scandinavian-wide movement with similar aims.

Formation. The movement was formed in November 1981, when a group burned their military service books and conscription papers.

Activities. The Campaign undertakes demonstrations and other non-violent actions against military bases and the imprisonment of conscientious objectors. In 1983 it established a refugee camp for fugitive Norwegian conscripts in Sweden. It has taken the issue of imprisonment of Norwegian conscientious objectors to the European Commission of Human Rights.

Publications. Rundbrev, 10 times a year; occasional pamphlets and booklets.

Affiliations. Associate membership of War Resisters' International (with whose full Norwegian affiliate, People's Resistance Against War, it co-operates closely; member of Norwegian Peace Council.

Christian Peace Movement
Kristent Fredslag

Address. Grensen 8, Oslo 1, Norway

Aims and objectives. As the Norwegian section of the International Fellowship of Reconciliation, this Christian pacifist movement stands for international peace, reconciliation and the renunciation of war. It supports conscientious objection to military service and opposes the trade in arms, which it regards as "cynical" irrespective of the destination of the arms. It also stands for observance of human rights by all political regimes.

Activities. The Movement co-operates with other Norwegian peace groups "after studying their proposed actions" and is also active in human rights work, notably in respect of the situations in Eastern Europe and Central America. The Movement undertakes world-wide co-operation with *Servicio Paz y Justicia* as well as humanitarian aid work.

Publication. Fredsbladet, quarterly.

Affiliations. International Fellowship of Reconciliation.

International Peace Research Institute, Oslo (PRIO)
Institutt for Fredsforskning

Address. Rådhusgata 4, 0151 Oslo 1, Norway

Aims and objectives. The PRIO undertakes research with the aim of contributing to conflict resolution and the establishment of peaceful relations between nations, groups and individuals.

Formation. The Institute became an autonomous body in 1966, after seven years of existence as a department of the Social Research Institute. It is financed principally by the Norwegian Government.

Activities. The Institute's research programme, dealing with both structural violence and conflict between groups and states, is intentionally given an international focus. Particular themes which have been studied include the potential effects of nuclear war on Norway and the economic consequences of disarmament.

Publications. *Journal of Peace Research*, quarterly; *Bulletin of Peace Proposals*, quarterly; *PRIO Report*, occasional research papers.

No to Nuclear Weapons
Nei til Atomvapen

Address. Youngstørget 7, 0181 Oslo 1, Norway

Aims and objectives. This movement favours the gradual dismantling of nuclear weapons in East and West, through the achievement of binding arms reduction agreements between the two superpowers. It is particularly opposed to further deployments of nuclear weapons, including the stationing of new US and Soviet missiles in Europe. The movement is campaigning for the Norwegian Parliament to pass a law making illegal the deployment of nuclear weapons on Norwegian territory.

The group supports the creation of a Nordic nuclear-weapon-free zone, to be established by treaty as recommended in the final act of the UN first special session on disarmament (UNSSOD I) in 1978. Such a treaty would include commitments by all states participating in the zone that they would not permit the stationing of nuclear weapons inside the zone, as well as undertakings from states armed with nuclear weapons that they would refrain from using them against states in the zone.

Formation. *Nei til Atomvapen* was formed in 1979 in response to the planned deployment of US cruise and Pershing II missiles and of Soviet SS-20 missiles. It was established as a permanent campaigning organization in 1980.

Activities. A petition campaign launched by the group in favour of a Nordic nuclear-free zone in 1981–82 collected a total of 540,000 signatures. After carrying out a preliminary study of the free zone question in 1982, the group together with other Nordic peace organizations, published a joint proposal on the subject in April 1983.

The campaign for a Nordic nuclear-free zone has remained the principal focus of the group's activities since 1983, although it has participated closely in the North Atlantic Network of movements opposed to the militarization of the North Atlantic (see entry under International Organizations) and has also recently launched a new campaign against the US Strategic Defence Initiative (SDI).

Membership. Nei til Atomvapen claims to have a "supportive membership" of approximately 100,000, operating in 300 local groups.

Publications. Regular publications include the *Campaigns* newspaper, with a circulation of around 300,000, and a journal with some 25,000 subscribers: The group also publish an English-language newsletter entitled *Nuclear Disarmament News*.

Nei til Atomvapen has also produced five pamphlets, as follows: *Norway and the Struggle for Nuclear Disarmament*, by Jon Grepstad; *A Nuclear-Weapon-Free Zone in the Nordic Countries*, by Erik Alfsen; *The Peace Movement in the Nordic Countries— Policies, Forms of Action, Impact*, by Jon Grepstad; *A Nordic Nuclear-Weapon-Free Zone*; and *Freeze and Withdrawal of Nuclear Weapons*, by Erik Alfsen.

Affiliations. Nei til Atomvapen is affiliated to the International Peace Communication and Co-ordination Network.

Norwegian Peace Council
Norges Fredsråd

Address. Rosenkrantzgata 18, 0160 Oslo 1, Norway

Aims and objectives. The Norwegian Peace Council co-ordinates the work of the 14 Norwegian peace organizations and disseminates information. Although it is not a policy-making organization, members share a desire for "positive peace" and an interest in forms of non-nuclear defence.

Formation. The Council was founded in 1945, at which time it served five or six organizations. Membership has growth rapidly since the late 1970s.

Activities. The Council's main activities involve fostering better communications between organizations working for peace and channelling information to government bodies and non-governmental organizations. It has given support to various peace and disarmament campaigns (including that for a Nordic nuclear-free zone) and also participated in a letter campaign prior to the Norwegian elections in September 1985, when all politicians were sent letters raising the issue of the nuclear situation in Norway.

Membership. The Council consists of a board of 10 members and each of the 14 member organizations has two representatives at the Council.

Affiliations. The Norwegian Peace Council is a member of the International Peace Bureau in Geneva and has links with Scandanavian and Nordic campaigns.

People's Resistance Against War
Folkereisning Mot Krig (FMK)

Address. Goteborggata 8, Oslo 5, Norway

Aims and objectives. The FMK seeks an end to militarism, the use of violence to resolve social conflict, and of "structural violence" caused by oppression and exploitation. It supports the international solidarity of radical non-violent liberation movements.

Formation. Originally established on Jan. 17, 1937, the FMK went underground during the Second World War and the period of German occupation (1940–45); it was re-launched in 1946.

Activities. These are principally (i) the encouragement and defence of conscientious objectors; (ii) active opposition to Norwegian membership of NATO; (iii) the creation of a model for local community-based "non-violent popular defence"; and (iv) contacting and supporting similar groups in third-world countries.

In May 1985 the seven editorial staff of the FMK journal *Ikkevold* were found guilty on charges of "endangering state security" by publishing information about a US anti-submarine warfare base on Andoya (northern Norway); one received a nine-month prison sentence and the others suspended sentences and fines. However, all seven were acquitted by an appeal court 12 months later on May 23, 1986, and their sentences quashed.

Membership. Currently the FMK has about 1,300 members. (Membership reached a peak, at about 2,000 in the 1960s, but fell sharply after the 1968 convention voted to support liberation fronts employing violence. This issue has remained controversial within the organization.)

Publications. Ikkevoldsaktivisten (The Non-Violent Activist), an internal publication; *Ikkevold* (Non-Violence), bi-monthly, which is sold in the streets and in book-cafes, etc.

Affiliations. In Norway: membership of the Norwegian Peace Council and observer status on other groups; internationally: War Resisters' International, International Peace Bureau.

Women's International League for Peace and Freedom (WILPF)
Internasjonal Kvinneliga for Fred og Frihet (IKFF)

Address. Fastingsgata 5, Oslo 3, Norway

Aims and objectives. As the Norwegian section of the world-wide WILPF (see entry under International Organizations), the IKFF seeks to involve women in the struggle for peace, disarmament and a non-violent society.

Activities. The IKFF has participated with other peace groups, in Norway and elsewhere in Europe, in a series of actions and campaigns in support of nuclear disarmament and the creation of a Nordic nuclear-free zone.

Publication. Fred og Frihet (Peace and Freedom), quarterly.

Affiliations. Women's International League for Peace and Freedom.

Portugal

capital: Lisbon   **population: 10,300,000**

Portugal was an original signatory on April 4, 1949, of the treaty creating the North Atlantic Treaty Organization (NATO), together with Belgium, Canada, Denmark, France, Iceland, Italy, Luxembourg, the Netherlands, Norway, the United Kingdom and the United States (later adherents being Greece and Turkey in 1952, the Federal Republic of Germany in 1955 and Spain in 1982). Portugal has, together with Spain, declared its wish to join the Western European Union (WEU), which was created as such in 1955 by Belgium, France, the Federal Republic of Germany, Italy, Luxembourg, the Netherlands and the United Kingdom, and which under the French-initiated Rome Declaration of October 1984 was to be reactivated with a view to increasing security co-operation between member states. Portugal is also a party to (i) the world's oldest surviving military alliance, namely the treaty of friendship and mutual military assistance concluded with England in 1373; and (ii) a bilateral military co-operation agreement with Spain under the 10-year treaty of friendship and co-operation signed by the two countries in November 1977.

Portugal participates in NATO's integrated military structure, there being a NATO-designated naval base in Lisbon and a US military base at Lajes on the island of Terceira in the Azores. Under an agreement concluded in December 1983 the United States was to have continued use of the Lajes base, in exchange for military and economic aid over the seven-year term of the agreement (from February 1984), which stipulated that no nuclear weapons were to be installed on Portuguese territory. A further agreement signed in March 1984 provided for the installation of a US satellite tracking station in southern Portugal, and the United States has also expressed a wish to negotiate for military bases on the Portuguese mainland for its Rapid Deployment Force. Under agreements with other NATO partners, West Germany has use of the Beja air base in northern Portugal and France has a missile-tracking station on the island of Flores in the Azores.

As at end-1985 the Portuguese armed forces totalled 73,000 men, consisting of 45,700 army, 14,000 navy and 13,300 air force personnel; in addition, para-militaries (National Republic Guard, Public Security Police and Fiscal Guard) numbered some 37,000 and reserves 175,000. About two-thirds of the armed forces were conscripts, there being compulsory military service of 16 months for the army, 21–24 months for the air force and 24 months for the navy. The defence budget for 1985 amounted to 115,000 million escudos, representing about 11 per cent of total government expenditure.

Anti-Militarist and Ecologist Group
Grupo Anti-Militarista e Ecológico

Address. Apartado 158, 3000 Coimbra, Portugal

Aims and objectives. This university-based Group campaigns against "ecocide", the "supremacy of state power" and the "system which destroys human nature".

Within this framework it opposes militarism and the "waste of huge sums" in government spending on armaments; it also fights for the right of conscientious objection from military service.

Formation. The Group was formed in 1976 within the framework of the Academical Association of university students.

Activities. The Group has engaged in a broad programme of information and publishing activities, concentrating on ecological and anti-nuclear power themes but also including output on anti-militarism and a guide for conscientious objectors.

Publications. Abordagem, periodical; pamphlets and books on relevant subjects.

Independent Association of Men and Women Conscientious Objectors
Associação Livre dos Objectores e Objectoras de Consciencia (ALOOC)

Address. Apartado 21122, 1128 Lisbon, Portugal

Aims and objectives. ALOOC has campaigned for the enactment of legislation affording the right of conscientious objection from military service. Following the introduction of such a law in March 1985, it decided to pursue its campaign for full recognition of conscientious objection as a human right and also to broaden its scope to include a campaign against government expenditure on armaments.

Activities. ALOOC has operated against a background in which, although the 1976 constitution guaranteed the right of conscientious objection, no actual legislation was forthcoming until 1985. In that period the number of COs increased from one in 1976 to an estimated 25,000 by mid-1985. The Association provides support for COs and also seeks to ensure that acceptable arrangements exist for alternative service and also for "total resisters".

Affiliations. ALOOC has links with War Resisters' International, although it is not formally affiliated.

Pax Christi Portugal

Address. Apartado 1423, 1012 Lisbon, Portugal

Aims and objectives. As the Portuguese section of Pax Christi International (the "international Catholic movement for peace"), this organization seeks to educate and involve Catholics in peace and development issues. As part of the country's peace movement, it urges disarmament, and particularly the abolition of nuclear weapons, as prerequisites for a just world order.

Formation. The Portuguese section was initiated in 1983 and formally established on May 19, 1985.

Activities. In 1985 the group organized a weekend study meeting on peace and education followed by a "week for peace" in a Lisbon parish. In 1986 it hosted an international conference on peace and education.

Membership. About 25 people.

Publication. Alicerce, quarterly.

Affiliations. Pax Christi International.

Spain

capital: Madrid   **population: 38,500,000**

Spain became the 16th member of the North Atlantic Treaty Organization (NATO) on May 30, 1982, following ratification of the Spanish protocol of accession (signed in December 1981) by Spain itself and by the 15 existing member states (Belgium, Canada, Denmark, France, the Federal Republic of Germany, Greece, Iceland, Italy, Luxembourg, the Netherlands, Norway, Portugal, Turkey, the United Kingdom and the United States). Accession to the alliance was opposed at the time by the (then opposition) Spanish Socialist Workers' Party (PSOE) as well as by the Communist Party, and following the PSOE's accession to power in October 1982 negotiations to integrate Spain into NATO's military command structure were suspended pending the holding of a referendum on the membership issue.

The PSOE then underwent a policy reversal, taking a majority decision at its 30th congress in December 1984 in favour of Spain remaining in NATO. On Dec. 27, 1985, the Congress of Deputies approved a resolution in favour of continued NATO membership by 278 votes to five (Communists and one Basque Left deputy) and in the referendum on March 12, 1986, the electorate did likewise by a margin of 52.5 to 39.8 per cent, with 7.6 per cent of the ballots left blank or spoilt. The turn-out was 59.5 per cent, reflecting the call of the conservative (and pro-NATO) Popular Coalition for abstention on the grounds that the referendum was unnecessary.

In the referendum voters were asked whether they thought it appropriate for Spain to remain in NATO under the terms set out by the Government, which as listed on the ballot papers were (i) that Spain would not be integrated in the alliance's military command structure; (ii) that the prohibition on deployment, stockpiling or introduction of nuclear weapons on Spanish territory would be maintained; and (iii) that the US military presence in Spain would be progressively reduced. In this last respect, negotiations were already under way to reduce the 12,500-strong US military contingent in Spain by means of a revision of the July 1982 US-Spanish friendship, defence and co-operation agreement (itself a revision of earlier agreements dating back to 1953). Under the existing five-year agreement, US forces had use of three air bases in Spain (at Torrejón de Ardoz, Morón and Saragossa), a naval base at Rota (on the Atlantic coast of southern Spain) and a military firing range (at Bárdenas Reales). Under a 1976 revision the United States had been obliged to withdraw its nuclear submarines from Rota by mid-1979 and had also undertaken not to store nuclear devices or their components on Spanish soil. In February 1985, following publication of a report that US contingency defence plans included one to store 32 nuclear depth charges in Spain for anti-submarine warfare in the Strait of Gibraltar, the United States stated that nuclear weapons would not be deployed without the prior agreement of the host country. (For the September 1984 incident involving the collision of a Soviet nuclear submarine in the Strait of Gilbraltar, see introduction to Gilbraltar section.)

As at end-1985 the Spanish armed forces numbered 320,000, consisting of 230,000 army, 57,000 navy and 33,000 air force personnel; there were also 110,000 para-militaries in the Civil Guard and the National Police. About two-thirds of the armed forces were conscripts, there being compulsory military service for men of 15 months; reserves totalled over 1,000,000. Under reforms introduced in late 1983 to establish full political control over the armed forces, the strength of the army was to be reduced by a quarter of its officers and a third of its men over a five-year period, with the air force also being reduced in numbers; the term of military service for the army was to be reduced to 12 months by 1987 and the right of conscientious objection was to be recognized (legislation to this effect being adopted in December 1984). The defence budget for 1985 was approximately 612,000 million pesetas, representing about 10 per cent of total government expenditure.

Spain has, together with Portugal, declared its wish to join the Western European Union (WEU), which was created as such in 1955 by Belgium, France, the Federal Republic of Germany, Italy, Luxembourg, the Netherlands and the United Kingdom, and which under the French-initiated Rome Declaration of October 1984 was to be reactivated with a view to increasing security co-operation between members states. Within the European framework, Spain is currently a party to (i) a bilateral military co-operation agreement with Portugal under the 10-year treaty of friendship and co-operation signed by the two countries in November 1977; and (ii) a military co-operation agreement with France, originally concluded in June 1970 and most recently renewed under a joint declaration of friendship and co-operation signed in July 1985.

Andalusian Assembly for Non-Violence
Asamblea Andaluza de Noviolencia

Address. Pasaje Pezuela 1, 7°, 20010 Malaga, Spain

Aims and objectives. The central principles of the Assembly are: (i) total opposition to war; (ii) struggle against economic exploitation and social injustice, political repression and all forms of authoritarianism and privilege, as well as racial, geographical, sexual or religious discrimination; (iii) the development of a way of life based on respect for all cultures and the creation of fundamental democratic organizations enabling all people to participate directly and have real responsibility in the exercise of power; and (iv) the safeguarding of cultural values and the environment.

Activities. The Assembly acts as a co-ordinating and directing body for regional peace groups, particularly conscientious objection and other pacifist movements. In December 1985 the Assembly was accepted as an associated member of War Resisters' International.

Affiliations. War Resisters' International (associated member).

Andalusian Pacifist Co-ordination
Coordinadora Pacifista Andaluza

Address. Apartado 733, 41080 Seville, Andalucia, Spain

Aims and objectives. This group aims to act as a co-ordinating body for peace groups in Andalusia and to assist in formulating joint plans of action and promoting non-violent methods of action.

Activities. The group's main activity is the distribution of pacifist and non-violent material and the planning of initiatives with other peace groups.

Membership. The group has no membership structure as such but its activities are directed by a working group.

Anti-NATO Commission
Comisión Anti-OTAN

Address. Calle Campomanes 13, 2° izda, 28013 Madrid, Spain

Aims and objectives. The main objective of the Commission is to achieve Spain's withdrawal from the NATO alliance, the dismantling of US bases in the country, the establishment of neutral status and a reallocation of the military budget. The Commission also works for the disarmament of the great military powers and for the rights of conscientious objectors.

Formation. The Commission was formed by Spain's anti-NATO committees in January 1981 when it organized a mass demonstration and march from Madrid to Torrejón de Ardoz (12 km from the capital and the site of the most important US base in Spain), in which 100,000 people participated.

Activities. The Commission's principal activity involves the organization of peace demonstrations (more than a million people being mobilized in a demonstration against President Reagan's visit to Spain in May 1985). The Commission also organizes cultural and educational events for the promotion of peace.

The Commission co-ordinated the (in the event unsuccessful) anti-NATO campaign leading up to the March 1986 referendum on whether Spain should withdraw from the alliance. It argued that staying in NATO would imply Spanish foreign policy being subordinated in particular to that of the United States and could implicate Spain in conflicts which did not affect its direct interests.

Membership. The Commission embraces a large network of peace groups (the Spanish peace movement as a whole claiming to have over a million active supporters throughout the country).

Publication. Zone Cero (Zero Zone), bi-monthly.

Affiliations. The Commission co-operates with all Spanish groups working for peace, including left-wing political parties and progressive Christian organizations.

Big Eye
Begi Haundi

Address. Apartado 1449, San Sebastian, Spain

Aims and objectives. Big Eye operates as a "service agency" for Spanish peace groups.

Formation. It was set up in mid-1983 on the initiative of peace and ecological activists of the Basque region.

Activities. Independent and self-financing, Big Eye acts as a channel for information about the Spanish and international peace movement and assists local peace groups with support materials, speakers, technical assistance etc. Initially centred on the Basque region, the agency is seeking to extend its network across Spain and also to develop contacts with peace research institutes in other countries.

Publication. Begi Haundi, bi-monthly newsletter.

Conscientious Objection Movement
Movimiento de Objeción de Conciencia (MOC)

Address. Calle Desengaño 13, 1° izda, 28004 Madrid, Spain

Aims and objectives. As an affiliate of War Resisters' International, the MOC is primarily opposed to militarism in all its forms and aims to achieve a non-violent strategy for defence. The organization is also against militaristic values permeating through society and being expressed in repression, élitism, class divisions and forms of authoritarian behaviour. The MOC's main objective is to achieve a non-militaristic society in which alternative forms of social organization can develop.

Formation. The MOC emerged in 1977 as a co-ordinating body for conscientious objectors fighting for recognition of their beliefs. With the change of government in Spain in 1977 all conscientious objectors were released from prison but the MOC continued to campaign for the rights of objectors to be recognized.

Activities. In December 1984 the Socialist Government passed the first Spanish law on conscientious objection and the following year the MOC carried out a campaign of "collective objection" to the new law. The law obliged objectors to complete civilian service and did not recognize their rights as civilians, as the MOC would have liked. More than 1400 objectors continue to protest against the law through acts of civil disobedience.

The MOC has also carried out a Peace Tax Campaign and completed studies of non-violent defence.

Membership. The MOC is not a legally recognized body so it has no enrolled members; it has around 1,500 activists.

Publications. The MOC has no publications as such but various independent groups sympathetic to the aims of the movement publish their own papers, including *Oveja Negra, Maldito Pais, Anvex* and *La Pulga y el General.*

Affiliations. Internationally the MOC is a member of War Resisters' International; within Spain it is a member of the National Co-ordination of Pacifist Organizations (CEOP) and in contact with the Non-Violent Action Group (GANV).

Ecologist and Pacifist Disarming Group (GEPD)

Address. Calle Entrenga, 30 atic 1era A, 08015 Barcelona, Spain

Aims and objectives. The GEPD detects and opposes threats to the environment and to peace.

Formation. The Group was set up in 1984 by a group of high-school students to arouse fellow students.

Activities. These have included a Christmas campaign against consumerism, defence of Barcelona's green spaces and endangered flora and of the Catalan forests, opposition to NATO and to staging the 1992 Olympic Games in Barcelona.

Extremadura Assembly for Non-Violence
Asamblea Extremeña de Noviolencia

Address. Apartado 31, Plasencia, Cáceres, Spain

Aims and objectives. This organization seeks to disseminate the concept of a non-violent alternative (especially at the educational level), to promote anti-militarism and conscientious objection, to co-ordinate the activities of non-violent groups in Extremadura and to organize actions in favour of peace and disarmament.

Formation. The Assembly was constituted in 1982, initially as the Extremadura Assembly of Conscientious Objectors.

Activities. In addition to pursuing its basic concern for the right of conscientious objection, the Assembly has also been actively involved in promoting "fiscal objection" to military expenditure, in peace education and in other campaigns and demonstrations deriving to the basic principles of non-violence.

Membership. Most members are in the 18–30 age bracket, with workers and students predominating.

Publication. Anvex, monthly review of non-violence and related developments.

Affiliations. Conscientious Objection Movement (MOC); National Co-ordination of Pacifist Organizations (CEOP); Extremadura Co-ordination of Pacifist Organizations.

Foundation for Peace
Fundació per la Pau

Address. Calle Pau Claris 72, 3er/2a, 08010 Barcelona, Spain

Aims and objectives. The Foundation seeks to encourage the tide of public opinion in favour of peace and disarmament, particularly through peace education work.

Formation. The Foundation came into existence in 1983.

Activities. In addition to fund-raising to finance itself (by private donations), the Foundation has mounted a major peace exhibition in Barcelona which subsequently toured Catalonia. It also organizes conferences and seminars and maintains an archive of printed and other material for use by peace activists and others.

Membership. The Foundation has a 14-member board and "collaborators".

Publication. A fortnightly bulletin is published.

Affiliations. International Peace Bureau.

Initiatives for Disarmament and the Emancipation of Peoples
Iniciativas por el Desarme y la Emancipación de los Pueblos

Address. Calle Abades 5/2a derecha, Jean, Spain

Aims and objectives. This movement seeks to build a broad campaign against the threat of nuclear war, for peace and disarmament, and for solidarity with liberation movements in the Third World.

Formation. The movement emerged from a Latin American support committee and a group opposed to Spain's membership of NATO.

Activities. The movement has concentrated on establishing links between existing and new peace groups, and with sympathisers in areas such as the trade unions, the political parties, the environmentalist movement, religious groups and feminist organizations.

Publication. Compromiso, newsletter.

Movement for Peace, Disarmament and Liberty
Movimiento por la Paz, el Desarme y la Libertad (MPDL)

Address. Calle Valle de Suchil 15, 28015 Madrid, Spain

Aims and objectives. The MPDL seeks general world disarmament and the dismantling of military blocs; it is opposed to Spain's membership of NATO and the presence of US bases in the country.

Activities. The MPDL played a prominent role in the anti-NATO camp in the campaign leading up to the referendum on Spanish membership held in March 1986. In mid-October 1985 it issued a document entitled *Opportunities for Peace* which had over 100 prominent signatories, including the secretaries-general of the General Workers' Union (UGT) and of the Young Socialists. The document opposed the pro-NATO policy of the ruling Socialist Workers' Party.

National Co-ordination of Pacifist Organizations
Coordinadora Estatal de Organizaciones Pacifistas (CEOP)

Address. Plaza Tirso de Molina 8, 28012 Madrid, Spain

Aims and objectives. CEOP seeks to co-ordinate the actions and campaigns of local pacifist groups, with particular reference to the campaign to secure the withdrawal of Spain from NATO.

Activities. Together with the Anti-NATO Commission (see separate entry), CEOP played a prominent role in the campaign leading up to the March 1986 referendum on whether Spain should remain a member of NATO.

Non-Violent Action Group
Grupo de Acción Noviolenta (GANV)

Address. Puente la Palmilla 1–3° C, 29011 Malaga, Spain

Aims and objectives. The GANV aspires to a world society of free men and women, classless, demilitarized and ecological.

Formation. The Group came into being in 1972 under the Franco dictatorship.

Activities. Since the advent of democracy in Spain, the GANV has campaigned for recognition of the right to conscientious objection, against the arms race and the arms trade, against civil nuclear power and for the withdrawal of Spain from NATO and the closure of US bases on Spanish territory. In its propagation of non-violent principles it concentrates on peace education in particular, and is also involved in a "fiscal objection" campaign whereby state tax destined for military purposes is withheld. The GANV also participated in protests against the US bombing of Libya in April 1986.

142

Membership. The "components" of the GANV fluctuate between 15 and 20. Most of the members are workers.

Affiliations. Andalusian Assembly for Non-Violence.

Peace and Co-operation
Paz y la Cooperación

Address. Calle Melandez Valdes 68–4, 28015 Madrid, Spain

Aims and objectives. This group works for peace, international aid and development, and a global approach to world problems.

Formation. It was formed in December 1982.

Activities. The group has promoted annual "Culture for Peace" events in Madrid and other peace-related campaigns, especially in schools. It has also been active in Guinea and Malabo (Equatorial Guinea), and promoted a campaign under the slogan "Friendship with Morocco". It participated in the campaign against NATO membership leading up to the March 1986 referendum.

Membership. 350 (mainly in Spain).

Publications. The group has published various leaflets.

Affiliations. Spanish organizations to which the group is affiliated include the National Co-ordination of Pacifist Organizations (CEOP).

Peace Education Permanent Working Group
Seminario Permanente Educaciôn para la Paz

Address. Calle San Gregorio 1, 1°, 41004 Seville, Spain

Aims and objectives. This Group promotes peace education in schools and elsewhere.

Formation. The group came into being in 1983.

Activities. The Group is involved in the designation of January 30 each year as a day of non-violence and peace in schools (see also entry for School Day of Non-Violence and Peace) and in the organization of seminars and conferences on peace education themes. It has a substantial research and publications programme.

Membership. The Group has about 12 members (teachers and education graduates).

Publications. The Group has published a dossier entitled *Educaciôn para la Paz*.

School Day of Non-Violence and Peace
Dia Escolar de la No-Violencia y la Paz (DENYP)

Address. Apartado 126, S'Arenal, 07000 Majorca (Balearic Islands), Spain

Aims and objectives. DENYP's aim is to have one day a year set aside in schools for the celebration and consideration of peace. It hopes thereby to act as a catalyst for the institution of "a pacifying and non-violent education".

Formation. DENYP was established in 1964.

Activities. DENYP's suggested activities for the day of non-violence and peace include meditation and discussion around the theme of "universal love, non-violence and peace: universal love is better than selfishness, non-violence is better than violence, peace is better than war". It also suggests that schoolchildren could engage in "pacifying meditation or personal reflection in silence", "expressive activities" and "individual or group prayer for love, non-violence and peace among men and between peoples", and that their teachers might lead discussions in the classroom on the ideas and achievements of Mahatma Gandhi.

In the northern hemisphere, DENYP is celebrated on January 30 (the anniversary of the death of Gandhi) and in the southern hemisphere (where this date coincides with summer holidays) on March 30.

Membership. Although DENYP is not a membership organization as such, its work is supported by *Amigos del DENYP y de la Educacion Pacificadora* (Friends of DENYP and of Peace Education). DENYP's founder and principal proponent is Llorenc Vidal. Its aims have been publicly supported by the Romanian writer Eugen Relgis, the Italian pacifist Lanza del Vasto, and several university professors in Spain and in West Germany.

Publications. *Ponent*, a magazine covering activities undertaken on the day of non-violence and peace.

Other Movements

Christians for Peace
Cristianos por la Paz

Address. Santa Catalina 8, 28014 Madrid, Spain

Commission for the Celebration of International Year of Peace
Comisión para la Celebracion del Año Internacional de la Paz

Address. Plaza Tirso de Molina 8, 28012 Madrid, Spain

Conscientious Objection Movement of Seville
Movimiento de Objeción de Conciencia de Sevilla

Address. Apartado 496, Seville, Spain

International Peace University
Universitat Internacional per la Pau

Address. Ajuntament de San Cugat del Valles, Barcelona, Spain

Justice and Peace General Commission
Comisión General Justicia y Paz

Address. Rivadeneyia 6, 10°, Barcelona 2, Spain

Pacifist Collective of Arganzuela
Colectivo Pacifista de Arganzuela

Address. Calle General Lacy 15, 28007 Madrid, Spain

Pacifist Co-ordination of Valencia
Coordinadora Pacifista de Valencia

Address. Pasaje Dr Bartuel 9, Pta 29, 46010 Valencia, Spain

Pax Christi

Address. Apartado 5454, Barcelona, Spain

Peace Co-ordination of Soria
Coordinadora por la Paz de Soria

Address. Caro 7, 5°B, 42001 Soria, Spain

Peace and Disarmament Action Group
Grup d'Acció per la Pau i el Desermament

Address. Montenegro 8, Palma de Majorca, Spain

Peace and Disarmament Action Committee
Comité de Acción por la Paz y el Desarme

Address. San Cosme y San Damian 24, 2°, 28012 Madrid, Spain

Peace and Disarmament Assembly of Salamanca
Asamblea Paz y Desarme de Salamanca

Address. Apartado 925, Salamanca, Spain

Peace and Disarmament Association
Asociación Paz y Desarme

Address. Calle Silva 20, 28013 Madrid, Spain

Peace and Disarmament Information Group
Grupo de Información sobre Paz y Desarme

Address. José Ortega y Gasset 77/2A, 28006 Madrid, Spain

Peace and Disarmament Platform of Zamora
Plataforma por la Paz y el Desarme de Zamora

Address. Apartado 339, Zamora, Spain

Teachers for Peace
Educadores por la Paz

Address. Apartado 577, Vigo, Ponteveda, Galicia, Spain

Sweden

capital: Stockholm   population: 8,335,000

Sweden has a longstanding policy of neutrality, maintained in both World Wars of the 20th century and reaffirmed by successive governments since 1945. While renouncing nuclear weapons, Sweden devotes substantial resources to maintaining a defensive capability against threats to its territorial integrity from whatever quarter. At the same time, Swedish statesmen have played a prominent role in UN and other international fora for disarmament negotiations, Sweden being the first country to have appointed (in 1966) a government minister specifically responsible for disarmament. In April 1985 the Government denied press reports that Sweden had carried out secret nuclear weapons research as late as 1972, two years after it had ratified the nuclear non-proliferation treaty and in violation of a 1957 parliamentary ban on such research.

The Social Democratic minority administration re-elected in September 1985 reiterated its support for a freeze on East-West nuclear weapons deployment and for the creation of a Nordic nuclear-weapons-free zone, while conceding that growing tension between the superpowers had heightened the strategic importance of the Nordic region. In the latter context, a particular Swedish concern in recent years has been the frequent detection of foreign submarines in Swedish territorial waters, both before and after the grounding on the south-eastern Swedish coast (in a restricted military zone near the Karlskrona naval base) of a Soviet submarine which was believed to be carrying nuclear weapons. (Sweden has given particular attention to civilian defence against a nuclear attack and has fall-out shelters capable of holding 5,000,000 people.)

As at end-1985 the Swedish armed forces totalled 65,650 personnel (army 47,000, navy 9,650 and air force 9,000) and the para-military coast guard 550. About three-quarters of the total were conscripts, there being compulsory military service for men of $7\frac{1}{2}$ to 15 months for the army and navy and of eight to 12 months for the air force; there were 735,500 reserves and 500,000 voluntary auxiliaries. There is legislative provision for conscientious objectors to military conscription to undertake alternative service. The defence budget for the 1985–86 financial year was some 25,000 million kronor, representing about 8 per cent of total government expenditure.

Anti-Weapons Association
Vapenvargförbundet (VVF)

Address. c/o SPAS, Brännkyrkgatan 76, S–117 23 Stockholm, Sweden

Aims and objectives. This pacifist movement is opposed to all forms of militarization and advocates total resistance to involvement in the military activities of the state. It became an associated member of War Resisters' International in December 1985.

Affiliations. War Resisters' International (associated member).

Campaign Against Conscription
Kampanjen Mot Verneplikt

Address. Svartmossevagen 14, S-436 00 Askim, Sweden

Aims and objectives. This movement campaigns for an end to compulsory conscription into the armed forces and for recognition of the right of conscientious objection.

Formation. The Swedish movement was established as part of a Scandinavian-wide initiative which began with the formation of a Norwegian movement of the same name in 1981.

Affiliations. The Scandinavian-wide Campaign is an associated member of War Resisters' International.

Christian Peace Movement
Kristna Fredsrörelsen (KrF)

Address. Götgatan 3, S-752 22 Uppsala, Sweden

Aims and objectives. As the Swedish section of the International Fellowship of Reconciliation, the Movement works for peace, justice and general and total disarmament, in accordance with the Christian gospel.

Formation. The movement was formed in 1919 under the name "Swedish World Peace Mission".

Activities. The organization works primarily through the churches, at both national and local levels, to encourage awareness of peace issues. It also co-operates with *Servicio Paz y Justicia* in Latin America. At present it is working to build better relations between East and West through the churches, is involved in peace education, supports conscientious objectors etc.

Membership. Membership reached the peak of 5,000 in 1931, and then declined steadily until recovering strongly 1977–83, since when it has stabilized at 4,300.

Publications. *Fred och Framtid* (Peace and Future), newsletter.

Affiliations. International Fellowship of Reconciliation; War Resisters' International.

Peace Forum of the Swedish Labour Movement
Arbetarrörelsens Fredsfrom

Address. S-105 53, Stockholm, Sweden

Aims and objectives. The Peace Forum encourages international disarmament within the framework of active support for peace campaigns mounted by the various branches of the Swedish labour movement.

Formation. The Forum was established in September 1981 under the presidency of Alva Myrdal as a working group of the Social Democratic Party and of the Swedish Trade Union Confederation (LO), following calls for the establishment of such a group by the congresses of the two organizations.

Activities. The Forum has organized a series of seminars and meetings on various aspects of disarmament issues. It has also set up a library of information resources on such issues.

Membership. All branches of the Swedish labour movement participate to some extent in the Forum's activities.

Publications. Freds Fakta (Facts About Peace) is published about eight times a year; several booklets and study materials have also been produced.

Satyagraha Workshop

Address. c/o Jorgen Johansen, Krossekärr 6822, S-450 81 Grebbestad, Sweden

Aims and objectives. This Workshop undertakes peace work in the spirit of Gandhi.

Formation. It was established in 1983.

Activities. The Workshop publishes pamphlets and books.

Affiliations. It has links with War Resisters' International.

Stockholm International Peace Research Institute (SIPRI)

Address. Pipersväg 28, S-171 73 Solna-Stockholm, Sweden

Aims and objectives. SIPRI has as its purpose the carrying out of independent research and information work on the major questions of international peace and security.

Formation. The Institute was set up in 1966 as an independent body, financed by the Swedish Parliament but with an international governing board and staff.

Activities. Since its foundation SIPRI has specialized in research on armaments and possibilities for disarmament, producing ongoing studies on the arms race and the proliferation of armaments around the world as well as on the progress, or lack of it, in various disarmament negotiations. It convenes regular seminars on specific topics and maintains contact with other peace research bodies throughout the world.

Publications. The main SIPRI publication is its yearbook *World Armaments and Disarmament*; it also publishes a range of studies (in English, Spanish, French, German, Japanese, Dutch and Russian, as well as Swedish).

Swedish Architects Against Nuclear Weapons (SAANW)

Address. Birkagatan 25/2, S-113 Stockholm, Sweden

Aims and objectives. SAANW believes (i) that governments should redirect resources from war to improving social conditions; (ii) that disarmament and peace "are not only prerequisites for the survival of the rich countries but also for redistribution towards a dignified life for the people of the world"; and (iii) that action by architects "can help mobilize forces for peace, break the arms race and transfer resources to peaceful activities".

Swedish Peace and Arbitration Society (SPAS)
Svenska Freds- och Skiljedomsföreningen

Address. Brännkyrkagatan 76, S-117 23 Stockholm, Sweden

Aims and objectives. The SPAS campaigns for independent, unilateral peace initiatives and is opposed to nuclear weapons and to the arms trade. It supports the establishment of a Nordic nuclear-free zone.

Formation. The SPAS was founded in Stockholm in 1983.

Activities. Since its formation, the SPAS has organized a series of nationwide demonstrations directed principally against the deployment of cruise and Pershing II missiles in Western Europe, and also calling for the establishment of Nordic and European nuclear-free zones. It also co-ordinated protest blockades aimed at preventing the export from Sweden of cranes built by the Hiab-Foco company for use as part of the transportation system for Pershing II missiles. In support of the Nordic nuclear-free zone proposal, the SPAS in September 1984 participated in a meeting at Orebro with representatives of other Nordic peace groups and with groups from the Balkans advocating a similar proposal for their area.

In late 1984, the SPAS initiated a petition campaign in an effort to gain support for its demand that all arms exports from Sweden be halted. At the opening of the campaign, SPAS researchers announced that weapons of Swedish manufacture had been employed in 39 wars since 1950.

An SPAS working group is currently researching into alternative defence policies, with a view to influencing the content of the five-year national defence plan for the period 1987–91, which is currently being discussed by a parliamentary committee.

As part of its continuing campaign against the Soviet military presence in Afghanistan, the SPAS organized a series of protest actions in December 1984 to coincide with the fifth anniversary of Soviet intervention. The group has also sought to mobilize public opinion in connection with the conference to review the state of the nuclear non-proliferation treaty held in October 1985, and with East-West disarmament negotiations in Geneva.

The SPAS has also conducted a fund-raising campaign to finance the production of a film on the international peace movement by Peter Watkins, director of *The War Game* (a film on the likely effects of a nuclear attack on Britain, commissioned in 1965 by the British Broadcasting Corporation, but not broadcast until August 1985). The film's première took place in Hiroshima on August 6, 1985 (the 40th anniversary of the first use of the atomic bomb).

Towards the end of 1985 the SPAS, in co-operation with the International Peace Bureau, launched an "International Testing Information Service" involving the provision of detailed information by telex on every nuclear explosion immediately after it takes place. The free service, aimed at peace movements throughout the world, includes data on the place, time and magnitude of each nuclear test (as established by the Swedish National Defence Research Institute) and is accompanied by suggestions for protest actions designed to mobilize public opinion against the continuation of underground testing by the nuclear-weapons powers.

Membership. SPAS's current membership totals some 15,500, the majority of whom are under 25 years of age. The activities of 120 local groups are co-ordinated by a central office in Stockholm, which employs seven full-time workers.

Publications. PAX, the group's newsletter, is published 10 times per year. It has a circulation of approximately 18,000 copies and is widely sold in news-stands and bookstalls.

Affiliations. Internationally: International Peace Bureau; War Resisters' International; International Peace Communication and Co-ordination Network. Within Sweden, the SPAS maintains contact with various political and religious bodies which are broadly sympathetic to the movement's aims.

Swedish Peace Committee
Svenska Fredskommitten

Address. P.O. Box 681, S-101 29 Stockholm, Sweden

Aims and objectives. The Committee is opposed to the arms race, nuclear weapons and other weapons of mass destruction. It seeks to mobilize public opinion on this issue, particularly in support of the proposed Nordic nuclear-free zone.

Formation. The Committee was founded in December 1949.

Activities. The Committee was instrumental in organizing the session of the 1950 World Peace Council which produced the "Stockholm Peace Appeal" the following year. It has since taken part in numerous conferences on disarmament. An "anti-imperialist" group, the Committee is also committed to assisting third-world liberation struggles.

Membership. Individual members number about 2,500, while some 400 trade unions, political and cultural organizations are affiliated.

Publications. Peace and Solidarity, a bi-monthly magazine; several booklets on disarmament.

Affiliations. World Peace Council.

Women for Peace
Kvinnor för Fred

Address. Klara N. Kyrkogatan 26, S-111 22 Stockholm, Sweden

Aims and objectives. This independent movement seeks to involve women in the campaign for peace and disarmament, working in co-operation with sister organizations in other European countries.

Formation. Following the formation of the Swiss movement of the same name in 1976, a Swedish section was established shortly thereafter.

Activities. The Swedish movement has been involved in various actions and demonstrations by the Swedish peace movement, including the organization of the "Great Peace Journey" series (see entry for Women's International League for Peace and Freedom).

Women's International League for Peace and Freedom (WILPF)—Swedish Section
International Kvinneforbundet für Fred och Frihet

Address. c/o Renate Schäffer, Packhusgränd 6, S-111 30 Stockholm, Sweden

Aims and objectives. The WILPF seeks to bring women together to study the causes of war and to work for total and universal disarmament.

Activities. The Swedish section of the WILPF is at present campaigning for a Scandinavian nuclear-free zone and against the sale of Swedish arms to other countries. In collaboration with other movements, it carried out a "Great Peace Journey" to all European member-states of the UN in May 1985, and in 1986 has organized a further "Great Peace Journey" to areas outside Europe, including the USA and the Soviet Union. The central aim of the journeys is to encourage the people of the countries en route to ask their governments a number of pertinent questions concerning their attitude to peace and disarmament. The idea for the journeys came from Astrid Einarsson, a Swedish peace activist and teacher in Ronneby.

Membership. About 2,000, principally but not exclusively women.

Publications. Fred och Frihet (Peace and Freedom), quarterly.

Affiliations. Women's International League for Peace and Freedom; Swedish Peace Committee; Swedish UN Association.

Switzerland

capital: Berne   **population: 6,500,000**

Switzerland has pursued a policy of permanent neutrality since 1815 and therefore belongs to no military alliances. Although both houses of the Swiss Parliament voted during 1984 in favour of Switzerland becoming a member of the United Nations Organization (UNO), a national referendum held on March 16, 1986, resulted in a three-to-one majority against membership. (While not a member of the UNO as such, Switzerland has UN observer status and is a member of various UN agencies, several of which have their headquarters in Geneva.)

As at end-1985 the Swiss armed forces had a total mobilizable strength of some 1,105,000 (army 580,000, para-military civil defence units 480,000 and air force 45,000). Apart from a small permanent complement of some 1,500 officers and training personnel, there is no "standing army" in Switzerland; the country's defence capability is based on the "militia" concept involving compulsory military service for men of about 12 months in total, spread over basic training (17 weeks) and subsequent refresher courses. There is no right of conscientious objection from military service. Particular attention is given to civil defence, there being nuclear fall-out shelter capacity for virtually the entire civilian population. The overall defence budget for 1985 was 5,043 million Swiss francs, representing about 22 per cent of federal government expenditure.

French-speaking Federation of Non-Violent Movements/Fédération Romande des Mouvements Non-Violents—see entry for Martin Luther King Centre (MLKC)

Geneva International Peace Research Institute (GIPRI)
Institut International de Recherches pour la Paix à Genève
Genfer Internationales Friedensforschunginstitut

Address. 41 rue de Zurich, CH-1201 Geneva, Switzerland

Aims and objectives. The Institute undertakes "scientific research, in both the exact and the human sciences, in all areas which involve the problems of peace and security or related problems, in order to contribute to the establishment of a genuine peace".

Formation. GIPRI was created as an association in 1980 and was transformed into a foundation in 1984.

Membership. Those interested in the Institute's work and publications can become members of the "PRO-GIPRI" network.

Publications. GIPRI's *Cahiers de Recherches* series had included *Le Nouvel Ordre Militaire* (The New Military Order), by Jan Øberg (1982); *Children and War*, by Edouard Dommen and David Pitt (1982); *Verhüting von Nuklearkrieg* (Preventing

Nuclear War), by Dietrich Fischer (1984); *Computers in the Settlement of International Disputes*, by Jacob Bercovitch and Herbert Ohlman (1984); *Sur la "Guerre Juste"* (On the "Just War"), by Ivo Rens (1984); *Die Kontinuität der Nuklearen Beziehungen zwischen Argentinien und Deutschland seit dem Zweiten Weltkrieg* (The Continuity of Nuclear Co-operation between Argentina and Germany since the Second World War), by Ralf Siedler (1984); *Commercial Fast Breeders: Towards an Integrated European Nuclear Force?*, by Michel de Perrot (1984); *Nuclear War Effects in Switzerland*, by Allan Din and Jacques Diezi (1985); and *Jean-Jacques de Sellon, Pacifiste et Précurseur de "l'Esprit de Genève"* (Jean-Jacques de Sellon, Pacifist and Precursor of "the Spirit of Geneva"), by Ivo Rens and Klaus-Gerd Giesen.

Affiliations. International Peace Research Association.

Group for a Switzerland Without Army
Gruppe für Eine Schweiz Ohne Armee (GSOA)

Address. P.O. Box 221, CH-8307 Effretikon, Switzerland

Aims and objectives. This Group has as its central objective the dissolution of the Swiss army and its replacement by "the development of a comprehensive peace policy by the people and the Government" involving the building of "a social model based on a new world order of federal linked states without armies". It forms part of a Swiss peace movement which "tries to being a new dimension into the European peace discussion based on Switzerland's neutral isolation as a small state".

Activities. In March 1985 the Group published a petition for the dissolution of the Swiss army which it aims to have submitted to a national referendum. To oblige the Government to hold such a referendum the petition required at least 100,000 signatures by September 1986 (about half having been collected by the end of 1985). The Group argues that the allocation of 20 per cent of total state expenditure to the military budget "is no longer acceptable", that its initiative is being taken seriously in Swiss political and establishment circles and that the army issue "is no longer taboo".

Publication. The Group publishes a newsletter 10 times a year.

Martin Luther King Centre (MLKC)
Centre Martin Luther King

Address. Avenue de Béthusy 56, CH-1012 Lausanne, Switzerland

Aims and objectives. The Martin Luther King Centre houses documentation and provides information on the theme of non-violence. It aims to increase public awareness of peace issues and co-ordinates the activities of other peace groups, acting as the secretariat of the *Fédération Romande des Mouvements Non-Violents* (French-speaking Federation of Non-Violent Movements).

The Centre also provides information and support for conscientious objectors, who are still subject to imprisonment in Switzerland.

Formation. The Centre was founded in 1968 just after the assassination of Martin Luther King.

Activities. Since its formation the Centre has participated in numerous activities including: an anti-militaristic film festival; a tour of Switzerland by conscientious objectors; petitions and non-violent direct action.

The Centre is currently sending Swiss peace brigades to Nicaragua and backing the Nicaragua Solidarity Campaign. It has also organized a campaign to refuse payment of taxes which go to military spending and demanding the creation of an official peace research centre in Switzerland. The Centre is also trying to achieve legal status for conscientious objectors and continues to work for non-violence between people and nations.

Membership. The Centre is not a membership organization but has around 1,500 people on its mailing list.

Publications. Feuille d'Information du Centre Martin Luther King is published 4 to 6 times a year; the Centre also collaborates on the publication of *RPmensuel*, which comes out every month.

Affiliations. The Centre has links with War Resisters' International and the International Fellowship of Reconciliation.

Military Denial Advisory Board
Beratungsstelle für Militärdienstverweigerer

Address. Sulzerstrasse, 16, CH-4054 Basel, Switzerland

Aims and objectives. This Board gives advice and support to those who have objections or difficulties relating to conscription (which is compulsory in Switzerland and without right of conscientious objection).

Formation. The Board was founded in 1975 by a group of people who rejected military service.

Membership. The Board had five members in mid-1985 (a doctor, a theologian, a gardener, a retailer and a member of Women for Peace—see separate entry).

Pax Christi—French-speaking Swiss Section
Pax Christi—Section Suisse Romande

Address. 3 rue Argand, CH-1201 Geneva, Switzerland

Aims and objectives. As the French-speaking Swiss section of Pax Christi International (the "international Catholic movement for peace"), this organization seeks to involve and educate Catholics in work for peace and disarmament. It is particularly active in human rights campaigns.

Activities. The organization has undertaken investigations of the human rights position in a number of countries (including Paraguay, Haiti, Timor and Sri Lanka). It also participates in activities of the Swiss peace movement, most recently those marking 1986 as International Year of Peace.

Publication. Si Tu Veux la Paix (If You Want Peace), quarterly.

Affiliations. Pax Christi International.

Pax Christi—German-speaking Swiss Section

Address. Bordackerstrasse, 66, CH-8610 Uster, Switzerland

Swiss Peace Council
Schweizerische Friedensrat

Address. P.O. Box 6386, CH-8023 Zurich, Switzerland

Aims and objectives. This independent umbrella organization advocates a "flexible" rather than "absolute" defence policy and opposes the "increasing militarization" of Swiss society, which it seeks to humanize and to make nuclear-free. It also acts as a clearing-house for information about the peace movement and pursues a policy of solidarity with peace movements abroad, being particularly concerned to develop contacts with the independent peace movement of Eastern Europe.

Activities. The Swiss Peace Council has demonstrated solidarity with peace actions in other countries, such as the campaigns in Belgium, West Germany, Italy, the Netherlands and the United Kingdom against the deployment of new US/NATO nuclear missiles. In 1983 it launched a campaign for the creation of a nuclear-free Switzerland. In November 1985 it co-organized a symposium in Berne on the theme "Finding alternatives to the bloc system"; aimed at stimulating public discussion on "the themes of independent peace initiatives in relation to the East European opposition and dissidents, and tearing down prejudice and enemy images in our countries about Eastern Europe", the symposium was attended by representatives of several independent East European peace groups.

Publication. Friedenszeitung, monthly.

Women for Peace
Femmes pour la Paix
Frauen für den Frieden

Address. Maison sur le Roc, CH-1812 Rivaz, Switzerland

Aims and objectives. This movement seeks to involve women in the campaign for peace and disarmament and to build a network of likeminded groups in other countries.

Formation. The Swiss movement (the first in a network which has groups of the same name in several other West European countries) was established in 1976.

Affiliations. International Peace Bureau.

Women's International Peace Camp
Camp International des Femmes de la Paix

Address. Place des Nations, Avenue de la Paix, CH-1202 Geneva, Switzerland

Aims and objectives. The Camp's participants are united by a rejection of violence and the desire to find new ways of living together in harmony with each other and with the earth.

Formation. The Camp came into being in September 1983 as International Peace Camp and became Women's International Peace Camp on March 8, 1985 (International Women's Day).

Activities. Women staying at the camp are involved in daily tasks and group activities of an everyday nature, as well as attending the United Nations Disarmament Conference sessions across the road twice a week.

Membership. The Camp's membership is fluid, participants come and go, and there is no hierarchy.

Publications. The Camp produces a bulletin on an approximately monthly basis, in French, English and German.

Affiliations. The Camp has no formal affiliations but stresses its solidarity with all women.

Other Movements

International Movement of Reconciliation
Mouvement International de la Réconciliation (MIR)

Address. Avenue de Morges 121, CH-1004 Lausanne, Switzerland

Service Civil International

Address. P.O. Box 246, Waldhohenweg 33A, CH-3000 Berne, Switzerland

Women's International League for Peace and Freedom

Address. 1 rue de Varembe, P.O. Box 28, CH-1211 Geneva 20, Switzerland

Turkey

capital: Ankarra   **population: 50,200,000**

Turkey became a member of the North Atlantic Treaty Organization (NATO) on Feb. 15, 1952, at the same time as Greece, thereby joining in military alliance with Belgium, Canada, Denmark, France, Iceland, Italy, Luxembourg, the Netherlands, Norway, Portugal, the United Kingdom and the United States (later adherents being the Federal Republic of Germany in 1955 and Spain in 1982). Being one of only two NATO countries with a common frontier with the Soviet Union, Turkey participates fully in NATO's integrated military structure. However, longstanding tensions with Greece in the eastern Mediterranean have proved a major complication in the NATO framework, notably as a result of the Turkish occupation of northern Cyprus since August 1974. Another cause of strain in Turkey's relations with its NATO partners has been its periodic reversion to military rule, most recently following the seizure of power by the military leadership in September 1980.

There are some 3,900 US military personnel stationed in Turkey and there are NATO-designated naval bases at Istanbul and Gölcük. Under a US-Turkish agreement signed on July 3, 1969 (and replacing earlier accords on the status of US bases in Turkey), Turkey's absolute sovereignty over all military installations in its territory was emphasized, in addition to which Turkey would, within the general framework of NATO defence policies, have co-determination with the United States on the number of US troops and their weapons and equipment to be stationed in Turkey. Following the Turkish invasion of Cyprus in 1974, the US Government suspended military aid to Turkey and imposed an arms embargo, but these measures were lifted by the end of the decade notwithstanding the continuing Turkish military presence in Cyprus. Under a new defence and economic co-operation agreement concluded on March 29, 1980, defence co-operation between Turkey and the United States was limited to obligations arising from the NATO alliance; a total of 12 military bases in Turkey were to be used by US forces, although only within the framework of NATO and each being under the command of a Turkish officer. In October 1984 Turkey began work on the construction of a joint US-Turkish plant for the manufacture of 120 US F-16 fighter-bomber warplanes, as originally agreed the previous December.

As at end-1985 the Turkish armed forces numbered 630,000 (the second largest complement in NATO after the United States), consisting of 520,000 army, 55,000 navy and 55,000 air force personnel; there were also 125,000 members of the para-military Gendarmerie. Over 80 per cent of the armed forces were conscripts, there being compulsory military service for men of 18 months; total reserve strength was some 940,000. The defence budget for 1985 was 860,800 million liras, representing about 16 per cent of aggregate government expenditure.

Turkish Peace Association (TPA)
Türkiye Baris Dernegi

Address. c/o Campaign for the Defence of the Turkish Peace Association, 13 Bolton Walk, Andover Estate, London N7 7RW, United Kingdom

Aims and objectives. The TPA monitors and promotes observance of the 1975 Helsinki Final Act of the Conference on Security and Co-operation in Europe (CSCE), signed by Turkey. Its prime objective is the abolition of all nuclear weapons and weapons of mass destruction and the dissolution of all military blocs. It advocates that funds at present allocated to armaments should be redistributed to ameliorate social and economic problems. The Association is also concerned with human rights issues and seeks the implementation of UN resolutions concerning matters of peace, security and human rights, as well as calling for an end to all forms of racism and colonialism.

Formation. The TPA was founded in April 1977, under the auspices of the Istanbul Bar Association, and was registered with the state authorities. Its activities continued after the declaration of martial law in December 1978 but its operations were suspended on the day of the military takeover in September 1980. The Association was formally banned in November 1983 (and all its assets confiscated), as a result of which it was obliged to continue its operations in exile.

Activities. During the first two years of its existence the TPA organized over 40 seminars and conferences in Turkey, principally directed at increasing public awareness of the provisions of the Helsinki Final Act. It represented Turkey at a conference of the Afro-Asian People's Solidarity Organization and was active in seeking dialogue with Mediterranean peace movements, including those of Greece and Cyprus. It promoted peace research on the Balkans, notably on the concept of Balkans nuclear-free zone, and was also prominent in development and anti-apartheid campaigns.

In February 1982 most of the TPA leadership was arrested by the military authorities and accused of propagating communist ideas through association with the Helsinki-based World Peace Council (see entry under International Organizations). Those arrested included the Association's president, Mahmut Dikerdem (a former ambassador), Orhan Apaydin (president of the Turkish Bar Association), Nurettin Yilmaz (a presidential candidate in 1980), Mrs Reha Isvan (a prominent educationalist), Dr Erdal Aterbek (president of the Turkish Medical Association), Orhan Taylan (a painter) and five former members of the Turkish Parliament.

After the first military prosecutor assigned to the case had demanded up to 30 years' imprisonment for the accused, the trial opened on June 24, 1982, with a new prosecutor who demanded that the defendants should be questioned in conditions of isolation and that they should be barred from attending their own trial. The court rejected this latter request, however, and after a period of adjournment the trial resumed on Aug. 17, 1982, with the defendants in attendance. It concluded on Nov. 14, 1983, with sentences of eight years' imprisonment (followed by two years and eight months of internal exile) being imposed on 18 members of the Association, while a further five received five years' imprisonment, five were acquitted and two were not present. Among those convicted was Mahmut Dikerdem, who had been diagnosed as suffering from cancer in July 1982.

Various appeal hearings followed, and amid complex processes before various military courts over the next two years the imprisoned TPA leaders were gradually released, the last six being freed in March 1986. Meanwhile, however, a further 48 TPA members had been brought to trial in November 1984 accused of being involved in the formation of the movement and of attempting to change the "constitutional" order.

After observing part of the trial at which the TPA leaders were originally convicted, two British Labour MPs, Roland Boyes and Ann Clwyd, set up a

Campaign for the Defence of the Turkish Peace Association based in London. This framework is now one of the means by which the TPA continues to exist in exile.

Membership. The TPA had about 500 members in Turkey before being banned, mainly prominent public personalities and with a strong intellectual component.

Publications. *Peace News from Turkey*, monthly; the TPA has also published pamphlets on such questions as security in the Mediterranean, the arms trade and economic development, Turkish foreign policy, the medical consequences of nuclear war, peace education in schools and the 1975 Helsinki Final Act.

Affiliations. (Current Turkish law prohibits any affiliations with foreign organizations.)

United Kingdom

capital: London   **population: 56,000,000**

The United Kingdom was an original signatory on April 4, 1949, of the treaty creating the North Atlantic Treaty Organization (NATO), together with Belgium, Canada, Denmark, France, Iceland, Italy, Luxembourg, the Netherlands, Norway, Portugal and the United States (later adherents being Greece and Turkey in 1952, the Federal Republic of Germany in 1955 and Spain in 1982). The United Kingdom participates fully in NATO's integrated military organization, there being some 66,000 British forces (army and air force) stationed in West Germany and a further 3,000 in West Berlin, while about 27,000 US air force personnel are stationed in Britain. There are NATO-designated naval bases at Chatham, Portsmouth, Portland and Devonport (in England) and at Faslane, Holy Loch and Rosyth (in Scotland), while the naval bases at Gibraltar and Bermuda (both UK dependencies) and at Akrotiri and Dhekelia (in the British sovereign base area of Cyprus) also come under the NATO structure.

The United Kingdom is also a member of the Western European Union (WEU), which was established as such in 1955 when the Federal Republic of Germany and Italy joined the Brussels Treaty Organization created in 1948 by Belgium, France, Luxembourg, the Netherlands and the United Kingdom. In October 1984 the UK Government was a party to the French-initiated Rome Declaration, which envisaged the reactivation of the WEU with a view to increasing security policy co-operation between the seven member states (prospectively to increase to nine with the accession of Portugal and Spain).

Outside the European and NATO theatres the United Kingdom is party to (i) the South-East Asia Collective Defence Treaty signed in Manila on Sept. 8, 1954, with Australia, France, New Zealand, Pakistan, the Philippines, Thailand and the United States, which remains in force despite the dissolution of the South-East Asia Treaty Organization (SEATO) in mid-1977 following the earlier withdrawal of France and Pakistan; and (ii) the 1971 five power ANZUK agreements under which Australia, New Zealand and the United Kingdom established a joint force for the defence of Malaysia and Singapore (although the British component of this force was withdrawn in 1975–76). The United Kingdom also has active defence assistance agreements with Belize, Brunei, Kenya, Oman and Zimbabwe and significant force contingents stationed not only in Belize and Brunei but also in the Falkland Islands and Hong Kong. There are British naval and air force units at Ascension Island in the Atlantic and a Royal Navy presence in the Indian Ocean and the Antarctic.

As at end-1985 the British armed forces totalled some 327,000, made up of 163,000 army, 93,000 air force and 71,000 navy personnel; there were in addition some 300,000 reserves. Within the overall active total about 10,000 were recruited abroad (mainly Gurkhas from Nepal) and about 16,000 were women. All services are wholly professional, military conscription having been discontinued in the early 1960s. The UK defence budget for the 1985–86 financial year (outturn) was £18,200 million, representing 13.1 per cent of total government expenditure.

The United Kingdom is a nuclear-weapons power, its strategic capability being, since the phasing out of the "V-bomber" force, the Polaris missile system (purchased from the United States) carried in nuclear submarines, of which the Royal Navy possesses four, each equipped with 16 nuclear missiles. British nuclear weapons tests are periodically conducted at the underground US testing site in Nevada (having in the 1950s been carried out in the atmosphere at two sites in Australia). The United Kindgom is party to the 1963 nuclear test-ban treaty banning atmospheric tests, to the 1967 treaty banning nuclear and other mass destruction weapons from outer space and celestial bodies and to the 1971 treaty prohibiting the deployment of such weapons on the seabed. It is also a party to the 1968 nuclear non-proliferation treaty which came into force in March 1970.

Under a decision taken by the then Labour administration in the late 1970s (and not made public at the time), Polaris missiles deployed by the United Kingdom were upgraded with Chevaline penetrating aids by 1982. The Conservative Government in power since 1979 is committed to replacing Polaris with the more advanced Trident system (also to be purchased from the United States) in accordance with the Conservative Party's belief in the need for an independent British nuclear deterrent. In contrast, since going into opposition in 1979 the Labour Party has adopted a non-nuclear defence policy under which the United Kingdom would, while remaining in NATO, rely on conventional arms for its defence and the United States would be required to withdraw all nuclear weapons from British territory. Of the two Alliance formations, the Liberals have voted at recent party conferences in favour of a unilateral non-nuclear defence strategy, whereas the Social Democratic Party, while opposed to Trident, favours retention of a British nuclear deterrent until an acceptable multilateral nuclear disarmament agreement can be concluded.

NATO's December 1979 "twin-track" decision on the modernization of intermediate-range nuclear missiles provided for the deployment of 160 US cruise missiles in the United Kingdom (at the Greenham Common and Molesworth air force bases in Berkshire and Cambridgeshire respectively). On Oct. 31, 1983, the House of Commons approved by 362 votes to 218 a motion proposed by the Conservative Government reaffirming support for the 1979 decision, strongly backing the West's "efforts to achieve a balanced and verifiable agreement at the Geneva [US-Soviet] negotiations" and confriming that "in the absence of agreement on the zero option cruise missiles must be operationally deployed in the United Kingdom at the end of 1983". The motion was opposed not only by the Labour members but also by the Liberals, the Social Democrats and the Scottish and Welsh Nationalists.

Alternative Defence Commission (ADC)—see entry for **Bradford University School of Peace Studies**

American Peace Network in Britain (APNB)

Address. c/o Antioch University, Regent's College, Inner Circle, Regent's Park, London, NW1 YNS, United Kingdom

Aims and objectives. The aim of the APNB is to work towards peace, justice and the end to world hunger. Their goal is to build a network of Americans living in Britain and Europe who will oppose the deployment of nuclear weapons and demand an immediate freeze.

Through non-violent direct action, they aim to change US government policy towards achieving a higher standard of living for those in third-world countries.

Formation. The APNB was formed in September 1984 to plan an action in conjunction with the US presidential election.

Activities. In November 1984 the APNB, in conjunction with Christian CND, staged a 24 hour vigil at the US embassy with the aim of delivering individual statements to the newly elected President.

In March 1985, 15 Americans from Britain went to Brussels, where they joined Americans living in Europe and European peace organizations, to protest against the deployment of US/NATO cruise missiles. During the three-day visit APNB members had discussions with officials at the US embassy as well as giving interviews to the national media.

The APNB holds periodic meetings and is working on a newsletter, while concentrating efforts on increasing the size of their group.

Membership. The APNB has five core members, who are Americans living in London, and 100 contact members (Americans living in other parts of Europe).

Publication. The APNB produced an "Open Letter to the People of Belgium" in *NATO Watch* (April 1985), published by the NATO Interest Group of the European Mennonite Peace Committee.

Anglican Pacifist Fellowship

Address. St Mary's Church House, Bayswater Road, Headington, Oxford, OX3 9EY, United Kingdom

Aims and objectives. The Fellowship's aim is to witness to the belief that all war is contradictory to the teachings of Christ. Members sign a declaration as follows: "We, communicant members of the Church of England, or of a Church in full communion with it, believing that our membership of the Christian Church involves the complete repudiation of modern war, pledge ourselves to renounce war and all preparation to wage war, and to work for the construction of Christian peace in the world."

Formation. The Fellowship was founded in June 1937.

Activities. The Fellowship offered counselling and support to conscientious objectors during the Second World War and organized the Hungerford Club, a project of aid to vagrants in London which was based in the church of St Martin-in-the Fields. The Fellowship was active in lobbying at the Lambeth (Anglican bishops) conferences in 1958, 1968 and 1978, contributing to the passage of the resolution on war and violence at the latter conference. In 1974 it launched the "Week of Prayer for World Peace". It also played a part in establishing the working party which produced the report on *The Church and the Bomb* in February 1983.

Membership. There are 1,350 members. An autonomous branch of the Fellowship has recently been established in South Africa and another exists in New Zealand; in the United States the Episcopal Peace Fellowship is an autonomous sister organization.

Publications. Challenge, bi-monthly newsletter; the Fellowship also publishes irregular pamphlets on the Christian doctrine of war and peace.

Affiliations. Fellowship of Reconciliation; National Peace Council; Week of Prayer for World Peace; World Conference on Religion and Peace; and other Christian organizations working for social, political and economic change.

Architects for Peace

Address. c/o Ian Abbott, 41 St James Road, Sevenoaks, Kent, TN13 3NG, United Kingdom

Aims and objectives. Architects for Peace calls for the abolition of nuclear arms and of all other weapons of mass destruction. It is opposed to all civil defence preparations, which it sees as giving "a false sense of security". It works to educate the architectural profession and the public as to the effects of nuclear war.

Formation. Architects for Peace was established in June 1981.

Activities. The group organizes regular meetings at the headquarters of the Royal Institute of British Architects, and it operates a speakers' panel.

Membership. There are approximately 400 members, while sponsors include Sir Hugh and Lady Casson, Berthold Lubetkin, Richard MacCormac, Peter More, Richard Rogers and Sir Peter Shepheard.

Publication. A regular *Newsletter* is distributed to members.

Affiliations. The group is a member of Professions for World Disarmament and Development, the National Peace Council and the UN Association Disarmament and Development Network. It maintains ties with Architects/Designers/Planners for Social Responsibility in the USA.

Armament and Disarmament Information Unit (ADIU)

Address. SPRU, Mantell Building, University of Sussex, Falmer, Brighton, BN1 9RF, United Kingdom

Aims and objectives. The ADIU is an independent source of information and research on a wide range of subjects related to defence policy, arms control negotiations, disarmament, military technology and the defence industry. It aims to foster informed discussion on defence and arms control issues by collecting and disseminating information from a wide variety of sources, for use by researchers, journalists, politicians, governmental and non-governmental organizations, and members of the general public.

Formation. The ADIU was set up in 1978 with the support of the Joseph Rowntree Charitable Trust and is part of the Science Policy Research Unit (SPRU) of Sussex University.

Activities. Claiming to be one of the most comprehensive non-governmental information banks in its field, the Unit monitors over 100 specialist and non-specialist periodicals, the national and international press, commercial intelligence, books, conference papers and a wide range of official publications, with particular attention being paid to UK parliamentary and US congressional proceedings. From this database the ADIU provides (i) accurate, factual information on defence policies worldwide, arms production and trade, weapon characteristics, disarmament and arms control negotiations, and defence spending; (ii) contacts with academics, researchers, government officials, interest groups and other organizations worldwide; (iii) reading lists and further sources of information; and (iv) consultancy work.

During its period of operation the Unit has developed particular expertise in the following areas: (i) British and US defence policy; (ii) the structure and doctrines of NATO and the Warsaw Pact; (iii) European defence debates; (iv) military technology; (v) chemical and biological warfare; (vi) arms control negotiations; (vii) alternative defence and disarmament proposals; (viii) economic aspects of defence; and (ix) the UK defence industry.

Publications. *ADIU Report*, bi-monthly journal; *ADIU Factsheets; ADIU Occasional Papers.*

Artists for Peace

Address. Roughwood Barns, Roughwood Lane, Chalfont St Giles, Bucks, United Kingdom

Aims and objectives. The group seek "to work for peace through our art" and thereby influence public opinion "by making them think more and feel more as a result of our exhibitions".

Formation. The present Artists for Peace arose out of a letter sent to 800 Royal Academy exhibitors in September 1983: its committee was formed in April 1984. A previous organization of the same name had been formed in 1951 by British members of the (pro-communist) Artists International Association.

Activities. The group has thus far staged a single exhibition, at St James's Church, Piccadilly, London, in May–June 1985. Similar events are planned for the future.

Membership. Working members number around 100.

Publications. Exhibition catalogues.

Affiliations. Professions for World Disarmament and Development.

Baptist Peace Fellowship

Address. c/o Fellowship of Reconciliation, 9 Coombe Road, New Malden, Surrey, United Kingdom

Aims and objectives. The Baptist Peace Fellowship aims to "stir the minds and consciences of Baptists to see that war cannot be reconciled with Christ's teaching". It provides a fellowship for British Baptist pacifists.

Formation. Founded in 1932 as the Baptist Peace Fellowship for Ministers, its scope was extended to include all Baptist pacifists in 1934. In 1940 it became affiliated to the Fellowship of Reconciliation. The Baptist Peace Fellowship is an official Baptist organization as recognized by the Baptist Union of Great Britain.

Activities. The Baptist Peace Fellowship produces items for church magazines and makes suggestions for Baptist services on Remembrance Day and similar occasions. A small committee meets regularly to stimulate discussions among Baptists on pacifist issues. The Fellowship holds an annual meeting during the Baptist Union Assembly; it also organizes an annual one-day conference.

Membership. Over 900 members or adherents of Baptist churches are members of the Fellowship; 200 of these are Baptist ministers.

Publications. The Fellowship produces a regular newsletter and occasional inserts for publication in magazines of Baptist churches.

Affiliations. Fellowship of Reconciliation.

Bertrand Russell Peace Foundation

Address. Bertrand Russell House, Gamble Street, Nottingham, NG7 4ET, United Kingdom

Aims and objectives. The Foundation was formed to further the cause of peace, and to assist in the pursuit of freedom and justice. It has sought to identify and counter the causes of violence, and to identify and oppose the obstacles to worldwide community. It was designed to promote research into disarmament, wars and threats of war, and to publish the results. It has consistently laboured to carry on the work of its founder in a spirit of fidelity to the standards of reason and tolerance which he did so much to advance. Accordingly, it has always struggled for freedom of thought and opinion, and for non-exploitative forms of human association.

Formation. The Foundation was established in 1963 by Bertrand Russell (the eminent British philosopher and peace campaigner who subsequently died in 1970 at the age of 97). It took its present shape in 1966, being incorporated as a limited company. Initially the Foundation was sponsored by nine heads of state or government (including Pandit Nehru of India and Kwame Nkrumah of Ghana) and other prominent people (notably Albert Schweitzer); but time depleted the board of sponsors by death, while four statesmen resigned during a controversy over the Foundation's condemnation of the US role in Vietnam in the 1960s.

Activities. The Foundation's work on the Vietnam War in the 1960s arose out of reports received by Russell from Foundation members sent to investigate, as a result of which the first Russell International War Crimes Tribunal was established in 1966. This held two authoritative sessions in 1967, in Stockholm and Copenhagen, to "try" the United States for its actions and policies in Vietnam. Many distinguished people took part (notably Jean-Paul Sartre, Lelio Basso, Peter Weiss and Vladimir Dedijer) and the verdict was unanimous that the United States was guilty of war crimes in Vietnam. (In 1965 Bertrand Russell had publicly torn up his Labour Party membership card in protest against the Wilson Government's support for US policy in Vietnam.)

Further Russell Tribunals, organized by the Foundation, were set up—in 1974 to examine repression in Latin America, in 1978 to investigate allegations of infringement of civil liberties in the Federal Republic of Germany, and in 1980 to examine the situation of the American Indians in both North and South America. The Foundation has also carried out numerous research projects on the political/human rights situation in various countries and regions, on the economic exploitation of the Third World and on disarmament questions—on all of which international seminars have been held regularly. A particular activity has been the organization of appeals and support actions on behalf of political prisoners and persecuted minorities in different parts of the world.

In view of the worsening of East-West relations in the late 1970s and the intensification of the arms race, the Foundation in 1980 joined with the Campaign for Nuclear Disarmament in Britain and the International Confederation for

Disarmament and Peace to launch a new campaign for European Nuclear Disarmament (END)—see separate entry in this country section—which has attracted widespread support all over Europe. The international END campaign has been co-ordinated by the Foundation.

Membership. The Foundation is not a membership organization; its policy is decided by the six-member board of directors.

Publications. The Spokesman, twice a year; numerous books and pamphlets under the Spokesman imprint. The Foundation also handles the publications of the Institute for Workers' Control (IWC).

Affiliations. European Nuclear Disarmament (international liaison committee); informal links with Campaign for Nuclear Disarmament, Amnesty International and other groups.

Book Action for Nuclear Disarmament (BAND)

Address. Flat 2, 45 Trinity Rise, London SW2, United Kingdom

Aims and objectives. BAND aims to encourage those in the book trade to consider the realities of nuclear war and to recognize that this issue cannot be separated from their professional lives. BAND aims to put its members' professional skills at the disposal of other sections of the peace movement so that published material is presented to the public as persuasively and effectively as possible.

Formation. BAND was founded in April 1983.

Activities. Its first major action was the "Read Around the Clock for Peace" 24-hour vigil in Trafalgar Square, London, in September 1983. This featured readings by 75 writers, including Melvyn Bragg, Jill Tweedie and Ian McEwan. BAND holds regular bi-monthly meetings on all aspects of the nuclear issue, with particular reference to the book trade's involvement. It held a "National Peace Book Week" in April 1985 to promote published books on peace issues.

Membership. BAND is open to all members of the book trade, including writers, publishers, agents, booksellers and librarians. Current strength is about 300.

Publication. A bi-monthly newsletter is mailed to members and other peace organizations.

Affiliations. BAND is affiliated to the Campaign for Nuclear Disarmament, Writers and Publishers Alliance for Nuclear Disarmament (USA) and Professions for World Disarmament and Development.

Bradford University School of Peace Studies

Address. University of Bradford, Bradford, West Yorkshire, BD7 1DP, United Kingdom

Aims and objectives. The main thrust of the School of Peace Studies, which as a university department is "precluded from being a dominantly activist organization", is academic but "not . . . in a purely speculative sense". "It sets out to be a centre of applied studies in which a scientific and scholarly thrust is applied to issues of peace and war, non-violent methods of social change, the costs of violence and the worth of human co-operation. Ideally, those who graduate through the School will carry with them all their lives an informed commitment to peace. Hopefully, the School itself will set the goal for its members of reflecting on issues crucial to human peace and will carry on dialogue and collaboration with all those interested in such issues."

Formation. Following discussions in the 1960s about the possibility of establishing a university department in Britain devoted to the study of peace, in 1972 members of the Society of Friends (Quakers) collaborated with the Bradford University administration to found Britain's first chair of peace studies at the University. Concerned Friends set up the Quaker Peace Studies Trust, which raised £75,000 in less than 10 weeks, and the University matched this contribution to incorporate the chair, to which Prof. Adam Curle was appointed in 1973. He retired in 1978 and was succeeded by James O'Connell. From 1973 Bradford University provided the means to build up a department around the chair, commencing with an MA course in peace studies in 1974 and a BA course the following year.

Activities. The School runs a three-year undergraduate course in peace studies and a postgraduate MA course of one year full-time or two years part-time; students who do not have the necessary graduate entry qualifications may register for a non-graduate diploma in peace. In addition, the School is involved in a wide range of research projects, many of them being pursued by students reading for research degrees (MPhil or PhD). Recent research degree projects have covered the following themes: the origins, development and critical appraisal of British civil defence programmes; nuclear weapons and British defence policy; nuclear weapons and nuclear war doctrines; conflict over mineral resources in central Africa; the foreign policy evolution of OPEC member states; the EEC and the Arab-Israeli conflict; water resources on the Palestinian West Bank; women and the peace movement; Asian education in Bradford; prisons and convicted insurgents in Northern Ireland; the Falklands war and the future of the Royal Navy.

The School is co-sponsor, with the Lansbury House Trust, of the Alternative Defence Commission (ADC), which was established in late 1980 to develop proposals for non-nuclear British defence policy alternatives. In its first major report, *Defence Without the Bomb* (published in 1982), the ADC suggested a series of steps for the denuclearization of NATO, including acceptance of a no-first-use policy, withdrawal of battlefield nuclear weapons, withdrawal of all nuclear weapons from Europe, and the decoupling of European NATO defence from US strategic nuclear weapons; it further proposed that if NATO did not agree to take these steps within a specified period the United Kingdom should withdraw from the alliance.

The School has also established a Nuclear Strategy Research Group, which co-ordinates independent research on aspects of nuclear weapons policies and developments, and on proposals for unilateral and multilateral nuclear disarmament.

Another important aspect of the School's activities is to act as a resource centre for peace groups, the media and the wider community. It has a full-time resources and information officer (funded by the Rowntree Trust) and the University Library houses the Commonwealth Collection of over 4,000 books, pamphlets and journals on peace studies and activities.

Publications. In addition to a twice-yearly newsletter, the School produces three series of publications: *Peace Studies Papers, Peace Research Reports* and *Peace Studies Background Briefing Documents.*

Affiliations. The School has established links with other institutions, particularly in Europe and North America.

British Peace Assembly (BPA)

Address. 3rd Floor, 5–11 Lavington Street, London, SE1 0NZ, United Kingdom

Aims and objectives. The Assembly seeks to mobilize public opinion to work for an end to the arms race, for disarmament negotiations and for peaceful co-operation between countries. In particular it calls for unilateral disarmament by the UK as a first step towards general disarmament, and for the removal of US bases from the country. It also demands the full implementation of the 1975 Helsinki Final Act (*i.e.* of the Conference on European Security and Co-operation). The Assembly supports the anti-apartheid movement and other "liberation struggles" since it is "convinced that peace cannot finally be won while oppression continues anywhere in the world".

Formation. The BPA was established in 1980 as the successor to the All-Britain Peace Liaison Group (ABPLG), itself formed in 1974.

Activities. The BPA concentrates on working with trade unions and the labour movement to divert expenditure from the arms industry toward socially useful production. It maintains links with peace activists in other countries including the Soviet Union, East Germany, Czechoslovakia, Finland, Australia and the USA, and it has participated in the international peace march from Kiev to Vienna in March 1982 and the World Assembly for Peace and Life Against Nuclear War in Prague in 1983.

The BPA organizes meetings, conferences and film shows in the UK.

Membership. Over 130 organizations are affiliated to the BPA, including trade unions, political parties, peace groups and "national liberation organizations". Individuals join as associate members. The BPA has a president (currently James Lamond MP) and three vice-presidents (including Alfred Lomas MEP, and Ernie Ross MP).

Publications. BPA Newsletter, bi-monthly; the BPA also acts as UK distributor for World Peace Council publications.

Affiliations. World Peace Council; UN Association of Great Britain. The BPA is accepted as a non-government organization by the UN Special Committee on Disarmament.

British Society for Social Responsibility in Science (BSSRS)

Address. 25 Horswell Road, London, N5 1XL, United Kingdom

Aims and objectives. The BSSRS fights for science and technology to be used responsibly for the benefit of all members of society and aims to demystify science by making scientific and technical knowledge available to working people.

Formation. The Society was founded in 1969 "out of a concern with the way that the military harnesses science and technology for its own needs and how the majority of scientific research and development money is for military purposes".

Activities. In addition to its publishing activities, the BSSRS has a number of local and working groups, the latter dealing with computers, the technology of political control, food, public health, feminism and science, and work hazards. The Society holds regular conferences and seminars.

Membership. There are about 600 individual members.

Publications. Science for People, quarterly, "the only magazine in Britain to deal with the issues raised by science and technology from a socialist standpoint"; *Science on Our side*, booklet; *Technocop*.

Affiliations. Campaign for Nuclear Disarmament.

Campaign Against Arms Trade (CAAT)

Address. 11 Goodwin Street, London, N4 3HQ, United Kingdom

Aims and objectives. CAAT is a broad coalition of groups and individuals committed to the following basic objectives: (i) an end to the international arms trade, and the key role played in it by Britain (currently the world's fourth largest arms exporter); and (ii) the conversion of military industry to socially useful production. CAAT makes no essential political or moral distinction between arms suppliers, being opposed to all arms exports; neither does it prescribe any one specific means for reducing and eventually eliminating arms exports. Within CAAT there is a diversity of opinion on such wider issues as military defence, non-violence and political security, but sponsors, affiliates and supporters of the Campaign are expected to support CAAT's basic objectives, doing this according to the resources and priorities of their own particular concerns.

Formation. CAAT was set up in 1974 by a number of peace and other organizations concerned about the growth in the arms trade in the wake of the 1973 Middle East war.

Activities. In pursuit of its objective of ending the arms trade, CAAT has initiated a number of campaigns with specific themes. Under the heading "arms trade and development", it launched a successful "Bread Not Bombs" week in 1985 (jointly with Oxfam) and organized a repeat campaign in 1986 during the "peace and development" quarter of UK events to mark International Year of Peace, this time co-sponsored not only by Oxfam but also by Christian Aid, Voluntary Service Overseas and other peace and development organizations. Other major themes of CAAT campaigning include (i) the connexion between the arms trade and human rights, and (ii) the need for conversion of the arms industry to socially useful purposes, in which field it works in particular with trade union representatives from the relevant factories.

CAAT maintains comprehensive files on the international arms trade categorized by company, country and topic. These are available to the general public by appointment.

Membership. CAAT has no formal membership structure, although it has some 4,000 supporters, various affiliated local peace groups and a number of national sponsoring organizations. The latter are: Campaign for Nuclear Disarmament, Christian Movement for Peace, *Dawn*, Fellowship of Reconciliation, London Greenpeace, Methodist Division of Social Responsibility, National League of Young Liberals, National Peace Council, Pax Christi, Peace Pledge Union, Quaker Peace and Service, Third World First, UN Association and Women's International League for Peace and Freedom.

Publications. CAAT publishes a bi-monthly newsletter as well as leaflets and other publicity materials.

Campaign Against Militarism—see entry for **Peace Pledge Union (PPU)**

Campaign for Nuclear Disarmament (CND)

Address. 22–24 Underwood Street, London, N1 7JG, United Kingdom

Aims and objectives. CND's aim is to achieve "the unilateral abandonment by Britain of nuclear weapons, nuclear bases and nuclear alliances as a prerequisite for a British foreign policy which has the worldwide abolition of nuclear, chemical and biological weapons leading to general and complete disarmament as its prime objective." Being opposed to all nuclear alliances, CND calls for Britain's withdrawal from NATO "as a positive step in the unravelling of both NATO and the Warsaw Pact".

CND is "opposed to the manufacture, stockpiling, testing, use and threatened use of nuclear, chemical and biological weapons by any country, and the policies of any country or group of countries which make nuclear war more likely, or which hinder progress towards a world without weapons of mass destruction".

Formation. CND was established in February 1958. Its forerunners include the British Peace Committee, which in 1950 collected some 1,000,000 signatures in support of the Stockholm Peace Appeal demanding "an unconditional prohibition of atomic weapons", and the Hydrogen Bomb National Campaign, which was set up in April 1954 and which collected 1,000,000 signatures to a petition calling for the convening of a summit-level disarmament conference and for the strengthening and extension of the UN's powers.

CND had its direct origins in the National Committee for the Abolition of Nuclear Weapons Tests (NCANWT), which had been set up in February 1957 as a co-ordinating body for a large number of local groups, the first of which, the Golders Green Committee for the Abolition of Nuclear Weapons Tests, had been formed by Gertrude Fishwick two years previously.

Other groups established at this time included the Direct Action Committee, set up in April 1957, originally to support and publicize the action of two Quakers planning to sail into a test area at Christmas Island in the Pacific, and the Labour Hydrogen Bomb Committee, formed later the same year.

The immediate trigger for CND's formation took the form of an article by J. B. Priestley, *Britain and Nuclear Bombs*, which appeared in a November 1957 edition of the *New Statesman*. Public response to the piece led Kingsley Martin, the magazine's editor, to call for a meeting to discuss the formation of a mass movement opposed to nuclear weapons. The question was discussed at an NCANWT meeting on Jan. 16, 1958, which was attended by, among others, Bertrand Russell, Canon John Collins, Rose Macauley, Michael Foot, James Cameron, Sir Julian Huxley, Sir Richard Acland, Ritchie Calder and Peggy Duff. The meeting agreed to transform the NCANWT into the Campaign for Nuclear Disarmament. Bertrand Russell was appointed president, with Canon Collins as national chairman and Peggy Duff as general secretary. The inaugural meeting, held on Feb. 16, 1958, in Central Hall, Westminster, attracted 5,000 people.

Activities. CND's activities since its formation have included marches, rallies and demonstrations, meetings, seminars and conferences, at both local and national level. In recent years, it has moved towards support for non-violent direct action tactics. A brief history of the movement follows below.

Its first major demonstration, the march from London to Aldermaston (site of the Atomic Weapons Research Establishment) in March 1958, had been organized (prior to CND's formation) by the NCANWT, the Direct Action Committee and the Labour Hydrogen Bomb Committee, although it was approved of by CND. The CND symbol—a composite of the semaphore signals for "N" and "D"—was designed for this occasion.

During its first year of existence, CND held over 270 public meetings. The second march, from Aldermaston to London during Easter 1959, attracted 20,000 participants. Similar marches in 1961 and 1962 numbered about 150,000, although this dropped to 70,000 the following year. The Campaign received encouragement from the passage of a resolution supporting its aims at the Labour Party conference in 1960, although this was overturned the following year.

Bertrand Russell resigned from CND in 1960, after differences with Canon Collins, and founded the breakaway "Committee of 100 for civil disobedience against nuclear weapons". It staged a number of "sit-downs" outside government buildings in London and at military bases. It was disbanded in 1968, after several years of inactivity.

Support for CND began to decline from 1963 onwards until a recovery in the late 1970s. This decline occurred against a background of the signature of the partial test-ban treaty of 1963 and the election of a Labour Government in 1964, even through the latter remained committed to both the Polaris nuclear submarine programme and to the presence of US nuclear bases in the country. In both the 1959 and 1964 elections, CND had drawn up lists of candidates sympathetic to the Campaign's aims and had organized election forums, but with little eventual impact on Labour Government policy.

CND became involved in the campaign for the withdrawal of US forces from Vietnam during the mid-1960s. In 1966 it staged protests outside the Chinese embassy after China had exploded its first H-bomb, and mounted demonstrations at the launchings of Polaris submarines in 1966–68.

As its support continued to drop away, the Campaign started a national membership scheme in 1966. It continued to hold annual Easter demonstrations during the late 1960s, although on a much smaller scale than several years previously. They included: marches from High Wycombe (1965–6), further Aldermaston marches (1967–8) and a coach tour of England and Wales (1970). In the early 1970s, the Campaign concentrated on local activities and on festivals, including the "Festival for Life" in Victoria Park, London, in 1970, which attracted 20,000 people. In terms of national support, however, 1971 was a low point, with membership standing at just 2,047.

A limited revival began on Clydeside, Glasgow, in 1973, and the Campaign became increasingly active nationwide from 1976 onwards, initially, in response to the US Government's plans to develop the neutron bomb, which was intended to be based in Europe. The real revival, however, followed the NATO announcement in 1979 of the planned deployment of US cruise missiles in Britain and the publication by the UK Government in early 1980 of *Protect and Survive*, the civil defence information booklet. Membership grew from 3,220 in 1978 to 20,000 in 1981 and 50,000 in 1982. A march through London in October 1980 attracted 80,000 people. A large number of local groups were founded at this time, while others which had been part of the Anti-Nuclear Campaign (an organization campaigning against both nuclear arms and nuclear power) or the locally based "Against the Missiles" movement affiliated to CND.

From 1981 onwards, the Campaign has organized local and national demonstrations, and has supported other initiatives such as the women's peace camp at the Greenham Common US Air Force base. Marches through London in October 1981 and June 1982 attracted 200,000 people, while a rally in Hyde Park, London, in October 1983 was attended by an estimated 400,000. A further march through London, organized to coincide with a visit by President Reagan in June 1983, drew approximately 100,000. Some 20,000 supporters travelled to Barrow, Scotland, in October 1984, for a rally at the site of construction of the Trident missile. During Easter 1985 a demonstration at RAF Molesworth, where cruise missiles were due to be deployed, also drew some 20,000 participants.

In August 1985 Meg Beresford was appointed CND general secretary in succession to Mgr Bruce Kent (a Roman Catholic priest who had held the post for six years), while at the CND annual conference in November 1985 Paul Johns (of Christian CND) was elected national chairman in succession to Joan Ruddock (both Kent and Ruddock being elected vice-chairmen of the Campaign). The conference adopted new policies (i) of making links between third-world poverty and expenditure on nuclear weapons, (ii) for campaigning against the proposed second UK cruise missile base at Molesworth and (iii) for campaigning against the US strategic defence initiative (SDI). Resolutions were adopted on the nuclear weapons capability of Israel and South Africa, on nuclear weapons testing in the South Pacific and on uranium mining in Namibia. In addition, a major new initiative was launched called "Basic Case", involving a co-ordinated nationwide public education campaign to communicate CND's positive arguments for nuclear disarmament by Britain.

Membership. CND membership currently totals approximately 360,000, of whom 110,000 are members of the national organization with a further 250,000 belonging to local groups, of which there are 1,400.

Major policy decisions are formulated at the annual delegate conference, which elects the CND council, which meets quarterly. This in turn chooses the national executive committee, which meets monthly.

There are a number of specialist sections, including Labour CND, Green CND, Liberal CND, Trade Union CND, Christian CND, Student CND and Youth CND.

Publications. CND produces two monthly periodicals: *Sanity*, a mass circulation magazine of general coverage; and *Campaign*, which deals with practical questions of tactics, strategy etc., for CND activists.

CND Publications Ltd publishes a range of books and pamphlets on nuclear disarmament and related subjects, including *Protest and Survive*, by E. P. Thompson.

Affiliations. CND is formally affiliated to the National Peace Council, the International Peace Bureau and the International Peace Communication and Co-ordination Network. It maintains active links with many other peace movements, British and foreign, notably European Nuclear Disarmament (END).

Campaign for the Demilitarization of the Indian Ocean (CDIO)

Address. 29 Elsie Road, East Dulwich, London, SE22 8DX, United Kingdom

Aims and objectives. CDIO campaigns for a nuclear-free Indian Ocean and for the non-proliferation of nuclear weapons by the coastal and hinterland states of the Ocean. It is also opposed to the dumping of nuclear waste in the area. CDIO demands the closure of US bases on Diego Garcia and elsewhere in the Indian Ocean, and the return of the island of Diego Garcia to Mauritius.

Formation. CDIO was launched in December 1982.

Activities. CDIO takes part in promotional work within Western peace movements in an effort to persuade them to take up the issue of the superpower military presence in the Indian Ocean. A resolution in support of the aims of CDIO has been passed by the Campaign for Nuclear Disarmament. The group also encourages discussion of the issue within trade unions and the Labour and Liberal parties.

CDIO members have been invited to speak to various organizations on the militarization of the Indian Ocean, and it has organized workshops on the theme of disarmament and development. The group has also set up a mini-exhibition on the "Militarization of the Indian Ocean and the People of Diego Garcia". Petitions have been circulated against the British Government's recruitment of Mauritians to work on the base at Diego Garcia.

Membership. CDIO has approximately 50 members worldwide.

Publications. Arming and Disarming the Indian Ocean by Paul Todd and "Raven". CDIO has also published a number of leaflets, including *The Uprooted Ilwa of the Indian Ocean* and *Demilitarize the Indian Ocean.*

Affiliations. Campaign for Nuclear Disarmament; the CDIO is in the process of establishing a network with other peace movements in the Indian Ocean and the Pacific (there being a group of the same name now active in Mauritius).

Catholic Peace Action (CPA)

Address. 7 Putney Bridge Road, London SW18, United Kingdom

Aims and objectives. Catholic Peace Action is a small group working for peace and social change for justice. It is committed to non-violent direct action and civil disobedience based on Christian belief.

Date of formation. CPA was established as an "affinity group" at the end of a three-day retreat in September 1982, when members prayed and discussed non-violent direct action.

Activities. Since its formation, CPA has undertaken nine "actions" for which members have spent over 120 days in prison between them. CPA leaflets the Ministry of Defence twice a month and has built up some dialogue with workers there. It held a four-day vigil outside the MoD in 1985 in remembrance of Hiroshima and Nagasaki. Members meet regularly to pray for peace.

Membership. At present the group has eight regular members.

Publications. CPA produces a newsletter which is sent to around 250 people every two to three months.

Affiliations. The CPA is affiliated to Christian CND and Pax Christi.

Centre for International Peacebuilding

Address. Southbank House, Black Prince Road, Lambeth, London, SE1 7SJ, United Kingdom

Aims and objectives. This Centre seeks "to bridge the gap between academic peace research and activist movements" by (i) "undertaking projects advancing international understanding and peaceful coexistence between nations", (ii) providing a "working base and resource centre" for the activist groups and individuals, (iii) providing resource materials for schools and (iv) holding mixed seminars for parliamentarians, military officers, churchmen, diplomats, academics etc.

Formation. The Centre was established in 1983.

Publication. The War Games that Superpowers Play: Verification Technologies: the Case for Surveillance by Consent.

Affiliations. Christian Action; Week of Prayer for World Peace; International Physicians for the Prevention of Nuclear War; Greater London Conversion Council; Peace Through Parliament.

Centre for Peace Studies

Address. S. Martins College, Lancaster, LA1 3JD, United Kingdom

Aims and objectives. The Centre's aims are (i) to assess national needs in relation to education for peace and world studies; (ii) to promote awareness of issues relating to peace and conflict within education; (iii) to interpret and clarify the existing educational responses to such issues: education for peace, world studies, multicultural education, development education, education for international understanding; (iv) to identify the priorities for curriculum development and innovation in these fields at both primary and secondary level; (v) to provide educational resources and support for the development of peaceful strategies and skills to cope with both global and local change in the 1980s and beyond; and (vi) to reinforce, and build on, existing regional, national and international networks that are concerned with education about, and for, peace.

Formation. The Centre was established in 1980 within S. Martins. The campus of this Church of England college was formerly the headquarters of the Lancashire Regiment, the Centre being situated on the top floor of the keep, in what was once the regimental armoury.

Activities. The Centre contributes to regional, national and international developments in education for peace, world studies and multicultural education in a variety of ways, including (i) an advice and enquiry service for individual teachers, schools and local education authorities; (ii) a series of occasional papers and other publications; (iii) responsibility for the Schools Council project *World Studies 8–13: A Teacher's Handbook* (published by Oliver & Boyd in 1985); (iv) programmes of specialized in-service training for teachers; (v) lectures and workshops on various issues relating to education for peace and world studies; and (vi) international links and contacts with educators interested in education for peace and world studies.

Publications. The Centre's publications include an annual report on its work and occasional papers.

Christian Campaign for Nuclear Disarmament (Christian CND)

Address. 22–24 Underwood Street, London, N1 7JQ, United Kingdom

Aims and objectives. Christian CND "works to alert the Christian community to the moral and theological implications of a defence policy based on the threat of nuclear weapons".

Formation. After initially being established with the foundation of CND in 1958, Christian CND was reformed in the late 1970s.

Activities. As the largest of CND's specialist sections, Christian CND holds conferences and workshops, takes part in demonstrations and non-violent direct actions, and organizes petitions and lobbies of Parliament. A particular feature of its campaigns has been the conducting of religious services outside military bases. It held "Peace Pentecost" celebrations in 1983 and 1985 and an "Easter Peace Pilgrimage" in 1984.

Membership. There is a mailing list of 5,000 people, mostly CND members; 200 local groups are affiliated to Christian CND.

Publications. Ploughshares, a bi-monthly newsletter; several leaflets and study guides have been produced.

Affiliations. It is represented on the British Council of Churches Peace Forum.

Christian Movement for Peace (CMP)—British Section

Address. c/o Mrs L. Green, Stowford House, Bayswater Road, Oxford, OX3 95A, United Kingdom

Aims and objectives. CMP works for the promotion of international understanding through international Christian work camps whose members perform voluntary service in an area of need.

Formation. CMP was founded in 1923 as a means of bringing together people of different nationalities following the First World War. A British branch was established in 1961.

Activities. CMP's main activities in the UK revolve around the organization of international workcamps in which volunteers from various countries undertake manual or social work on placements.

Membership. There are approximately 50 British members of CMP. Workcamp volunteers themselves are under no obligation to join the Movement.

Publications. Grapevine, bi-monthly newsletter.

Affiliations. Christian Movement for Peace; Christian Organizations for Social, Political and Economic Change (COSPEC); Campaign for Nuclear Disarmament.

Churches Lateral Committee for European Nuclear Disarmament

Address. 4 The Square, Clun, Shropshire, SY7 8JA, United Kingdom

Aims and objectives. This Committee seeks (i) to promote the general aims of the European Nuclear Disarmament (END) movement (see separate entry) within the Churches and amongst Christians generally; (ii) to spread information on specifically Christian peace and disarmament initiatives both in and beyond Europe; (iii) to initiate and/or sponsor Christian peacemaking projects whenever possible, particularly with regard to links between Eastern and Western Europe; and (iv) to collaborate with other Christian peace organizations in the UK and elsewhere.

Formation. The Committee was set up early in 1982 as a response to the declared aim of END to promote a "healing process" in Europe.

Activities. The Committee acts as a clearing-house for its constituent members, who together represent most of the specifically Christian peace organizations in Britain. Its most ambitious initiative to date has been an international seminar on "Towards a Theology of Peace" held in Budapest, Hungary, in September 1984, involving participation from 30 countries and producing deliberations which subsequently influenced Christian work for peace in many parts of the world.

Membership. Movements represented on the Committee include Quaker Peace and Service, Christian CND, the Anglican Pacifist Fellowship, the Fellowship of Reconciliation, Pax Christi and Clergy Against Nuclear Arms.

Publication. END Churches Register, ecumenical quarterly for Christians.

Affiliations. European Nuclear Disarmament (END).

Clergy Against Nuclear Arms (CANA)

Address. 38 Main Road, Norton, Evesham, Worcs., WR11 4TL, United Kingdom

Aims and objectives. CANA is seeking a commitment from the Government that it will not make first use of nuclear weapons, and that it will renounce their possession within a given period of around five years. It is opposed to the deployment of cruise missiles in Britain and to the purchase of Trident, and in favour of a Europe-wide nuclear-free zone. It also demands an end to the sale of British arms overseas and to the conversion of arms-producing capacity to "socially useful" production.

Formation. CANA was founded at Christmas 1982.

Activities. CANA acts principally as an ecumenical group working to support, educate and serve as a resource for clergy. It has held consultative meetings and established links with other professional peace groups.

Membership. CANA has approximately 400 members, composed of clergy of all denominations, full-time church workers and members of religious orders.

Affiliations. CANA has links with other professional peace groups through Professions for World Disarmament and Development.

Coalition Against Star Wars

Address. c/o WDC, 45–47 Blythe Street, London, E2 6LX, United Kingdom

Aims and objectives. The stated aims of the Coalition are (i) the ending of the UK Government's support for the US Strategic Defence Initiative (SDI), commonly referred to as "Star Wars"; (ii) the cancellation of the US–UK memorandum of understanding on British participation in the SDI and the redirection of Britain's high-technology industry towards socially useful ends; (iii) to oppose the further militarization of space and above all the development, testing or deployment of space weapons by any government or agency; and (iv) to support existing treaties and agreements which restrict the militarization of space and to press for such restrictions to be strengthened and enlarged.

Formation. The Coalition was officially launched on June 26, 1986.

Activities. Addressing the launch press conference, opposition Labour Party leader Neil Kinnock condemned the SDI as strategically unsound, a potential major escalation of the arms race and an immense waste of money. The Social Democratic and the Liberal parties also associated themselves with the Coalition, which includes a wide range of peace organizations and churches as well as academics, doctors, environmentalists and development groups. It was envisaged that the Coalition would provide the focus for a programme of campaigns against "the folly" of the SDI.

Committee on South African War Resistance (COSAWR)

Address. Box 2190, London, WC1N 3XX, United Kingdom

Aims and objectives. COSAWR "supports the international campaign to isolate" South Africa and aims to assist and support South Africans opposed to being conscripted into that country's armed forces.

Formation. COSAWR was founded in 1978.

Activities. In addition to its anti-conscription activities, COSAWR "researches into the militarization of South Africa and helps to expose the threat to peace constituted by the Botha regime".

Publications. Register, bi-monthly journal.

Council on Christian Approaches to Defence and Disarmament (CCADD)—British Group

Address. Edinburgh House, 2 Eaton Gate, London, SW1W 9BA, United Kingdom

Aims and objectives. CCADD seeks to study problems relating to defence and disarmament within a Christian context, and to bring "an ethical viewpoint to bear on disarmament, arms control and related issues". In doing so, it reflects "the diversity of views" on disarmament held by Christians.

Formation. CCADD was set up in 1963 by the Rt Rev. Robert Stopford, then Bishop of London.

Activities. CCADD arranges regular discussion meetings, with one major "open meeting" taking place annually. Previous speakers at such meetings have included two US ambassadors (Eliot Richardson and Kingman Brewer), Fred Mulley (when Minister of Defence) and Field Marshal Lord Carver.

CCADD has advised the international affairs division of the British Council of Churches on defence and disarmament matters and has assisted in the preparation of two of the Council's recent reports, *The Sale and Transfer of Conventional Arms Systems and Related Technology* (1977) and *The Future of the British Nuclear Deterrent* (1979 and 1983). The group encouraged the establishment of a lectureship in ethical aspects of warfare at King's College, London University.

Membership. Membership is limited to 500 persons, with admission dependent upon nomination by another member. The Council meets annually to appoint honorary officers and elect a committee of management, which in turn appoints working groups to organize international conferences and other meetings.

CCADD groups have been established in the USA, West Germany, France, the Netherlands and Norway, and there are also members in Sweden and

Finland. While each group is autonomous, CCADD meets as an international body once a year.

Publications. CCADD publications include *Ethics and Power in International Politics* by Prof. Michael Howard, *Ethics and Nuclear Deterrence*, a collection of essays, and several booklets by John Habgood, Sydney Bailey and others.

East-West Peace People

Address. 1 Hampstead Hill Gardens, London NW3, United Kingdom

Aims and objectives. As outlined in its "Peace Charter", East-West Peace People aims to build up contacts between the people (as opposed to the governments) of the two super-power blocs, on the basis of a declared mutual renunciation of war and of the East-West divide. It is committed to working for the extension of human rights, notably those of free expression and communication, as outlined in the 1975 Final Act of the Helsinki Conference on Security and Co-operation in Europe.

The group supports total nuclear and conventional disarmament, "to be carried out in balanced stages without giving any military advantage" to either side. It sees its main focus, however, as breaking down "cold war" barriers, and in this respect criticises some British peace movements for being "hypnotized" by nuclear weapons.

Formation. The group was founded in 1978 as an extension of the work of Peace Action—Atlantic to the Urals, which had been set up by Peter Cadogan, the group's secretary, 18 months previously. Its founders include two Soviet exiles, Vladimir Bukovsky and Alexander Sthromas. The group took its name from the Peace People organization in Northern Ireland.

Activities. The group's principal activities are centred around maintaining and expanding contact with people in Eastern Europe and the Soviet Union. To this end, it provides briefings for visitors to the East and acts as host for people coming to London. It also established contact with the Moscow-based Independent Group for Establishing Trust. The group holds regular monthly meetings and organizes weekend schools. Its members have on occasion engaged in non-violent direct action, notably as part of the demonstration in June 1984 at the Lancaster House economic summit meeting.

It is currently placing an increasing emphasis on contacts with third-world countries and the non-aligned movement, and has held meetings on this matter with the Indian high commission in the UK.

Membership. There are around 100 members, "with nearly as many additional contacts".

Publications. An occasional newsletter is produced between two and four times a year, as well as a number of leaflets, including one in both English and Russian which was designed to be distributed in Moscow during the 1984 Olympic Games.

Affiliations. East-West Peace People is formally affiliated to the National Peace Council, the Human Rights Network and the General Committee on Human Rights, while it also has connections with War Resisters' International, European Nuclear Disarmament (END), Quaker Peace and Service and the UK Trustbuilders, which it helped to establish. It also maintains links with Solidarity activists in Poland.

Electronics for Peace (EfP)

Address. Townsend House, Green Lane, Marshfield, Chippenham, Wiltshire, SN14 8JW, United Kingdom

Aims and objectives. EfP aims to provide a link for electronic engineers who are concerned about the military implications of their profession and to co-ordinate action to reduce the industry's involvement in arms manufacture and development. It encourages plans for the conversion of industry from military to civilian production and for "socially useful" applications of electronics. The group also aims to promote public awareness of the links between the electronics and arms industries.

Activities. Founded in October 1982, EfP has provided technical advice and information for other peace groups, and members have appeared on radio and television. It has recently launched an "Exchange Resources Employment Agency" under which peace-oriented electronics and computing professionals who wish to work with like-minded people and with organizations that "recognize social and moral issues" are notified to potential employers, who can themselves thereby "choose from highly-skilled, talented and motivated people who care about their work and its consequences".

Membership. Approximately 250 members, most of whom are electronic or computing engineers; there are several local branches.

Publications. A twice-yearly journal and a bi-monthly newsletter; the group has also produced a booklet, *The Ground Launched Cruise Missile—A Technical Assessment.*

Affiliations. World Disarmament Campaign; Professions for World Disarmament and Development.

Engineers for Nuclear Disarmament (EngND)

Address. c/o Paul S. Woods, 115 Riversdale Road, Highbury, London, N5 2SU, United Kingdom

Aims and objectives. As laid down in its constitution, EngND's objectives are as follows: (i) reaffirming the aims of the Institution of Civil Engineers, as defined in its royal charter of 1828, which defines the profession as "the art of directing the great sources of power in nature for the use and convenience of man"; (ii) working for the abolition of nuclear arms and other weapons of mass destruction as being contrary to the aims set out in the charter; (iii) awakening the profession and the public to the effects of nuclear war, especially in the field of engineering; (iv) publicity of the diversion of resources from civil expenditure to nuclear weaponry; (v) co-operating with similar professional groups in the fields of engineering, science, architecture, medicine etc.; and (vi) making representations on these issues to appropriate authorities and to the media.

The group does not take a position on the question of whether multilateral or unilateral disarmament should be adopted as the preferred means of achieving its aims. It regards itself as a learned society, and as such does not engage in active campaigning work. It is seeking official recognition from the Institution of Civil Engineers (similar to that extended to the Medical Campaign Against Nuclear Weapons by the British Medical Association), and hopes to persuade it and other engineering bodies to take over its research.

Formation. A meeting of civil engineers at Hebden Bridge (West Yorkshire) in October 1982 resulted in the formation of Civil Engineers for Nuclear Disarmament. Due to the interest generated by the group among mechanical and other engineers, the term "civil" was dropped from the title in November 1984.

Activities. EngND has organized meetings and seminars on matters related to its aims, including a fringe meeting at the Institution's "Engineer in Society" congress at Brighton in 1984 and a meeting on the ethical considerations of engineers working on nuclear defence in Central Hall, Westminster, in January 1985.

Shortly after its formation, working parties were set up to study the effects of nuclear war on the civil infrastructure. These covered water supply, transportation, energy and structures.

Membership. There are approximately 300 members, mostly chartered engineers from the civil, mechanical, structural, chemical and electrical institutions. Regional groups have been formed centred on London, Edinburgh, Leeds and Liverpool. The group holds an annual general meeting, while routine matters are dealt with by an executive committee of eight officers. A number of eminent engineers act as sponsors.

Publications. *The Effect of a Nuclear Attack upon the Water Services of the United Kingdom*, a report of the working party edited by D. M. V. Aspinwall.

Affiliations. EngND is formally affiliated to Professions for World Disarmament and Development, and maintains close links with Architects for Peace, Electronics for Peace, and Scientists Against Nuclear Arms.

European Nuclear Disarmament (END)

Address. 11 Goodwin Street, London, N4 3HQ, United Kingdom

Aims and objectives. The aims of END were set out in its 1980 launch document, the "END Appeal". This demanded the withdrawal "from Poland to Portugal" of all nuclear weapons, air and submarine bases and of all institutions concerned with the research or manufacture of nuclear weapons. It appealed directly to the Soviet Union and the USA to halt the planned deployment of cruise, Pershing and SS-20 missiles in Europe, and it called on both countries to ratify the second strategic arms limitation talks (SALT II) agreement "as a necessary step towards the renewal of effective negotiations on general and complete disarmament".

The Appeal stressed the need for citizens of Europe in both East and West to be free to work for the achievement of these goals, calling for "a European-wide campaign", with formal and informal contacts and exchanges between different organizations and individuals across the ideological divide. It stated that "we must commence to act as if a united, neutral and pacific Europe already exists . . . and disregard the prohibitions and limitations imposed by any national state", although each people of necessity would "decide upon its own means and strategy, concerning its own territory". The movement would, however, "offer no advantage, either to NATO or to the Warsaw Pact", since its ultimate objective was the dissolution of both alliances.

Formation. END was established in early 1980 on the initiative of British activists; it rapidly became the focus of a Europe-wide network of peace groups.

Activities. END concentrates on educational activities (in the UK) and on fostering and maintaining links with peace groups in both Eastern and Western

Europe. While demanding general nuclear disarmament across Europe, its campaigning activities have tended to focus on the deployment of cruise, Pershing II and the SS-20s.

END maintains contacts, through correspondence, group or individual visits, and participation in conferences, with both the "official" (i.e. government-approved) and unofficial peace movements of the Eastern bloc. Such contacts have included meetings or exchanges with the Hungarian Peace Group for Dialogue, the Polish Solidarity union and KOR group, the Czechoslovak Charter 77 group, the Moscow-based Group for Establishing Trust, and peace activists in Yugoslavia and East Germany. END was responsible for much of the publicity surrounding the Berlin Appeal. It has campaigned on behalf of imprisoned peace activists in Eastern Europe, and in particular for the release of members of the Turkish Peace Association. The group was also closely involved in organizing the North Atlantic Network of peace movements in North America, Britain and Scandinavia.

END is the principal organizer of the annual European Nuclear Disarmament conventions, held in Brussels in 1982, in Berlin in 1983, in Perugia (Italy) in 1984, in Amsterdam in July 1985 and at Evry near Paris in June 1986. These have included representatives from numerous European peace groups, with an "official" Soviet delegation taking part since 1984.

END issued a "European Declaration for Peace" in late 1984, which called in particular for: (i) "the furtherance of every possible measure of demilitarization, whether by unilateral national initiatives or by multilateral agreements"; (ii) "the unrestricted flow of communication between the people of both halves of the continent"; and (iii) "the progressive and agreed withdrawal of all foreign forces from the territories of other nations".

During 1985 END expanded its parliamentary work, briefing Westminster MPs and members of the European Parliament in Strasbourg on the US Strategic Defence Initiative and on the possibilities of a realistic alternative foreign policy. END was represented at a conference in Beijing in June 1985 on the theme "Safeguarding World Peace" (organized by the Chinese People's Association for Peace and Disarmament), while END's East European working groups maintained contacts with a wide range of peace opinion in Czechoslovakia, East Germany, Hungary, Poland and the Soviet Union. Through its European network END was involved in the Belgian and Dutch campaigns against the deployment of cruise, and in October 1985 it co-organized a well-attended "Third World War" conference which examined the likelihood of nuclear war starting from a third-world conflict in which the superpowers intervened.

Membership. There is no formal individual membership system; each subscriber to the *END Journal* (see below) is entitled to full voting rights at annual supporters' conferences. Activities are organized under the general direction of a national co-ordinating committee, with a large number of specialized committees and working groups, under such headings as Churches, Women, Higher Education, Parliament, North-South, Netherlands-Belgium, Hungary, Soviet Union, Czechoslovakia, Poland and the GDR. Among END's leading members are Mary Kaldor and E. P. Thompson.

Publications. The *END Journal* (formerly the *END Bulletin*) is published six times a year and acts as the main forum for discussion and communication within the organization. Other regular publications include the *END Churches Register* and *END papers* (published by Spokesman books in co-operation with the Bertrand Russell Peace Foundation). It has also produced a number of special reports (usually in collaboration with Merlin Press) on peace movements in Turkey, Czechoslovakia, Moscow, Hungary and Comiso (Sicily). Other publications include *Beyond the Cold War* and *The Defence of Britain* by E. P. Thompson and *Symbols of War* by Andrew White.

Affiliations. END has formal affiliations to the National Peace Council and the International Peace Communication and Co-ordination Network. It maintains close links with the Campaign for Nuclear Disarmament and the Bertrand Russell Peace Foundation.

Fellowship of Friends of Truth

Address. c/o Ruth Richardson, 52 Green Meadow Road, Birmingham, B29 4DE, United Kingdom

Aims and objectives. The Fellowship of Friends of Truth aim to unite people of all faiths to share their religious traditions and work together for world peace and social justice. The Fellowship takes part in non-violent action to achieve these aims. Members also try to identify themselves, as far as possible, with the oppressed and the disinherited.

Formation. The Fellowship was founded in India in 1949 and set up in England in 1959.

Activities. The Fellowship holds an annual conference and meetings are held in Birmingham every month. It holds a voluntary work week once a year and work weekends. Members also meet for study and meditation.

Membership. There are around 200 members of the Fellowship who are of various nationalities and many religions, although the group is predominantly Christian.

Freeze—see entry for Nuclear Freeze

Fellowship of Reconciliation

Address. 40 Harleyford Road, Vauxhall, London, SE11 5AY, United Kingdom

Aims and objectives. As the UK section of the International Fellowship of Reconciliation, this non-denominational Christian pacifist organization works on the premise that Christians are forbidden to wage war and must work and witness for love as the basis of all relationships, personal, social, commercial and national.

Activities. The Fellowship has participated in numerous campaigns of the British peace movement, notably within the Churches Lateral Committee for European Nuclear Disarmament and in opposition to the British arms trade. It has also sought signatures for a simple declaration worded: "I am prepared to live without the protection of military armaments. I wish to take a stand in our country for the political development of peace without arms." The Fellowship has additionally promoted the development of peace education in schools.

Publications. Newspeace, monthly; *Reconciliation*, quarterly; *Peace Education Newsletter*, for schools.

Affiliations. International Fellowship of Reconciliation; War Resisters' International.

Fellowship Party

Address. Woolacombe House, 141 Woolacombe Road, Blackheath, London, SE3 8QP, United Kingdom

Aims and objectives. The policy aims of this pacifist party include total world disarmament; common ownership of the means of production and distribution; environmental conservation; the pooling of the world's resources for use by all; support for international law and the United Nations; and the dismantling of NATO and the Warsaw Pact.

Formation. The party was founded in June 1955.

Activities. The party was prominent in early campaigns against the H-bomb and nuclear weapons testing by governments leading to the establishment of the Campaign for Nuclear Disarmament in 1958. It has opposed military conscription, the rearming of Germany, Italy and Japan, the wars over Suez, Vietnam and the Falklands, and the invasions of Hungary, Czechoslovakia, Vietnam, Afghanistan and Grenada. It has contested numerous elections without, however, ever winning any parliamentary representation.

Publication. Day by Day, monthly.

Greenham Common Women's Peace Group

Address. outside USAF Greenham Common, nr Newbury, Berkshire, United Kingdom

Aims and objectives. To maintain a vigil outside the base where US cruise missiles are sited. Each woman goes to the camp as an individual and has her own aims and objectives.

Formation. The camp was started in September 1981 at the end of a march from Wales by women protesting about the decision to site cruise at Greenham.

Activities. A number of major demonstrations have been centred round the camp, including the "Embrace the Base" action in December 1982, when over 30,000 women surrounded and sealed off the base. The camp remains in spite of recent attempts by the local authorities to evict the women.

Membership. The camp is open to all women and its membership is constantly changing.

Publications. An occasional newsletter is prepared by women at the camp.

Jews Organized for a Nuclear Arms Halt (JONAH)

Address. 21 Edmunds Walk, London, N2 0HU, United Kingdom

Aims and objectives. JONAH seeks to develop and publicize a Jewish response to the arms race, educating members of the Jewish community about the dangers of nuclear proliferation and providing a forum of discussion on this issue. JONAH believes in a global nuclear freeze and the eventual dissolution of NATO and the Warsaw Pact, while maintaining a "strong, just and non-provocative defence for Britain".

Formation. JONAH was formed in London and Leeds in 1981.

Activities. JONAH holds meetings and debates, organizes vigils and has taken part in mass peace demonstrations, including the Greenham "Embrace the Base" action in 1982.

Membership. Approximately 200 members, although it is "not essentially a membership organization".

Just Defence

Address. The Rookery, Adderbury, Banbury, Oxon., United Kingdom

Aims and objectives. Just Defence seeks to promote "serious and informed discussion" on the question of defence policy, based on an acceptance of five principles that defence should be (i) effective, (ii) non-provocative, (iii) non-nuclear, (iv) morally just, and (v) part of a strategy for the achievement of world security.

Activities. Regular public meetings are held at different locations throughout the UK, and a number of study weekends have been organized. The group emphasizes the importance of involvement with political parties, trade unions and professional organizations, "to ensure that Just Defence perspectives are taken into account". In September 1986 the group was scheduled to co-sponsor (with the Richardson Institute for Conflict and Peace Research) a conference at Lancaster University on the theme "Britain's role in Europe: defence strategies for the 1980s".

Membership. There are approximately 500 members, many of whom are serving or former military officers.

Publications. The group produces a regular newsletter and briefing paper, as well as an explanatory leaflet, *What is Just Defence?* It is associated with the Defence Research Trust, the first publication of which was *Avoiding Nuclear War* (1985).

Lawyers for Nuclear Disarmament (LND)

Address. 2 Garden Court, Temple, London, EC4Y 9VL, United Kingdom

Aims and objectives. Lawyers for Nuclear Disarmament was established to research into and publicize the "legal implications and consequences of the production, possession, deployment and use of nuclear weapons and other weapons of mass destruction". It aims to provide support to groups and local authorities who are opposed to nuclear weapons and to the production of materials for the manufacture of nuclear weapons. It also seeks to encourage the passage of legislation in furtherance of these aims.

Activities. LND participates in numerous conferences and seminars on the question of the legality of nuclear weapons. It was instrumental in setting up the Nuclear Warfare Tribunal, held in London in January 1985. The tribunal was charged with ruling as to whether the use of nuclear weapons is in breach of international law and whether the strategies of NATO and the Warsaw Pact are lawful.

Membership. There are currently approximately 500 members of Lawyers for Nuclear Disarmament, including barristers, solicitors, academics and several students. Membership is open to anyone who is or has been engaged in the legal profession, or related callings.

Publications. The group produces a bi-monthly newsletter for its members, and also the following four pamphlets: *The Illegality of Nuclear Warfare*; *Trade Unionism and Nuclear Disarmament*; *The Legal Status of Nuclear Weapons*; and *A Tax on Peace.* It has also published a series of six working papers on the legal implications of nuclear-free zones and a *Law of Direct Action* pack.

Affiliations. Formally affiliated to the Campaign for Freedom of Information, LND maintains informal links with other peace organizations, notably through Professions for World Disarmament and Development.

Medical Association for Prevention of War (MAPW)

Address. 238 Camden Road, London, NW1 9HE, United Kingdom

Aims and objectives. MAPW studies the causes and effects of war, and examines the "psychological mechanisms by which people are conditioned to accept war as a necessity". It formulates the ethical responsibilities of doctors in relation to war and opposes the use of medical science for any purpose other than the prevention and relief of suffering. The MAPW urge that the energy and finance spent in preparation for war be diverted for work against disease and malnutrition.

Formation. MAPW was founded in 1951 as a result of concern among doctors as to the course of the Korean war and the danger of the use of nuclear weapons in that conflict.

Activities. One of MAPW's first campaigns was against the embargo on medical supplies to China in 1952. The campaign claims partial success to the extent that the embargo on antibiotics and anti-malaria drugs was lifted. A later campaign was directed against the use of napalm and defoliants in the Malayan peninsula. MAPW declared itself opposed to the nuclear test programme in 1955 on the grounds that "nuclear warfare is tantamount to the annihilation of human society".

The group holds regular annual conferences which have included discussion of topics such as: atmospheric contamination due to radioactive fall-out from nuclear tests; the relationship between disarmament and development; the efficacy (or otherwise) of civil defence precautions; and the ethical responsibility of doctors in relation to warfare. MAPW participated in the "Industry and the Bomb" conference in November 1983, making contributions on the theme of the effects of nuclear war on industry and agriculture and on the question of technology transfer to developing countries. It also took part in the International Physicians for the Prevention of Nuclear War Congresses in Helsinki (Finland) in June 1984, in Budapest in mid-1985 and in Cologne in mid-1986. Other conferences in which MAPW has participated, or plans to participate, include: (i) Professional Responsibility in the Nuclear Age (held in 1985 in conjunction with Professions for World Disarmament and Development); and (ii) the Medical Consequences of Chemical and Biological Weapons, scheduled for 1986.

In October 1984 the group established a "speakers' bank" to provide speakers for meetings of such organizations as the United Nations Association and the Campaign for Nuclear Disarmament as well as religious organizations.

In the longer term, MAPW plans campaigns for: (i) the creation of a "We the People" second assembly at the UN; (ii) the worldwide implementation of Article 9 of the Constitution of Japan, which states that "the right of belligerency of the state will not be recognized"; and (iii) an international agreement on a comprehensive ban on "methods and means of warfare designed to induce human disease".

Membership. There are corrently over 500 full members of MAPW, of which membership is open to doctors, dentists, medical scientists and members of allied professions (including psychologists, opticians, pharmacists, nurses, social workers, other health care workers and students in any of these professions). An "associate membership" category is open to people in other fields who are sympathetic to the aims of MAPW.

Publications. MAPW has issued regular bulletins since its inception. These have been variously known as: *Bulletin of MAPW* (until 1964); *Proceedings of MAPW* (until 1981); *Journal of MAPW* (until 1984); and (from 1985 onwards) *Medicine and War: A Journal of International Medical Concern on War and other Social Violence.*

Affiliations. MAPW is affiliated to the International Physicians for the Prevention of Nuclear War, Professions for World Disarmament and Development, National Peace Council, UN World Disarmament Campaign, and the UN Association Disarmament and Development Network.

Medical Campaign Against Nuclear Weapons (MCANW)

Address. Tress House, 3 Stanford Street, London, SE1 9NT, United Kingdom

Aims and objectives. The MCANW is an association of doctors and health care workers which advocates progressive nuclear disarmament as the only means to safeguard people from the medical consequences of nuclear war. In particular, the Campaign argues that its members have a special role to play in securing this objective since they have an ethical responsibility for the health of their patients and for preventative medicine, while also possessing the expertise to judge the likely medical effects of a nuclear attack.

The MCANW endorses a motion passed at the British Medical Association's 1984 annual representative meeting, which demanded "a massive and progressive reduction in world arms spending, both nuclear and conventional, with the diversion of the resources thus freed to health care and welfare, at home and in the developing countries".

Formation. The MCANW was founded in October 1980.

Activities. The Campaign has produced a large amount of resource material, in both published and film form, and has staged several seminars in cities around the UK. It also has four permanent mobile touring exhibitions.

MCANW members gave evidence for the BMA's Board of Science and Education report on the medical effects of nuclear war which was endorsed by the 1983 annual representative meeting and which broadly concluded that health services would be incapable of dealing with the casualties resulting from the lowest anticipated level of nuclear strike against Britain.

Together with the Medical Association for the Prevention of War (MAPW) the Campaign has formed a joint parliamentary committee which has established contact with MPs of both Houses. A lobby held in connexion with the civil defence debate in October 1983 was attended by over 100 MPs.

Also in collaboration with the MAPW, the Campaign has formed a Medical Educational Trust under the auspices of the Lionel Penrose Trust (a registered charity) to undertake further educational work related to the effects of nuclear weapons. MCANW members are also undertaking research projects into the psychological effect on children of living under the threat of nuclear war, and into the lack of perceived urgency among members of the public with regard to the dangers of nuclear weapons. The group has produced a programme on nuclear civil defence for the BBC's "Open Space" series. It has working groups on strategy, civil defence, psychological effects and international relations.

Contact is maintained with similar organizations in both East and West, and a number of visits have been organized to the Soviet Union. MCANW delegates regularly attend congresses of International Physicians for the Prevention of Nuclear War. The Campaign also took part in the Conference on Social Responsibility held in October 1985 under the auspices of Professions for World Disarmament and Development.

Future plans include a growing emphasis on work to educate people to the effects of nuclear weapons, increased support for nuclear freeze policies as providing the best chance for a halt in the arms race and the establishment of a journal to be published jointly with the MAPW.

Membership. The MCANW has approximately 3,500 members, most of whom are doctors, although the Campaign is open to all health care workers, with an additional "supporters" category for people outside the profession.

MCANW policy is decided at general meetings, while the day-to-day administration is carried out by an executive committee under the guidance of a national council; there are 48 regional branches.

Publications. In addition to slide sets, the Campaign has produced two books: *The Human Cost of Nuclear War*, a collection of papers presented at an MCANW symposium in 1983, and *The Medical Consequences of Nuclear Weapons.*

Affiliations. International Physicians for the Prevention of Nuclear War; Professions for World Disarmament and Development.

Meteorologists Against the Bomb

Address. 11 Lambourn Way, Tunbridge Wells, Kent, TN2 5HJ, United Kingdom

Aims and objectives. This group seeks (i) to inform itself of the possible effects of a nuclear war on weather and climate, (ii) to make such information known as widely as possible and (iii) to campaign for the abolition of nuclear armaments.

Formation. The group came into being in late 1984 on the initiative of John Morris.

Activities. The group has held discussion meetings, particularly with a view to devising a popular presentation of the nuclear winter concept.

Affiliations. Campaign for Nuclear Disarmament.

Methodist Peace Fellowship

Address. 9 Coombe Road, New Malden, Surrey, KT3 4QA, United Kingdom

Aims and objectives. The Methodist Peace Fellowship is composed of Methodist members of the Fellowship of Reconciliation (see separate entry) who wish to maintain a separate identity in order to influence other Methodists to accept the aims of the Fellowship of Reconciliation. While renouncing violence and refusing to take part in fighting, members of the Methodist Peace Fellowship are also committed both to finding alternatives to a posture of "weak acquiescence" and to "positive, practical peacemaking".

Formation. The Methodist Peace Fellowship was formed in 1933.

Activities. During the Second World War, the Fellowship provided guidance and counselling for Methodist conscientious objectors, and helped to organize alternatives to military service, including the "Pacifist Forestry and Land Units". Since 1945, it has concentrated on providing a focus within Methodism for the aims and activities of the Fellowship of Reconciliation.

Membership. There are over 720 members of the Methodist Peace Fellowship, all of whom are either full members of the Methodist Church, or are listed on a Church's community role as supporters, sympathizers or church attendants.

Publications. The Methodist Peace Fellowship's literature, which includes leaflets and booklets, is for the most part published on its behalf by the Fellowship of Reconciliation. In 1956, the Methodist Fellowship produced a book entitled *I Am Persuaded*, "a Methodist statement of the case for Christian pacifism".

Affiliations. Fellowship of Reconciliation, with which the Methodist Fellowship has a joint membership arrangement, all subscriptions going to the Fellowship of Reconciliation's general fund, out of which the Methodist Fellowship's expenses are met. The group has representatives on the Fellowship of Reconciliation's general committee.

Mothers for Peace

Address. 30 Gledhow Wood Grove, Leeds, LS8 1NZ, United Kingdom

Aims and objectives. To build bridges of friendship between mothers of different nations and thereby help to increase mutual understanding and reduce the fear and suspicion which impede disarmament. By such means, the group also hope to dispel some of the myths and misinformation presently existing in East-West relations.

Formation. Mothers for Peace was founded in 1981 by two Quaker women (Lucy Behenna and Marion Mansergh) who used the bulk of their life savings to set up a fund enabling mothers to travel to the USA and the Soviet Union with messages of peace and friendship.

Activities. Four mothers travelled to each country in May 1981. Groups of Soviet and American mothers paid return visits to Britain in May of the following year.

A part-time office was established in September 1982. The group hosted a "discussion week", attended by representatives from the USA, the Soviet Union, West Germany and Sweden, in April 1983. Three supporters travelled to the Soviet Union in April-May 1984 as the guests of the Soviet Women's Committee, while four toured the USA at the same time in the company of mothers from Denmark and the Soviet Union. A further ten mothers visited the Soviet Union in October 1984. The group has also sent delegates to peace conferences in East Germany, Bulgaria, Czechoslovakia and Hungary.

Further visits to the Soviet Union, as well as visits to Britain by Soviet women and mothers from other Eastern bloc states took place in 1985. In March 1986 the group participated with American and Soviet mothers in the completion of the Boise Peace Quilt.

Membership. There is no formal membership structure; about 250 groups and individuals are on the mailing list.

Publications. Bridge Builders for Peace, an account of the contacts during 1981–82, and *Fears and Rainbows*, dealing with the 1983 discussion week.

Affiliations. Campaign for Nuclear Disarmament.

The Muriel Davis Youth Peace Fund

Address. c/o Joyce Simpson, 10 Osprey Close, Farlington, Portsmouth, PO6 1LP, United Kingdom

Aims and objectives. To involve young people in various individual and collective projects working for peace.

Formation. After the well-known Quaker activist Muriel Davis died in 1979, the Fund was initiated by Quakers in Hampshire to continue her work for peace with her main priority: the involvement of the young.

Activities. The Fund has helped to establish a full-time peace worker in Dorset; it has also financed young people's participation and attendance at various peace conferences, seminars, demonstrations and job interviews involving peace work. At present it is making a grant to a Quaker youth work camp and exploring means to reduce East-West tension and to create links.

Membership. The Fund is administered by a committee of six, appointed by the Hampshire, Isle of Wight and Channel Islands General Meeting of the Religious Society of Friends (Quakers).

Publications. A leaflet *Working for Peace.*

Affiliations. Religious Society of Friends.

Musicians Against Nuclear Arms (MANA)

Address. c/o Ms C. Mellor, 28 Hydethorpe Road, Balham, London, SW12 0HY, United Kingdom

Aims and objectives. MANA provides musicians for peace groups' benefit events and organizes concerts of classical and pop music as the expression of opposition to nuclear arms.

Date of formation. March 21, 1983.

Activities. MANA has presented concerts in support of the anti-nuclear campaign and has provided musicians for events organized by other peace groups.

Membership. 400 musicians from various walks of musical life.

Affiliations. Campaign for Nuclear Disarmament; Professions for World Disarmament and Development; close links with Members of Equity for Nuclear Disarmament and with Musicians for Peace groups in Europe, Australia and the United States.

190

National Peace Action Foundation for the Promotion of Peace and Racial Harmony

Address. 435A, Kingswood Road, Nuneaton, Warwickshire, United Kingdom

Aims and objectives. The Foundation works for peace and racial harmony. It is a non-party political, non-denominational, multi-racial organization which emphasizes educational work.

Formation. It was launched at Coventry Cathedral on September 23, 1983.

Activities. The Foundation stages lectures and workshops in churches, schools, youth clubs etc. It has a secretary-organizer and a community adviser/press officer. It holds a poetry competition for the C.L.R. James race and peace prize.

Membership. The Foundation is a "collective" rather than a membership organization.

Publications. Information packs; poetry booklets (in conjunction with the Brotherhood Church).

National Peace Council (NPC)

Address. 29 Great James Street, London, WC1N 3ES, United Kingdom

Aims and objectives. The Council's constitution states that its purposes shall be:
"(*a*) To educate people in the ways of peace and the prevention of war. To promote the study of good relations between peoples and of approaches to international co-operation in their religious, scientific, economic, political and social aspects. To consider the policies necessary for the settlement of disputes, the maintenance of peace and the prevention of war, and to promote these policies at all appropriate levels.
"(*b*) To sponsor or encourage the provision of facilities for fostering these aims through foreign travel, international holiday and leisure activities, schemes of mutual aid between nations and individuals, the relief of distress caused by wars and international disputes, and in other relevant ways.
"(*c*) For the securing of greater economy and effectiveness to facilitate co-operation and co-ordination amongst groups and organizations in Great Britain concerned to foster these aims and to provide informational and other services for their common use.
"(*d*) To encourage the full co-operation of British organizations in these aims with similar bodies abroad and to act as a representative body for them in this field."
The constitution also states that the policies of the NPC "shall be independent of and not aligned with those of any particular government or of any political, social or religious grouping".

Formation. The NPC was founded in 1908 at an international peace congress held in London.

Activities. One of the NPC's first resolutions following its creation in 1908 expressed opposition to the spending of £63,000,000 by the British Government on war preparations. During the First World War the Council campaigned against conscription and in the 1930s opposed German rearmament. During the Second World War it held a "peace aims" conference and issued a series of pamphlets on that theme. The Council opposed the descent into cold war in the late 1940s and condemned the Anglo-French Suez invasion of 1956. It protested against the US military intervention in Vietnam and the Soviet-led invasion of Czechoslovakia in 1968.

With the growth in the 1960s of single-focus peace campaigns, the priorities of the NPC changed, as member organizations became in need of reliable information about each other's policies and activities and about the issues at stake. Since then the central role of the Council has been to provide such information, to act as a clearing-house and thereby to encourage and facilitate the work of individual peace groups. Each month a mailing goes out to member organizations containing the Council's newsletter as well as information on new policies and initiatives, together with special briefings on current topics. The latter have ranged from Northern Ireland to the Falklands and the Lebanon, from nuclear disarmament and nuclear power to world development and human rights. The NPC also provides a forum where co-operation and co-ordination among member organizations can be achieved, with consultation at pre-planning stages ensuring, for example, that two major events are not being scheduled for the same date.

Through its representation on international bodies, the NPC provides a link between British peace movements and other independent, non-aligned organizations in the fields of peace, disarmament, energy and human rights. The Council attended both the 1978 and the 1982 special sessions of the UN General Assembly on disarmament.

The NPC's research and educational activities are pursued in part through its United World Trust, which was established in 1955 for such purposes and which has recently launched a new programme of publications and seminars. The NPC is also responsible for the London Peace Information Unit, funded by a capital grant from the (now defunct) Greater London Council.

Membership. Over 180 organizations are affiliated to the NPC, including national and local peace movements, trade unions and other bodies.

Publications. As stated above, the NPC has a monthly mailing of its newsletter and other literature.

Affiliations. International Peace Bureau; UN Non-Governmental Organizations' Committee on Disarmament.

Northern Friends Peace Board

Address. 1 The Grange, Hall Lane, Horsforth, Leeds, LS18 5EH, United Kingdom

Aims and objectives. The Board works as a grass-root campaign within the British peace movement trying to "communicate Quaker attitudes of non-violence and reconciliation to others in the peace movement" and "stressing the need for disarmament in general". Its main field of specialization is East–West relations.

Formation. The Board was established in 1913, when Friends in the north of Britain were concerned about the drift to war.

Activities. The Board's activities have included: (i) aiding conscientious objectors; (ii) reconciliation work involving parties to the conflict in Northern Ireland; (iii) international disarmament work, especially through the International Peace Bureau; (iv) grass-roots peace work in Britain to help the broader peace movement.

At present the Board is "seeking to deepen and widen its relationships with Soviet bodies, especially the Soviet Peace Committee, and use this basis for mutual trust to overcome important barriers in the way of East–West communication". The Board also seeks to "tackle infringements of religious freedom [in the Soviet Union] which create a bad image in the West".

Membership. The Board serves the members of the Religious Society of Friends in the north of England, who number about 6,000.

Publications. The Board has published various studies and pamphlets.

Affiliations. National Peace Council; United Nations Association; World Disarmament Campaign; International Peace Bureau; United Nations Non-Governmental Organizations' Committee on Disarmament.

Nuclear Freeze

Address. 82 Colston Street, Bristol, BS1 5BB, United Kingdom

Aims and objectives. This new movement seeks a comprehensive worldwide freeze on the testing, deployment and production of all categories of nuclear weapons—and, as steps towards this end, a comprehensive test ban and a freezing of the space weapons programme. A key objective is "to help create international co-operation for the freeze specifically amongst NATO countries and non-nuclear countries with the aim of third-party intervention in the nuclear arms race". Accepting that a freeze would not in itself banish the threat of nuclear war, the movement believes that it would be "a positive first step towards arms reduction" and seeks to mobilize the "massive" public support for a freeze into political action.

Formation. After a loose coalition of pro-freeze groups had in September 1984 formed itself into the Nuclear Weapons Freeze Clearing House based in Bristol, a national Nuclear Freeze campaign was launched on Nov. 13, 1985, at a meeting chaired by the actress Jane Asher. The campaign has drawn support from MPs of all four main parties and is also backed by numerous people prominent in the arts and the Church.

Activities. On the basis that opinion polls have shown over 70 per cent of the UK electorate as being in favour of a nuclear freeze, the movement is conducting a "Freezevote" campaign, consisting of a door-to-door referendum of registered voters; results obtained have consistently shown a positive response to the basic freeze proposal of around 80 per cent. Another major initiative is the "Freeze Nuclear Testing Campaign", involving the lobbying of MPs to persuade them to sign an early day motion (placed before the Commons on March 26, 1986, by two Labour members, two Conservatives, a Liberal and a Social Democrat) calling on the Government to seek a resumption of US–Soviet–UK trilateral negotiations towards the achievement of a comprehensive test ban treaty. The movement has also initiated a "Freeze Dialogue" campaign, involving the elaboration of detailed proposals for presentation at seminars and in discussions with leading policy makers.

At the movement's second national assembly, held at Warwick University on April 5–6, 1986, it was decided to launch a "Freeze Bandwagon" mobile publicity campaign which would tour the country with the aim of making Freeze "a household name". Other priorities include the expansion of the campaign within the Churches, the development of national and international contacts and networking, letter-writing campaigns and the preparation of educational material for sixth-form pupils and teachers. With a view to developing the campaign's international dimension, a freeze conference was held in Geneva in September 1985, sponsored jointly with the US Nuclear Freeze movement.

Membership. By mid-1986 the Nuclear Freeze campaign had some 5,000 national supporters, together with 120 local contacts and 320 patrons.

Publications. *Freeze Update*, monthly newsletter; various pamphlets and broadsheets.

Affiliations. National Peace Council.

Oxford Project for Peace Studies

Address. 30 Sunderland Avenue, Oxford OX2 8DX, United Kingdom

Aims and objectives. This Project acts as a charitable trust promoting peace studies at university level.

Formation. The Project was launched in 1980.

Activities. During 1984–85 the Project developed links with academic institutions in Oxford and elsewhere, held an essay competition for students in higher education on the subject of "The Search for Peace", and organized a series of lectures at St Antony's College, Oxford. It is currently raising funds in hope of establishing a Centre for Peace Studies at Oxford.

Membership. There are seven trustees (Mary Allsebrook, Sir Richard Doll, Dr Frank Ellis, Prof. John Ferguson, Dr George Johnson, Elaine Kaye, Prof. Kenneth Kirkwood), who appoint a 14-member executive committee. The committee can invite observers and subcommittees may include co-opted members. There is a small group of Friends of the Project.

Peace Advertising Campaign (PAC)

Address. P.O. Box 24, Oxford, OX1 3JZ, United Kingdom.

Aims and objectives. An organization which is "dedicated to using the media for peace", PAC aims to identify issues suitable for use as advertising images which would be easily accessible to the public at large and which would provide the peace movement with support for its campaign.

Formation. PAC was set up in 1980 by a group of Quakers in Oxford who were involved in media work.

Activities. PAC produces advertising material for the peace movement in a wide range of media. Its principal focus to date has been billboard posters which are designed, produced and marketed by PAC. It has also sponsored a poster-designing competition. PAC has undertaken national publicity campaigns for CND demonstrations and has also designed advertising material for the World Disarmament Campaign.

In 1983, PAC assisted in the financing and marketing of a cinema commercial made by Parallax Pictures. The commercial urged filmgoers to join CND or any peace group. PAC is planning to market a further Parallax commercial, arguing the case against the planned purchase of Trident missiles.

A series of advertisements and poster campaigns were produced to support the unilateral disarmament conclusions of the report produced by the Church of

England working party on *The Church and the Bomb*. PAC has also produced a range of smaller posters, badges, postcards and stickers.

It is currently acting as advertising agent for organizations outside the confines of the mainstream peace movement, including the Guatemala Committee for Human Rights and Oxfam's "Hungry for Change" campaign.

Future projects include liaison with television producers to encourage a wider coverage of nuclear issues on television and closer co-operation with nuclear-free zone authorities, trade unions and specialist peace organizations in order to produce advertising materials targeted to their needs.

Membership. PAC is composed of seven or eight regular members, including media workers and designers, with one full-time salaried administrator.

Publications. Billboard posters, smaller posters, stickers and badges.

Affiliations. PAC is affiliated to the Campaign for Nuclear Disarmament, to the National Peace Council and to the World Disarmament Campaign.

Peace Chariot

Address. 7 Furnace Cottages, Crow Edge, Sheffield, S30 5HF, United Kingdom.

Aims and objectives. This group seeks to live in harmony with the earth, animals and plants and to learn to be self-sufficient.

Formation. It was launched in 1983.

Activities. The group is involved in various issues ranging from peace and anti-nuclear campaigns, to ecology issues and to spiritualism.

Publications. Various leaflets.

Peace Education Network (PEN)

Address. 33 Churchill Avenue, Kenton, Middlesex, HA3 0AY, United Kingdom.

Aims and objectives. The Network exists to promote research and development in the field of peace education and to provide support and a means of communication for teachers and others interested in making education a force for peace. It seeks to promote the concept of peace education among the general public and to develop links with those similarly involved in other countries.

Formation. The PEN was established at an inaugural meeting at the United World College of the Atlantic in Glamorgan, Wales, in June 1981.

Activities. Conferences have been staged annually since the group's inception, that for 1985 (at Beechwood College, Leeds) having as its main theme the evaluation of experiences in peace education and the development of effective strategies for promoting education for peace. Members have also attended conferences and other meetings organized by other groups on related subjects. The Network has sought to counter criticisms of the concept of peace education made in the press and elsewhere.

Membership. There are some 350 members, comprising teachers, lecturers, parents and others involved in education.

Publications. *Newsletter*, three times a year, a recent issue of which took the form of a comprehensive list of resources for peace education.

Peace Education Project (PEP)

Address. Dick Sheppard House, 6 Endsleigh Street, London, WC1H 0DX, United Kingdom.

Aims and objectives. The Peace Education Project works to develop in schoolchildren the ability to recognize conflict and understand its causes; it encourages them to search for alternative solutions to problems which lead to conflict. Its statement of principles contains a quotation from the writer H. G. Wells: "Human history becomes more and more a race between education and catastrophe".

Formation. The Project was set up in 1981 by the Peace Pledge Union.

Activities. PEP's principal activity is the design and distribution of teaching materials, usually taking the form of workpacks, which the Project claims are "objective and without dogma". It has organized several workshops for teachers, including a series on "co-operative games" and on approaches to teaching about subjects such as racism, sexism, human rights and non-violence. It has produced an exhibition on its work, and its members, on occasion, give talks in schools. Through the media of seminars, conferences and interviews, it also attempts to foster and maintain contact with schools' inspectors, college lecturers, parent-teacher associations and, where possible, the public at large.

Publications. A quarterly journal, *PEP Talk*, which the Project is currently planning to develop "into a professional educational journal".

Workpacks produced to date have included ones on Martin Luther King, Gandhi, and general topics such as "Heroism", "War and Society", "Law and Order" and the Antarctic treaty. It has also published factsheets.

Membership. The Project is supported and promoted by the Peace Pledge Union and the Lansbury House Trust. Its current membership is composed of 50 individuals and 20 affiliated organizations. Policy is decided by a co-ordinating group whose meetings are open to the public.

Affiliations. The Project is formally affiliated to the Peace Education Network, and maintains close links with Pax Christi, Quaker Peace and Service and Teachers for Peace.

Peace Pagoda of Nipponzan Myohoji

Address. Willen Lake, Milton Keynes, United Kingdom.

Aims and objectives. Nipponzan Myohoji is a Buddhist foundation working for the elimination of nuclear weapons and other weapons of mass destruction, and the establishment of world peace and social, cultural and racial justice.

Activities. Founded in China by Nichidatsu Fujii in 1917, the first *Nipponzan Myohoji* was established in Japan in 1924. Fujii met Mahatma Gandhi in India in 1933, since when there has been a close association between *Nipponzan Myohoji* and the Gandhian philosophy of non-violent revolution. After the Second World War the construction of "peace pagodas" was begun in 1946 as part of an effort to prevent the outbreak of a further war by reviving Buddhist peace teachings. The first pagoda was completed in Hanaukayama, Japan, in 1954, and there are now a total of 60 pagodas in that country, together with four in Sri Lanka, two in India and one each in Austria and Britain (Milton Keynes). Currently four pagodas are under construction in Japan, two in Sri Lanka and one each in India, Britain (Battersea) and the United States (Boston, Massachusetts).

A joint pilgrimage with members of the Christian faith from Canterbury Cathedral to London is planned to accompany the opening of the Battersea pagoda. It is hoped that many more pagodas will be built all over the world, in order that "gradually the mental and spiritual illness of the age" will be replaced by a time of "enlightenment and harmony".

Members of *Nipponzan Myohoji* have also organized peace marches of "continuous prayer", which have included a continental march across the USA in 1976, the "Pilgrimage for Humanity" in 1983 (involving marches to Berlin from Warsaw and Brussels) and the Aldermaston to Faslane walk in 1979, when members held fasting and prayer ceremonies outside military bases and arms factories. Monks and nuns of the group have also staged regular marches from Tokyo to Hiroshima since 1946.

Membership. Approximately 300 Buddhist monks and nuns are members of *Nipponzan Myohoji*, and these enjoy the support of around 3,000 "followers and helpers".

Publication. Sarvodaya, monthly magazine.

Affiliations. Nipponzan Myohoji has numerous affiliations with international and national peace organizations.

Peace Pledge Union (PPU)

Address. Dick Sheppard House, 6 Endsleigh Street, London, WC1H 0DX, United Kingdom.

Aims and objectives. Members of this pacifist organization sign a pledge as follows: "I renounce war and I will never support or sanction another." Members of all religions, atheists and agnostics, can equally commit themselves through the pledge to the renunciation of war, to research into the causes of war, and into non-violent solutions, to the repudiation of discrimination against others, and to striving for reconciliation and goodwill as positive alternatives to the methods which bring about war. Against this background the PPU seeks to change the attitudes which encourage violence, opposes military conscription and supports the right of conscientious objection and the right to allocate tax payments to peaceful purposes. The Union also gives high priority to peace education work, through its Peace Education Project (see separate entry).

Formation. The PPU was founded in October 1934 by Dick Sheppard, who took the above-quoted pledge from a US Armistice Day sermon and appealed for individuals to commit themselves to it.

Activities. Basing itself on "the individual decision to start the process of disarmament by a personal renunciation of war and violence", the PPU has over the years been involved in various campaigns "to explore and promote non-violent methods of resistance to oppression and injustice, and alternative ways of living that will alter the existing nature of a society that, as currently organized, breeds war".

These have included (i) an ongoing Campaign Against Militarism which "aims to create an awareness of the nature of militarism and its implications for the struggle for a just and warless world"; (ii) trying to make young people aware of the implications of joining the armed forces and to discourage them from joining, while at the same time searching for creative and socially useful alternative employment; (iii) advising and supporting people in the armed forces who for reasons of conscience want to leave but find this difficult; (iv) campaigning for the abolition of compulsory military service where it exists and supporting conscientious objectors; (v) supporting women's campaigns against militarism; (vi) encouragement of new, creative, more accurate and less dogmatic approaches to the study of peace, war and related issues in schools; (vii) campaigning against the availability of "war toys" and promoting "co-operative" games; (viii) participating in the search for racial justice and harmony through non-violent means (in which connection the Union has produced and distributed a range of material on Martin Luther King); (ix) seeking a deeper understanding of the Northern Ireland problem and encouraging "a creative community-based approach aiming at the withdrawal of all troops and para-militaries"; (x) campaigning against the trade in armaments, particularly in association with the Campaign Against Arms Trade; and (xi) opposing nuclear power "because of its inherent dangers and its intimate relationship with nuclear weapons".

The PPU has also established (in 1984) a Young Peacemakers Club, which under the slogan "Tomorrow is ours and tomorrow is made today" aims to involve younger children in thinking about what "peace" may mean.

Membership. The PPU has some 1,250 members.

Publications. The Pacifist, monthly journal; *Studies in Non-Violence,* three times a year; a range of other literature, including a Young Peacemakers newsletter (10 a year) and the output of the Peace Education Project (see separate entry).

Affiliations. The PPU is a British affiliate of War Resisters' International; within Britain it has links with a range of peace organizations and is a member of the National Peace Council.

Peace Tax Campaign (PTC)

Address. 13 Goodwin Street, London, N4 3HQ, United Kingdom.

Aims and objectives. The Campaign seeks to secure for the individual the legal right to choose, on grounds of conscience, not to pay taxes for military purposes but to direct an equivalent proportion of tax payments into a "peace-building fund" which would be used exclusively for non-military peacemaking.

The Campaign's statement of principle stresses the fact that the individual's personal responsibility for acts of inhumanity, even if ordered by a "lawful" authority, was established at the Nuremburg war crimes trials following the Second World War. It also points out that the traditional right of conscientious objection to military service is becoming outdated since future wars are likely to be fought by a relatively small number of professional soldiers with sophisticated weapons of mass destruction, the use of which would constitute an act of inhumanity. The Campaign demands that the right of conscientious objection be extended to the right to refuse to pay for the construction and maintenance of these and other weapons.

The role of the "peace-building fund" is as yet undecided, although suggested uses include the development of international mediation processes, funding of peace and conflict research, conversion of military industries into socially useful ones and provision for more contacts and exchange visits between different peoples. The fund would not be used to support any existing services or projects, since this could release money for arms manufacture.

Formation. In 1969 Lord Fenner Brockway suggested in the House of Lords that conscientious objection should be extended to paying for war. The issue lay dormant until 1979, when an appeal for the institution of a peacemaking fund received support from several MPs and six bishops. By 1981, 47 MPs had declared their sympathy for the campaign and in the same year the first annual general meeting adopted a constitution and appointed a committee.

Activities. The first attempt to divert a portion of income tax away from military expenditure was made by a supporter of the campaign in 1981 by means of sending two separate cheques to the Inland Revenue. In the same year, amendments to the Finance Bill to provide for an individual refusal to pay for war were tabled by two Labour MPs.

The PTC aims to concentrate on securing sufficient support among MPs to ensure a full debate in Parliament. On March 26, 1986, Dennis Canavan and 11 other Labour MPs introduced in the Commons a bill "to allow people to withhold that portion of their tax which is at present spent on arms and related purposes, and to facilitate the payment by them of sums so withheld to peaceful non-governmental purposes"; however, introduced under the 10-minute rule, it failed to secure a second reading on April 11.

In September 1986 PTC representatives attended the first International Peace Tax Conference, held in Tübingen (West Germany).

Membership. Approximately 5,500 full supporters, with a further 2,000 who have stated that they support the Campaign in principle. A large number of organizations have declared their support, including the following: Anglican Pacifist Fellowship; Campaign for Nuclear Disarmament; Christian Action; Green Party; Fellowship of Reconciliation; Greenpeace; National League of Blind and Disabled; Pax Christi; Peace Pledge Union; *Plaid Cymru*; Quaker Peace and Service (who also provide the Campaign with a grant); Scottish Council for Civil Liberties; Women's International League for Peace and Freedom; and the Woodcraft Folk.

Publication. Peace Tax Campaign, a bi-monthly newsletter.

Peace Through Parliament

Address. 9 Beaverbrook Road, London, N19 4QG, United Kingdom.

Aims and objectives. Peace Through Parliament aims to encourage and assist people in Britain to communicate to their member of Parliament their concerns on the dangers of the continuing nuclear arms race. They hope to convince the population at large of the value of lobbying individual MPs to achieve peace.

Formation. The group started work in 1983 by producing 15,000 copies of a basic leaflet which was circulated through peace and environmental groups.

Activities. Peace Through Parliament is primarily involved in assisting other peace groups in their parliamentary work. Periodically they publish literature concerning people's experiences of seeing their MP which is circulated through other peace groups.

Membership. Peace Through Parliament has no members as such but around 200 people have contacted the group with donations.

Publications. The group produces a leaflet *Peace Through Parliament* which encourages people to contact their MP and gives advice on how to go about it. They also produce discussion sheets.

Peacemakers Relief Society

Address. 6 Endsleigh Street, London WC1 0DX, United Kingdom

Aims and objectives. The Society seeks to assist people who suffer financial hardship as a consequence of non-violent action for peace.

Formation. The Society was established in 1982.

Activities. The Society administers a fund from which resources are available to peace activists, or their dependants, whose own means of support are exhausted. Beneficiaries are asked to contribute money back in to the fund as soon as they are able, so that others can be assisted without straining the Society's resources.

Membership. Membership of the Society is open to both groups and individuals, all of whom contribute to the fund. The Society's activities are co-ordinated through a national committee which co-operates with locally based contacts.

Pensioners for Peace International—see entry under International Organizations

Philosophers for Peace

Address. c/o Thomas C. Daffern, 108 Ledbury Road, London, W11 2AH, United Kingdom

Aims and objectives. This organization seeks to provide "a decentralized global communications network to help facilitate the effective sharing of ideas, perspectives and research among all those people interested in exploring the philosophical issues involved in the whole question of peace in the widest sense".

Formation. The group emerged in 1984 out of discussions between Thomas C. Daffern and John-Francis Phipps following publication of the latter's book *Time and the Bomb.*

Activities. The group has organized various seminars and discussion groups on the underlying causes of conflict, considering ways to heal such conflicts and the role of philosophy in relation to peace issues. The group's seminar and lecture programme aims to encourage eminent thinkers, as well as members of the general public, to engage in dialogue towards the peaceful reconciliation of divergent philosophical opinions underlying contemporary conflicts.

The group is currently preparing a register of interested bodies to assist in the building of a Co-operative Peace Research Network, which is projected as an umbrella organization for peace-minded practitioners of philosophy and other academic disciplines such as history, theology and linguistics.

Membership. The group has no formal membership structure, being open to all who have "a personal interest and commitment to philosophy".

Affiliations. Philosophers for Peace acts as convenor for the formation of a UK section of International Philosophers for the Prevention of Nuclear Omnicide.

Professions for World Disarmament and Development (PWDD)

Address. 139 Vauxhall Street, London, SE1 1SL, United Kingdom

Aims and objectives. PWDD seeks to co-ordinate the actions of groups of professionals opposed to nuclear war and to develop strategies for relating disarmament to development programmes.

Membership. PWDD links Architects for Peace, Book Action for Nuclear Disarmament, Clergy Against Nuclear Arms, Electronics for Peace, Engineers for Nuclear Disarmament, Journalists Against Nuclear Extermination, Lawyers for Nuclear Disarmament, Medical Association for Prevention of War, Medical Campaign Against Nuclear Weapons, Members of Equity for Nuclear Disarmament, Musicians Against Nuclear Arms, Psychologists for Peace and Scientists Against Nuclear Arms. These groups have an aggregate membership of about 5,000.

Psychologists for Peace (PFP)

Address. c/o Ms M. Hilton, Department of Psychology, St George's Hospital Medical School, Jenner Wing, Cranmer Terrace, London SW17, United Kingdom

Aims and objectives. PFP aims to apply the principles of psychology and the results of psychological research to the process of peace. The group also works to increase the level of public debate and awareness about this aspect of the peace process. In addition, PFP assists other peace organizations needing information on psychological issues.

Formation. PFP has existed since 1981.

Activities. PFP organizes conferences and lectures and runs seminars at British Psychology Society conferences. A one-day PFP conference in London 1984 drew about 80 participants.

Membership. Around 550 psychologists, ranging from students to professors, are members of PFP.

Publications. Quarterly newsletter.

Affiliations. PFP assists the Medical Campaign Against Nuclear Weapons and the Campaign for Nuclear Disarmament in their work; it is an affiliate of Professions for World Disarmament and Development.

Quaker Peace & Service (QPS)

Address. Friends House, Euston Road, London, NW1 2BJ, United Kingdom

Aims and objectives. QPS is the department of the Religious Society of Friends in Britain and Ireland concerned especially with international understanding, world development and peace work and witness. It "gives expression to the corporate experience of Friends (Quakers) that the Holy Spirit moves people as individuals or groups to serve the needs of their fellows and to promote peace". The Service works for non-violent solutions to social injustices and against poverty; for disarmament and against the arms race; for sustainable development and against ecological degradation; for human rights and responsibilities and against exploitation and torture; for international understanding and "against confusion and misrepresentation". In its peace work, QPS bases itself on the 1660 Quaker "Peace Testimony" (written by George Fox and presented to Charles II) rejecting "all outward wars and strife, and fightings with outward weapons, for any end, or under any pretence whatever".

Activities. The central activity of QPS is its network of over 50 "practical peace-building projects and programmes" in some 15 countries, notably in Africa, seeking to assist the self-development of people, including refugees and the victims of natural disasters. "Projects are planned with the long-term goal of devolving full responsibility to local people. The initial stages of participation are often assisted by the network of Quaker contacts, which has been developed over centuries as a result of both the Society's active international work and its historic concern for peaceful conflict resolution."

QPS is also closely involved in the activities of the UK and European peace movements. It has participated in vigils protesting against the deployment of new missiles in Europe and supported the Campaign Against Arms Trade, the Peace Tax Campaign and the Campaign for Nuclear Disarmament. Since April 1980 the Service has run the "Quaker Peace Action Caravan", which gives performances on the street, at fairs and at shows seeking to involve the general public in the concerns of the peace movement. The Caravan also conducts workshops exploring the principles of non-violence, working in particular with fourth-to-sixth form school pupils and their teachers.

Publication. *QPS Reporter*, quarterly.

Affiliations. Friends World Committee for Consultation; International Peace Bureau.

Richardson Institute for Conflict and Peace Research

Address. Dept. of Politics, University of Lancaster, Lancaster, LA1 4YF, United Kingdom

Aims and objectives. The Richardson Institute conducts and promotes peace studies and conflict research at the academic level; it also seeks to extend its activities into the broader community through popular publications, conferences and public meetings. The Institute seeks to redress the imbalance of a situation in which "in Britain more money is spent on weapons research in one hour than is spent on peace research in a whole year".

Formation. The Institute has its origins in the Lancaster Peace Research Centre founded in 1959. In 1965 the newly established Lancaster University was the first British university formally to include peace research in its prospectus, through the appointment of a fellow in the politics department. The Institute is named after Lewis Fry Richardson, a British Quaker who pioneered peace studies in the aftermath of the First World War.

Activities. The Institute's research activities have resulted in dozens of articles and papers appearing both in academic journals and in popular form, covering topics such as the nuclear arms race, alternative work for military industries and alternative defence policies for Britain. Current plans include the continued development of the post-graduate research programme and of two new research projects, namely (i) Alternative Work for Military Industries, involving an examination of the particular conversion problems associated with the Trident submarines being built at Barrow-in-Furness and the Tornado programme based at the British Aircraft Corporation's works near Preston; and (ii) Computer-Based Peace Studies Packages, including the "Worldwise" micro-computer atlas and the "Worldwise: Nuclear Weapons" package from which all the world's nuclear weapons systems can be displayed with text and computer graphics giving details of size, range, numbers and accuracy.

In conjunction with the Conflict Research Society, the Richardson Institute organized a Conference on Accidental Nuclear War at Manchester Town Hall in November 1985, resulting in a decision to work for the establishment of an

International Committee on Accidental Nuclear War. A further conference was scheduled to be held (in conjunction with the Just Defence organization) at Lancaster University in September 1986 on the theme "Britain's role in Europe: defence strategies for the 1980s". The Institute has also been involved with a group of Sheffield-based lecturers in a project to establish peace studies as an advanced-level option in schools.

Publications. In addition to a regular newsletter and its "Worldwise" material (see above), the Institute has published a series of monographs and completed MSc and PhD dissertations. The monographs include *Alternative Work for Military Industries: Military Spending and Arms Cuts—Economic and Industrial Implications* (contributors: Dave Elliot, Mary Kaldor, Dan Smith, Ron Smith); *Target North-West: Civil Defence and Nuclear War in Cumbria, Lancashire, Manchester, Merseyside and Cheshire* (by Robert Poole & Steve Wright); *Peace Education in Great Britain: Some Results of a Survey* (by Hanns Fred Rathenow & Paul Smoker); *Swords into Ploughshares: A Study of the Conversion Problems associated with the Trident and Tornado Programmes* (by Barbara Munske); *Trident Town: A Study of the Opinions of the People of Barrow*.

Affiliations. International Peace Research Association.

Schools Against the Bomb

Address. 22–24 Underwood Street, London, N1 7JQ, United Kingdom

Aims and objectives. This group aims to educate schoolchildren as to the dangers of nuclear war and to ensure that they have access to "the full and unbiased facts" about nuclear weapons. It also organizes and participates in demonstrations on nuclear issues.

Formation. Schools Against the Bomb was set up in 1981 by pupils at two private schools, with an inaugural conference being held at Frensham Heights school in the same year.

Activities. The group repeatedly pressed the BBC to agree to screen *The War Game* (a film commissioned by the BBC from Peter Watkins in 1965, which was eventually transmitted in August 1985). A demonstration to this effect was held in 1982, and the group also launched a petition campaign on the subject. Members of the group made their own television programme in 1982 for the BBC's Open Door series, this being subsequently shown in a number of schools and colleges throughout the country.

In 1984 representatives of the group met with Michael Foot MP (Labour) for a lobby of the House of Commons in order to protest against provisions of an Education Bill proposed by Edward Leigh MP (Conservative), which sought among other things to outlaw "peace education" activities in schools. A subsequent petition campaign called for "balanced and fair" discussion of the nuclear issue as part of the educational curriculum.

Schools Against the Bomb holds occasional conferences (including one in 1983 which was addressed by E. P. Thompson). In the future, the group intends to hold a number of debates on the nuclear weapons' issue in schools around the country.

In 1985 it undertook a series of activities to coincide with International Youth Year, including leaflet production and distribution and the convening of an international youth peace camp in co-operation with Youth CND. Other plans for the future include the institution of regular exchanges between pupils in the

UK and the Netherlands with those of East Germany and the Soviet Union. It also intends to set up a pen-pal network with pupils from Eastern bloc countries.

Membership. Schools Against the Bomb has some 400 members, with over 25 individual school groups, each comprising between ten and 50 members.

Publications. The group produce a regular newsletter and a factsheet outlining its activities. They have also published a leaflet entitled *Opportunities for School Leavers.* They intend to expand their publishing programme to include broadsheets on various aspects of nuclear disarmament.

Affiliations. The group work closely with Youth CND, and it is also expanding its links with similar groups overseas.

Scientists Against Nuclear Arms (SANA)

Address. London Production Centre, Broomhill Road, Wandsworth, London, SW18 4JQ, United Kingdom

Aims and objectives. SANA exists to promote and co-ordinate the activities of scientists wishing to assist moves to reverse and halt the arms race. It seeks to provide reliable factual information and well-informed speakers, and attempts to promote awareness among members of the scientific community of their "special responsibility" towards achieving disarmament. Since much technical information relating to defence and disarmament is contained in technical reports and specialist journals, SANA aims to make this material more readily available to, and understandable by, a wider audience.

Although SANA's title refers only to nuclear weapons, the group believes that nuclear disarmament cannot be considered in isolation from other disarmament measures and that the dangers from other weapons of mass destruction (notably chemical and biological weapons) cannot be overlooked.

Formation. SANA was formed in 1981.

Activities. SANA is active nationally and locally in providing information to various peace and disarmament organizations and to members of Parliament, church and trade union leaders, county and borough councillors and other individuals with influence on public policy. It has provided briefing notes for MPs and parliamentary candidates, and also speakers for numerous meetings, debates, symposia, television and radio programmes. Over 20 SANA research and study groups have been set up.

SANA has set up a Local Authorities Advisory Service to provide these bodies with information, advice and practical assistance on the effects of nuclear weapons, the effectiveness of civil defence and related matters. It provided technical briefing to the Campaign for Nuclear Disarmanent and to local authorities for the "counter-exercise" Operation Hard Luck, which played a part in the cancellation of the Home Office's Operation Hard Rock civil defence exercise. The group also provided evidence and advice to the British Medical Association's inquiry into the medical effects of nuclear war. It gave scientific and technical advice to television producers, notably for the BBC's *A Guide to Armageddon* programme.

In November 1984 SANA, in conjunction with the national steering committee of nuclear-free-zone authorities, organized a national briefing tour on nuclear winter theories in which Prof. Paul Ehrlich, Dr Anne Ehrlich and Dr Richard Turco spoke about these theories to public meetings, in university lectures and seminars and in briefings for MPs and local authorities.

SANA convened an international symposium of scientists on the problems and prospects of nuclear disarmament in September 1983, and a further "disarmament conference" was held in 1985.

Membership. SANA has some 1,000 members in the UK, including natural and social scientists, engineers and technologists. General policy is decided by a national co-ordinating committee elected by an annual membership conference. SANA has a council of sponsors, who include 27 fellows of the Royal Society.

Publications. SANA has published a range of material on the nuclear winter concept, including a video and several booklets and information leaflets. It also acts as distributor for material on this subject produced by other sources. The group has also produced general information material on nuclear weapons.

Affiliations. SANA maintains contacts with scientists in other countries who have similar aims, including the USA, Canada and the Soviet Union. It has been a prime mover in the establishment of a European Network of Scientists for Nuclear Disarmament and encouraged and supported the formation of Science for Peace in Canada and of Scientists Against Nuclear Arms in Australia. It is a member of Professions for World Disarmament and Development.

Shareholders Question Investment in the Arms Race (SQIAR)

Address. Pump Close, Shilton, Oxon, OX8 4AB, United Kingdom

Aims and objectives. SQIAR aims to bring together a group of people who will buy small numbers of shares in UK defence contract companies. These people will then attend AGMs, follow company reports and activities, raise questions and open debate about UK company involvement in nuclear weapons production.
     The group believes that the decision-making process in public companies can be very undemocratic and wishes to raise debate and democracy within companies.

Activities. SQIAR was set up when eight Greenham Common women bought 16 shares in Tarmac. This civil engineering contractor built the silos for cruise missiles at Greenham Common, the A90 complex for Trident warheads' fabrication at Aldermaston and the fence at the Molesworth proposed cruise base. Questions have been raised at three of Tarmac's AGMs.
     SQIAR hopes to develop this idea to major defence contract companies. The group is still small, but some shares in British Aerospace have been acquired and a SQIAR supporter attended the AGM.
     SQIAR held its first supporters' meeting in 1985.

Affiliations. SQIAR is not officially affiliated to any other groups but contacts are made through the Ethical Investment Research and Investment Service (EIRIS).

Snowball Civil Disobedience Campaign

Address. Green Fields, 48 Bethel Street, Norwich, United Kingdom

Aims and objectives. The primary objective of the Snowball Campaign is to make the British Government take steps towards the reduction of weapons of mass destruction. To this end the Campaign asks that Britain starts voting in favour of multilateral disarmament proposals at the United Nations, regardless of how the USA votes; that Britain publicly encourages the USA to accept freeze proposals; and that Britain takes some unilateral step towards a freeze or reduction in arms.

Activities. The Snowball Campaign's activity consists of cutting the perimeter fences of military bases and installations. Each person cuts one strand of the fence and each time more people participate in this act of civil disobedience. The Campaign covers at least ten different bases.

In March 1985, 81 people symbolically cut one of the strands of the wire at USAF Sculthorpe. No attempt was made to enter the base. After the cut was complete each of the 81 went to their chosen police station and handed in their statement explaining why they had cut the wire.

After each stage of the Snowball, letters are written to the authorities explaining their actions and pledging that the Snowball will stop if action is taken to stop the arms race.

Student Peace Project

Address. 77 Hungerdown Lane, Lawford, Manningtree, Essex, CO11 2LX, United Kingdom

Aims and objectives. The Project aims to encourage students of all disciplines to relate their dissertations, theses or other projects to the resolution of conflict and the establishment of peaceful relations at local, national and international levels. Awards are granted "for all quality work".

Formation. The Project was founded in 1979 by "some of Britain's leading educationalists", who believe that all arts, sciences and other studies can be related to the establishment of peaceful relationships.

Activities. The Project refunds, upon receipt of any work sent to them, the cost of photocopying and postage, and it also makes small grants of up to £100 for most of the work thus submitted, providing it is of a reasonable standard.

Publications. A collection of abstracts of work received by the Project has recently been printed, while the Project also makes available the complete work of each student for the cost of photocopying and postage.

Teachers for Peace

Address. c/o 22–24 Underwood Street, London, N1 7JQ, United Kingdom

Aims and objectives. A national organization of teachers, lecturers, youth workers, parents and others with an interest in education, Teachers for Peace aims to answer young peoples' questions about nuclear war; it believes that information about the dangers of nuclear war and the possible alternatives to such a war should be widely available in schools and colleges in forms designed for each age group. The group believes that teachers have a duty to discuss the means by which disarmament could be achieved, whether unilateral or multilateral, although it is opposed to the use of the classroom as a suitable recruiting ground for any organization.

Formation. Teachers for Peace was formed in May 1981 at a CND conference.

Activities. The group distributes peace education materials and is currently producing material for use in science lessons, consisting of a series of exercises on the questions of choice and decision-making about the applications of science with special reference to the nuclear threat. The group seeks to persuade education authorities to support peace education in their area. It acts as an information centre for teachers preparing their own resources for peace education, and in co-operation with Professions for World Disarmament and Development it contributed to a study paper reproduced in the National Union of Teachers' *Education for Peace.*

Teachers for Peace is developing links with teachers' organizations overseas who also wish to see the issues of peace and disarmament introduced into school and college curricula. It participates in international conferences when possible.

Membership. There are some 700 individual members and 60 school groups, some of whom produce their own newsletter relating to the educational situation in their area.

Publications. The group publishes a termly (three times a year) newsletter, which gives news about developments in peace studies and also acts as a cumulative resource on materials for teaching; about 50 local education authority libraries subscribe to this newsletter.

The group also publishes *Dovepax,* a resource pack for peace studies.

Affiliations. National Peace Council, Campaign for Nuclear Disarmament, Professions for World Disarmament and Development, and the Society of Teachers Opposed to Physical Punishment. Teachers for Peace is recognized as a non-governmental organization by the UN.

Trade Union CND (TUCND)

Address. 22–24 Underwood Street, London, N1 7JQ, United Kingdom

Aims and objectives. As a specialist section of the national Campaign for Nuclear Disarmament, the group works "to promote CND's aims and objectives within the British trade union movement".

Activities. Trade Union CND has carried out research and campaign work on issues such as civil defence and the conversion of the arms industry. It co-operates closely with CND's trade union affiliates and gives support to union members wishing to form workplace CND groups. Its long-term focus is to achieve the integration of nuclear disarmament concerns and issues into the general industrial and political work of trade unions.

Membership. There is no individual membership separate from that of national CND, to which 26 trade unions and 500 other union organizations are affiliated.

Publications. TUCND News, bi-monthly newsletter; the group has also produced *Working for Peace,* a guide to workplace campaigning.

Affiliations. Labour Disarmament Liaison Committee, National Trade Union Defence Conversion Committee.

Women for Life on Earth (WFLOE)

Address. 2 Bramshill Gardens, London NW5 1JH, United Kingdom

Aims and objectives. WFLOE is a network promoting the links between feminism, peace and ecology through the means of non-violent direct action, public education and information exchange.

Activities. WFLOE supports and encourages non-violent direct action, such as a march from Cardiff to Greenham Common USAF Base in 1981 which resulted in the establishment of the Women's Peace Camp at the base. It has inspired the setting up of many more peace camps in Britain, Europe and the US.

WFLOE provides speakers and educational material on eco-feminist issues for conferences, workshops and local meetings. It puts women in touch with each other locally, nationally and internationally and publishes a quarterly magazine. The WFLOE has been instrumental in the setting up of groups all over the country.

Membership. WFLOE has about 360 women members world-wide and six men.

Publications. WFLOE publishes a quarterly magazine and has produced an international anthology of women's writings on the environment entitled *Reclaim the Earth.*

Women for World Disarmament (WWD)

Address. c/o Kathleen Tacchi-Morris, North Curry, Taunton, Somerset, TA3 6HL, United Kingdom

Aims and objectives. Women for World Disarmament seeks to "enable women to express their concern at the long delay in implementing world disarmament, and to assist in alerting the public mind to its urgent need and its possibility in this day and age". It supports the achievement of "general and complete disarmament" through the machinery of the UN.

Formation. The organization was set up in Sheffield (UK) and Warsaw (Poland) in 1950.

Activities. It holds regular meetings, usually in Taunton or London, including an annual joint session with the UN Association on International Women's Day (March 8) at the House of Commons. Speakers at recent meetings have included Brig. Michael Harbottle and guests from the Soviet Union. It was represented at the UN Women's Conference in Nairobi (Kenya) in July 1985.

Affiliations. WWD is affiliated to the UN Association in the UK, the UN Non-Governmental Organizations' Committee on Disarmament, the National Peace Council and the British Peace Assembly; it is "twinned" with the UN Association in Weimar, East Germany. It co-operates with the Church of England's Community Programme and is part of the Women's Peace Alliance network.

Women's International League for Peace and Freedom (WILPF)—British Section

Address. 17 Victoria Park Square, London, E2 9PB, United Kingdom

Aims and objectives. As the British section of the WILPF, this movement seeks to eradicate the political, social, economic and psychological causes of conflict and to create the conditions for peace, including complete and universal disarmament and the renunciation of violent or coercive methods of settling disputes.

Formation. The British section dates from the time of the establishment of the International League in 1915.

Activities. The British WILPF participates in the major campaigns of the UK peace movement, notably opposition to the British nuclear deterrent and the

208

presence of nuclear missile bases on British soil. It has an active branch structure wherein peace issues are looked at from the particular perspective of women.

Membership. The British section has about 350 members.

Publications. Peace and Freedom, quarterly; *Current Affairs*, monthly newsletter.

Affiliations. Women's International League for Peace and Freedom.

Women's Peace Alliance (WPA)

Address. P.O. Box 240, *Peace News*, 8 Elm Avenue, Nottingham 3, United Kingdom

Aims and objectives. The WPA exists to promote peace by enabling women to support each others' initiatives for disarmament. It serves as an umbrella organization for numerous women's peace groups, satisfying a demand for communication between them so as to avoid duplication and to gain strength from an exchange of ideas and a pooling of resources.

Formation. WPA was founded in December 1981.

Activities. WPA's various actions have included the mass lobby of Parliament by Families Against the Bomb in May 1982, the "Embrace the Base" action at Greenham Common in December 1982, the Stock Exchange "die-in" in June 1982 and the mass phone-in to the *Sun, Daily Mail* and *Daily Telegraph* in November of that year. Members have also taken part in Women's Day for Disarmament and International Women's Day events over the last four years, both in Britain and overseas.

The WPA also runs workshops on non-violent direct action and use of the media, and operates a "telephone tree" for rapid exchange of information. It also has an exhibition called "Herstory of the Women's Peace Movement".

Membership. WPA groups include: Women for Life on Earth, Women's International League for Peace and Freedom, Mothers for Peace, Women Oppose the Nuclear Threat, Women's Peace and Protest Group and the peace camps at Greenham and at La Ragnatela (Comiso, Italy). A large number of independent local groups are also affiliated to the WPA.

Publications. History of the Women's Peace Movement by Anne Piper.

Affiliations. National Peace Council.

World Disarmament Campaign (WDC)

Address. 45–47 Blythe Street, London, E2 6LX, United Kingdom

Aims and objectives. The WDC's principal objective is to gather support for the disarmament proposals as contained in the Final Document of the UN Special Session on Disarmament of 1978 (UNSSOD I). The main recommendations were as follows: (i) the abolition of nuclear weapons and weapons of mass destruction; (ii) the phased abolition of conventional weapons over a period of years, leading to general and complete disarmament, excepting weapons necessary for internal security and as contributions to a UN peacekeeping force; and (iii) the transfer of military expenditure to development, with a view to ending world poverty.

Formation. The WDC was set up in 1979.

Activities. A petition circulated in the UK in support of the UNSSOD I recommendations gathered over 2,250,000 signatures. It was presented to the UN Secretary-General in 1982 before the holding of UNSSOD II in September of that year. In view of the "disappointing but not disastrous" outcome of the second UN session, it was decided to keep the Campaign in being and to give it a proper organizational structure.

The WDC has recently concentrated its campaigning activities on the nuclear freeze issue, organizing public meetings, sponsoring advertisements and producing material in support of an immediate halt to the testing, production and deployment of further nuclear weapons as a first step towards reversing the global arms race. It is currently promoting the "World Peace Action Programme", a comprehensive programme for disarmament, which has been prepared as a basis for common campaigning following discussion with other peace movements in Britain and abroad. By the end of February 1986 the Programme had been endorsed by some 130 peace movements throughout the world.

The WDC also runs a letter-writing campaign (based on its *Letternews* publication), which provides information and guidance on writing to the media and to elected representatives.

Membership. The WDC has approximately 3,000 individual members and some 200 affiliated organizations, drawn from all political and denominational spectra. Lord Fenner Brockway and the Rev. Dr K. G. Greet serve as co-chairmen, with Prof. Frank Barnaby as director.

Publications. Network and *Letternews.*

Young Peacemakers Club—see entry for Peace Pledge Union (PPU)

Youth Campaign for Nuclear Disarmament (Youth CND)

Address. 22–24 Underwood Street, London, N1 7JQ, United Kingdom

Aims and objectives. A specialist section of CND, Youth CND works to promote the movement's aims among young people.

Formation. The group was "re-launched" in 1981.

Activities. Youth CND's first major act was a festival in Brockwell Park, London, in 1983, which featured pop groups such as the "Style Council" and "Madness" and which was attended by over 70,000 people. In the summer of 1984, the group organized a 200 mile march around nuclear bases in southern England, which was completed by 135 members. During 1985 it staged a number of events to tie in with International Youth Year.

Membership. There are 14,000 national members; many more are active in the 200 or so local Youth CND groups; members must be under the age of 21.

Publications. Sign of the Times, quarterly newsletter; *Protest,* a monthly publication sent to local groups.

Other Movements

Buddhist Peace Fellowship

Address. Gilletts, Smarden, nr. Ashford, Kent, TN27 8QA, United Kingdom

Chilwell Women's Peace Camp

Address. outside USAF Chilwell, Nottingham Road, nr. Beeston, Notts., United Kingdom

Committee for International Justice and Peace of the Catholic Bishops' Conference of England and Wales

Address. 39 Eccleston Square, London, SW1V 1PD, United Kingdom

Committee for Nuclear Issues of the Catholic Bishops' Conference of England and Wales

Address. 39 Eccleston Square, London, SW1V 1PD, United Kingdom

Cruisewatch

Address. P.O. Box 28, Newbury, Berks., United Kingdom

European Proliferation Information Centre (EPIC)

Address. 258 Pentonville Road, London, N1 9JY, United Kingdom

Ex-Services Campaign for Nuclear Disarmament Group

Address. 15 Mangotsfield Road, Mangotsfield, Bristol, BS17 3JG, United Kingdom

Feminism and Non-Violence Study Group

Address. 69B Landor Road, London SW9, United Kingdom

Gandhi Foundation

Address. 68 Downlands Road, Purley, Surrey, CR2 4JF, United Kingdom

Green Campaign for Nuclear Disarmament

Address. c/o Linda Churnside, 120 Hartfield Road, Forest Row, East Sussex, United Kingdom

International Voluntary Service (IVS)

Address. Ceresole House, 53 Regent Road, Leicester, LE1 6YL, United Kingdom

Journalists Against Nuclear Extermination (JANE)

Address. c/o NUJ, Acorn House, 314 Gray's Inn Road, London, WC1X 8DP, United Kingdom

Labour Action for Peace

Address. 37 Hollingworth Road, Petts Wood, Kent, BR5 1AQ, United Kingdom

Labour Campaign for Nuclear Disarmament

Address. c/o Labour Party, 144–152 Walworth Road, London, SE17 1JT, United Kingdom

Members of Equity for Nuclear Disarmament (MEND)

Address. 98A Uplands Road, London N8, United Kingdom

Mennonite Centre

Address. 14 Shepherds Hill, London, N6 5AQ, United Kingdom

Menwith Hill Peace Camp

Address. outside US Base, Menwith-with-Darley, nr. Harrogate, N. Yorks., United Kingdom

Molesworth Peace Camp

Address. Peace Corner, Old Weston Road, Brington, nr. Huntingdon, United Kingdom

Network on Militarization and Development (NOMAD)

Address. 57 Upper Lewes Road, Brighton, Sussex, BN2 3FG, United Kingdom

Pax Christi—British Section

Address. St Francis of Assisi Centre, Pottery Lane, London, W11 4NQ, United Kingdom

Peace and Animal Welfare (PAW)

Address. 5A Grangewood Close, Shiney Row, Houghton-le-Spring, Tyne & Wear, DH4 4SD, United Kingdom

Peace Prayer Centre

Address. Seniors Farmhouse, Semley, Shaftesbury, Dorset, United Kingdom

Polariswatch

Address. c/o Campaign ATOM, 35 Cowley Road, Oxford, United Kingdom

Prolifers for Peace

Address. 26 Parkfield Road, London, NW10 2BG, United Kingdom

Student Campaign for Nuclear Disarmament

Address. c/o CND, 22–24 Underwood Street, London, N1 7JG, United Kingdom

Unitarian and Free Christian Peace Fellowship

Address. 3 Lower Whitley Farm, Farmoor, Oxford, United Kingdom

Upper Heyford Peace Camp

Address. Portway, Camp Road, Upper Heyford, Oxon., United Kingdom

Whores Against Wars

Address. c/o English Collective of Prostitutes, King's Cross Women's Centre, 71 Tonbridge Street, London WC1, United Kingdom

Women Oppose the Nuclear Threat (WONT)

Address. c/o CND, 22–24 Underwood Street, London, N1 7JG, United Kingdom

Wales

Campaign for Nuclear Disarmament—Wales
CND Cymru

Address. 2 Plasturton Avenue, Pontcanna, Cardiff, CF1 9HH, United Kingdom

Aims and objectives. CND Cymru subscribes to the objectives laid down in national CND's constitution, although it reserves the right to make alterations to these at its annual conference.

Formation. After functioning as a region of national CND for many years, CND Cymru was established as a separate section in 1982.

Activities. Prior to its formal establishment as a separate section, CND Cymru's members took part in organizing the march from Wales which resulted in the establishment of the women's peace camp at USAF Greenham Common. Recent activities have included actions related to civil defence measures and leafleting outside factories where components for the Trident missile system are assembled. In February 1985, it held a "Nuclear-Free Wales Week" in celebration of the third anniversary of the passage of nuclear-free zone resolutions by all eight county councils in Wales. CND Cymru takes part in the national Eisteddfod festivals.

Membership. There are approximately 3,000 individual and 120 group members; 60 organizations, including trade unions, churches, political parties and local councils are affiliated.

Publications. Its monthly newspaper, *Campaign Wales*, is distributed to groups and affiliates; various leaflets and other material are also published; all material is printed in both Welsh and English.

Fellowship of Reconciliation in Wales
Cymdeithas y Cymod yng Nghhymru

Address. 14 Kenilworth House, Heol y Port, Cardiff, CF1 1DJ, United Kingdom

Aims and objectives. The Fellowship aims "to state positively and constructively the message of reconciliation of man to God through Christ, to apply unflinchingly Christ's revolutionary principle of love however impractical it may seem under present conditions, and to pursue a common quest after an order of society in accordance with the mind of Christ".

Formation. The Fellowship in Wales dates from the time of the origination of the International Fellowship of Reconciliation at a meeting in Cambridge in 1914, at which at least one Welshman was present. The Welsh Fellowship became autonomous in 1974.

Activities. The Fellowship in Wales grew quickly because the Christian pacifist tradition was already strong in that country. For 60 years the Welsh section worked alongside its English counterpart, but in 1974 it became autonomous and now has its own general secretary and executive committee and is responsible for its own fund-raising and activities. Current activities include retreats twice annually, sponsored pilgrimages and other fund-raising methods, talks on the Fellowship to church groups and others, and participation in Christian witness to reconciliation as being the heart of peace-making.

Membership. There are currently about 170 members, two-thirds of the generation with direct memories of war and connections with the Welsh Christian pacifist tradition and a third younger members "identifying with the new call to peace through reconciliation and non-violent protest".

Affiliations. International Fellowship of Reconciliation.

Scotland

Anti-Trident Campaign

Address. 420 Sauchiehall Street, Glasgow G2, United Kingdom

Aims and objectives. This "single weapon" campaigning group focuses on the submarine-launched Trident nuclear missile system, seeking to reverse the decision of the Conservative UK Government to purchase and deploy the system (which is to be based on the River Clyde in eastern Scotland).

Formation. The group was created in 1981 as the Scottish Campaign Against Trident (SCAT) and subsequently modified its name to convey its decision to broaden its organization and activities to encompass the whole of Britain.

Activities. The Campaign acts as an umbrella organization for opposition to Trident, which is centred in the non-Conservative political parties, trade unions and local councils as well as in the peace movement. Methods used include political lobbying, mass petitioning, demonstrations and actions, and media work.

Faslane Peace Camp

Address. below St Andrew's School, Shandon, nr. Helensburgh, Dumbartonshire, United Kingdom

Aims and objectives. The Faslane Peace Camp was established to protest against nuclear weapons and the society which breeds them. It also aims to inform people about nuclear weapons and show the links between defence spending and deprivation at home and abroad. It seeks to demonstrate an alternative way of life based on non-violence, caring, honesty, openness and trust.

The Camp aims to serve as a constant reminder of the nuclear threat and members are committed to learning about peace while opposing all forms of exploitation such as racism and sexism. The Camp also acts as a base for peace actions and a focal point where people can meet to exchange ideas.

Formation. The Camp was established on June 12, 1982. The site was granted a licence by Dumbarton district council in October 1982 with 13 conditions attached. In the spring of 1985 the Camp was given a five-year site licence with only two conditions. In January 1982 the peace campaigners set up another camp at Holy Loch which lasted for nine months.

Activities. The protesters at the Faslane Peace Camp have organized numerous activities since 1982, including: a fast and vigil on the Hiroshima weekend in 1982; a blockade in November 1982; the first Scottish women's demonstration, attended by 2,000 women in March 1983; a four-day Fast for Life to coincide with Hiroshima-Nagasaki day in 1983; removing a 40-ft fence on more than one occasion; a march and blockade in December 1983; a fast for Namibia in 1984; organizing a month of action "Turn the Tide Against Trident" in November 1984; stopping the Polaris warhead convoy several times.

Members of the Faslane Peace Camp plan to keep up their activities in order to stop the extension of the Faslane and Coulport bases and aim eventually to close down the base altogether.

Membership. The camp has a fluid population but between ten and 25 women and men are present at any one time.

Publications. The Peace Camp produces a magazine, *Faslane Focus* and has produced a book, *Faslane: Diary of a Peace Camp*, written by the campers and published by Polygon Books.

Affiliations. The Peace Camp has friends all over the world and is affiliated to the Alternative Employment Study Group, Helensburgh CND, Edinburgh Justice and Peace Group, Scottish CND and the Scottish National Party.

Scottish Campaign for Nuclear Disarmament (SCND)

Address. 420 Sauchiehall Street, Glasgow G2, United Kingdom

Aims and objectives. Scottish CND shares the same objectives as national CND.

Formation. It was set up as a Scottish counterpart to British CND in the early 1960s.

Activities. The movement's main period of growth has occurred since 1979. Since that time it has staged various demonstrations at bases such as Faslane and Holy Loch. It held an Easter demonstration and "die-in" in Glasgow and Faslane in 1983, and in the following year staged "Easter Alert Scotland 1984", which linked ten US bases around Scotland. It co-operated with Youth CND in a two-day festival to mark International Youth Year at the beginning of June 1985. Other aspects of Scottish CND's campaigns include ones against sea-launched cruise missiles and for the creation of a nuclear-free North Atlantic. It also holds regular parliamentary lobbies.

Membership. In mid-1986 individual membership was around 12,000; many others are active in Scotland's 150 local CND groups. Over 180 organizations are affiliated to the movement, including peace groups, religious bodies, trade unions and political parties.

Publications. SCND News; Fortress Scotland—A Guide to the Military Presence (by Malcolm Spaven).

Affiliations. National Peace Council; Scottish Council for Civil Liberties. Scottish CND also works closely with the Scottish branch of the Nuclear Freeze Campaign and the Anti-Trident Campaign (which, as the Scottish Campaign Against Trident, was in part set up by Scottish CND).

Other Movements

Fellowship of Reconciliation in Scotland

Address. 16 Claremont Gardens, Milngavie, Glasgow, G62 6PG, United Kingdom

Parents for Survival

Address. 8 Blackburn Crescent, Glasgow, G66 3PQ, United Kingdom

Peacemaking in a Nuclear Age

Address. Bishop's House, Fairmount Road, Perth, PH2 7AP, United Kingdom

Northern Ireland

Community of the Peace People

Address. "Fredheim", 224 Lisburn Road, Belfast, BT9 6GE, United Kingdom

Aims and objectives. The Peace People are working for the creation through non-violent means of a just and peaceful society in Northern Ireland. They aim to promote dialogue between different political groups, to inform people on political and social issues and to provide support for people organizing locally to solve local problems. They also campaign for the establishment in Northern Ireland of a judicial system based on the highest standards of justice and respect for human rights and human dignity.

Formation. The Community of the Peace People arose out of an incident in August 1976 when the driver of an IRA getaway car was shot dead by a pursuing British Army patrol. The car crashed, killing three young children and gravely injuring their mother. Following a number of rallies to protest against this incident in particular and the continuing violence in general, the Peace People movement was established by Ciarán McKeown, Betty Williams and Mairead Corrigan (the aunt of the dead children). The latter two were awarded the Nobel Peace Prize in December 1977.

Activities. The group has a full-time welfare officer, supported by a team of volunteers, organizing such events as a daily minibus service for prison visiting, and social events and holidays for prisoners' families. The Peace People resettlement scheme provides the opportunity for ex-prisoners and others under pressure from para-military groups to move away from Northern Ireland.

Peace People's "Youth for Peace" group organizes social events, street theatre, fasts and vigils and educational sessions on political and social issues. It also runs summer camps in Norway, where teenagers from different parts of Northern Ireland can get to know one another away from the pressures of the province. The group also runs a "Peace People Junior Football League". Future plans include the establishment of a farm project to bring Protestant and Catholic youth together in a rural setting.

Through public debate and meetings with government and other interested parties, the Peace People work for a reform of the province's judicial system, and in particular for improvements in prison conditions and for the repeal of the emergency legislation, since this "serves to bring the judicial system and the security forces into disrepute".

Membership. Peace People has 120 adult members, while 100 young people are members of Youth for Peace; members participate in the activities of local groups, while general policy is decided at an annual assembly.

Publications. A fortnightly newspaper, *Peace by Peace*, is sold door-to-door; the group also produces various publications allied to its judicial campaign.

Affiliations. International Fellowship of Reconciliation.

Fellowship of Reconciliation in Ireland

Address. 24 Pinehill Road, Ballycairn, Lisburn, Northern Ireland, United Kingdom

Aims and objectives. This Christian pacifist movement shares the objectives and principles of the International Fellowship of Reconciliation, with particular reference to the situation in Northern Ireland.

Formation. The movement was established in Northern Ireland in 1949 from among members of the Peace Pledge Union.

Activities. The Fellowship has been active in anti-nuclear weapons campaigns and has also undertaken various activities aimed at reconciliation in Ireland, including (from the 1950s until 1969) annual North–South conferences with the

Irish Pacifist Movement based in Dublin. It runs summer play-schemes and work-camps which bring Catholic and Protestant children together as well as their parents.

Membership. The Fellowship has about 100 members, mostly in the North but with a few in the Republic.

Affiliations. International Fellowship of Reconciliation; the Fellowship works closely with other Christian peace movements and is represented at the monthly liaison meetings of the Northern Ireland Peace Forum.

Northern Ireland Campaign for Nuclear Disarmament (NI CND)

Address. 10 Stanmillis Park, Belfast, United Kingdom

Aims and objectives. NI CND shares the aims of both British and Irish CND, and it also stands for "the promotion of non-violence in a violent society".

Formation. NI CND was set up in 1980.

Activities. NI CND has held several rallies and carried out non-violent direct actions, including the occupation of the civil defence bunker in Belfast. It helped to set up the peace camp outside RAF Bishopscourt and has taken part in campaigns leading to the declaration of "nuclear-free zones" by a number of district councils.

Membership. Total membership is approximately 500; two of the province's political parties are affiliated to the movement.

Northern Ireland Peace Forum

Address. 8 Upper Crescent, Belfast 7, United Kingdom

Aims and objectives. The Northern Ireland Peace Forum acts as a co-ordinating body for approximately 20 groups engaged in peace and reconciliation work in the province.

Formation. The Peace Forum was set up in 1976.

Activities. The Forum holds regular monthly general meetings with occasional specialist meetings to deal with particular topics. The Forum also acts as a clearing-house for the exchange of information and ideas between its member groups, and helps to ensure that activities are scheduled so as not to clash with each other. If sufficient groups are interested in a particular idea or campaign, this can be adopted as an activity by the Forum as a whole. The Forum also attempts to maintain a dialogue with political parties and other groups.

Membership. Membership of the Forum is open to any group concerned with peace and reconciliation work in Northern Ireland. Potential members participate in Forum activities as "prospective members" for an initial three-month period, following which they become eligible for full membership if regarded as suitable candidates. On occasion the Forum invites certain groups to become members. It also operates an "honorary membership" system for leading individuals working in the peace and reconciliation field.

The Forum has a formal organization, headed by a chairperson, and it has a full-time secretary. The following groups are currently members, the majority being based in or near Belfast: Action for Peace, All Children Together, The

Corrymeela Community, Northern Ireland Campaign for Nuclear Disarmament, *Dawn* (a monthly magazine), Dutch–Northern Irish Advisory Committee, East Belfast Community Council, Fellowship of Reconciliation in Ireland, Glencree Belfast House, Lifeline, Community of the Peace People, Protestant and Catholic Encounter, Pax Christi, Peace and Reconciliation Group, Peacepoint, Ulster Quaker Peace Committee, Witness for Peace, Women Together, and Sydenham Community Group.

Ulster Quaker Peace Committee

Address. 11 Rennore Avenue, Portadown, Co. Armagh, Northern Ireland, United Kingdom

Aims and objectives. The Committee expresses the views of Quakers in Ulster on peace issues and other current concerns.

Activities. The Committee's activities have been centred on conferences and educational meetings, including a recent one-day conference on the Quaker peace testimony. Members of the Committee have corresponded with members of both the British and European Parliaments. It is currently organizing a "peace day" in Belfast, and it has also initiated a "peace poster" competition in Sunday schools.

Membership. The Committee has nine members, including a convenor and secretary, each representing different Quaker meetings in Northern Ireland.

Publications. The Committee has produced a pamphlet, *The Quaker Peace Testimony.*

Affiliations. Dublin Quaker Monthly Meeting Peace Committee and the Quaker Peace and Service in London. The Committee also has representatives on the Northern Ireland Peace Forum, and maintains links, including financial support, with Christian CND and with the World Disarmament Campaign.

3. EASTERN EUROPE AND THE SOVIET UNION

Bulgaria

capital: Sofia   **population: 9,000,000**

Bulgaria is a founder signatory of the East European Mutual Assistance Treaty (or Warsaw Pact) concluded in the Polish capital on May 14, 1955, with Albania (which subsequently formally withdrew in September 1968), Czechoslovakia, the German Democratic Republic, Hungary, Poland, Romania and the Soviet Union. As at end-1985 the Bulgarian armed forces numbered an estimated 148,000 (including 94,000 conscripts) and the defence budget for 1985 was estimated at about 1,000 million leva.

National Committee for the Defence of Peace

Address. 39 Doundukov Boulevard, Sofia, Bulgaria

Aims and objectives. The Committee is the "official" co-ordinating body of the country's peace movement, advocating nuclear and general disarmament, détente and peaceful coexistence.

Affiliations. World Peace Council.

Czechoslovakia

capital: Prague   **population: 15,500,000**

Czechoslovakia is a founder signatory of the East European Mutual Assistance Treaty (or Warsaw Pact) concluded in the Polish capital on May 14, 1955, with Albania (which subsequently formally withdrew in September 1968), Bulgaria, the German Democratic Republic, Hungary, Poland, Romania and the Soviet Union. In August 1968 Soviet forces together with Bulgarian, East German, Hungarian and Polish contingents carried out a military intervention in Czechoslovakia because of fears that the liberalization programme introduced by Alexander Dubček would lead eventually to the detachment of Czechoslovakia from the "socialist community". Since then Czechoslovakia has been guided by the need to maintain friendly relations with the Soviet Union and other socialist countries. As at end-1985 Czechoslovakia's armed forces numbered an estimated 203,000 (half of them conscripts) and the defence budget for 1985 was estimated at 27,500 million koruna.

Charter 77

Address. c/o P.O. Box 222, London, WC2H 9RP, United Kingdom

Aims and objectives. Having originally emerged in 1977 as an opposition group seeking observance by the Czechoslovak Government of the 1975 UN covenants on civil and political rights and on economic, social and cultural rights (ratified by Czechoslovakia in December 1975), Charter 77 in recent years has become increasingly involved in peace issues as an "independent" movement distinct from the "official" Czechoslovak Peace Committee (see below). It has developed contacts with the European Nuclear Disarmament (END) movement in support of the demand for the withdrawal of NATO and Warsaw Pact missiles in the European theatre stretching from "Poland to Portugal", and is seen by END and other West European peace movements as an ally in the furtherance of their aims.

Activities. In a statement issued on Aug. 21, 1985 (the 17th anniversary of the Soviet-led intervention in Czechoslovakia), Charter 77 said inter alia: "The presence of Soviet troops in Czechoslovakia has by now become a tactical component in the deployment of military forces and part of the calculations of each of the blocs. The withdrawal of these troops is feasible only within the framework of a process of ending the bloc division of Europe. We therefore pose the question whether the withdrawal of these troops, or at least a reduction of their numbers, might not be an exemplary unilateral step towards military disengagement. Its initiators would not win support in Czechoslovakia alone, for it would help replace rigid bloc attitudes by measures designed to promote a dynamic approach to peaceful coexistence as the basis of peace and co-operation."

Czechoslovak Peace Committee
Ceskoslovensky Mirovy Vybor

Address. Panská 7, 11669 Prague 1, Czechoslovakia

Aims and objectives. The Committee advocates general and nuclear disarmament, establishment of demilitarized and nuclear-free zones and the prevention of the militarization of outer space.

Formation. The Committee was established in 1949 as the "official" co-ordinating body of the country's peace movement.

Activities. Having acted as host for the 1949 "World Congress of Peace Defenders", the Czechoslovak Committee has organized a range of actions, including peace marches, rallies and seminars. In 1983 it hosted the "World Assembly for Peace and Life Against Nuclear War".

Membership. There are some 10,000 elected members of local peace councils throughout the country.

Publication. Mir (Peace), monthly.

Affiliations. World Peace Council.

German Democratic Republic

capital: Berlin   **population: 17,000,000**

The German Democratic Republic (East Germany) is a founder signatory of the East European Mutual Assistance Treaty (or Warsaw Pact) concluded in the Polish capital on May 14, 1955, with Albania (which subsequently formally withdrew in September 1968), Bulgaria, Czechoslovakia, Hungary, Poland, Romania and the Soviet Union. As at end-1985 the East German armed forces numbered an estimated 175,000 (over half of them conscripts) and the defence budget for 1986 was set at 14,045 million marks.

Peace Committee of the GDR
Friedensrat der DDR

Address. Clara–Zetkinstrasse 103, 1080 Berlin, German Democratic Republic

Aims and objectives. The Committee is the "official" co-ordinating body of the East German peace movement, advocating nuclear and general disarmament, détente and peaceful coexistence.

Publication. Information, monthly.

Affiliations. World Peace Council.

Women for Peace
Frauen für den Frieden

Address. n.a.

Aims and objectives. This independent movement seeks to involve women in the campaign for peace and disarmament and to build a network of like-minded groups in other countries, across the East-West divide.

Formation. Following the establishment of the prototype Women for Peace movement in Switzerland in 1976, similar groups were quickly formed in other European countries, including East Germany, where several members have spent periods in detention for offences arising from their peace campaigning activities.

Hungary

capital: Budapest   **population: 10,700,000**

Hungary is a founder signatory of the East European Mutual Assistance Treaty (or Warsaw Pact) concluded in the Polish capital on May 14, 1955, with Albania (which subsequently formally withdrew in September 1968), Bulgaria, Czechoslovakia, the German Democratic Republic, Poland, Romania and the Soviet Union. Hungary withdrew from the Warsaw Pact on Oct. 31, 1956, at the time of the popular uprising which brought the reformist Imre Nagy briefly to power, but returned to the organization under the pro-Soviet regime installed after the insurrection had been quashed by Soviet forces. As at end-1985 the Hungarian armed forces numbered an estimated 106,000 (about half of them conscripts) and the 1986 defence budget was 40,300 million florints, representing about 7 per cent of total government expenditure.

Hungarian Peace Council

Address. P.O. Box 440, 1395 Budapest, Hungary

Aims and objectives. The Council is the "official" co-ordinating body of Hungary's peace movement, advocating nuclear and general disarmament, détente and peaceful coexistence.

Publication. Peace News and Views, quarterly.

Affiliations. World Peace Council.

Peace Group for Dialogue

Address. n.a.

Aims and objectives. This independent group shares the basic aims of the Hungarian Peace Council (see previous entry) but seeks to develop its own contacts with Western peace movements, among which the European Nuclear Disarmament (END) network is an important point of reference.

Poland

capital: Warsaw   **population: 37,000,000**

Poland is a founder signatory of the East European Mutual Assistance Treaty (or Warsaw Pact) concluded in the Polish capital on May 14, 1955, with Albania (which subsequently formally withdrew in September 1968), Bulgaria, Czechoslovakia, the German Democratic Republic, Hungary, Romania and the Soviet Union. As at end-1985 the Polish armed forces numbered an estimated 320,000 (including 190,000 conscripts) and the defence budget for 1985 was estimated at 288,700 million zlotys.

Freedom and Peace Group

Address. West European representative: Jan Minkiewicz, Reguliersgracht 46″, 1017 LS Amsterdam, The Netherlands

Aims and objectives. This independent movement takes as its first foundation "the struggle for civil rights, for religious freedom and for national independence" and as its second a determination to make the Polish people aware of "the threat of nuclear war, of militarism and militaristic education", in which task it is committed to non-violence. The movement advocates the demilitarization of Central Europe and making the region a nuclear-free zone, coupled with the democratization of the East European states. The movement also believes that "legally enforced military service is contrary to the demands of the people's conscience" and urges that every conscript should have the right "to opt for a civilian type of national service which does not envisage the taking of life".

Formation. The Group was formed in March 1985 following a fast at Podkowa Lesna (a village outside Warsaw) by supporters of an imprisoned conscientious objector (Marek Adamkiewicz).

Activities. In October 1985 28 members of the Group publicly returned their military papers in solidarity with Adamkiewicz and the following month the Group issued its programme on the occasion of a ceremony to mark the anniversary of the death of Otto Schimek, an Austrian soldier executed during the Second World War for refusing to fight. In February two prominent Group members, Jacek Czaputowicz and Piotr Niemczyk, were arrested and charged with membership of an unauthorised organization and with spreading false information in Poland and abroad (Niemczyk having returned from the West after an unsuccessful attempt to represent the Group at the triennial conference of War Resisters' International). In March 1986 six women members of the Group observed a week-long fast in Podkowa Lesna in support of the right of conscientious objection, and in May 1986 members of the Group staged a protest in Warsaw against Poland's first nuclear power station (being built at Zarnowiec on the Baltic and due to come into service in 1991).

Affiliations. The Group has developed contacts with West European peace movements, particularly within the European Nuclear Disarmament (END) network.

Polish Peace Committee
Ogolnopolski Komitet Pokoju (OKP)

Address. ul. Rajcow 10, 00-220 Warsaw, Poland

Aims and objectives. The OKP defines its role as the "promotion of ideas of peace, friendship, co-operation and disarmament, in particular nuclear disarmament, and the voicing of the opinions and consensus of Polish society" in these regards. It supports the development of peace education and research.

Formation. Founded in 1949 as the Polish Committee of Defenders of Peace, the organization changed its name to the Polish Peace Committee in 1958. It has since organized numerous peace marches and rallies, as well as plebiscites, seminars and artistic competitions. It has also acted as host for several international meetings, including the second World Peace Congress of 1950 and the World Assembly of Builders of Peace in 1977.

The main focuses of its present campaigns are (i) opposition to the deployment of cruise and Pershing missiles in Western Europe and (ii) support for the creation of nuclear-free zones, notably in central Europe. It organized an international seminar on "Culture and Art in Peace Education" in mid-1985.

Membership. The OKP acts as the "official" umbrella organization for relevant activities of other groups such as party organizations, youth and student unions, trade unions, co-operatives and churches and religious bodies.

Publications. The OKP publishes a monthly magazine, *Widnokregi,* and a bi-monthly bulletin.

Affiliations. World Peace Council.

Ranks of Peace and Solidarity

Address. n.a.

Aims and objectives. Formed as a section of the banned Solidarity trade union movement, this group demands the withdrawal of all nuclear weapons and Soviet troops from Polish territory and the reduction of arms production and military manpower levels. It urges Western peace movements to give "open support" to the independent East European peace movements, believing that "only a simultaneous and universal peace movement both in the West and in the East can save the world".

Romania

capital: Bucharest population: 22,600,000

Romania is a founder signatory of the East European Mutual Assistance Treaty (or Warsaw Pact) concluded in the Polish capital on May 14, 1955, with Albania (which subsequently formally withdrew in September 1968), Bulgaria, Czechoslovakia, the German Democratic Republic, Hungary, Poland and the Soviet Union. Romania has, however, pursued a relatively independent line in the area of external policy and, for example, did not participate in the 1968 military intervention in Czechoslovakia by the Soviet Union and four other Warsaw Pact states. As at end-1985 the Romanian armed forces numbered an estimated 190,000 (over half conscripts) and the defence budget for 1985 was 12,278 million lei.

National Committee for the Defence of Peace
Comitetul National Apararea Pacii

Address. 29 rue Biserica Amzei, 70172 Bucharest, Romania

Aims and objectives. The Committee is the "official" Romanian body seeking to promote peace on the basis of UN principles and the right of sovereign states to determine their own domestic policies.

Formation. The Committee was set up in 1949.

Activities. The Committee organizes rallies, meetings and conferences on problems of peace and disarmament and participates in various international gatherings devoted to peace themes.

Membership. The Committee has 200 members representing different social categories and organizations.

Publications. The Council publishes a quarterly information bulletin in English and French.

Affiliations. World Peace Council.

Union of Soviet Socialist Republics

capital: Moscow   **population: 275,000,000**

The Soviet Union is a founder signatory of the East European Mutual Assistance Treaty (or Warsaw Pact) concluded in the Polish capital on May 14, 1955, with Albania (which subsequently formally withdrew in September 1968), Bulgaria, Czechoslovakia, the German Democratic Republic, Hungary, Poland and Romania. The Soviet Union also has treaties providing for mutual assistance in the event of either of the parties being attacked with the People's Republic of Mongolia and with the Democratic People's Republic of (North) Korea, and a "stationing of forces agreement" with Afghanistan (concluded in April 1980 some four months after substantial numbers of Soviet troops were deployed in that country in support of the Communist regime).

As at end-1985 the Soviet armed forces were estimated to total 5,300,000 and the officially declared defence budget for 1985 was 19,063 million roubles. Soviet nuclear weapons capability includes inter-continental ballistic missiles, submarine-launched missile systems and a strategic nuclear bomber force.

Moscow Trust Group

Address. n.a.

Aims and objectives. This independent peace movement believes that governmental efforts alone cannot end the current state of armed "unpeace" between the super-powers and accordingly seeks to create new forms of peace activity within the Soviet Union.

Formation. The Group came into being in June 1982.

Activities. Since its formation the Group has faced severe harassment from the Soviet authorities. By late 1985 eight members had been forced into exile, some imprisoned and others placed in psychiatric hospitals. The group's meetings have been disrupted and its members submitted to physical intimidation. Despite these difficulties, however, the Group has developed contacts with visiting peace activists from the West, circulated petitions, staged demonstrations, held seminars and published a series of peace proposals. In the wake of the Chernobyl nuclear reactor disaster in April 1986 the Group issued a statement opposing civilian nuclear power programmes.

Soviet Committee for European Security and Co-operation

Address. 3 Kropotkin Street, 119889 Moscow, USSR

Aims and objectives. This Committee aims to improve co-ordination between the Soviet public and between European peoples to secure a durable peace in Europe. It promotes active public participation in carrying out the provisions of the 1975 Helsinki Final Act.

Formation. The Committee was formed in 1971 by agreement between various organizations of the USSR: the Parliamentary Group, trade unions, youth and women's organizations, unions of journalists, scientists, writers and artists. The Committee is sponsored by the Soviet Peace Fund.

Activities. The Committee exchanges delegations with similar organizations in Europe. It participates in international non-governmental events to promote détente and disarmament in Europe and publishes various reports.

The Committee organizes bilateral and multilateral meetings of representatives of the Soviet public with their counterparts abroad to discuss topical European problems.

Membership. The Committee has around 300 individual members.

Publications. The Committee has published the following reports: *The Threat to Europe* (1982); *How to Avert the Threat to Europe* (1983); *December is Near: Europe Must Choose* (1983); *Helsinki—10 Years After. The Results and Prospects of the Process of European Security and Co-operation. Report of the Soviet Committee for European Security and Co-operation* (1985).

Affiliations. The Committee takes part in the activities of the International Committee for European Security and Co-operation, based in Brussels. It maintains extensive contacts with national committees and other organizations abroad and with political and public figures and scientists working for peace, disarmament and détente in Europe.

Soviet Peace Committee (SPC)
Sovyetskii Komityet Zaschiti Mira

Address. 36 Mira Prospekt, 129010 Moscow, USSR

Aims and objectives. The Committee seeks "general disarmament and détente".

Formation. The SPC was formed in 1949 by the First All-Union Peace Conference in Moscow.

Activities. The SPC holds rallies, torchlight processions, contests and festivals of anti-war songs and posters, peace marathons, concerts, "peace-watch shifts" at factories. Participation in major events is claimed to be "tens of millions". The Committee maintaining contacts with other groups in more than 100 countries.

Membership. There are 445 elected members; the SPC is a co-ordinating body for the peace movement in the Soviet Union and its members are elected by the All-Union Peace Conferences, which are the supreme body of the Soviet peace movement.

Publications. *Twentieth Century and Peace* (in English, French, German, Russian, Spanish).

Affiliations. World Peace Council; UN Non-Governmental Organizations' Committee on Disarmament.

Yugoslavia

capital: Belgrade   **population: 23,000,000**

Having broken with the Soviet Union in 1948, Yugoslavia did not join the Warsaw Pact on its creation in 1955 but rather became one of the principal founders of the Non-Aligned Movement in 1961. It maintains a balanced relationship with each of the two military blocs and has no military alliances. As at end-1985 the Yugoslav armed forces numbered an estimated 240,000 (including 154,000 conscripts) and the defence budget for 1985 was some 765,000 million dinars.

Working Group for Peace

Address. n.a.

Aims and objectives. This independent movements seeks the dismantling of military blocs leading to demilitarization and disarmament. It has been particularly involved in campaigns for the demilitarization of the Alps-Adria region (spanning regions of Yugoslavia, Italy and Austria) and the withdrawal of nuclear weapons and offensive troops from southern Central Europe (see also entry for Alps-Adria Peace Network under International Organizations).

Yugoslav League for Peace, Independence and Equality of Peoples
Jugoslovenska Liga za Mir, Nezavisnost i Ravnopravnost Naroda

Address. Narodnog Fronta 45, 11000 Belgrade, Yugoslavia

Aims and objectives. The League aims to promote the philosophy of non-alignment and the UN Charter; to support disarmament, solidarity with national liberation movements and the democratization of international relations; and to oppose all forms of oppression.

Formation. The League was established in 1959.

Activities. In its early years the League was orientated primarily towards international relations and in 1964 was a co-sponsor of the International Confederation for Disarmament and Peace (which was merged into the International Peace Bureau in 1983). The League has paid more attention to domestic activities in recent years. It organized its first major peace event ("Rock for Peace") in Belgrade in 1982, and has since organized exhibitions, domestic and international round tables, lectures etc.

Membership. Members of the presidency and assembly of the League are delegates from various social and citizen organizations and unions, and from religious groups.

Publications. The League issues occasional publications on various current problems, as well as assembly resolutions in English and Serbo-Croat.

Affiliations. International Peace Bureau.

4. NORTH-AMERICA

Canada

capital: Ottawa   **population: 25,150,000**

Canada was an original signatory on April 4, 1949, of the treaty creating the North Atlantic Treaty Organization (NATO), together with Belgium, Denmark, France, Iceland, Italy, Luxembourg, the Netherlands, Norway, Portugal, the United Kingdom and the United States (later adherents being Greece and Turkey in 1952, the Federal Republic of Germany in 1955 and Spain in 1982). Canada participates fully in NATO's integrated military structures, there being some 5,000 Canadian troops stationed in West Germany and NATO-designated naval bases at Argentia (Newfoundland) and Halifax (Nova Scotia).

Canada also participates with the United States in the North American Air Defence Command (NORAD), which was originally set up in 1958 for a 10-year term and which has been extended subsequently, most recently for a five-year term from May 1986. Under the 1975 extension of NORAD, the establishment of a second control centre at Edmonton, in addition to the existing one at North Bay (Ontario), meant that all Canadian air space came under the control of centres located in Canada and manned by Canadian personnel. In March 1985 a US-Canadian agreement was signed providing for a new chain of 52 ground radar stations across the Canadian Arctic and northern Alaska, to be known as the North Warning System and intended to replace the obsolescent Distant Early Warning (DEW) line dating from the mid-1950s.

Under a framework agreement signed in Washington in February 1983, the United States was authorized to test cruise missiles in northern Alberta. This decision provoked a series of major demonstrations by peace movements and others groups, a coalition of which initiated a legal suit against the federal Government on the grounds that the missile testing constituted a violation of the right to life, liberty and security guaranteed in the Canadian Charter of Rights and Freedoms. Nevertheless, the first test flight over Canadian territory of four unarmed cruise missiles (mounted on a B-52 bomber) took place on March 6, 1984, and the following year further successful test flights of air-launched cruise missiles were made after the protest coalition had failed to secure a restraining injunction from the Canadian Supreme Court. However the Progressive Conservative administration which came to power in September 1984 continued its Liberal predecessor's policy of allowing only unarmed missiles to be tested and also emphasized that there was no intention of permitting nuclear weapons to be re-deployed on Canadian territory (the last US nuclear weapons having been removed in mid-1984).

As at end-1985 the Canadian armed forces (which were unified in 1968) totalled some 85,000 personnel, which was to be increased to 90,000 by 1989; there were also about 8,000 para-militaries and 25,000 reserves. Military service is voluntary. The defence budget for the 1985–86 financial year was C$9,383 million, representing about 9 per cent of overall government expenditure.

Alliance for Non-Violent Action

Address. c/o 436 Lisgar Street, Ottawa, Ontario, K1R 5H1, Canada

Aims and objectives. This Alliance has the long-term aim of constructing a non-oppressive and non-exploitative world, believing that militarism is "rooted in hierarchical and dehumanizing forms of power that are used to maintain and expand privilege based on sex, race, class and imperialism".

Activities. The group plans and participates in educational and direct-action events to promote the cause of non-violence, focusing on opposition to expressions of militarism and other forms of oppression. Its methods include fasting, leafletting, public demonstrations, boycotts, tax resistance, street theatre and civil disobedience. In 1985 it initiated the War Toys Boycott Campaign (see separate entry).

Membership. The Alliance is a collective of groups active in Ontario and Quebec.

Publications. The Alliance has study kits on non-violent direct action, the arms race and women and militarism, as well as a civil disobedience campaign handbook.

Canadian Friends Service Committee (CFSC)

Address. 60 Lowther Avenue, Toronto, Ontario, M5R 1C7, Canada

Aims and objectives. This Committee of the Canadian Quaker community is responsible for carrying out peace and social action programmes in Canada and abroad.

Formation. The CFSC was established in 1931.

Activities. In addition to participating in the broader Canadian peace movement, the CFSC has been particularly active in organizing refugee assistance programmes and third-world development projects (notably in south-east Asia), often in association with Quaker groups of other countries. In 1963 the Committee founded the Grindstone Island peace conference centre (now an independent collective).

Publication. Quaker Concern, quarterly.

Affiliations. Through the Friends World Committee for Consultation in London, the CFSC is in contact with other Quaker groups around the world, particularly Quaker Peace and Service in the UK and the American Friends Service Committee.

Canadian Peace Alliance (CPA)

Address. 736 Bathurst Street, Toronto, Ontario, M5S 2R4, Canada

Aims and objectives. The CPA is the main umbrella organization for Canadian peace movements and "seeks to involve Canadians in the worldwide movement to stop the arms race, ensure the non-violent settlement of disputes and guarantee the security and wellbeing of all peoples".

Formation. The Alliance was formed in November 1985 at a four-day convention hosted by the Toronto Disarmament Network.

Activities. The founding convention of the Alliance drew up a seven-point basis for unity of action within the Canadian peace movement. This included support for a nuclear-weapons freeze, the declaration of Canada as a nuclear-weapons-free zone and support for "conversion" of the arms industry. A statement was also adopted stressing the special responsibility of the two superpowers to end the arms race. It was stressed that the Alliance would not seek to be a "supergroup" but would facilitate co-operative action between participating movements, information exchange and national-level discussion on peace issues.

In early 1986 the CPA launched a campaign to oppose any Canadian participation in the US Strategic Defence Initiative (SDI), either through contracts being awarded to Canadian companies or through integration of SDI into the NORAD system. It was intended that an anti-SDI petition would be presented to the Canadian Prime Minister and that a "Star Wars Watch" committee of the Alliance would monitor any SDI contracts given to Canadian companies and whether any such companies were in receipt of government grants.

Membership. The CPA links some 250 separate peace groups and has a representative and geographically-balanced steering committee.

Canadian Peace Research and Educational Association (CPREA)

Address. c/o Prof. V. M. Naidu, Political Science Dept., Brandon University, Brandon, Manitoba, R7A 6A9, Canada

Aims and objectives. The CPREA aims to promote peace research and peace education, mainly at universities.

Formation. The Association was formed in 1965.

Activities. A yearly conference is held at Learned Societies and the Association also works with the Social Science Federation of Canada, preparing briefs for the Social Science and Humanitarian Research Council. There are plans for it to co-operate with the Canadian Institute for International Peace and Security.

Membership. There are 100 members, who are mainly university professors.

Publications. Peace Research, three times a year since 1975; *CPREA Newsletter.*

Affiliations. The group is affiliated to the International Peace Research Association and to the Social Science Federation of Canada.

Christian Movement for Peace (CMP)

Address. 427 Bloor Street West, Toronto, Ontario, M5S 1X7, Canada

Aims and objectives. As the Canadian section of the international Christian Movement for Peace, the CMP aims to provide resources and personnel for education on disarmament and the latter's relationship with economic development. The Movement is also concerned with human rights and "the phenomenon of globally increasing militarization".

Activities. The CMP conducts a number of programmes, including (i) development of a peace studies curriculum for senior school pupils; (ii) an international youth exchange programme designed to promote understanding between nations; and (iii) provision of a resources centre.

Publication. Calumet, quarterly.

Affiliations. The CMP is affiliated to the international Christian Movement for Peace, based in Paris.

Coalition for World Disarmament

Address. 1414 West 12th Avenue, Vancouver, British Columbia, V6H 1M8, Canada

Aims and objectives. The Coalition is a non-partisan organization founded with the aim of raising public awareness of the dangers of the arms race and of the need for mass influence for nuclear disarmament through the implementation of the final document of the first UN Special Session on Disarmament (1978). The Coalition also seeks Canadian withdrawal from NATO and from NORAD, and an end to Canadian involvement in the arms trade.

The Coalition's campaign priorities are (i) the achievement of a bilateral freeze on research, production and deployment of nuclear weapons systems, (ii) the promotion of the UN World Disarmament Campaign, (iii) worldwide agreement on a UN comprehensive programme of world disarmament, and (iv) the prohibition of chemical weapons.

Formation. The Coalition was established in Vancouver in 1977.

Activities. The Coalition works on the basis of an information and communications network to encourage individual and collective action to counter the nuclear threat. It organizes province-wide conferences to stimulate co-operation and intensify activity among disarmament groups, and acts as a co-ordinating body for the distribution of peace literature in the province. It organizes literature stalls and displays in libraries and shopping centres.

The Coalition promotes UN disarmament initiatives, notably the UN disarmament campaign. It sponsors speakers on topics such as "The Russian threat—its myths and realities", and its members take part in local and national peace demonstrations.

Membership. The Coalition has approximately 120 members, although "active members number about eight". The following groups are "founding sponsoring organizations": Global Concerns Division, United Church; Faculty Association, Langara College; Religious Society of Friends; Fellowship of Reconciliation; Vancouver Unitarian Church; British Columbia Peace Council; Voice of Women; Women's International League for Peace and Freedom; Vancouver and District Labour Council; Pacific Life Community; United Nations Associations; Canadian Coalition for Nuclear Responsibility; British Columbia Federation of Labour; Vancouver Status of Women; and the Canadian Catholic Organization for Development and Peace.

Publications. The Coalition produces regular factsheets on disarmament.

Cruise Missile Conversion Project

Address. 730 Bathurst Street, Toronto, Ontario, M5S 2R4, Canada

Aims and objectives. The Project's primary aim is to achieve the conversion of Litton Industries (Canada) from military production to "socially useful" production. (Litton Industries produces the guidance system for the US cruise missile.) In more general terms, the Project opposes militarism in daily life and in the community.

Formation. The campaign was launched in 1980.

Activities. The Project has organized actions and demonstrations on the Litton site since its inception. It organizes a bi-weekly leafletting of workers at the factory and works for the support of trade unions and of the local community for the conversion idea. In future, the Project intends to stage more actions on particular days (Hiroshima Day—Aug. 6, for example). It is forming a conversion team to develop an "alternate use plan" for the Litton factory production.

Membership. The Project has an active membership of 30, organized into six collectives. There is a "supporting membership" of around 3,000 volunteers and financial contributors.

Publications. The Project publishes a newsletter three or four times per year; it has also produced a booklet, *Arms Maker, Union Buster: Litton Industries, A Corporate Profile*.

Affiliations. Alliance for Non-Violent Action (an Ontario-wide network); Toronto Disarmament Network; and the Weapons Facilities Conversion Network (comprising groups in Toronto and upstate New York, USA). The Project also maintains links with groups based in Michigan (also in the USA).

Global Issues Committee, Ontario Federation of Students (OFS)

Address. 643 Yonge Street, Toronto, Ontario, M4Y 1Z9, Canada

Aims and objectives. The Committee aims to inform and educate student leaders on peace and international issues. It provides a network with campus peace groups in the province of Ontario.

Activities. The Committee conducts workshops on peace and international issues at conferences of the Ontario Federation of Students. It has investigated the extent of military research being conducted at universities.

Membership. Five students are elected by the OFS membership and there is one staff resource person. (The OFS consists of 200,000 college and university members.)

Affiliations. The Committee has informal connections with campus peace groups and with the Toronto Disarmament Network.

Island Peace Committee

Address. 81 Prince Street, Charlottetown, Prince Edward Island, C1A 4R3, Canada

Aims and objectives. The Committee works to discourage activities which contradict the ideal of a just and peaceful society by practising non-violence in everyday life.

Formation. It was founded in March 1982.

Activities. The Committee conducted a ten-day "Walk for Peace" across Prince Edward Island in October 1983 and has sponsored annual public forums on peace issues in the context of International Women's Day, Mother's Day, Hiroshima Day, Disarmament Week and the War-Toys Boycott. The Committee has also campaigned to make Prince Edward Island a nuclear-free zone, and is taking part in the opposition to the establishment of a weapons component manufacturing plant on Prince Edward Island. It has also given support to popular movements in Central America.

Membership. There are approximately 50 fully paid-up members.

Affiliations. Project Ploughshares; Canadian Peace Alliance; Central American Anti-Intervention Coalition.

Operation Dismantle

Address. P.O. Box 3887, Station C. Ottawa, Ontario, K1Y 4M5, Canada

Aims and objectives. Operation Dismantle seeks balanced, multilateral nuclear disarmament as a precursor to a gradual, phased and balanced general disarmament. Towards this end, it supports the holding of a global referendum on disarmament under the auspices of the UN. Particular goals on which Operation Dismantle concentrates include an end to Canadian participation in cruise missile testing; the declaration of a Canada-wide nuclear-free zone; a nuclear weapons freeze; and a worldwide comprehensive test ban.

Activities. Operation Dismantle lobbies the Canadian Government on the achievement of these goals, and is involved in the court case which was brought in an effort to establish the illegality of cruise testing in Canada. Its lobbying activities during the 1984 federal elections were concentrated on promoting the nuclear freeze proposal. It organized a local referendum on disarmament in 192 Canadian muncipalities, and launched Project Ploughshares to encourage municipalities to declare themselves nuclear-free zones. It is currently opposing the US strategic defence initiative and any Canadian participation therein.

Membership. Operation Dismantle's paid-up membership totals over 6,300.

Publications. The Dismantler, quarterly.

Pacifist Union of Quebec
Union des Pacifistes du Québec (UPQ)

Address. 1264 rue St Timothee, Montreal, Quebec, H2L 3N6, Canada

Aims and objectives. The UPQ strives for the abolition of the root causes of war and for the development of ways of living that lead to peace. It seeks to persuade the Quebecois populace to become pacifists, opposed to all wars and all preparations for war, and favourable to unilateral and international disarmament.
The UPQ lays particular stress on the application of non-violent action in the pacifist struggle, and supports defence policies based on non-violent, non-military civil defence methods. It supports a non-aligned position in international politics and is opposed to Canadian membership of NATO. It also works for the demilitarization of Quebec.
The UPQ seeks to emphasize and publicize the links between feminism and pacifism.

Formation. The UPQ was founded in Montreal on June 26, 1982.

Activities. The UPQ has organized or taken part in a number of pacifist and political demonstrations, notably the civil disobedience action at Griffis military base in New York state (USA) in July 1983 and in Hiroshima and Nagasaki remembrance ceremonies in August of that year. In October 1983 the Union organized a "human chain" demonstration linking the US and Soviet consulates in Montreal and co-ordinated civil disobedience actions outside the consulates and the Defence Department. It took part in a further human chain action in October 1984.

Since its inception, the group has held public vigils for peace on a weekly basis.

The UPQ organized a series of conferences and meetings on the question of non-violence and pacifism in March and April 1984. Throughout 1984 it also produced publicity material on the relevance of George Orwell for pacifists. The Union took part in the Youth Summit in June and August 1983 and in the March for Employment in June of that year.

It helped organize a visit to Quebec in May 1983 by a group of Belgian representatives of non-violent and pacifist organizations. In June 1984, five UPQ members visited Belgium for further discussions with pacifist groups there.

Since October 1984, the UPQ has been involved in the peace tax campaign in Canada, and in particular with the setting up of a "peacemaking fund" as an alternative to paying taxes for military preparations. It also stages training sessions in non-violent direct action techniques.

Membership. The UPQ has some 175 members from varying social and professional backgrounds.

Publications. La Pacifisme: Son Histoire et son Sens d'Aujourd'hui (Pacifism: Its History and its Meaning for Today), the text of a paper presented to the UPQ conference in Montreal in September 1982. The UPQ has also published two books by Dmitri Roussopoulos: *Le Militarisme Mondiale—La Note* (World Militarism—The Bill) and *Le Vrai Orwell . . . Orwell vu par un Pacifiste* (The Real Orwell . . . Orwell as seen by a Pacifist).

Affiliations. War Resisters' International.

Peace Education Resource Centre (PERC)

Address. 10 Trinity Square, Toronto, Ontario M5G 1B1, Canada

Aims and objectives. PERC exists to provide interested parties with reference information on peace issues.

Formation. PERC, which is a co-operative project sponsored by Holy Trinity Church in Toronto, originated as an educational collective known as the Canadian Disarmament Information Service (CANDIS).

Activities. PERC maintains a press clipping archive and other material on peace-related matters, for use by students, researchers, peace movements and the general public.

Publications. PERC has published a bibliography of books on peace as well as regular factsheets.

Peace Research Institute, Dundas (PRID)

Address. 25 Dundana Avenue, Dundas, Ontario, L9H 4EH, Canada

Aims and objectives. PRID abstracts information "relevant to the questions of war and peace" from newspapers and journals with the objective of eliminating "folklore and mere opinion and to replace them with knowledge".

Formation. Established in 1962 as the Dundas office of the Canadian Peace Research Institute, PRID was reconstituted in its present form in 1976.

Activities. PRID's sole activity is the publication of abstracts, which are currently being entered onto computer. PRID is a sponsor of the Canadian School of Peace Research.

Publications. PRID's two publications are (i) the *Peace Research Abstracts Journal*, which has been published monthly since 1964, and (ii) the *Peace Research Reviews Journal*, an irregular series of monographs on topics related to peace research.

Project Ploughshares

Address. Conrad Grebel College, Waterloo, Ontario, N2L 3G6, Canada

Aims and objectives. The Project takes its name from the biblical phrase in the book of Isaiah: "And they shall beat their swords into ploughshares and their spears into pruning hooks. Nation shall not lift up sword against nation, neither shall they learn war any more."

Its three stated aims are (i) to analyse the effect of military spending on development in both Canada and the developing countries and to identify links between disarmament and development; (ii) to propose alternatives to existing policies with a view to diverting resources from the arms race to development needs; and (iii) to increase awareness of the consequences of the arms race among the churches, development community and general public in Canada and to enlist their resources in the search for alternatives.

Formation. The Project was founded in 1976 with the aid of finance from Canadian University Services Overseas (CUSO) by Murray Thomson, then executive director of CUSO, and Ernie Regehr, author of *Making A Killing: Canada's Arms Industry* and a member of the Mennonite Central Committee. Shortly after its formation the Project amalgamated with the Canadian Defence Alternatives Group, a church-based group set up earlier the same year, after which it was placed under the sponsorship of the Canadian Council of Churches. Other organizations involved in the Project's establishment included Oxfam and the United Nations Association.

Activities. The Project carries out research work on its areas of concern, and maintains a reference library. It is currently establishing a database on Canadian military industries. It is also responsible for the "peace and security" section of the Canadian churches' submission to the Government's foreign policy review.

The Project has carried out consultancy work, including the submission of briefings to the (Canadian) House of Commons standing committee on external affairs and national defence. A member of the Project's staff served as special advisor to the Canadian delegation to the 34th session of the UN General Assembly, and the group was part of the External Affairs Department's consultative group on disarmament and arms control. It took part in both of the UN's special sessions on disarmament (1978 and 1982).

The Project has participated in various seminars and conferences, notably the Canadian Council for International Co-operation's conferences on disarmament and development. It organizes events and meetings annually during the UN Disarmament Week (Oct. 24–31). It has co-operated with other peace groups in the Election Priorities Project—a questionnaire—mailing to MPs seeking their views on various disarmament and army sales issues.

Membership. There is a mailing list of 5,000. In addition to being sponsored by the Canadian Council of Churches, the Project receives the support of various religious, development and peace groups, including the Canadian Catholic Organization for Development and Peace, the Christian Movement for Peace, the Native Council of Canada and the Development Education Centre.

Publications. *Monitor*, the Project's own journal, appears quarterly. It has also produced pamphlets, "background kits" and working papers, on topics such as Canadian military sales and policy, cruise missiles, nuclear-free zones and the proposal for a demilitarized zone in the Arctic.

Quebec Coalition for Peace and Disarmament
Coalition Québécoise pour la Paix et le Désarmement (CQPD)

Address. 1264 St Timothée, Montreal, Quebec, Canada

Aims and objectives. A loose grouping of 10 peace organizations, the CQPD takes an independent, non-aligned stance on peace issues (in opposition to the Quebec Peace Council).

Quebec Project for Disarmament
Projet Québécois pour le Désarmement (PQD)

Address. 49 boulevard Tache, Hull, Quebec, J8Y 3N7, Canada

Aims and objectives. The Quebec Project for Disarmament seeks to involve the public in the process of peace and disarmament by campaigning for a referendum on general disarmament, as proposed by the United Nations in 1961, and a nuclear freeze. Its aim is to hold such a referendum in Quebec initially then in Canada as a whole, leading eventually to a series of international referendums controlled by the United Nations.

Formation. The Quebec Project started out in 1982 as the Quebec Committee for Disarmament, aiming to be a middle-ground Quebec version of the (English-speaking) group Operation Dismantle. The Committee was later disbanded and two groups formed by consensus—the PQD, to campaign for the referendum, and *Option Paix*, which produces a magazine on peace issues every two months.

Activities. The Project's activities centre on campaigning for a referendum and lobbying political and other groups. The idea of a referendum has been endorsed by the Quebec National Assembly (on June 22, 1982) and supported by the *Parti Québécois* (in June 1984).

Membership. The Project's membership fell from over 100 in 1983 has fallen to only 15–20, five of whom are activists.

Affiliations. The PQD is part of the Quebec Coalition for Peace and Disarmament; it is also closely connected with Operation Dismantle.

Science for Peace (SFP)

Address. University College, University of Toronto, Toronto, Ontario, M5S 1A1, Canada

Aims and objectives. Science for Peace is dedicated towards providing members of the public with factual information on the dangers of nuclear war and the likely consequences of such a conflict. It conducts research (and encourages others to do so) into the dangers of a war waged with any weapons of mass destruction, and monitors "destabilizing developments" in the arms race. SFP provides support for scientific activities directed towards peace and for the publication and distribution of the findings of peace research.

Formation. Science for Peace was established in February 1981. Its origins lay in a Toronto-based ad hoc committee which had organized a public forum on "Science, Religion and the Arms Race" at Toronto University in January of that year, and which had been instrumental in securing the passage of a resolution, calling for a reduction in "reliance on weapons of mass destruction", by the annual meeting of the American Association for the Advancement of Science in the same month. Guest of honour at the inaugural meeting was Bernard Feld, the editor of the *Bulletin of Atomic Scientists.*

Activities. In the educational field, Science for Peace has co-operated with the University College in establishing a chair of peace studies at Toronto University. It has worked with the City of Toronto board of education on the latter's advisory committee on "Thinking and Deciding in the Nuclear Age". The aim of this co-operation has been the evolution of a secondary and primary school curriculum designed to deal with issues such as arms control, disarmament and "the quality of the nuclear future". SFP has also drawn up a course on Nuclear War—Facts and Implications, which is offered in the School of Continuing Studies at Toronto University.

SFP maintains a roster of speakers, who are available to give talks to churches, schools and other organizations, on subjects related to its field of activity.

Since its formation, SFP has held regular workshops and symposia, on occasion in co-operation with other groups. These have covered subjects such as chemical warfare, the militarization of space, economic conversion proposals, nuclear-free zones and peace education. It sponsors an annual series of six public lectures at Toronto University. Previous lecturers have included William Epstein, Anatol Rapoport and Alfonso García Robles. SFP's sponsorship of the lectures has been assisted by grants from the arms control and disarmament division of the (Canadian) Department of External Affairs. SFP also hold weekly public seminars at the University.

SFP co-operated with two US organizations—the Union of Concerned Scientists and United Campuses to Prevent Nuclear War—in holding Remembrance Day (Nov. 11) convocations on a number of campuses in the USA and Canada. Activities at the convocations have included lectures, films and panel discussions.

Since its inception, SFP has carried out a large number of research projects. These have included the following: (i) the causes of war and the management of conflicts; (ii) laboratory studies of crisis management techniques; (iii) computer simulations of a nuclear attack on Canada; (iv) technology of anti-submarine warfare; (v) the implications of the cruise missile for Canada; (vi) study of the likely effects of a "nuclear winter"; (vii) the threatened militarization of outer space; (viii) the establishment of a committee to advise the Government on the state of the (nuclear) non-proliferation treaty; (ix) a study of the means required to verify compliance with the proposed comprehensive nuclear test ban treaty; (x) technical research for the External Affairs Department on verification measures required for a chemical and biological warfare treaty.

Membership. SFP's members include physical, life, behavioural and social scientists and engineers, who are organized in local chapters across Canada. National policy is determined by a board of over 50 directors.

Publications. In addition to numerous research papers and reports, SFP produce a regular news bulletin for members.

Affiliations. SFP was a founder of Science for Peace International Network.

Veterans for Multilateral Nuclear Disarmament (VMND)

Address. P.O. Box 8252, Halifax, Nova Scotia, B3K 5L9, Canada

Aims and objectives. VMND is a pressure group of ex-servicemen and women which aims to promote multilateral nuclear disarmament.

Formation. VMND began in March 1982 when four Halifax veterans obtained the names and financial contributions of 28 other Halifax ex-servicemen to publish a newspaper advertisement calling for public support for the peace march to take place in Halifax on May 20, 1982.

Activities. VMND's principal activities focus on drawing public attention to Canada's participation in the nuclear arms race. This is done through press conferences, meetings, lectures and articles in the local and national press.

The group has also established a dialogue with the Soviet War Veterans Committee and has had contact with US and West German ex-service people working for disarmament. They have also established relations with Ex-Services CND in Britain.

Members have participated in peace marches and joint activities with other peace groups. The president of VMND has participated in the consultative group to Canada's ambassador for disarmament.

With the help of a federal government grant the group has established an office and conference room/library for the holding of discussion groups. Future plans include a recruitment drive, a speakers' bureau and an enlarged community education programme.

Membership. VMND has around 350 members; 95 per cent are ex-service men and women or people who served in wartime services such as the merchant marine or civil defence. A few are spouses or other relatives of deceased veterans. Members range in past rank from private to lieutenant-general.

Publications. VMND has produced various publications including an introductory pamphlet, press releases, briefs to government bodies and an annotated bibliography on the nuclear arms race and nuclear disarmament.

Voice of Women

Address. 175 Carlton Street, Toronto, Ontario, M5A 2K3, Canada

Aims and objectives. This group aims to provide a focus for women to exert pressure for international negotiations to achieve general disarmament and to eliminate the threat of war. It supports the declaration of Canada as a nuclear-weapons-free zone and the holding of a national referendum on disarmament.

Publication. The group publishes a regular newsletter.

War Toys Boycott Campaign

Address. c/o 9 Melbourne Avenue, Toronto, Ontario, M6K 1K1, Canada

Aims and objectives. This Campaign seeks to bring about the disappearance of children's toys with violent or military associations.

Formation. The Campaign was launched in 1985 by the Alliance for Non-Violent Action (see separate entry) and drew support from some 300 peace groups.

Activities. The Campaign has agitated in particular for the creation of "war toys free zones" in Canada. It also sponsored an International Day Against War Toys on Nov. 20, 1985.

Women's Action for Peace

Address. c/o 436 Lisgar Street, Ottawa, Ontario, K1R 5H1, Canada

Aims and objectives. This feminist collective shares the same general aims as the Alliance for Non-Violent Action (see separate entry), while at the same time giving particular attention to challenging "patriarchal domination", which it sees as a root cause of violence and militarism.

Publication. The group has published a bibliography of feminism and non-violence.

Other Movements

Campaign Against Nuclear and For Disarmament Universal (CANDU)

Address. c/o 2033 boulevard St Laurent, Montreal, Quebec, H2X 2T3, Canada

Canadian Coalition for Nuclear Responsibility

Address. P.O. Box 236, Snowdon Post Office, Montreal, Quebec, H3X 3T4, Canada

Canadian Study Group in Arms Control and Disarmament

Address. 15 King's College Circle, Toronto, Ontario, M4K 2P4, Canada

Catholic Organization for Development and Peace

Address. 2111 rue Centre, Montreal, Quebec, H3K 1J5, Canada

Fellowship of Reconciliation

Address. 4536 West 8th Avenue, Vancouver, British Columbia, Canada

Institute of Peace and Conflict Studies

Address. c/o Conrad Grebel College, Waterloo, Ontario, N2L 3G6, Canada

Mennonite Central Committee

Address. 201–1483 Pembina Highway, Winnipeg, Manitoba, R3T 2C8, Canada

Peace Education Network

Address. P.O. Box 71, Student Union Building, University of British Columbia, Vancouver, British Columbia, V6T 2A5, Canada

Physicians for Social Responsibility

Address. 360 Bloor Street West, suite 406, Toronto, Ontario, M5S 1X1, Canada

Quebec Peace Council
Conseil Québecois de la Paix

Address. C.P. 475, Station Outremont, Montreal, Quebec, J8Y 3N7, Canada

Students for Peace and Disarmament

Address. 643 Yonge Street, second floor, Toronto, Ontario, M4Y 1Z9, Canada

Trade Unionists' Peace Committee

Address. 77 Essex Street, Toronto, Ontario, M6G 1T4, Canada

Women's International League for Peace and Freedom

Address. 1310 West 13th Avenue, Vancouver, British Columbia, V6H 1N8, Canada

United States of America

capital: Washington　　　　　　　　　　　　　　　　　**population: 236,500,000**

The United States was an original signatory on April 4, 1949, of the treaty creating the North Atlantic Treaty Organization (NATO), together with Belgium, Canada, Denmark, France, Iceland, Italy, Luxembourg, the Netherlands, Norway, Portugal and the United Kingdom (later adherents being Greece and Turkey in 1952, the Federal Republic of Germany in 1955 and Spain in 1982). As the world's strongest military power, the United States leads the NATO alliance, having some 350,000 military personnel (all services) stationed in Western Europe and a network of bilateral agreements covering US military bases and other defence co-operation (see introductory sections for the European NATO countries for details). In the United States there are NATO-designated naval bases at Brunswick (Maine), Boston (Massachusetts), Newport (New Hampshire), New London (Connecticut), New York, Philadelphia (Pennsylvania), Norfolk (Virginia), Charleston (South Carolina), Brunswick (Georgia) and Mayport/Jacksonville (Florida). The United States participates with Canada in a NATO regional planning group for North America and also in the North American Air Defence Command (NORAD) arrangement.

Outside the NATO area the United States has a further 144,000 military personnel (including 33,500 afloat) stationed in the Pacific and Far East regions, where the United States is party to (i) the tripartite Pacific Security Treaty (or Anzus Pact) signed in September 1951 with Australia and New Zealand, although the participation of the latter country was effectively frozen in mid-1986 (see introductory section for New Zealand); and (ii) the South-East Asia Collective Defence Treaty signed in September 1954 with Australia, France, New Zealand, Pakistan, the Philippines, Thailand and the United Kingdom, and still in force despite the dissolution of the South-East Asia Treaty Organization (SEATO) in June 1977 following the earlier withdrawal of France and Pakistan. There are major concentrations of US forces in Japan (52,000), South Korea (40,000) and the Philippines (15,000), with each of which the United States has mutual security treaties dating from September 1951, October 1953 and August 1951 respectively.

Other important US overseas force deployments include 13,000 in the Indian Ocean (based at Diego Garcia), 10,000 in the Panama Canal Zone, 2,500 at the Guantánamo Bay base on Cuba (the only sovereign state in the world with both US and Soviet military personnel stationed therein) and 2,400 in Egypt, including 1,100 members of the multinational peacekeeping force (MFO) in Sinai. Non-MFO US forces in Egypt form part of the US Rapid Deployment Force created in 1980 with a view inter alia to resisting possible Soviet penetration of the Gulf area and the Indian Ocean, in which connection the United States also has access to bases in Oman, Somalia and Kenya under agreements concluded in mid-1980. Elsewhere in the Middle East theatre, the United States is committed to providing support to Israel in the event of any violation of the 1979 Egyptian-Israeli peace treaty "deemed to threaten the security of Israel" and is party to a "strategic co-operation agreement" with Israel, which as eventually concluded in November 1983 commits both sides to giving "priority attention" to the threat to their mutual interests posed by "increased Soviet involvement in the Middle East".

Within its own region, the United States is a party to the 1947 Inter-American Treaty of Reciprocal Assistance (or Rio Treaty) and also to the 1948 Charter of the Organization of American States (OAS), which as amended in 1967 provides that OAS member states should take common action in the event of extra-continental aggression against any of their number. In this framework successive US administrations have been highly sensitive to any encroachment of communism in the OAS area, particularly since the establishment of a pro-Soviet communist regime in Cuba in 1959.

As at end-1985 the US armed forces totalled some 2,153,000 men and women, consisting of 780,000 army, 604,000 air force, 569,000 navy and 200,000 marine corps personnel; there were also some 1,200,000 active reserves and about 1,000,000 other reserves. Para-military forces (coast guard, civil air patrol and state militia) numbered about 120,000. The US armed forces are entirely professional, compulsory military service (the draft) having been abolished in 1973. The defence budget for the fiscal year beginning on October 1, 1985, as approved by Congress on August 1, 1985, was $302,500 million in authorizations for military spending, representing about 31.3 per cent of total federal government expenditure and a 4 per cent inflation-linked increase over the previous year.

The United States has the world's largest nuclear weapons capability, its nuclear forces consisting of US-based inter-continental ballistic missiles (ICBMs), the Poseidon and Trident submarine-launched missile systems and a strategic nuclear bomber force, as well as various theatre and battlefield nuclear weapons. US medium-range theatre nuclear weapons include ground-launched cruise and Pershing II missiles, deployment of which in five European NATO countries began in 1983–84 amid substantial political controversy (see country introductions for Belgium, Federal Republic of Germany, Italy, the Netherlands and the United Kingdom). Nuclear weapons tests are regularly conducted at the US underground testing site in Nevada and continued in 1985–86 notwithstanding the unilateral Soviet moratorium on such tests declared in July 1985. The United States is party to the 1963 nuclear test-ban treaty (banning atmospheric tests), to the 1967 treaty banning nuclear and other mass destruction weapons from outer space and celestial bodies, and to the 1971 treaty prohibiting the deployment of such weapons on the seabed. It is also a party to the 1968 nuclear non-proliferation treaty (NPT) which came into force in March 1970. On March 23, 1983, President Reagan publicly launched the US Strategic Defence Initiative (SDI)—dubbed "Star Wars"—involving "long-term research and development programmes" into the creation of a defence shield in outer space against hostile missiles or satellites. The SDI was presented as essentially defensive in intent and held not to violate the 1972 US-Soviet ABM treaty banning the development of anti-ballistic missile systems, since it was a research programme. It was also described as matching similar research being undertaken by the Soviet Union, which nevertheless strongly condemned the US SDI as a further escalation of the arms race.

Abalone Alliance

Address. 2940 16th Street, room 310, San Francisco, California 94103, USA

Aims and objectives. The Abalone Alliance describes its objective as being to "involve people in non-violent direct action against nuclear power and weapons and the corporate mindset (maximizing profits) that brings us both".

Formation. It was formed in 1977 to oppose the construction and licensing of the Diablo Canyon nuclear power reactor in California.

Activities. These are currently (i) to oppose the operation of the Diablo Canyon plant; (ii) to campaign against the use of the Vandenberg air force base in California for military applications of the space shuttle; (iii) to work in solidarity with the indigenous people of Big Mountain, Arizona, to prevent their removal from their land.

Membership. The Alliance links 50 local groups in California.

Affiliations. American Friends Service Committee; Movement for a New Society; Mobilization for Survival.

ACCESS

Address. 1755 Massachusetts Avenue NW, Washington, DC 20036, USA

Aims and objectives. ACCESS is an information service on international peace and security issues.

Activities. ACCESS provides information to organizations and individuals on a wide range of topics, including weapons systems and contractors, alternative security options, non-proliferation and international relations generally. The free service also provides data on available resources such as factsheets, articles, speakers or films and helps non-profit-making groups in finding fund-raising, computer and lobbying assistance.

American Friends Service Committee (AFSC)

Address. 1501 Cherry Street, Philadelphia, Pennsylvania 19102, USA

Aims and objectives. The AFSC, basing itself on the pacifist principles of the Quaker community (Friends), aims to develop opposition to war and militarism in all forms and to promote non-violent alternatives, in respect of both the United States and the world at large.

Activities. The AFSC is involved in a broad range of peace work, particularly directed at proposals for the "conversion" of military industries to peaceful production, with emphasis being given to local projects. It participates with other US peace movements in campaigning for nuclear and general disarmament and conducts programmes of meetings and educational initiatives to that end. For the purposes of lobbying Congress and the Administration, there is a Friends Committee on National Legislation (see separate entry).

The AFSC is also active on the international plane, working with peace movements in other countries in various initiatives. In February 1986, for example, it co-sponsored (with Dutch, Italian and French organizations) a Middle East Study Conference in Amersfoort (Netherlands) which was attended by Israeli and Palestinian representatives.

A major project of the AFSC is National Action/Research on the Military Industrial Complex (NARMIC), which was launched in 1969 as a national clearing house for information on the research, production and distribution of US military technology and weaponry; such information is made available (by subscription) to a wide range of people, including journalists, educators, students and peace activists.

Publications. NARMIC has published a wide range of factsheets, reports and other material on various facets of US military-industrial complex.

Affiliations. The AFSC is part of the international Quaker movement through the London-based Friends World Committee for Consultation, of which there is a Section of the Americas.

American Peace Test (APT)

Address. PO Box 10255, Las Vegas, Nevada 89126, USA

Aims and objectives. The APT is "a national organization aimed at adding direct action (including civil disobedience) to the mix of activities undertaken by Freeze supporters" in support of a halt to the testing and deployment of nuclear weapons.

Formation. The movement was launched in January 1986 with the official endorsement of the Nuclear Weapons Freeze Campaign (see separate entry), although it is a distinct organization.

Activities. The APT organized a major protest demonstration on May 31, 1986, at the Nevada nuclear testing site (65 miles north of Las Vegas), where the previous month a further US test had been carried out (notwithstanding the moratorium on Soviet tests announced by General Secretary Mikhail Gorbachev in July 1985).

Architects/Designers/Planners for Social Responsibility (ADPSR)

Address. 225 Lafayette Street, New York, NY 10012, USA

Aims and objectives. ADPSR seeks to propagate and act upon its conviction that its professional constituencies have a special responsibility to spread awareness of the threat posed by nuclear weapons and the waste of resources represented by the arms race.

Activities. ADPSR is active in the United States in the fields of publicity and educational work, organizing regular meetings and other events focusing on the concerns and proposals of architects, designers and planners in relation to nuclear weapons and the arms race. In the international sphere the organization has sought to develop contacts with fellow-professionals in the Soviet Union, to which end an ADPSR delegation visited Moscow in May 1986 for talks with the USSR Union of Architects. The meeting resulted in a provisional agreement that an organization to be called International Architects/Designers/Planners for the Prevention of Nuclear War should be established to promote the reduction and eventual elimination of nuclear and chemical weapons and other means of mass destruction, both on earth and in space.

Artists for Survival

Address. 147 Moody Street, Waltham, Massachusetts, USA

Aims and objectives. Artists for Survival hopes to alert the general public to the dangers inherent in the nuclear arms race by making an "emotional and intellectual appeal to the sanctity of life on the planet and the danger and pain of a holocaust".

Formation. The group was established in January 1972.

Activities. It has held over 70 exhibitions, including ones staged in venues such as the Senate and House of Representatives, the Massachusetts statehouse and Harvard University medical school. The group have designed posters and participated in "posters for peace" rallies, including one on the occasion of the UN's second special session on disarmament (UNSSOD II) in New York in

1982. It has recently initiated a series of "poster exchanges" between schoolchildren in the USA and the Soviet Union.

Membership. Current membership totals approximately 200 individuals, including professional artists and schoolchildren.

Publication. A newsletter is produced twice a year.

Affiliations. The group is linked to the Nuclear Weapons Freeze Campaign and the National Day of Peace network.

Athletes United for Peace

Address. PO Box 1776, Lawrence, Kansas 66044, USA

Aims and objectives. The group seeks to improve relations between the USA and the USSR through sporting contacts.

Formation. Athletes United for Peace was formed in 1983.

Activities. In April 1983 Athletes United for Peace hosted the visit of a Soviet team to the Kansas relays; a "Declaration of American and Soviet Athletes United for Peace", drafted during the event, was subsequently signed by athletes from more than 40 countries. This "Lawrence Declaration" proved the inspiration for further Athletes United for Peace conferences in West Germany, Japan and elsewhere. In 1985 the group organized a "Journey for Peace", including a reunion of US and Soviet veterans who met at the Elbe in 1945.

Membership. The group has 500 members and contributors.

Baptist Peace Fellowship of North America

Address. First Baptist Church, Granville, Ohio 43023, USA

Aims and objectives. The Fellowship aims to unite Baptists who believe themselves to be "called by God to witness to the gospel of peace". Its practical goals are the establishment of peace groups within the Baptist community at local, associational and regional levels and, by so doing, to encourage the growth of pacifist ideas within the North American Baptist community.

Formation. A Baptist peace fellowship in the early 1940s was formed by a group of US Baptists who had become convinced that the New Testament forbade them from killing or taking up arms. The grouping became the Baptist Peace Fellowship of North America in 1984 (see below).

Activities. During the 1950s membership of the Fellowship expanded rapidly against the background of the Cold War. Over the succeeding years, several Fellowship members became presidents of the American Baptist Churches. In 1983 a 50-member delegation from the Fellowship visited the Soviet Union. Discussions which took place following the return of the delegation culminated in a meeting at Deer Park Baptist Church in Louisville, Kentucky (a southern Baptist congregation which had established the *Baptist Peacemaker*—see separate entry), at which representatives from the Baptist Peace Fellowship, the *Baptist Peacemaker* group and local Baptist groups, together with other concerned pastors and lay people, took the decision to establish the Baptist Peace Fellowship of North America.

Membership. The Fellowship is controlled by a steering committee composed of equal representation from each American Baptist tradition together with a representative of the Baptist World Alliance. Activities are co-ordinated by a four-member executive committee.

Publication. Peaceworks, the Fellowship's newsletter, is published quarterly; the Fellowship also has partial responsibility for the distribution of the *Baptist Peacemaker*.

Affiliations. Baptist Peacemaker Group; Baptist World Alliance.

Baptist Peacemaker Group

Address. 1733 Bardstown Road, Louisville, Kentucky, USA

Aims and objectives. Centred on the quarterly publication *Baptist Peacemaker*, this Group aims to support and encourage Baptists from the southern states in "the mission of peacemaking". The Group concentrates on the spiritual aspects of peace work, seeking to "explore the biblical basis of peacemaking, to foster a peacemaking lifestyle and to examine the peacemaker's inward and outward journey".

Formation. Baptist Peacemaker was set up on Feb. 17, 1980, at the initiative of Robert Broome following the first meeting of the Deer Park Baptist Church World Peacemakers.

Activities. The Group's main regular activity consists of publishing *Baptist Peacemaker*, a quarterly tabloid. It also provides information resources to Baptist and other peace groups in the USA and overseas. It co-operated with the Religious Society of Friends (Quakers) in a national colloquy on "Prayer and Holy Obedience in a War-racked World" in June 1981. In August 1982 it organized a national peace conference on "strategies for Peacemaking".

Baptist Peacemaker has co-sponsored Baptist Peace Friendship Tours to the Soviet Union annually since 1983, and it also sent a delegation to the first West German Baptist Peace Conference in April 1984. It has recently set up an international division and is planning further tours to China, Nicaragua and El Salvador. The Group is currently exploring the possibility of a Baptist liaison peace representative in the All-Union Council of Evangelical Christians in Moscow.

Membership. There is no formal membership system in operation, but the Group claims to reach about 20,000 people, the majority southern Baptists, through the *Baptist Peacemaker* journal.

Publications. In addition to the *Baptist Peacemaker*, the Group have published *Journey into Peacemaking* by Glen Stassen and *Peacemaking and A Tangled Wing* by Robert Broome (the organization's founder). It has also produced reports on its conference and joint meeting with the Quakers.

Affiliations. The Group has direct links with the Baptist Peace Fellowship of North America and with the Baptist Peace Resource Centre.

Campaign for Peace and Democracy/East and West

Address. PO Box 1640, Cathedral Station, New York, NY 10025, USA

Aims and objectives. The Campaign aims to unite peace and democratic movements in the East, the West and the Third World. Its objective is to create an alternative to the superpower system and it opposes militarism, interventionism and repression.

The organization supports movements working for peace, democracy and social justice in the United States and in countries within the American sphere of influence such as South Africa, Chile and Turkey. It also supports the Polish Solidarity movement and defends independent peace movements in the Eastern bloc.

In late 1985 the Campaign co-operated with the California-based journal *Across Frontiers* to secure international support for a statement denouncing the Reagan administration's "escalating war on Nicaragua" and protesting against "this ominous heightening of the Cold War". Published as an advertisement in the *New York Times* of December 1, 1985, the statement was signed by 34 leading independent peace and human rights activists in Eastern Europe and the Soviet Union as well by prominent individuals from the West, including Daniel Ellsberg, E. P. Thompson, Petra Kelly, Simone de Beauvoir and Günter Grass.

Formation. The Campaign was founded in 1982.

Activities. The organization arranges meetings and discussion groups to promote the exchange and development of ideas on peace issues. It also produces publications and provides the media with information about international peace and democratic movements.

Membership. The Campaign has 1,500 active members from various peace, labour, religious and women's rights movements.

Publications. Peace and Democracy News, three times a year.

Catholic Peace Fellowship (CPF)

Address. 339 Lafayette Street, New York, NY 10012, USA

Aims and objectives. The Catholic Peace Fellowship aims to initiate action and educational projects among Catholics in the spirit of non-violence. Its ultimate objective is to turn the Catholic Church into a "peace church". It seeks in particular to make Catholics aware of the pacifist, non-violent tradition of the pre-Constantinian Church and of the subsequent Catholic attitudes towards such concepts as the "just war". It is currently working towards the development of a "theology of peace" and of principles and techniques of non-violent resistance.

Members of the CPF subscribe to the six principles outlined in the statement of purpose of the Fellowship of Reconciliation (see separate entry).

Formation. The CPF was formed in 1964 (in the wake of Pope John's encyclical letter *Pacem in Terris*) by Catholic members of the Fellowship of Reconciliation.

Activities. The group was actively involved in the opposition to the Vietnam War and it has since supported campaigns of civil disobedience and of draft resistance. It works with other peace groups for the abolition of the draft legislation. The CPF provides a counselling service to Catholic conscientious objectors.

The CPF supports the Nuclear Freeze campaign in the USA, and publicizes the pastoral letter, *The Challenge of Peace: God's Promise and Our Response*, approved by the US national conference of Catholic Bishops, which effectively calls for a "no first use" of nuclear weapons policy. The CPF encourages civil disobedience as a means of working for nuclear disarmament.

The CPF also works to prevent US military intervention in Central America. It has participated in demonstrations against US policy in the region and helped to organize an "emergency response network" to oppose any invasion that might take place. The group has sponsored trips to the area.

Membership. The CPF has 5,500 members, all of whom are Catholic pacifists.

Publications. The group publishes two newsletters: *Catholic Peace Fellowship Bulletin* and *Catholic Peace Fellowship Organizers News*. It has also produced a booklet, *Catholics and Conscientious Objectors* (by Jim Forest), and various supplements on peace education.

Affiliations. Fellowship of Reconciliation.

Center for Defense Information (CDI)

Address. 303 Capitol Gallery West, 600 Maryland Avenue SW, Washington, DC 20024, USA

Aims and objectives. The primary purpose of the CDI is to provide reliable and timely information concerning US national security policies and programmes to Congress, the media and the general public.

The CDI is a private, non-partisan research organization which analyses US national security policies and programmes based on the experience of senior retired members of the armed services.

CDI also provides information to the public through an active media programme; to the Congress in testimony to various committees and through an active outreach programme.

Formation. The CDI was founded in 1972 by Admiral Gene R. La Rocque, a retired rear admiral in the US Navy.

Activities. The CDI is involved in providing the public with information on military and defense issues, based on careful analysis and research and in lobbying Congress.

Membership. The CDI is not a membership organization, but circulates its journal to over 70,000 people in the US and abroad.

Publications. *The Defense Monitor* is published 10–12 times a year and covers a relevant defense or arms control issue.

Center for Peace Studies

Address. Room 410, Maguire Building, Georgetown University, Washington, DC 20057, USA

Aims and objectives. The Center seeks to integrate peace studies into the broader curriculum at Georgetown University through an interdisciplinary peace studies programme, and to develop a Christian response to the arms race.

Formation. The peace studies programme at Georgetown was begun in 1965 in response to the debate over the morality of US involvement in the war in Vietnam and the instruction of Vatican II to teachers "to regard as their most weighty task to instruct all in a new understanding of peace".

Activities. The Center is concerned with developing the interdisciplinary peace studies programme and working with similar groups elsewhere to promote such studies.

Affiliations. The Center is affiliated to Pax Christi USA and also the UN University for Peace (in Costa Rica).

Center for Peaceful Change

Address. Kent State University, Kent, Ohio 44242, USA

Aims and objectives. The Center offers a course of university study leading to a major in "integrative change".

Formation. The Center for Peaceful Change was founded in 1971 as a "living memorial" to four students killed by National Guardsmen during a protest against the war in Vietnam at Kent State University in May 1970.

Activities. In addition to running its course, the Center is involved in efforts to extend the study of peace issues and conflict management in Ohio education.

Publication. Peace and Change: A Journal of Peace Research.

Affiliations. Consortium on Peace Research, Education and Development (COPRED); Consortium on Peace Research in History; Society of Professionals in Dispute Resolution (SPIDR).

Center for War, Peace and the News Media, New York University

Address. 1021 Main Building, New York University, New York, NY 10003, USA

Aims and objectives. The Center aims to correct what it regards as the inadequacy of the news media's coverage of the arms race and related issues by evaluating the reporting and suggesting ways to improve it.

Activities. In addition to its press monitoring and publications work, the Center holds regular symposia and conferences on subjects germane to its field of work.

Publications. The Center produces a bulletin called *Deadline* which appears as a supplement to the bi-monthly journal *Nuclear Times*. It also publishes scholarly papers and books.

Center for War/Peace Studies (CW/PS)

Address. 218 East 18th Street, New York, NY 10003, USA

Aims and objectives. The CW/PS has as its basic objective the carrying out of "applied research towards a world of peace with justice", seeking to develop concepts which would "influence the global political process in the direction of a peaceful and just world order".

Activities. The Center works with individuals and organizations on various research and educational projects, focused in recent years on (i) arms control and disarmament; (ii) reform of the United Nations system; (iii) the Law of the Sea; and (iv) conflict in the Middle East. It has in particular developed the "Binding Triad" proposal under which the UN General Assembly would have the authority to make binding decisions (by weighted votes) and thus become a genuine decision-making body in the sphere of disarmament.

Publications. Global Report, quarterly newsletter; occasional special studies.

Central Committee for Conscientious Objectors (CCCO)

Address. 2208 South Street, Philadelphia, Pennsylvania 19146, USA

Aims and objectives. CCCO aims to provide information and counselling to those subject to US military and draft law and, in particular, to conscientious objectors.

Formation. The Committee was set up in 1948, originally to assist conscientious objectors under the 1948 draft law.

Activities. In addition to its work with conscientious objectors, CCCO also provides counselling directly to military personnnel, with particular emphasis on discharge counselling. It also works with young people of military age who may be considering enlistment with the services.

CCCO acts as advocate of the rights of conscientious objectors before the relevant government agencies and, in certain cases, the law courts. It has trained some 3,000 military lawyers and counsellors in the USA and abroad, who provide advice to all its target groups. The Committee is developing its counselling activities near US military bases overseas and increasing its "outreach work" to young people of enlistment age.

Membership. CCCO is not a membership body, but has a mailing list of some 40,000 people who have acted as draft or military counsellors, who have registered with the organization as a conscientious objector, who have contributed to it financially, or in some other role represent an "interested party" in its work.

Publications. CCCO produces two regular journals, *CCCO Notes* (a quarterly) and *The Objector* (ten times per year). Four books have been produced: *Handbook for Conscientious Objectors*; *Advice for Conscientious Objectors in the Armed Forces*; *Military Counsellor's Manual*; and *Draft Counsellor's Manual*. It has also produced a large number of brochures, leaflets etc.

Children's Campaign for Nuclear Disarmament

Address. 14 Everit Street, New Haven, Connecticut 06513, USA

Aims and objectives. The Children's Campaign for Nuclear Disarmament seeks to educate young people about nuclear war. Its stated objective is to set up "a network of kids working for world peace and helping each other to grow up in the nuclear age".

Formation. The Campaign was established by a group of friends in Vermont in May 1981.

Activities. The Campaign is concentrated on efforts to talk to children in schools and to encourage them to be active on the nuclear issue. It has sponsored childrens' letter-writing campaigns to the US President, and has organized a number of rallies, vigils and other actions against nuclear war and militarism.

Membership. The Campaign has approximately 3,000 members, all of whom are between the ages of six and 18, organized into 80 separate chapters in the USA and elsewhere.

Publications. The Campaign publishes a bi-monthly *CCND Newsletter*, which is prepared by the CCND central group and despatched to the individual chapters and to other peace organizations.

Citizens Against Nuclear War (CAN)

Address. 1201 16th Street NW, Washington, DC 20036, USA

Aims and objectives. CAN works with the national membership organizations which support it to encourage their individual members to become active in the anti-war movement. All the supporting organizations favour a bilateral freeze on nuclear weapons, and emphasis is placed on demonstrating the falsity of the perception that all people in the nuclear disarmament movement are middle class and white.

Activities. CAN has sought to stimulate awareness of the nuclear arms issue in its member organizations. It has lobbied in particular for the continuation of the ABM and SALT treaties, and against the Strategic Defence Initiative. In early 1986 it held a conference on "The Nuclear Arms Race: Survival Dilemma for People of Colour", bringing together many groups and individuals linked by a common desire to promote nuclear disarmament for the benefit not only of the United States but also for people of colour around the globe.

Membership. CAN was formed under the leadership of the executive director of the National Education Association (the largest public school teachers' union) as a coalition of 27 national organizations representing teachers, trade unionists, senior citizens, women, churches, medical people and minorities (blacks, Hispanics, Asians and American Indians). The number of organizations holding membership in CAN had grown to over 60 (with a total of 20,000,000 members) by mid-1986.

Publications. A newsletter is issued to member organizations.

Affiliations. CAN has some 40 organizations as associated members, including the Federation of American Scientists, Union of Concerned Scientists, Jobs with Peace, Physicians for Social Responsibility, Student/Teacher Organization to Prevent Nuclear War, War Resisters' League, Women's International League for Peace and Freedom, World Peacemakers, and Women's Action for Nuclear Disarmament.

Clergy and Laity Concerned (CALC)

Address. 198 Broadway, New York, NY 10038, USA

Aims and objectives. CALC describes itself as "an interfaith peace and justice organization of people called to social action by religious faith or ethical principles".

Formation. The group was created in 1965 to oppose US policy in Vietnam and South-East Asia generally.

Activities. CALC participates with the major US peace movements in campaigns for nuclear and general disarmament and for the conversion of the armaments industry to socially useful purposes. The group has been particularly involved in actions to oppose the deployment of new nuclear missiles in Western Europe. It is also concerned with social, developmental and human rights issues both in the United States and abroad.

Publication. CALC report, monthly.

Affiliations. US affiliations include the Nuclear Weapons Freeze Campaign and the Jobs With Peace Campaign.

Coalition for a New Foreign and Military Policy

Address. 712 G Street SE, Washington, DC 20003, USA

Aims and objectives. The Coalition seeks to combine grassroots organizing with co-ordinated activity on Capitol Hill to reduce military spending, protect human rights, promote arms control, and establish a non-interventionist and demilitarized US foreign policy.

Formation. The Coalition was formed in 1976.

Activities. The Coalition maintains a computerized citizen action network data base which helps it to mobilize support within its member organizations for its lobbying activities in Washington. The Coalition's staff, in turn, maintains contact with active groups, providing them with help through training workshops, "outreach" and networking, and educational materials. Washington-based working groups of the Coalition set legislative priorities for key issues and develop the organizing and lobbying strategies to press for action.

Coalition policy is set by a board of directors, composed of one representative from each member organization, while an elected executive council meets monthly to oversee implementation of board decisions. There is also a small full-time staff.

An important part of the Coalition's work has been in following, and trying to influence, legislation in Congress of relevance to arms control, US sanctions against South Africa, US covert military intervention in Central America, and similar issues. The Coalition recognizes the importance of sustained pressure on congressmen from voters in their own districts as a factor in policy-making, and organizes that pressure through its "Field Programme".

The Coalition was strongly critical of the US air strike on Libya in April 1986, which it described as an "act of terror".

Membership. The Coalition has 55 member organizations and 15,000 "network" members (individuals and local groups). The member organizations include a broad range of church movements of Christian and other denominations, as well as peace, developmental, human rights and minority groups.

Publications. Coalition Close-Up, quarterly newsletter; *Budget Bulletin* (tracing the course of appropriations legislation for military purposes), 10–15 times a year; *Action Guides* and *Action Alerts*, mailed to members several times a year as issues arise; numerous pamphlets and other materials.

Coalition for a Nuclear-Free Harbour

Address. 135 West 4th Street, New York, NY 10012, USA

Aims and objectives. This Coalition opposes the US Navy's plan to base the *Iowa* nuclear battleship task force at the Staten Island harbour of New York City.

Formation. The Coalition was launched in August 1983.

Activities. With the participation of various groups and prominent individuals, the Coalition mounted a Campaign for a Nuclear Navyport Referendum in 1985, seeking to place the issue of the Staten Island base on the ballot paper in the Nov. 5, 1985, New York City elections. With a minimum of 50,000 signatures of registered voters being required, by early September 1985 nearly 112,000 had been obtained and over 60,000 had been declared valid. The intention was that Question 6 on the ballot paper would request support for the proposition that the city authorities should not volunteer funds or property for the proposed port; it would not, and could not, have prevented the US Navy from coming to New York. However, the campaign was strongly opposed at official level on the grounds of the "unconstitutionality of allowing New Yorkers to influence national defence policy" and five days before the elections a New York City judge ruled that Question 6 should not appear on the ballot paper. The Coalition responded by organizing an unofficial ballot and has stated its intention of continuing its campaign.

Committee Against Registration and the Draft

Address. 731 State Street, Madison, Wisconsin 53703, USA

Aims and objectives. The Committee seeks to build a broad grassroots movement opposed to registration for military service and the draft.

Formation. The Committee was formed in 1979 to oppose legislation for the return of draft registration.

Activities. The Committee gives legal and political support to draft resisters.

Membership. The Committee links 60 national and local organizations.

Publications. The Anti-Draft, bi-monthly; various brochures and leaflets.

Committee for a Sane Nuclear Policy (SANE)

Address. 711 G Street SE, Washington, DC 20003, USA

Aims and objectives. SANE is committed to total nuclear disarmament and to the conversion of military industry to civilian production.

Formation. SANE was established in 1957 as a campaign directed principally against the atmospheric testing of nuclear weapons.

Activities. SANE took part in the protest movement against the Vietnam War. It claims to have been instrumental in building widespread support for the Anti-Ballistic Missile (ABM) treaty of 1972. It has more recently played a leading part in the campaign against the development of the MX missile. SANE participates in campaigns for a nuclear freeze and for a nuclear testing ban, together with other disarmament proposals. It is currently involved with efforts to bring peace to Central America.

SANE conducts a number of educational campaigns related to military spending and the possibility of economic conversion, involving the transfer of resources currently allocated to defence expenditure. It carries out regular lobbies of Congress, and runs a political action committee during national election campaigns. It took part in the April 1985 peace demonstration in Washington and in 1986 launched a major new publicity campaign in support of a nuclear test ban, focusing on the fact that "thanks to billions of dollars in research and underground testing, it is now possible to fit a powerful nuclear warhead into an airline carry-on bag".

Membership. SANE has 100,000 individual members across the USA, while a further 35,000 participate as activities organized by congressional district.

Publications. *SANE World*, a newsletter despatched to members, is published monthly. The group also produces numerous leaflets and brochures on specific issues of concern to the campaign.

Affiliations. A member of the Coalition for a New Foreign and Military policy, SANE is also active in the Nuclear Weapons Freeze Campaign and the Rainbow Coalition; it has endorsed the Coalition on Block Grants and the Central America Peace Campaign.

Committee for National Security (CNS)

Address. 2000 P Street NW, Washington, DC 20036 USA

Aims and objectives. The Committee aims to advance and protect US national security while reducing the risk of nuclear war.

Formation. The CNS was formed in 1980.

Activities. The CNS believes that only through sustained educational efforts can the general public concern over nuclear war be turned into an active, informed constituency for alternative national security policies. As a result, it has initiated a "Community Visits" programme that pairs prominent Committee members with community leaders to discuss national security issues, such as "Star Wars" and the "nuclear winter" possibility.

The CNS has also organized press conferences and round table discussions on such topics as sea-launched cruise missiles; the US defence budget; the global campaign to halt underground testing; a national campaign to save the ABM Treaty; national security; not for men only; and spending for a sound defence: alternatives to the Reagan military budget.

Modelled on these conferences, the CNS also arranges regional ones, particularly directed at women throughout the United States. Many of these conferences are designed to provide women with the resources, training and expertise needed to draw them into active participation in national security policy. At the Third Annual Women's Leadership Conference on the Economics of National Security, participants came from 36 states and 126 organizations.

The Committee has organized a National Security and Foreign Policy Speakers' Bureau, composed of 14 arms control organizations. Over 3,000 requests have been filled since September 1983 and the CNS is currently supplementing the Bureau with names of Soviet experts. In co-operation with the Harriman Institute at Columbia University, the CNS is preparing a study series about the USSR. It is intended for use by foreign affairs organizations, churches, continuing education programmes in order to increase America's knowledge and understanding of the Soviet Union.

Membership. The Committee is a leadership group composed of about 100 prominent individuals.

Publications. *A Sensible Alternative for a Sounder Defence*; *Preventing Nuclear War— The Case for a Comprehensive Test Ban*; Fact Sheets and Common Questions series; Military Budget Resource Guide; Proceedings from Women's Leadership Conferences; *Soviet Women* (in the Soviet Studies series).

Common Cause

Address. 2030 M Street NW, Washington, DC 20036 USA

Aims and objectives. Common Cause is a non-party lobbying group concerned with nuclear arms control, accountability in government, tax reform and other policy issues.

Formation. Common Cause was founded in 1970 by John Gardner.

Activities. Past and current campaigns include the reform of presidential election funding, women's rights' issues, improved oversight of military spending, limitation of expenditure on the MX missile and "Star Wars" projects, and the control of the national deficit. Common Cause also gives annual public service achievement awards.

Membership. There are 250,000 members throughout the United States.

Publications. Common Cause Magazine, bi-monthly.

Conscience and Military Tax Campaign (CMTC)

Address. 44 Bellhaven Road, Bellport, New York 11713, USA

Aims and objectives. The CMTC's aim is to build up resistance to the payment of taxes for military purposes to a politically significant level, thereby assisting in the passage through Congress of the proposed US Peace Tax Fund Bill (see separate entry for National Campaign for a US Peace Tax Fund). Its immediate goal is to gather 100,000 signatories to its resolution, which pledges the signatory to refuse payment of military taxes upon being notified that 100,000 people have agreed to do so. Military tax refusal would continue until Congress had provided an alternative, such as the US Peace Tax Fund, for those who objected on conscientious grounds to having a portion of their taxes used for military purposes.

Formation. CMTC was set up in November 1979 by two members of the steering committee of the National Campaign for a World Peace Tax Fund (as it was then known). Certain members of the Campaign had argued that stronger measures, including civil disobedience, were required to focus congressional attention on the Peace Tax Fund Bill, while others felt that identification of the Campaign with a willingness to break the law would be detrimental. CMTC was created, therefore, as a separate organization in order to satisfy both these views.

Activities. CMTC concentrates on encouraging more people to sign its resolution—by late 1985, about 5,000 signatories had been collected in five years of campaigning. It gives support to individuals who are already withholding a part or all of their taxes, many of whom redirect their payments into the CMTC's escrow account, which has been created in anticipation of the passage of the Peace Tax Fund Bill or similar legislation.

Membership. CMTC has a mailing list of approximately 5,000 people.

Publications. The group publishes a quarterly newsletter and various information and campaign brochures; it has also published several books, including *The Illegality of War* and *People Pay for Peace*, both by William Durland.

Affiliations. National Campaign for a US Peace Tax Fund.

Consortium on Peace Research, Education and Development (COPRED)

Address. 911 West High Street, room 100N, Urbana, Illinois 61801, USA

Aims and objectives. COPRED seeks to provide "broad-based linkage and interchange among peace educators, researchers and professionals, activists and practitioners to maximize the effectiveness of common work for peace and social justice".

Activities. COPRED participates in networks in various sectors, organizing study groups, conferences and research projects as well as carrying on a publications programme.

Publications. COPRED *Peace Chronicle*; *Peace and Change: A Journal of Peace Research*.

Affiliations. International Peace Research Association; International Studies Association; Canadian Peace Research and Education Association; *Consejo Latinoamericano de Investigadores para la Paz*; Conference on Peace Research in History; American Association for the Advancement of Science.

Council for a Liveable World

Address. 20 Park Plaza, Boston, Massachusetts 02116, USA (national office); 100 Maryland Avenue NE, Washington, DC 20002, USA (legislative office)

Aims and objectives. The Council was established to combat the threat of nuclear war and to strengthen national security through rational arms control. It is a bi-partisan organization which seeks to achieve its aims principally through assisting in the election to the US Senate of candidates who favour arms control measures and in the progress of arms control legislation. The Council is particularly concerned with working for a mutual, verifiable nuclear weapons' freeze and for a complete nuclear test ban treaty; it is opposed to the Strategic Defence Initiative.

A Council for a Liveable World Education Fund has been set up to inform the public of the consequences of the use of nuclear weapons.

Formation. The Council was formed in 1962 by the nuclear physicist Dr Leo Szilard.

Activities. The Council has assisted in the election of 65 senators, including George McGovern, who credits the Council with facilitating his first election victory. The Council helps initiate and draft arms control legislation and provides expert witnesses for congressional hearings. Its lobbying office in Washington arranges "off the record" seminars for senators on foreign policy, military strategy and weapons systems (including in the latter case seminars on the neutron bomb, MX and "Star Wars" systems). In the 1984 elections the Council raised over $1,000,000 for Senate candidates committed to nuclear arms control.

The Council also lobbies the Administration, including representatives of the White House, the National Security Council, and State and Defence Departments and the Arms Control and Disarmament Agency.

The Education Fund, founded in 1980, distributes literature and organizes conferences on such matters as the medical effects of nuclear weapons and the consequences of a "no first use" policy.

In 1982 the Council established the Peace Political Action Committee (see separate entry) to undertake similar work in respect of the House of Representatives.

Membership. The Council has an estimated 85,000 supporters and is controlled by a board of directors who include Jerome B. Wiesner and John Kenneth Galbraith.

Publications. These include fact sheets, pamphlets, reprints of newspaper articles and two books—*The Final Epidemic* (a collection of papers presented at a number of symposiums on the medical and environmental consequences of nuclear war) and *MX—Prescription for Disaster* by Herbert Scoville.

Earth's Youth for Peace

Address. c/o 101 Richmond, suite A, Nicholasville, Kentucky 40356, USA

Aims and objectives. This group's main objective is to unite the people of the world as "one nation in the universe" in peace. It aims to do this by facilitating understanding between peoples through the youth of the world. Thus it works for improved communication between young people from different countries and peace projects.

Activities. Earth's Youth for Peace works to unite all peace movements and establish world-wide communication between them. The group is active in establishing programmes in schools and colleges for youth leadership in the community and in government.

Membership. The organization has 207,000 members throughout the world.

Publications. Earth's Youth for Peace produces various publications including *A Newsletter with Exchange of Country Ideas and Active programmes.*

Educators for Social Responsibility (ESR)

Address. 23 Garden Street, Cambridge, Massachusetts 02138, USA

Aims and objectives. ESR aims to bring together parents, teachers and individuals to respond directly and sensitively to children's questions and fears about nuclear war, "as well as addressing the related issues of the nature of peace and the importance of citizen participation".

Formation. ESR was set up on a national level in 1981.

Activities. Local "chapters" organize lectures, conferences and workshops for teachers on education techniques and international understanding in the nuclear age. ESR provides speakers and runs consulting services. It organized a national "Day of Dialogue" and a number of events based around the screening of the film *The Day After*. ESR has been particularly concerned to rebut accusations that it seeks to indoctrinate or scare children.

Membership. ESR has over 7,000 members and supporters in the USA, Canada and elsewhere; many of these belong to ESR's 95 local chapters.

Publications. Forum, quarterly newsletter. ESR also markets material on new forms of teaching technique based on conflict-resolution and multi-cultural understanding; these include *Perspectives, Dialogue and Decision-making in the Nuclear Age.*

Episcopal Peace Fellowship (EPF)

Address. 620 G Street SE, Washington, DC 20003, USA

Aims and objectives. The EPF "is a body of Episcopalians dedicated to discovering and practising what peace is and what is needed to end war and the militarism that feeds it". It "endeavours to develop, within the Church, a community of Christians pledged to renounce, so far as is possible, participation in war and to espouse non-violence in the works of reconciliation in parish and nation, as well as in the larger world community".

Formation. The EPF was founded on Armistice Day 1939.

Activities. During the Second World War the EPF gave support to Episcopalian conscientious objectors and their families; subsequently it "broadened its witness within the Church to oppose war, militarism and the legitimized uses of violence".

Under its current programme of activities, the EPF (i) introduces peace issue resolutions at the Episcopalian general convention and provides participants with educational and liturgical materials on peace; (ii) counsels young Episcopalians who are considering conscientous objection to military service and offers them support in their dealings with official military bodies; (iii) participates in nationwide efforts to end the death penalty; (iv) opposes the militarization of the church ministry to those in the armed forces; (v) works with other groups around the world in trying to halt the nuclear arms race; (vi) supports "war tax resistance"; and (vii) arranges for publications, workshops, speakers and conferences on peace initiatives.

Membership. Members of the EPF are encouraged to join or start a local chapter. The Fellowship's policies and programmes are determined by a 15-member national executive committee, one-third of which is elected each year by the membership at large.

Publications. The EPF publishes a quarterly newsletter as well as peace education materials.

Affiliations. Fellowship of Reconciliation (of the United States).

Fellowship of Reconciliation (FoR)

Address. P.O. Box 271, Nyack, New York 10960, USA

Aims and objectives. FoR seeks the abolition of war and to aid through non-violent means the victims of injustice and exploitation. It is the US section of the International Fellowship of Reconciliation.

Formation. The American FoR was established in November 1915 (a year after the movement was launched in Europe).

Activities. The activities of the US Fellowship have included support for the civil rights movement, non-violent resistance to the Second World War, opposition to the war in Vietnam in the 1960s and early 1970s, and work for disarmament and against nuclear weapons, particularly since the end of the 1970s. FoR's predominant concern at this time is to seek nuclear disarmament and Soviet–US reconciliation.

Membership. The US Fellowship has 11,000 pacifists in membership.

Publications. Fellowship, eight times a year.

Affiliations. International Fellowship of Reconciliation.

Freeze—see entry for **Nuclear Weapons Freeze Campaign**

Friends Committee on National Legislation (FCNL)

Address. 245 2nd Street NE, Washington, DC 20002, USA

Aims and objectives. The FCNL acts as a political lobbying agency on behalf of the pacifist aspirations of the US Quaker community (see also entry for American Friends Service Committee).

Publications. FCNL Washington Newsletter, monthly.

Gaudete Peace and Justice Center

Address. 634 Spruce Street, Madison, Wisconsin 53175, USA

Aims and objectives. The Center aims to encourage and support Christian non-violent resistance to the nuclear arms race, either through legal means or through civil disobedience/divine obedience.

Formation. The Center was founded in 1981.

Activities. The group holds weekly prayer vigils at the Wisconsin Federal Center and also organizes liturgies and symbolic witnesses. It provides counselling for people who wish to resist tax or who wish to engage in civil disobedience. The Center helps people in a variety of ways, such as encouragement of public speaking.

Membership. There is no specific membership as people participate in certain activities and do not feel bound to subscribe to any philosophy or platform except Christian non-violence. There are four people on the board of directors (two of whom are now serving 18-year prison terms for civil disobedience offences).

Publications. Harvest of Justice, bi-monthly.

Ground Zero

Address. 806 15th Street NW, suite 421, Washington, DC 20005, USA

Aims and objectives. Ground Zero "is a non-partisan, non-advocacy educational organization whose goal is to involve citizens in the effort to find creative solutions to the problem of preventing nuclear war".

Formation. Ground Zero was founded in 1981 by Dr Roger Molander, former staff member of the White House National Security Council (1974–81) whose principal area of responsibility was strategic nuclear policy; he served as chairman of the working group which prepared the analytical research for the SALT II negotiations.

Activities. The organization's first major activity was "Ground Zero Week" on April 18–25, 1982, during which over one million Americans participated in nuclear war educational activities in their communities. Since then Ground Zero has operated on the premise that "an informed public can make the right choices about our nation's security", that it is "not necessary that every citizen [should] have the level of technical knowledge that national security experts possess", but that "every citizen has the ability—and the obligation—to know the basic facts about our nation's nuclear weapons policies". To this end Ground Zero produces programmes and materials designed to make the facts about nuclear war accessible to citizens and with a broad popular appeal.

Ground Zero has worked to institutionalize nuclear war education in existing community structures such as schools, religious congregations and service organizations. Its particular contribution to public education is its "fuses and firebreaks" concept, which it describes as "a structured way of looking at the nuclear war problem" and which involves citizens being encouraged to ask two simple questions: (i) how might a nuclear war begin? and (ii) what are the resources available to prevent that from happening? In the latter respect Ground Zero advocates six "firebreaks" for preventing nuclear war, namely (i) nuclear non-proliferation; (ii) nuclear arms control; (iii) improved conflict resolution; (iv) control of conventional arms sales; (v) improved super-power crisis communication; and (vi) improved US–Soviet relations.

Within the foregoing framework Ground Zero works in communities throughout the United States, offering programmes which enable citizens to learn about the nuclear war issue and to share their knowledge with others. With the assistance of its local groups, the Ground Zero national office distributes a wide variety of resources, including three commercial paperback books, curriculum materials for teachers and a bi-monthly newsletter. Its "Firebreaks War/Peace Game", a role-playing crisis game for groups interested in learning about nuclear war prevention, has been played by over 7,000 groups nationwide.

Ground Zero has two ancillary bodies, namely (i) the Ground Zero Pairing Project (established in 1982), which seeks to pair US and Soviet cities "to form a framework for establishing bridge-building programmes wherein citizens in both countries may learn more about the other"; and (ii) the Ground Zero Resource Center (P.O. Box 19329, Portland, Oregon 97219), which produces and distributes games, educational packages and promotional materials all designed to publicize the movement's basic message.

Publications. In addition to a bi-monthly newsletter, Ground Zero and its ancillary bodies publish a wide range of material. Its basic primer, *Nuclear War: What's In It for You?*, has become a nationwide bestseller.

Gualala Nuclear Education (GENIE)

Address. 32830 Highway One, Gualala, California 95445, USA

Aims and objectives. GENIE aims to educate public opinion on the issue of nuclear disarmament. It also promotes the activities of local peace groups.

Formation. GENIE has been actively involved in peace work since 1982.

Activities. The group provides speakers for local schools and organizations and publishes its own educational materials. GENIE has testified at governmental hearings and worked actively for various candidates and bills at election time. It maintains a local telephone-tree network for action alerts.

Membership. GENIE has one full-time staff member who co-ordinates the activities of around 50 volunteers.

Publications. GENIE has produced postcards and stationery entitled *20 Steps Toward Peace* and a poster *In Case of Nuclear Attack* which is a satire on civil defence instructions.

High Technology Professionals for Peace (HTPFP)

Address. 639 Massachusetts Avenue, room 316, Cambridge, Massachusetts 02139, USA

Aims and objectives. HTPFP consists of scientists, engineers and technical workers who are concerned with the threat of nuclear war. Its main purpose is to provide information about the impact of weapons systems on national security, the environment, the economy and society. It is an active supporter of the nuclear freeze campaign.

Activities. HTPFP sponsors a lecture programme by scientists, policy experts and high-technology executives covering such topics as the history and capability of nuclear weapons systems and the relationship between technological research and its military applications. It has acted as co-sponsor in organizing a forum on possible diversification and conversion of the arms industry and also an interfaith conference concerned with counselling for employees in the defence industry. The group provides expert speakers for community, university and church groups on such matters as nuclear proliferation and the career implications of employment in the defence industry, and it also produces a number of research papers.

HTPFP members attend conferences on national security and provide information to legislators on weapons technology and related policy matters. It has also undertaken the analysis of political candidates positions on military research and arms control policy. It was represented at the US–Soviet conference on conversion of the military economy, held in Moscow in June 1984.

HTPFP has established a non-profit employment agency in the greater Boston area in order to facilitate the task of technology professionals seeking alternatives to weapons-related work. The agency was used by over 150 companies in its first year of operation.

Membership. Due to the fact that many of HTPFP's members work in jobs requiring security clearance, membership details are confidential; the group's general policies are decided at annual meetings.

Publications. Technology and Responsibility, the group's newsletter, is published four times a year.

Institute for Defense and Disarmament Studies (IDDS)

Address. 2001 Beacon Street, Brookline, Massachusetts 02146, USA

Aims and objectives. The IDDS is a non-profit research and education center which believes that "the principles of democracy and the rule of law should prevail among nations as well as within them". Its central purpose "is to study the nature and uses of armed force and the obstacles to and the opportunities for disarmament".

Formation. The Institute was founded in 1980.

Activities. The IDDS conducts a public education programme "intended to popularize and disseminate the results of the Institute's research through publications, public speaking and other activities". Major projects of its research programme include (i) a survey of the history, numbers and capabilities of the major weapons produced in all countries since the Second World War; (ii) a survey of weapons production capacity and projected rates of production in the future; (iii) an analysis of the main objectives of past and current military policies, relating objectives to force components, weapons systems and military spending; (iv) a history and monthly update of the positions of all governments in arms control negotiations since 1945; (v) a survey of the goals, activities and impact of non-governmental peace movements in the United States; and (vi) development of a theory of "how we might strengthen internalized constraints against the use of force so that the international system could evolve into a co-operative democratic system in which military forces, if they exist at all, are maintained only for defence, strictly and narrowly defined".

Publications. Arms Control Reporter, monthly reference report on disarmament negotiations and proposals; the Institute's other publications include the *American Peace Directory.*

Institute for Policy Studies (IPS)

Address. 1901 Q Street NW, Washington, DC 20009, USA

Aims and objectives. The IPS is a research and public education body seeking to increase knowledge and awareness of the underlying realities of the arms race.

Activities. The Institute's programmes have focused on disarmament proposals, the arms trade (especially US arms sales abroad) and the current status of the nuclear arms race and nuclear weapons deployment. It conducts seminars and conferences on these themes and also publishes papers and books on its research findings.

Publications. The IPS publishes pamphlets, research papers and books, as well as providing a press monitoring service on disarmament issues.

Interfaith Center to Reverse the Arms Race

Address. 132 N. Euclid Avenue, Pasadena, California 91101, USA

Activities. This Center runs a subscription service providing news and information on peace issues.

Jane Addams Peace Association (JAPA)

Address. 777 United Nations Plaza, New York, NY 10017, USA

Aims and objectives. JAPA seeks to promote international understanding and peace.

Formation. JAPA was formed in 1948.

Activities. Acting as the educational fund of the Women's International League for Peace and Freedom (see separate entry), JAPA has organized children's international art exchanges, various films, publications, conferences and children's book awards. It has also been active in promoting co-operation and contacts between US and Soviet women's groups.

Publications. Building Peace.

Affiliations. Women's International League for Peace and Freedom.

Jewish Peace Fellowship

Address. P.O. Box 271, Nyack, New York 10960, USA

Aims and objectives. The Fellowship is composed of Jews who hold the belief that Jewish ideals and experience provide inspiration for a non-violent way of life. Members refrain from participation in war or military service and engage in general work "to create a community of concern transcending national boundaries and selfish interests".

Formation. The Jewish Peace Fellowship was founded in 1941 by Rabbi Abraham Cronbach, Rabbi Isidor Hoffman and Jane Evans.

Activities. The Fellowship was concerned initially with establishing the right of Jews to be recognized as conscientious objectors, and in its early years it concentrated on this issue and on providing counselling to objectors. This developed into a campaign against the military draft laws. Although this has remained a major part of the group's activities, it has also campaigned for an end to capital punishment and for prison reforms. The Fellowship is opposed to all forms of nuclear power.

Particular campaigns have focused on the Vietnam war and on US military involvement in Central America. The Fellowship has also concerned itself with the status of Jewish communities in the Soviet Union, Syria, Iraq and Argentina. It supports the rights of conscientious objectors and of the Falasha community within Israel, and favours a political solution to the Arab–Israeli conflict based on principles of peaceful reconciliation.

The Fellowship supports the establishment of political, religious and social equality for women.

Membership. Members and "friends" of the Fellowship together number 3,000; among its former supporters were Albert Einstein and Rabbi Leo Baeck.

Publications. Shalom, the Fellowship's newsletter, is published quarterly; the Fellowship has also produced a pamphlet entitled *Roots of Jewish Non-Violence.*

Affiliations. Fellowship of Reconciliation.

Jobs with Peace Campaign

Address. 77 Summer Street, Boston, Massachusetts 02110, USA

Aims and objectives. The Campaign seeks to build a broad-based movement in support of reducing military spending by 20–25 per cent and transferring the money to create jobs in education, health care, transport, housing and other socially productive industries. The Campaign hopes to bridge the gap between the two movements of peace and economic justice, so that they become a more cohesive and powerful united movement.

Formation. The Jobs with Peace Campaign was launched in 1978 in San Francisco with the holding of a referendum on the above-mentioned aim of reducing military spending.

Activities. Since its birth the Jobs with Peace Campaign has initiated successful referendums in 85 cities, towns and counties throughout America. In Los Angeles, Baltimore and Pittsburgh the referendum result has been binding and each year the cities provide a study of the impact of military spending on the city. This is then published in all the local newspapers.

Since 1985 a central goal has been to build strong local Jobs with Peace campaigns, to influence how congressmen vote on the federal budget; the strategy has been to make the federal budget a local issue by showing the "trade-offs" at a local level. This involves having nationally-co-ordinated activities organized in late autumn until the spring. For the 1986 elections the Jobs with Peace Campaign has striven to make the federal budget a key issue and the group has also done legislative work on specific bills. The group also supports the Congressional Black Caucus Alternative Budget in Congress. Generally, the group prepares Jobs with Peace budgets and works with labour, low-income and third-world constituencies.

Membership. There are about 20 Jobs with Peace campaigns around the country.

Lawyers' Alliance for Nuclear Arms Control

Address. 43 Charles Street, apartment 3, Boston, Massachusetts 02114, USA

Aims and objectives. This group works to educate legal professionals and the public about the dangers of nuclear war and to encourage people to solve conflicts through negotiations rather than force.

Formation. The Alliance was formed in 1981.

Activities. The Alliance has held conferences between Soviet and American lawyers in both the USA and the Soviet Union. Local chapters do educational work in their own communities.

Membership. There are approximately 7,000 members (lawyers, judges, law librarians, law students etc.) organized in 57 chapters throughout the USA.

Publications. Many chapters publish their own newsletter and the Alliance has published three issue briefs and several bibliographies.

Affiliations. Professionals' Coalition for Nuclear Arms Control.

Lawyers' Committee on Nuclear Policy

Address. 225 Lafayette Street, suite 513, New York, NY 10012, USA

Aims and objectives. This Committee is dedicated to the prevention of nuclear war and the eventual abolition of nuclear weapons. It bases its stance on the view that policies based on the use or threatened use of nuclear weapons are in violation of (US) constitutional and international law and are "inconsistent with the fundamental tenets of a democratic society".

Specific objectives are as follows: (i) the establishment of an international consensus on the illegality of nuclear weapons; (ii) an end to foreign policies which rely on "unlawful" threats to start nuclear war; (iii) the development of an international programme for the abolition of nuclear weapons; and (iv) support for individuals who are attempting to enforce the "illegality" of nuclear weapons (whether through the courts or through participation in the policy-making process).

Activities. The Committee provides active assistance in the form of legal advice to organizations and individuals who are concerned with disarmament. This assistance is provided in a variety of ways.

A "Litigation Programme" involves members of the Committee in the preparation of arguments and witness statements for cases relating to nuclear weapons where constitutional or international laws are being cited. The Programme played an active part in the Greenham Women et al. v. Reagan et al. case, in which the members of Lawyers' Committee and the Center for Constitutional Rights represented the plaintiffs.

The Committee's "Homeporting Programme" has concentrated on the legal implications of the planned dispersal of nuclear-capable ships to urban ports. The Committee has served as a legal council to the (New York) Coalition for a Nuclear-Free Harbour. Members of the Committee have testified on the matter to the New York city council, and have also helped organize two public meetings on the homeport plan.

The Committee's "Nuclear-Free-Zone Project" involves the provision of assistance with the legal aspect of nuclear-free zone declarations. As legal adviser to the Nuclear Free America campaign, the Committee has assisted in the drafting and passage of nuclear-free-zone legislation in several states, including California, New Jersey, New York, Massachusetts and Michigan. It has recently produced a model nuclear-free-zone ordinance for distribution by Nuclear Free America.

Another major sphere of the Lawyers' Committee's activities is that of public discussion and debate. Members deliver lectures and participate in workshop discussions in law schools across the USA, while the Committee has also helped organize conferences at several law schools. Members have made presentations before such groups as the American Civil Liberties Union and the National Lawyers' Guild. Articles by members of the Committee on nuclear policy have been published in a number of law journals, several of which have published special issues dealing solely with the question of the legality of nuclear weapons. Articles have also appeared in other publications, including the *Bulletin of Atomic Scientists*, and members' work has been cited during congressional debates.

The Lawyers' Committee has taken part in several international conferences, including the "International Symposium on the Legal and Moral Dimensions of Nuclear Weapons", held in New York in 1982, which produced draft treaties on disarmament for submission to the UN second special session on disarmament (UNSSOD II). The Committee has also been represented at international nuclear-free-zone seminars and at the Nuclear Warfare Tribunal in London in January 1985. A conference with leading Soviet international lawyers was held in late 1985.

Future plans include detailed research into the possibilities of a credible and reciprocal "no first use" declaration and into the alternatives to nuclear deterrence as a system of national defence.

Membership. The Committee has approximately 600 members, who are either academics or practising lawyers, the vast majority American; its 31-member consultative council includes Seán MacBride, Anthony d'Amato, Ian Brownlie and, until his death in 1982, Lord Philip Noel-Baker.

Publications. The Committee produces a quarterly newsletter and has published a *Statement on the Illegality of Nuclear Weapons.*

Affiliations. The Committee works closely with the International Peace Bureau, Nuclear Free America, the North Atlantic Network and the National Campaign to Save the ABM Treaty.

Livermore Action Group

Address. 3126 Shattuck Avenue, Berkeley, California 94705, USA

Aims and objectives. This Group seeks (i) the abolition of all nuclear weapons, starting with a halt to their design, development and deployment; (ii) curtailment of the US military budget; (iii) the demilitarization of US society; and (iv) the reallocation of resources currently devoted to military purposes to socially constructive uses.

Formation. The Group was formed in late 1981 by peace activists of the San Francisco Bay area, being a direct-action coalition of "affinity groups" involved in campaigns against the Diablo Canyon and Livermore Laboratories nuclear research facilities.

Publications. Direct Action, monthly; handbooks and other materials.

Many to Many

Address. 151 Gonzales Road, apartment 34, Santa Fe, New Mexico 87501, USA

Aims and objectives. This project operates as a "receiving and transmitting station" for people throughout the world who wish to participate in the "process of restoring sanity, decency and caring in our relationship to one another, as individuals and as nations, and in our relationship to the precious planet we live upon, and of which we are the guardians". Peace and disarmament are major themes of such exchanges, although "the concerns voiced may be as broad as those encompassed by the United Nations".

Activities. The letters which the project receives are compiled and reproduced as a volume and then sent out to individuals and groups in more than 40 countries in Eastern and Western Europe, the Americas, Africa, Australasia, India, South-East Asia and the Far East.

Mennonite Central Committee Peace Section (MCCPS)

Address. 21 S. 12th Street, Akron, Pennsylvania 17501, USA

Aims and objectives. The MCCPS aims to inform the public about the Mennonite principles regarding pacifism which are rooted in the Bible and church history. It also tries to link the Christian service and political witness through peacemaking projects.

Formation. The Committee was formed in 1942 as part of the movement of historic peace churches (Brethren, Mennonites and Friends) to secure the right of conscientious objection to military service in the United States.

Activities. The MCCPS works towards securing the classification of conscientious objector for men; it also assists in alternative service work (such as military tax resistance), women's concerns, conflict management and conciliation, political action and ecumenical peace dialogue. The Committee has sponsored several peace study tours to the Middle East, the Soviet Union and Eastern and Western Europe and has also arranged tours of the United States by representatives of European peace movements.

Membership. There are approximately 200,000 members of the Mennonite religious bodies throughout the USA. The policy is set by representatives from the major groups.

Publications. Peace Section Newsletter, bi-monthly; *Washington Memo*; Committee on Women's Concerns report; *Conciliation Service Newsletter*; Draft Counsellor's Update.

Military Information Center (MIC) of the Council on Economic Priorities

Address. 84 Fifth Avenue, New York, NY 10011, USA

Activities. The MIC of the Council on Economic Priorities concentrates on research and information provision on the broad economic ramifications of expenditure on armaments and on US corporate involvement in the arms race and the arms trade. It also concerns itself with projects for the conversion of the arms industry to socially useful production.

Publication. MIC Update, quarterly.

Mobilization for Survival (MFS)

Address. 853 Broadway, room 2109, New York, NY 10003, USA

Aims and objectives. MFS seeks to "abolish nuclear weapons, nuclear power and military intervention, reverse the arms race and meet human needs". It describes itself as a "multi-issue coalition highlighting the connections between nuclear power, nuclear weapons, military intervention, military spending and the lack of commitment to social and economic justice". It endeavours to develop "a grassroots movement by working with community-based organizations".

Foramtion. MFS was set up in 1977 to organize activities connected with the first UN General Assembly special session on disarmament (in 1978).

Activities. These currently include campaigns against the development and deployment of first-strike nuclear weapons such as the MX and cruise missiles and against the US Strategic Defence Initiative. The organization also opposes US intervention in areas such as Central America, in which connection it has co-ordinated a "Pledge of Resistance" campaign. MFS also runs a "Deadly Connections" campaign which "seeks to unite anti-nuclear and anti-intervention groups . . . and raise awareness of the global nature of US policy".
MFS also works with the Rainbow Coalition of minority groups in support of common social and economic policies at both national and local levels. Opposition to the apartheid regime in South Africa is an important feature of the organization's work.
At a national MFS conference held in Washington in November 1985 (and attended by over 100 people), the organization decided to make domestic issues a

central focus over the coming year, while campaigning would continue against US first strike policy, the US naval build-up and US interventionism.

The US movement has developed an international dimension to its activities, there being an International Mobilization for Survival organization with headquarters at the MFS office in New York and also a European Mobilization for Survival office in France (96 rue Anatole France, F-92300 Levallois-Perret, France).

Membership. There are 175 MFS grassroots groups in the United States, the main task of the national office being to co-ordinate their activities.

Publications. The Mobilizer, quarterly magazine; *Weapons Facilities Network Bulletin*, quarterly newsletter; various pamphlets.

Affiliations. In addition to its international connections (see above), MFS has a number of US peace and other movements as affiliates or as campaigning partners on specific issues.

Movement for a New Society

Address. 4722 Baltimore Avenue, Philadelphia, Pennsylvania 19143, USA

Aims and objectives. This pacifist movement opposes militarism and is particularly involved in war tax resistance and support for conscientious objectors.

Publications. Grapevine, monthly; *Dandelion*, quarterly.

Affiliations. War Resisters' International (associated member).

Musicians Against Nuclear Arms (MANA)

Address. 2161 Massachusetts Avenue, Cambridge, Massachusetts 02140, USA

Aims and objectives. The group assists the work of the Nuclear Weapons Freeze Campaign through its Education Fund. It also contributes to other similar disarmament groups through their respective education funds.

Formation. MANA was formed in 1982 by Harvard University's composer-in-residence Earl Kim.

Activities. MANA organizes concerts to raise money for disarmament organizations. By mid-1985 it had arranged 16 concerts in 15 different cities, raising one million dollars (gross).

MX Information Center/SL Freeze

Address. 232½ University Street, Salt Lake City, Utah 84102, USA

Aims and objectives. This group works to educate the local community on the dangers of nuclear weapons and excessive military spending.

Formation. It was organized in November 1979 in response to development of MX missiles.

Activities. Activities include: lobbying congressional leaders against specific weapons systems; organizing peace rallies; maintaining a nuclear issues' library;

sponsoring lectures, debates, films and informal research on nuclear issues; and providing updated factsheets on the MX and Midgetman weapon systems.

Publications. The Desert Sun, quarterly newsletter.

Affiliations. Nuclear Weapons Freeze Campaign.

National Action/Research on the Military Industrial Complex (NARMIC)—see under entry for **American Friends Service Committee (AFSC)**

National Campaign for a US Peace Tax Fund

Address. 2121 Decatur Place NW, Washington, DC 20008, USA

Aims and objectives. This Campaign seeks the amendment of current tax law through the passage of the US Peace Tax Fund Bill. This would amend the Inland Revenue code to allow a taxpayer who was conscientiously opposed to participation in war in any form to have his or her income, estate and gift tax payments used for non-military purposes. Specifically, the Campaign envisages the establishment of a special trust fund, known as the US Peace Tax Fund, into which would be paid a percentage of the conscientious objector's taxes equivalent to the proportion of the budget allocated to military expenditure. The Fund would be under the control of 11 trustees who would "have demonstrated a consistent commitment to world peace and international friendship" and who would have had "Experience with the peaceful resolution of international conflict".

The Campaign has suggested a number of destinations for the money paid into the Peace Tax Fund. These include the following: (i) the establishment of "a national academy of peace and conflict resolution", such as the proposed "United States Institute for Peace"; (ii) disarmament efforts; (iii) research into the potential for non-military and non-violent resolution of international conflicts; (iv) retraining workers made redundant by the conversion of military industry into "socially useful" production; (v) funding improvements in international health and welfare; and (vi) the promotion of international exchanges for peaceful purposes. The fund's resources would also be employed on increasing public awareness of its activities.

Formation. The National Campaign was established as the National Campaign for a World Peace Tax Fund Bill by a group of "concerned citizens" in Ann Arbor, Michigan, in 1971. It changed its name to the National Campaign for a US Peace Tax Fund in early 1985.

Activities. The initial introduction of a World Peace Tax Fund Bill was in 1972, when 10 members of Congress presented it to the House of Representatives. Similar legislation was proposed in the Senate by Senator Mark Hatfield in 1977, and since that date the bill has been introduced in each succeeding Congress. There are currently 47 supporters of the bill in the House of Representatives, and at least five in the Senate.

Members of the Campaign engage in active lobbying of Congressmen, both in Washington and in the states. The Campaign also publicizes its objectives and achievements with other religious, civic and peace groups. The Campaign holds regular seminars and an annual membership meeting.

Membership. The Campaign has a current mailing list of 7,400 people, each of whom receives a copy of its newsletter. It is at present in the process of transforming itself into a membership organization, and aims to have 4,000 fully paid-up members by the end of 1986. The group has a formal organizational structure, with a national board of directors and professional lobbying staff based in Washington. Contact at local levels is maintained through regional co-ordinators and congressional district contacts. Among its supporters outside Congress are Linus Pauling, Noam Chomsky, Archbishop Raymond Hunthausen and several bishops.

Publications. The Campaign publishes a quarterly newsletter and a variety of brochures and leaflets, as well as badges, hand stamps etc. It has also published two books: *A History of the World Peace Tax Fund—And a Vision*, by David Bassett, the Campaign's founder, and *Affirm Life—Pay for Peace*, a handbook on methods of building support for a peace tax fund bill.

Affiliations. The Campaign maintains close links with similar campaigns in the UK, Canada, West Germany and New Zealand. It also has ties with groups supporting individuals who have chosen to withhold a portion of their taxes on conscientious grounds.

The following organizations are among those which have endorsed the Campaign: American Friends Service Committee, Fellowship of Reconciliation, Friends Committee on National Legislation, Church of the Brethren, General Conference Mennonite Church, Jewish Peace Fellowship, Mobilization for Survival, New Call to Peacemaking, Pax Christi, US Catholic Conference, and Women's International League of Peace and Freedom.

National Center on Law and Pacifism

Address. PO Box 308, Cokedale, Colorado 81032, USA

Aims and objectives. The Center provides legal and theological research, resources, representation and support work for people involved in conflict with law or legal institutions because of the exercise of their religious or moral conscience. The Center works principally with conscientious war tax resisters and others resisting the arms race and US militarism.

Formation. The Center was established in 1978.

Activities. The Center has brought four major constitutional cases on war tax resistance before the US Supreme Court, as well as a number of appellate cases at lower levels. It also provides counselling to people on an individual basis and has assisted individuals defending themselves in cases of conscientious objection.

Membership. The Center has no formal membership structure as such. It has counselled approximately 10,000 individuals over the past seven years, and it estimates that its publications reach an audience of about 3,000 (mostly in the USA, with some overseas). There is a staff of two—an attorney and an editor.

Publications. Center Peace, a bi-monthly news journal. The Center has also distributed three books by William Durland: *People Pay for Peace*, a military tax refusal guide, currently in its fourth edition; *Conscience and the Law*, a court guide; and *The Illegality of War*, a monograph on international treaties and constitutional provisions which argues that war preparations and the nuclear arms race are illegal.

Affiliations. The Center established the National War Tax Resistance Co-ordinating Committee as a means of improving information sharing within the

American war tax resistance movement. The Center is a religious organization but is not affiliated to any specific denomination or Church.

National Interreligious Service Board for Conscientious Objectors

Address. 800 18th Street NW, suite 600, Washington, DC 20006, USA

Aims and objectives. The Board is committed to serving the needs of conscientious objectors and to spreading understanding of the motivation and purpose of such objection. It is opposed to conscription during peacetime and to compulsory national service.

Formation. The Board was established in 1940 as a result of concern among pacifist Churches that the USA would shortly enter the Second World War. The churches were eager to ensure that conscientious objectors should be treated with greater respect than was accorded them during the First World War.

Activities. The organization assisted with the operation of civilian public service during the Second World War, providing non-military work for about 12,000 men. It took an active part in the drive to secure an amnesty for draft-dodgers following the Vietnam War. It provides information on many aspects of military recruitment, and gives training to "draft counsellors". The Board offers help and support to conscientious objectors in the armed forces who are seeking discharge or transfer to non-combatant service. It also provides professional counselling to people who are unsure of their attitudes towards military service and conscientious objection. It assists those who are serving prison terms for draft evasion.

The Board gives information on how to register with the US Selective Service System and on the techniques of documenting a claim of conscientious objection. It advocates the rights of conscientious objectors before the courts, Congress and the Administration, and publicizes any potential changes in laws on conscription.

The Board is currently discussing the nature of terms used in conscientious objectors' claim forms with the US Selective Service. It is also monitoring possible revisions in conscription regulations that if implemented would amount to a reinstitution of the military draft. The Board is also becoming involved in the peace tax campaign, principally by providing support for individuals facing the consequences of their refusal to pay a portion of their taxes in protest at their use for military expenditure. It is currently expanding its resources on conscientious objection, and is planning to work with a number of other peace groups on drawing up a set of educational curricula which address the problems of conscription and war.

Membership. A total of 35 religious organizations are represented on the Board's consultative council; there is no provision for individual membership.

Publications. The Board's newsletter, *The Reporter for Conscience's Sake*, is published monthly; other publications include *Words of Conscience—Religious Statements on Conscientious Objection* and *Draft Counsellor's Manual*. The Board also produces a variety of explanatory leaflets, as well as distributing material on conscientious objection produced by other publishers.

Affiliations. The Board has close links with the National Campaign for a US Peace Tax Fund and with the National War Tax Resistance Co-ordinating Committee.

National Peace Institute Foundation

Address. 110 Maryland Avenue NE, Washington DC 20002, USA

Aims and objectives. The National Peace Institute Foundation is a non-profit-making private educational organization, dedicated to promoting the process of co-operative conflict resolution in international disputes. It aims to educate leadership groups in the United States and other countries about the potential for avoiding nuclear and conventional war.

Formation. The Foundation was set up in 1982 under the name of National Peace Academy Foundation, as the education affiliate of the National Peace Academy Campaign. As such, the Foundation functioned in conjunction with its political sister organization. When the federally-chartered US Institute of Peace was created by Congress in October 1984, the name of the Foundation was changed from Academy to Institute.

Activities. The Foundation actively supports the US Institute of Peace which, as a public institution cannot accept private funds. Thus the Foundation provides a structural framework for the flow of funds and energies from the private sector, and gives the public institution the strong constituency it needs to achieve success.

The Foundation also lobbies directly for the US Institute of Peace, encouraging its development into a position of international leadership.

Membership. The Foundation has a nationwide membership of around 45,000.

Publication. The Foundation has published a handbook, *The United States Academy of Peace: a Long Step toward Real Security.*

National War Tax Resistance Co-ordinating Committee (NWTRCC)

Address. P.O. Box 2236, East Patchoque, New York 11772, USA

Aims and objectives. The MWTRCC is one of several US organizations campaigning for non-payment by citizens of that proportion of their taxes which is used for military purposes—see also entries for Conscience and Military Tax Campaign (CMTC), National Campaign for a US Peace Tax Fund and War Resisters League.

Activities. The NWTRCC concentrates on co-ordinating local group actions in resistance to taxation for military purposes, producing support materials of various kinds and also offering workshop and counselling sessions.

Natural Resources Defense Council (NRDC)

Address. 122 East 42nd Street, New York, NY 10168, USA

Aims and objectives. The NRDC is a non-profit organization principally concerned with environmental issues, in which context it works to eliminate the dangers posed by nuclear weapons and nuclear energy. It is currently campaigning in particular for a comprehensive nuclear test ban treaty.

Formation. The Council was established in 1970, by a group of 50 lawyers and scientists.

Activities. As part of the Council's campaign to eliminate nuclear weapons, an NRDC delegation visited Moscow in May 1986 and signed an agreement with representatives of the Soviet Academy of Sciences envisaging that US non-governmental scientists would staff stations in the Soviet Union to monitor underground nuclear tests, provided that permission was given for Soviet scientists to do likewise in the United States. The plan (reported to be the first time that the Soviet side had expressed readiness to implement a specific plan for on-site inspection) called for the speedy installation of up to three seismic stations in the area of the Soviet nuclear testing grounds to the west of Semipalatinsk in Kazakhstan, to be manned by US scientists; similar stations would be established near the US nuclear testing site in Nevada, to be manned by Soviet scientists.

The NRDC subsequently launched a campaign to raise financial support for its "Nuclear Test Ban Citizen Verification Team", claiming that the project "makes verification a reality not just a pipedream" and "could well be the turning-point towards a comprehensive test ban treaty between the superpowers". The campaign literature pointed out that the Soviet Academy of Sciences would cover the project's costs at the Soviet end, but that the NRDC needed to meet costs such as $10,000 for each seismometer and $3,500 for the passage of each US scientist to Semipalatinsk.

Membership. The NRDC has some 62,000 members.

The Nerve Center

Address. 2327 Webster Street, Berkeley, California 94705, USA

Aims and objectives. The Nerve Center is a research and educational organization focusing on chemical and biological warfare (CBW), and dedicated to helping achieve lasting chemical, biological and nuclear disarmament. The Center encourages the larger peace and disarmament movement to include chemical and biological disarmament on its agenda. To that end, it acts as a resource centre, providing information on CBW to that movement and to the public at large.

Formation. The Nerve Centre was established in 1982.

Activities. The Center carries out research and education on issues such as military use of biotechnology, chemical disarmament initiatives, strengthening the Biological Weapons Convention, environmental contamination from chemical weapons construction and disposal. The Center is currently campaigning against US production of binary nerve gas weapons.

Membership. There are about 50 members, both national and international.

Publications. *Unmask*, a quarterly journal concerned with chemical and biological warfare issues; occasional brochures on current issues.

New Call to Peacemaking

Address. PO Box 1245, Elkhart, Indiana 46515–1245, USA

Aims and objectives. The group's stated goals are: (i) to clarify and express the biblical basis for peace; (ii) to encourage all Christians to renounce violence and accept Christ's call to peacemaking; and (iii) to explore strategies which promote peacemaking in contemporary society.

Formation. The group arose out of a meeting in 1976 of representatives of the three "Historic Peace Churches"—i.e. the Society of Friends, the Mennonites and the Church of the Brethren—and it held its first national conference in Wisconsin in 1978, with further conferences taking place in 1980 and 1982.

Activitis. New Call has joined with other religious groups in promoting the "New Abolitionist Covenant" to serve as a focus for action and meetings in local churches. It organizes conferences and study groups, and sets up "task forces" to work on specific issues. These currently include meditation and conflict resolution, war taxes and conscription. The group is also concerned to move beyond anti-nuclear-weapons protest to a wider use of non-violent methods of resolving conflict and establishing justice.

Membership. While there is no fixed membership, New Call to Peacemaking groups operate locally and regionally. Overall direction is provided by a central planning committee with representatives from each of the three participating churches, while specific decisions are taken by a steering committee of three, working with a national co-ordinator.

Publications. Call to Peacemaking, quarterly newsletter; also several books and pamphlets on the group's activities and the biblical basis thereof.

Nuclear Age Peace Foundation

Address. 1187 Coast Village Road, suite 123, Santa Barbara, California 93108, USA

Aims and objectives. The Foundation seeks "the elimination of nuclear weapons and co-operative interchange among nations".

Formation. The Foundation was established in 1982.

Activities. The Foundation publishes the *Waging Peace* series of booklets which serve as the basis for school and community discussions and conferences; it presents an annual "distinguished statesman award" (given in 1985 to Admiral Gene La Rocque) and the "Swackhamer Prizes", an annual scholarship award for an essay on a peace-related theme.

Membership. The Foundation has 1,200 members.

Publications. Waging Peace, booklet series.

Nuclear Free America

Address. 325 East 25th Street, Baltimore, Maryland 21218, USA

Aims and objectives. Nuclear Free America exists to promote awareness of nuclear-free zones and to assist individuals, communities and states in efforts to create such zones as part of a process towards creating "a nuclear-free world".
As defined by the campaign, a nuclear-free zone consists of "any well-defined geographical area, regardless of size, in which no nuclear weapons shall be produced, transported, stored, processed, disposed of or detonated. Neither shall any facility, equipment, supply or substance for their production, transportation, storage, processing disposal or detonation be permitted within its borders."

Formation. Nuclear Free America was founded on Independence Day (July 4) 1982, as a response to the first nuclear-free-zone declarations in the USA (by

Garrett Park, Maryland, in May 1982 and by Skyesville, Maryland, in June 1982).

Activities. Nuclear Free America provides support and advice to individuals campaigning to have their communities declared nuclear free, and it provides assistance to those communities who have already done so. The group lays particular stress on providing legal support, notably through its legal advisory group, which is co-sponsored by the Lawyers' Committee on Nuclear Policy (see separate entry). In 1986 it launched a campaign for a public boycott of consumer products emanating from companies also involved in the production of nuclear weapons.

Publications. *The New Abolitionist*, Nuclear Free America's newsletter, is published bi-monthly. Other publications include the *Nuclear-Free Zone Organizing Packet*, *Nuclear Free Investments* (an information pack suggesting ways in which authorities which have declared themselves nuclear-free can avoid placing contracts with major nuclear weapons contractors), *Neighbourhood Nukes* (a guide to identifying nuclear weapons' installations in local communities) and *Nuclear-Free Zones on Campus*.

Nuclear Free America's legal advisory group have produced a series of publications on the legal implications of nuclear-free-zone declarations, including *Nuclear Weapons and the Law*, *Nuclear-Free Zones and the Law*, *In Defence of Nuclear-Free Zones*, and *Nuclear-Free-Zone Legislation*.

The campaign also produces badges and posters, including one which draws attention to the fact that the name "Ronald Wilson Reagan" is an anagram for "Insane Anglo Warlord".

Affiliations. Nuclear Free America works closely with the Lawyers' Committee on Nuclear Policy as well as with nuclear-free-zone campaigns across the USA and in 15 other countries around the world.

Nuclear Free Zone Registry

Address. 28222 Stonehouse Road, Lake Elsinore, California 92330, USA

Aims and objectives. This group promotes the declaration, and registers the creation, of nuclear-free zones (NFZs), also serving as a non-profit-making educational centre.

Formation. The Registry was set up on July 12, 1982.

Activities. The Registry assists local communities with NFZ campaigns, sponsors workshops and conferences on arms control and NFZs, assists schools and churches in becoming NFZs, and functions as a registry for all types of NFZs. At the end of 1985 the Registry stated that 104 cities and counties across the United States had adopted some form of NFZ declaration.

Publications. *News Flash*, bi-annual news report on NFZs; other publications: *Nuclear Free Zones; New Hope for Global Peace*.

Nuclear War Graphics Project

Address. 100 Nevada Street, Northfield, Minnesota 55057, USA

Aims and objectives. The group aims to produce and distribute graphic materials pertaining to the arms race.

Formation. The group started producing materials for distribution in 1981.

Activities. The group produces materials for distribution, such as four slide shows with a narrative tape, two packages of slides, a 16 mm film and other related materials.

Nuclear Weapons Freeze Campaign

Address. 220 I Street NE, suite 130, Washington DC 20002, USA

Aims and objectives. The Freeze Campaign's ultimate objective is to halt all testing, production and deployment of nuclear weapons by the USA and the Soviet Union. Its immediate aim is to activate public opinion so as to compel the US Administration to agree to a bilateral freeze, as a result of either a presidential or of a congressional initiative.

The Campaign also supports moves to prevent military intervention in other countries by both the USA and the Soviet Union, to reduce the world stockpile of nuclear weapons and to convert military industry to production for civilian purposes. It acts as a vehicle to co-ordinate activities of the various disparate peace groups in the USA, and seeks to mobilize coalitions of professional, labour and religious groups previously inactive on peace issues.

Formation. The Freeze Campaign has been active since 1980, arising in part out of an appeal by Randall Forsberg (director of the Institute for Defence and Disarmament Studies) for the USA and the USSR to halt all testing, production and deployment of nuclear weapons.

Activities. The Campaign has played an active part in campaigns leading to the passage of resolutions supporting the idea of a nuclear freeze in town meetings, city councils and state legislatures during 1981–82. Referendums were held in 10 states on the question of a nuclear freeze in 1982, all of them being approved. A resolution calling for a freeze was passed by the House of Representatives in 1982, and tabled in the Senate in 1983, while freeze resolutions have been adopted by over 20 state legislatures and by several hundred local councils.

The Campaign has organized or participated in a number of public demonstrations, including one in New York in 1982, in which up to one million people took part, and the "four days" actions in Washington in April 1985.

An independent political action committee, Freeze Voter, was set up to support candidates favourable to a freeze in the 1984 presidential and congressional elections. The Campaign supported the introduction of proposals in congress in early 1985 which called for a comprehensive bilateral freeze to be achieved through a congressional suspension of funds for the testing, production and deployment of nuclear weapons, to be contingent upon a similar demonstration of restraint by the Soviet Union.

The Campaign is currently urging support for legislation providing for a comprehensive test ban treaty, a halt to flight testing of missiles, the cancellation of the MX and of the anti-satellite programmes, and suspension of the deployment of cruise and Pershing missiles and of other single weapons systems.

In May 1986 the Campaign held a conference entitled "Common Sense Defence Budget", which examined the proposition that real security depended on progress in arms control, developing a quality educational system, ensuring a productive civilian economy and rebuilding the country's cities and infrastructure.

Membership. There are currently over 1,100 Freeze chapters across the country, with support coming from individuals as well as professional, religious and labour organizations. The Campaign claims that opinion poll evidence reveals that over 80 per cent of US citizens support a bilateral nuclear freeze.

Publications. Freeze Focus, monthly newsletter; *Local Organizer*, fortnightly bulletin for Freeze chapters. The Campaign has also produced *Freeze Fact Sheets* and other information material.

Affiliations. The Freeze Campaign has close contacts with most major American peace groups; its aims have been endorsed by all the major US churches.

Nukewatch

Address. 315 West Gorham Street, Madison, Wisconsin 53703, USA

Aims and objectives. Nukewatch, a public education project of the Progressive Foundation, seeks to foster public awareness, debate and discussion on nuclear power and weapons issues. It is "dedicated to the belief that an informed citizenry, rather than a select few, must make the crucial decisions on nuclear issues that may determine the fate of humankind and the planet itself".

Formatoin. Nukewatch was established in 1979 amid an attempt by the Government to suppress an article in *The Progressive* magazine "challenging the mystique of secrecy which surrounds nuclear weapons and prevents public participation in decision-making".

Activities. Nukewatch has pursued its basic objectives (i) by serving as a national clearing house for information on nuclear issues, particularly on "campus militarism and the recent increases in Pentagon-funded campus research"; (ii) by publishing a "nuclear reader" showing the links between nuclear power and weapons; (iii) by establishing a speakers' panel to offer talks on nuclear issues to campuses and groups across the country; (iv) by sponsoring public conferences, films, workshops and speakers on nuclear issues; and (v) by serving as a catalyst for local action, "sharing our experience and expertise with grassroots groups who need help or advice with organizing, fund-raising, publicity or special projects". Current priorities include support for the Nuclear Weapons Freeze Campaign (see separate entry) and for the creation of nuclear-free zones.

Publications. Nukewatch publishes a regular newsletter as well as other information and educational materials.

Pacific Campaign Against SLCMs

Address. 2085 Makiki Place, Honolulu, Hawaii 98622, USA

Aims and objectives. This group seeks the denuclearization of the Pacific Ocean and particularly the withdrawal of sea-launched cruise missiles (SLCMs) from the area.

Activities. This Campaign's recent activities have included participation in the international day of action against sea-launched cruise missiles on June 15, 1985, together with the North Atlantic Network and other peace movements.

Affiliations. The Campaign is part of the Nuclear-Free and Independent Pacific (NFIP) network (see entry under International Movements).

Pacific Concerns Resources Center (PCRC)

Address. 570 Auahi Street, room 222B, Honolulu, Hawaii 96813, USA

Aims and objectives. The PCRC seeks to strengthen the movement for a nuclear-free Pacific; it also supports the self-determination of the peoples of the region.

Formation. The PCRC was set up as a result of an initiative by the third conference for a nuclear-free Pacific held in Hawaii in 1980.

Activities. The PCRC has co-ordinated actions and activities by anti-nuclear groups in the Pacific region and also facilitated the exchange of relevant information and research. As part of the Nuclear-Free and Independent Pacific (NFIP) network, it participated in the organization of Pacific Ocean actions on the occasion of the international day of action against sea-launched cruise missiles held on 15 June 1985, in co-operation with the North Atlantic Network and other movements.

Membership. The PCRC's main centres are in Hawaii and Vanuatu; it has branches in Belau and New Zealand.

Publication. Pacific Bulletin.

Pax Christi USA

Address. 6337 West Cornelia Avenue, Chicago, Illinois 60634, USA

Aims and objectives. As the US section of Pax Christi International (the "international Catholic movement for peace"), this organization seeks to involve Catholics in work for peace and co-operation in accordance with the teachings of the Church of Rome. It urges international disarmament, particularly the abolition of nuclear weapons, as prerequisites for a just world order.

Activities. Pax Christi in the United States seeks to exert influence on the Government to reduce military expenditure and trading in armaments and to realign its priorities towards "policies which have as their chief concern the survival of all peoples". It organizes two major events every year, namely a National Assembly of the movement and a National Celebration of the International Day of Peace. The movement participates with other peace movements in campaigns and actions in favour of disarmament and is also particularly involved in the development of a programme for non-violent and social defence.

Publications. Pax Christi Newsletter, bi-monthly; *The Church and the Arms Race,* booklet.

Affiliations. Pax Christi International.

Peace Links

Address. 747 8th Street SE, Washington, DC 20003, USA

Aims and objectives. Also known as Women Against Nuclear War, the Peace Links organization seeks to raise women's consciousness of the threat of nuclear war and to develop strategies for preventing it, in particular through the abolition of nuclear weapons.

287

Activities. Peace Links works through local groups and established women's organizations, one particular project being the "Iowa Peace Quilt", which is described as "a meaningful image of the world drawn together . . . , tenderly appliqued, pieced and stitched". Peace Links has a "congressional wives" group, which together with the George Mason University Center for Conflict Resolution organized a conference in mid-1986 on the theme "US–Soviet Relations: Myths and Realities" as part of an effort to improve understanding between the superpowers.

The Peace Museum

Address. 432 W. Erie Street, Chicago, Illinois 60610, USA

Aims and objectives. The Peace Museum provides peace education through the visual, literary and performing arts. It serves as a gallery, resource centre and workshop.

Activities. The Museum organizes a wide range of different exhibitions. In the past, these have included: the first US exhibition of original drawings by Hiroshima and Nagasaki survivors; the history of folk and rock music and its relation to peace efforts; patchwork pictures from Chile; cartoons and caricatures; the artist as social critic from the 17th century to the present; and the life and times of Martin Luther King. The 12th major exhibition planned is on "child's play", when peace toys and games will be on display. The Museum has also participated in the production of a "Peace Ribbon", when in August 1985 10,000 embroidered, painted and coloured segments of cloth were placed end to end around the Pentagon.

Membership. About 600.

Publications. *Give Peace a Chance*; *Ribbon Book*; resource packs on teaching peace.

Peace Political Action Committee (Peace PAC)

Address. 100 Maryland Avenue NE, Washington, DC 20002, USA

Aims and objectives. Peace PAC works for the prevention of nuclear war by campaigning for the election to the House of Representatives of candidates who (i) support measures to freeze and reduce nuclear weapons and to diminish the risk of nuclear war and (ii) have previously played a leading role in debates on arms control and military spending.

Formation. Peace PAC was set up by the Council for a Liveable World (see separate entry) in April 1982 when it became clear that the House of Representatives was taking an unusually prominent role in issues of nuclear arms control, particularly concerning nuclear freeze proposals and the debate over the MX missile.

Activities. Candidates selected for Peace PAC support must sign a declaration committing themselves to work for: (i) an immediate, verified, mutual freeze on testing, construction and deployment of new nuclear weapons by both superpowers; (ii) termination of the MX, B-1 bomber and nerve gas programmes; (iii) the continuation in force of the 1972 anti-ballistic missile treaty; (iv) a negotiated end to all nuclear testing by all nuclear powers; and (v) a limit to the planned increases in military spending.

Membership. Peace PAC is supported by many who also support the Council for a Liveable World; its Board of Directors includes Admiral John M. Lee and Paul C. Warnke, the former director of the Arms Control and Disarmament Agency and chief US negotiator at the SALT II talks.

PeaceNet

Address. 1918 Bonita, Berkeley, California 94704, USA

Aims and objectives. PeaceNet describes itself as "an affordable, easy-to-use computer-based communications and information sharing system" which helps "to foster a new sense of community and co-operation within the peace movement".

Formation. PeaceNet was set up as a co-operative project of the Ark Communications Institute, the Center for Innovative Diplomacy, Community Data Processing and the Foundation for the Arts of Peace.

Activities. Users of PeaceNet with appropriate equipment can (i) hold "electronic conferences", circulating agenda proposals and background information in advance of meetings; (ii) input their activities and read those of other groups on an updated national and international calendar; and (iii) gain immediate access to information banks containing a variety of useful information. PeaceNet undertakes to work with its users and friends "to conduct polls, distribute software, support action alert networks, develop co-operative strategies and provide technical support".

Membership. By mid-1986 over 550 individuals and groups were using PeaceNet in support of peace projects.

Performing Artists for Nuclear Disarmament (PAND)

Address. 225 Lafayette Street, suite 207, New York, NY 10012, USA

Aims and objectives. PAND aims to educate the performing arts community about the dangers of the nuclear arms race and to use performance to make others aware of them.

Formation. The group was founded in 1982.

Activities. Shortly after its formation PAND was involved in the "June 12 Rally" in Central Park, New York. In 1983 it sent a company of 60 actors, dancers and singers on a tour of New York state, performing disarmament material. During the 1983–4 season, the group produced the "Music for Survival" series of chamber music concerts.

At present the group's major activity is providing performers, both celebrity and grassroots, for other peace groups' programmes. It is also working on a programme called "Unsell the Bomb", involving advertising professionals in producing items to be aired on television and radio.

Membership. PAND has about 200 fee-paying members in addition to the performers on its roster.

Publications. *PAND Alert*, a newsletter produced several times a year; PAND also participates in the production of the monthly *New York Peace Network Calendar*.

Physicians for Social Responsibility (PSR)

Address. 1601 Connecticut Avenue NW, suite 800, Washington, DC 20009, USA

Aims and objectives. PSR is an educational organization of medical practitioners and others which seeks to inform the general public about the hazards of nuclear weapons and of the nuclear arms race.

Activities. PSR undertakes a broad range of public educational work throughout the United States, holding regular symposia on the likely medical consequences of nuclear war and giving lectures to colleges, schools, churches, civic groups etc. It maintains an extensive library of printed and visual material for use by its members and by other interested groups. Since 1984 it has been particularly involved in the campaign for a comprehensive nuclear test ban treaty and has worked with like-minded organizations to initiate legislation which would suspend funds earmarked for US nuclear weapon testing for as long as the Soviet Union maintains its own moratorium on testing (operative since July 1985).

To increase grassroots support for a US suspension PSR has also launched a public education campaign—called Code Blue—"to stress the urgency of a bilateral moratorium and, ultimately, the comprehensive test ban treaty". On June 14, 1986, PSR physicians from around the country gathered in Washington to urge the need for a mutual testing moratorium, lobbying elected officials on the growing public support for a test ban and co-ordinating Code Blue strategies leading to Hiroshima Day on Aug. 6.

Publications. In addition to its quarterly newsletter, PSR publishes information packs on the medical hazards of nuclear weapons, based on authoritative clinical and scientific literature.

Affiliations. International Physicians for the Prevention of Nuclear War.

Pledge of Resistance Campaign—see under entry for Sojourners Peace Ministry

Poets for Nuclear Disarmament (POND)

Address. 66 Grove Hill Avenue, Newton, Massachusetts 02160, USA

Aims and objectives. The aim of POND is to encourage poets to write peace or disarmament poems and read them to the public or publish the works. The originator of the group was the poet Douglas G. Worth.

Activities. POND arranges poetry readings on peace and disarmament themes.

Professionals' Coalition for Nuclear Arms Control

Address. 1346 Connecticut Avenue NW, Washington, DC 20036, USA

Aims and objectives. The Coalition seeks to organize groups of professionals on the local level to lobby their members of Congress to vote for arms control. Its specific aim is to lobby in opposition to the MX missile and "Star Wars" space weapons, and in favour of a comprehensive test ban and a nuclear freeze.

Formation. The Coalition was formed in 1984.

Activities. The Coalition has conducted lobbies on behalf of professional peace groups such as Physicians for Social Responsibility, the Lawyers' Alliance for Nuclear Arms Control and the Union of Concerned Scientists. It also provides information about arms control legislation in the US Congress and training in effective lobbying techniques.

Membership. The Coalition encompasses 5,000 members (physicians, lawyers, scientists and others).

Publications. In addition to a quarterly newsletter and an annual record showing the votes cast by all members of Congress on arms control issues, the Coalition has published *Citizen Lobbyist Skills Manual.*

Progressive Space Forum (PSF)

Address. 1724 Sacramento Street No. 9, San Francisco, California 94109, USA

Aims and objectives. The PSF is opposed to the arms race in space, and particularly to the deployment of anti-satellite weapons and ballistic missile defence systems. It supports the peaceful use of space technology and international co-operation in space. The Forum aims to provide information and opinion on these issues to the public in the USA and elsewhere.

Formation. The PSF was founded under the name of Citizens for Space Demilitarization in San Francisco in 1979.

Activities. The PSF has conducted public forums and meetings on space policy and published literature on the subject. It has co-operated with other disarmament groups as well as organizations concerned with space policy, and participated in rallies against the arms race.

Membership. PSF has some 230 members in the USA and ten other countries. The group has a "grassroots" non-professional orientation.

Publications. *Space for All People*, quarterly; the Forum also produces campaign material including a slide presentation.

Prolifers for Survival

Address. PO Box 3316, Chapel Hill, North Carolina 27515, USA

Aims and objectives. To agitate, educate and organize men and women to oppose nuclear arms and abortion.

Formation. The Group was formed in 1979.

Activities. The group has participated in public protest at the Three Mile Island nuclear generator meltdown, civil disobedience at the Pentagon and in the annual "March for Life" in Washington (held to mark the anniversary of the 1973 Supreme Court decision to legalize abortion). It organizes lecture hours and various types of non-violent direct actions.

Membership. There are 3,000 members around the world (but mostly USA).

Publications. *PS*, bi-monthly journal; *Prolife Peace Styles*, bi-monthly pamphlet series; *Building Bridges*, a book; also an audio-visual programme "Rainbows Promise Life".

Affiliations. There are Prolifers for Survival groups in Australia, West Germany and the United Kingdom.

Promoting Enduring Peace

Address. P.O. Box 5103, Woodmont, Connecticut 06460, USA

Aims and objectives. Educational and religious in character, this group seeks to advance world peace through international understanding.

Formation. The group was founded in 1952 by a Quaker, Dr Jerome Davies.

Activities. As a "grassroots citizens peace organization", the group has concentrated on despatching reprints of press articles on peace issues. It was particularly active in circulating material opposed to US involvement in the Vietnam war, and today it sends out approximately one million articles annually on all aspects of peace and disarmament. It also conducts national and international conferences and seminars (including one on the CIA in 1975), and presents an annual "Gandhi peace award" for outstanding work in the field of world peace. Past recipients have included Helen Caldicott, Linus Pauling and Eleanor Roosevelt.

In recent years it has sponsored a "Peace Cruise" on the Volga River in the Soviet Union in an effort to bring US, Canadian and Soviet citizens together for discussion of peace issues, and it has also arranged tours of the Soviet Union by high school study groups.

Membership. Approximately 4,000 people are on the group's mailing list to receive reprint articles.

Psychologists for Social Responsibility (PSR)

Address. 1841 Columbia Road NW, No 207, Washington, DC 20009, USA

Aims and objectives. Dedicated to preventing the outbreak of nuclear war and to finding ways to build a lasting peace, PSR studies means to move from adversarial to co-operative models of international relations. It seeks to "promote activities which reduce world tensions and which create a psychologically more favourable climate for survival".

Formation. PSR was founded in early 1982.

Activities. PSR co-ordinates and co-operates with local groups of psychologists who are carrying out research into such fields as group leadership and conflict resolution. It provided a "hospitality suite" at successive American Psychological Association conventions. PSR took part in the "Day Before" programme, and it sent a delegation to the mass rally in New York in June 1983.

Membership. There are approximately 2,000 members, the majority of whom are resident in the USA, with some in other countries. Membership is open to practising psychologists or students studying the subject. Initially run by a single individual, its activities are now organized on a committee basis. Local PSR groups are in the process of being formed. The group is setting up an international network of psychologists who are interested in using their professional skills for peaceful purposes, and it is currently seeking to establish a working relationship with other professional groups.

Publications. PSR produces a quarterly newsletter.

Resource Center for Non-Violence

Address. P.O. Box 2324, Santa Cruz, California 95062, USA

Aims and objectives. The Resource Center for Non-Violence aims to provide a public educational programme in the history, theory, methodology and current practice of non-violence as a force for personal and social change. Its objectives include improved East–West relations, nuclear disarmament and the solution of conflicts in the Third World, with particular emphasis on the Middle East and Latin America.

Formation. The Resource Center was founded in 1976.

Activities. The Center offers various workshops and study groups in non-violence as well as providing speakers for interested groups. It has an extensive library and makes available films, videos and slideshows. It also offers many books, pamphlets and literature for sale, as well as a regular newsletter.

The Centre also organizes special projects and has co-sponsored educational and political delegations to the Middle East to promote non-violent alternatives to the armed conflict in the region. In order to increase the understanding of the role and responsibility of the US in Latin America, it has arranged an exchange programme, an inter-Americas newsletter and an urgent action network.

The Center is encouraging direct contact between American and Soviet citizens in the hope that human relations will help thaw the Cold War. Work is done in Santa Cruz to dispel myths about the Soviet Union, and with others in northern California to organize exchanges among American and Soviet peoples. The Center also offers support and counselling to conscientious objectors.

Membership. The Center has nine part-time staff and a local mailing list of 1,000.

Publications. The Center produces a quarterly non-violence newsletter as well as a variety of books, pamphlets, greetings cards, calendars and posters.

Seneca Women's Encampment for a Future of Peace and Justice

Address. outside Seneca Army Depot, 5440 Rt.96, Romulus, New York 14541, USA

Aims and objectives. Seneca is a feminist peace camp founded on principles of non-violence which aims to end the deployment of first-strike nuclear weapons in Europe. It is situated outside the Seneca Army Depot from which it is believed that Pershing II warheads are shipped to West Germany. The Depot is the largest US Army nuclear storage site in the world.

The campers seek to transform society through education and direct action in order to do away with social inequality and violence in society.

Formation. The women at the Seneca camp decided to set up the camp following the 1982 Conference on Global Feminism and Disarmament. The land was purchased in May 1983, the camp opened in July 1983 and it became a permanent peace camp in February 1984.

Activities. The Seneca campers participate in acts of civil disobedience and hundreds have been detained. The camp is open all year round for visits, workshops and actions.

Membership. All women who participate in the camp are considered to be members. Some make short visits and some have stayed for one-and-a-half years. There are 7,500 names on the camp's mailing list.

Publications. The camp has produced a *1983 Handbook of the Women's Encampment for a Future of Peace and Justice* and also two brochures: *Why a Women's Peace Camp?* and *Seneca Army Depot*. The minutes of all regional decision-making meetings are also available.

The Shalom Center

Address. Church Road and Greenwood Avenue, Wyncote, Pennsylvania 19095, USA

Aims and objectives. The Shalom Center aims to unite the wide spectrum of American Jewry in its efforts to end the nuclear arms race. Its main constituency is in North America and it provides a resource and organizing focus to give a specifically Jewish perspective on the problem and aim of preventing a nuclear holocaust.

Formation. The Center was founded in 1983.

Activities. The Center provides sermons, liturgies, school curricula, policy papers and adult education programmes to many Jewish groups and communities. In the spring it organizes "Rainbow Sign" observances and in the autumn "Sukkat Shalom" observances. In the future the Center hopes to broaden and intensify the work of these two observances. The Center is currently conducting a "Jewish Inquiry into Personal and Communal Responsibility for Action to Prevent a Nuclear Holocaust".

Membership. There are approximately 2,000 members; board members include leaders of every major religious and political group of American Jewry.

Publication. The Shalom Report, bi-monthly.

The Sierra Club

Address. 730 Polk Street, San Francisco, California 94108, USA

Aims and objectives. The primary aim of the Sierra Club is environmental protection, but in view of the gross environmental disruption that would be caused by nuclear war and of the role of environmental and natural resource problems in engendering conflict, it has made the environmental effects of warfare its priority issue. In this context, the Club seeks to end the arms race, reduce nuclear arsenals and lower the hostility between the superpowers.

Activities. The Club carries out public educational work through its local chapters and its publications. It has lobbied against particular weapons programmes, such as the MX missile, and in favour of arms reduction agreements and the comprehensive test ban treaty.

Membership. 365,000, mainly in the United States and Canada.

Publications. Sierra, bi-monthly magazine; *National News Report*, weekly newsletter; and about 22 books per year on environmental issues.

Affiliations. American Committee for International Conservation; International Union for the Conservation of Nature; Global Tomorrow Coalition.

Sojourners Peace Ministry

Address. P.O. Box 29272, Washington, DC 20017, USA

Aims and objectives. Based around *Sojourners*, a monthly peace magazine, this group of ecumenical Christians is committed to the principle of non-violence at all levels of human relationships, being particularly involved in campaigns against nuclear weapons.

Activities. In recent years the group has been in the forefront of the Pledge of Resistance Campaign, which developed in late 1983 when Christian peace activists feared that a US invasion of Nicaragua was imminent. In August 1984 *Sojourners* magazine published details of the pledge, which had two parts, one a civil disobedience pledge and the other a public protest pledge. Under the first section, signatories undertook "to join with others to engage in acts of non-violent civil disobedience" if the United States "sends combat troops, invades by proxy, bombs or otherwise significantly escalates its intervention in Central America". The second part committed the signatory, in such circumstance, "to engage in acts of public protest". By early 1986 there were some 80,000 signatories of the Pledge of Resistance and 400 local Pledge groups around the country. The group has also been closed involved in the "Sanctuary" movement, aimed at providing shelter for refugees feeling from political repression in Central America.

Publication. *Sojourners*, monthly magazine.

Student/Teacher Organization to Prevent Nuclear War (STOP)

Address. 636 Beacon Street, room 203, Boston, Massachusetts 02215, USA

Aims and objectives. STOP aims to educate secondary school pupils and their teachers as to the dangers of nuclear war, and to mobilize them to become involved in attempts to reverse the arms race.

Formation. STOP was founded in 1981.

Activities. STOP's principal focus of activity has been the dissemination of information to teachers and pupils about the nuclear threat. It is currently training groups of organizers from different parts of the USA.

Current endeavours include sponsoring visits of young people to the Soviet Union and working for the recognition of May 19 as "national student day of peace", on which appropriate demonstrations and actions would be staged.

Membership. STOP has approximately 2,500 members, scattered across 42 US states. Members are organized in local chapters based on individual schools. There are currently 100 of these chapters in existence.

Publications. *STOP News*, which is written by school pupils and published six or seven times a year.

Union of Concerned Scientists (UCS)

Address. 26 Church Street, Cambridge, Massachusetts 02238, USA

Aims and objectives. The UCS is "an independent, non-profit organization of scientists and other citizens concerned about the impact of new technology on society", with particular focus on nuclear arms control, nuclear power safety and national energy policy. The UCS recognizes "the need to protect America's national security interests" but believes that "the shortsighted development of certain weapons technologies—such as space weapons—will make the world less stable and our nation less secure".

Formation. The UCS originated in 1969 as an informal group of lecturers and students of the Massachusetts Institute of Technology.

Activities. Making use of its membership's scientific and technical expertise, the UCS seeks to influence policy debates by conducting independent research, sponsoring and participating in conferences and panels, testifying at congressional and regulatory hearings, and undertaking various forms of public education work.

In its early years the UCS actively opposed the deployment of both anti-ballistic missile systems (ABMs) and multiple-warhead technology for nuclear missiles (MIRVs). It helped to build public support for the US–Soviet ABM treaty of 1972 and called for a MIRV test ban, warning (correctly in the event) that US MIRV deployment would be reciprocated by the Soviet Union. In 1979 the UCS urged the ratification of the SALT II treaty in a declaration signed by several thousand scientists. Since 1979 the Union has actively opposed the MX missile "as an unwarranted weapon that would endanger arms control agreements and destabilize the nuclear arms race", and has also been a leading advocate of the United States and NATO adopting a no-first-use policy in respect of nuclear weapons.

UCS arms control efforts have most recently been concentrated on space weapons—both the US Strategic Defence Initiative (SDI, or "Star Wars") for a space-based defence system against ballistic missiles and also development of anti-satellite weapons. The Union has submitted two technical and political studies of space weapons to Congress, the scientific community and the public at large, and has also recast its study findings in a paperback entitled *The Fallacy of Star Wars* (1984) aimed at a general audience.

The UCS undertakes a variety of educational activities related to arms control. Since 1981, when it began co-ordinating autumn teach-ins at college and community locations across the country, the event has grown from a one-day programme into a full week of educational activities including panel discussions, speakers, and films. In 1984 a tele-conference entitled "Breaking the Stalemate" was the starting event. In an effort to educate younger Americans about the nuclear age, the UCS developed jointly with the National Education Association a junior high school curriculum entitled *Choices: A Unit on Conflict and Nuclear War.* More than 8,000 copies have been distributed.

Several thousand scientists have now joined a grassroots education and lobbying programme called the UCS Action Network. Several hundred of these scientists make up the UCS Speakers' Bureau, providing local groups with informed speakers. In addition, through the Professionals' Coalition for Nuclear Arms Control, UCS scientists work closely with physicians and lawyers in many communities. The Union also has a "legislative alert network" to let interested sponsors know about important arms control votes in Congress.

In 1984 the UCS received in Vienna the Bruno Kreisky Foundation Award for Human Rights. One of fourteen recipients, the UCS received the award for its work to halt the nuclear arms race.

Membership. The UCS is supported by donations from some 100,000 individuals nationwide, including many thousands of scientists; these sponsors provide more than 70 per cent of UCS revenues, the remainder coming from major gifts and grants from foundations.

Publications. The UCS quarterly newsletter *Nucleus* has a circulation of 125,000; the Union also publishes books, reports and briefing papers.

United Campuses to Prevent Nuclear War (UCAM)

Address. 1346 Connecticut Avenue NW, suite 706, Washington, DC 20036, USA

Aims and objectives. UCAM's "statement of principles" notes the dangers inherent in the "increase in number and complexity of nuclear weapons and delivery systems" and assumes that (i) "the continuing development, deployment and production of new weapons and delivery systems will make it more difficult to achieve an effective arms control agreement"; and (ii) "it is almost inevitable that any use of nuclear weapons will result in an escalation to all-out nuclear exchange, with all its devastating consequences". It concludes that "the United States and the Soviet Union must adopt far-reaching and absolute limits on the nuclear weapons and delivery systems which each side is permitted to retain", and that "as a first step, the United States should negotiate with the Soviet Union a halt to the testing, production and deployment of nuclear weapons and their delivery systems".

Formation. Following a series of "sponsored teach-ins" on nuclear war organized on 150 university campuses by the Union of Concerned Scientists in November 1981, UCAM was established by a group of students and staff in June 1982.

Activities. UCAM concentrates on education, lobbying and "non-partisan participation in the electoral process". Its activities are co-ordinated by a national office based in Washington.

In the electoral field, UCAM's first move was to circulate a questionnaire to congressional candidates in June 1982. It has taken part in lobbies for a nuclear weapons freeze and against the deployment of the MX missile. In March 1984, it held a "University Lobby to End the Arms Race" in Washington. UCAM groups lobbied Congress on arms control and the military budget in early 1985. Educational activities have included joint teach-ins with the Union of Concerned Scientists on "Solutions to the Nuclear Arms Race", while in December 1984 UCAM held meetings in 700 campuses in the USA and Canada.

It is currently concentrating on campaigns against the Strategic Defence Initiative and on education about US–Soviet relations, particularly "how to address fears about the Soviet Union".

Membership. Members are grouped in 60 university chapters spread throughout the USA and Canada. An individual membership programme has recently been introduced.

Publications. In addition to the membership journal, *UCAM Network News*, the group have produced several books, including *What About the Russians?* by Sanford Gottlieb and *Who Decides? A Citizen's Guide to Government Decision-making on Nuclear Weapons.* Other materials include information packs and campaign manuals, as well as a series of *UCAM Reports.*

United States Peace Council

Address. 7 East 15th Street, room 408, New York, NY 10003, USA

Aims and objectives. This Council advocates international disarmament and the dismantling of military blocs, being particularly opposed to what it regards as US militarism and interventionism.

Membership. Membership of the Council is drawn largely from the Communist Party of the USA and other Marxist groups.

Publications. Peace and Solidarity, monthly.

Affiliations. World Peace Council.

Volunteers for Peace (VFP)

Address. Belmont, Vermont 05730, USA

Aims and objectives. This group seeks to promote world peace through citizen exchange and voluntary service.

Formation. VFP was formed in 1980.

Activities. VFP sends American volunteers to work camps in 32 countries and receives about 200 foreign volunteers into the US every year. There are currently 14 work camps in 11 US states.

Membership. VFP has about 1,000 members.

Publications. Free, annual newsletter; *International Workcamp Directory* annual.

Affiliations. Service Civil International.

War Resisters' League

Address. 339 Lafayette Street, New York, NY 10012, USA

Aims and objectives. The League seeks to bring about disarmament and establish a "democratic society free of war, racism, sexism, and human exploitation".

Formation. The League was formed in 1923.

Activities. During its history the League has organized or participated in numerous anti-war actions and campaigns. During the Second World War it aided conscientious objectors. In the 1950s it supported civil rights efforts and opposed civil defence programmes. In 1963 it began a campaign against the Vietnam War involving marches, rallies, draft card burnings, war tax resistance and civil disobedience at induction centres, military bases and corporate headquarters. Since the mid-1970s the League has emphasized the issue of nuclear weapons and it has recently been closely involved in the National Campaign for a US Peace Tax Fund (see separate entry).

Membership. The League has 18,000 members.

Publications. The Non-Violent Activist, bi-monthly; *Peace Calendar*, annual; *WRL Organizers Manual*; *Guide to War Tax Resistance*; *High School Organizing Packet*; various booklets, brochures etc.

Affiliations. War Resisters' International; International Peace Bureau; Mobilization for Survival; Committee Against Registration and the Draft; Nuclear Weapons Freeze Campaign.

Women Against Military Madness (WAMM)

Address. 3255 Hennepin Avenue South, Minneapolis, Minnesota 55408, USA

Aims and objectives. WAMM works to counter militarism in US society, and the threat of both conventional and nuclear warfare, through education and non-violent direct action; also to oppose US intervention in other countries.

Formation. WAMM was formed in 1982 by women concerned about the threat of nuclear war and their inability, as women, to influence government decision-making on weapons and war.

Activities. WAMM campaigns through such techniques as door-to-door canvassing (the "outreach campaign"), pamphleteering, sponsorship of peace caravans and a touring anti-nuclear dance performance, demonstrations, talks to women's, civic and church groups and schools. It has four full-time employees. Most activity is in Minnesota.

Membership. WAMM has 2,000 on its mailing list (including 200 organizations and 300 men), predominantly in Minnesota.

Publications. Monthly newsletter and numerous pamphlets.

Affiliations. Mobilization for Survival.

Women Against Nuclear War—see entry for Peace Links

Women for Peace

Address. 2302 Ellsworth Street, Berkeley, California 94704, USA

Aims and objectives. This group seeks an end to the arms race and all nuclear tests; reductions in the military budget; and non-intervention by the USA in the affairs of other countries.

Formation. The group was founded in 1961 in protest against US and Soviet nuclear tests in the atmosphere.

Activities. The group lobbies Congress, distributes leaflets and petitions, places messages on TV and radio, engages in and organizes demonstrations. Current major issues include the campaign for a comprehensive nuclear test ban and opposition to US policy in Central America.

Membership. There are some 500 members.

Publications. The group publishes a regular newsletter.

Affiliations. Women Strike for Peace.

Women Strike for Peace (WSP)

Address. 145 S. 13th Street, room 706, Philadelphia, Pennsylvania 19107, USA

Aims and objectives. WSP endeavours to mobilize women against the arms race and for universal peace and justice.

Formation. The group was formed in 1961.

Activities. WSP is currently campaigning for: (i) a comprehensive nuclear test ban treaty; (ii) an end to the US Strategic Defence Initiative; and (iii) the "pledge of resistance" to US intervention in Nicaragua.

Membership. WSP has over 8,000 members and supporters, most of whom are women.

Publications. Peacelines, a national newsletter; *WSP Legislative Alert*; *A Basic Primer on Star Wars for the Legitimately Confused*; in addition all local branches publish newsletters.

Affiliations. Coalition for a New Foreign and Military Policy; Center for Defense Information.

Women's Action for Nuclear Disarmament (WAND)

Address. P.O. Box 153, New Town Branch, Boston, Massachusetts 02258, USA

Aims and objectives. WAND seeks a bilateral nuclear weapons freeze by the superpowers, as a crucial step towards general disarmament and world peace. The movement's founder, Dr Helen Caldicott, summed up its ethos in early 1986 as follows: "Who can snuff out the sickness of self-delusion and stop it from leading our world to hell? Maybe an aroused and unsentimental and steadfast international network of women has a chance."

Activities. WAND is a campaigning movement, working nationally and through its local groups to lobby Congress and the Administration on the need for nuclear and general disarmament, participating in this respect with other sections of the US peace movement. It also conducts programmes of education for its members and the general public, having an Education Fund for this purpose. WAND maintains contacts with women's peace movements in Europe and has helped to organize US speaking tours for European peace movement representatives.

Publications. WAND Bulletin, bi-monthly; *Organizing for Nuclear Disarmament*, a manual.

Women's International League for Peace and Freedom (WILPF)

Address. 1213 Race Street, Philadelphia, Pennsylvania 19107, USA

Aims and objectives. As the US section of the international movement of the same name, the WILPF aims to unite people in all countries in a determination to abolish the political, social, economic and psychological causes of war and to work for peace and disarmament. The League advocates non-violent change to secure the elimination of racial and sexual discrimination.

Formation. The US section dates from the foundation of the WILPF in 1915.

Publications. Peace and Freedom, monthly; *WILPF Legislative Bulletin and Alerts*, monthly.

Affiliations. Women's International League for Peace and Freedom.

World Without War Council (WWWC)

Address. 1730 Martin Luther King Way, Berkeley, California 94709, USA

Aims and objectives. Describing itself as "a kind of management consultant agency for enterprises that do not yet exist", WWWC carries out research and consultation work on world affairs with a view to influencing government and non-government bodies to adopt and support policies which favour the peaceful resolution of international conflict.

Formation. WWWC has its roots in California, where 12 national peace organizations established "Acts for Peace". In 1961 this became "Turn Toward Peace", a co-operative body composed of some 60 groups of various political stances. The organization became divided over US involvement in Vietnam, and in 1966 was superseded by the World Without War Council.

Activities. WWWC sponsors seminars and conferences and conducts education and training programmes. Its researchers provide background information on world affairs and carry out consultations on various disarmament and human rights issues, and on State Department and independent sector programmes. It also provides speakers and materials for local community programmes.

The Council's "American Initiatives Project" brought together several specialists in international affairs who drew up the following proposals as a basis for peaceful resolution of disputes: (i) the reform, strengthening and expansion of international, legal and political institutions; (ii) the development of a world political community sufficient to sustain international law; (iii) effective economic and political development in the Third World; (iv) worldwide protection of basic human rights; and (v) the formation of processes for effective mediation and intervention in regional crises.

In the "Historians Project", some 50 historians of peace organizations have co-operated to identify and assess the validity of the central ideas of the peace movement over the past fifty years. Seminars on this subject have been held in various parts of the country.

Membership. The Council has no membership as such, but has over the years trained some 300 interns who have subsequently taken up posts with organizations such as the State Department, the USIA, Peace Corps, the UN and other world affairs bodies, as well as peace organizations. There are approximately 30–40 staff members.

Publications. Books produced by WWWC include *To End War: A New Approach to International Conflict* (Robert Woito); *Americans and World Affairs*; *Exploring Soviet Realities: Problems in the Pursuit of Peace*; *War and Peace in Literature* (Lucy Dougall, ed.); *War and Peace Film Guide* (J. Dowling, ed.); and *Peace Archives: A Guide*.

Other Movements

American Committee on East–West Accord

Address. 227 Massachusetts Avenue NE, suite 300, Washington, DC 20002, USA

Arms Control Association (ACA)

Address. 11 Dupont Circle, suite 900, Washington, DC 20036, USA

Arms Race Education Project

Address. P.O. Box 76600, Washington, DC 20013, USA

Buddhist Peace Fellowship

Address. P.O. Box 4650, Berkeley, California 94704, USA

Carnegie Endowment for International Peace

Address. 30 Rockefeller Plaza, New York, NY 10112, USA

Center for National Security Studies

Address. 122 Maryland Avenue NE, Washington, DC 20002, USA

Center on Law and Pacifism

Address. P.O. Box 308, Cokedale, Colorado 81032, USA

Community for Creative Non-Violence

Address. 1345 Euclid Street NW, Washington, DC 20009, USA

Conference on Peace Research in History

Address. University College, Adelphi University, Garden City, New York 11530, USA

Covenant for Peace

Address. P.O. Box 1831, East Lansing, Michigan 48823, USA

Draft Action

Address. 1435 G Street, NW, suite 534, Washington, DC 20005, USA

Gandhi Institute

Address. P.O. Box 92, Cheney, Pennsylvania 19319, USA

Institute for Peace and Justice

Address. 4144 Lindell Street, St Louis, Missouri 63108, USA

Institute for Security and Co-operation in Outer Space (ISCOS)

Address. 201 Massachusetts Avenue NE, suite 102A, Washington, DC 20002, USA

Lutheran Peace Fellowship

Address. 2481 Como Avenue West, St Paul, Minnesota 55108, USA

Martin Luther King Jr Center for Non-Violent Social Change

Address. 449 Auburn Avenue NE, Atlanta, Georgia 30312, USA

Military Law Task Force

Address. c/o National Lawyers' Guild, 1168 Union Street, suite 202, San Diego, California 92101, USA

National Association of Atomic Veterans

Address. 1109 Franklin Street, Burlington, Idaho 52601, USA

Nurses' Alliance for the Prevention of Nuclear War (NAPNW)

Address. P.O. Box 319, Chestnut Hill, Massachusetts 02167, USA

Peace and Justice Action League

Address. 321 8th Avenue West, Spokane, Washington 99204, USA

Peaceworkers

Address. 3565 Mount Diablo Boulevard, Lafayette, California 94549, USA

People United to Save Humanity (PUSH)

Address. 930 East 50th Street, Chicago, Illinois 60615, USA

Refuse the Cruise Coalition

Address. P.O. Box 4212, Portland, Oregon 97208, USA

Service Civil International (SCI)

Address. P.O. Box 3333, New York, NY 10185, USA

Stop Cruise and Pershing II Clearing House

Address. 4722 Baltimore Avenue, Philadelphia, Pennsylvania 19143, USA

Task Force on Militarization in Asia and the Pacific

Address. Room 616, Inter-Church Center, 475 Riverside Drive, New York, NY 10115, USA

United Methodist Church Peace and World Order Department

Address. 777 UN Plaza, New York NY 10017, USA

United Presbyterian Peacemaking Programme

Address. 465 Riverside Drive, New York, NY 10115, USA

United States Pacific Network

Address. 942 Market Street, room 711, San Francisco, California 94102, USA

United States Pacifist Party

Address. 5729 South Dorchester, Chicago, Illinois 60637, USA

War/Watch Foundation .

Address. P.O. Box 487, Eureka Springs, Arizona 72632, USA

World Peacemakers

Address. 2025 Massachusetts Avenue NW, Washington, DC 20009, USA

World Policy Institute

Address. 777 UN Plaza, New York, NY 10017, USA

World Priorities

Address. P.O. Box 25140, Washington, DC 20007, USA

5. THE PACIFIC REGION

Australia

capital: Canberra   **population: 15,600,000**

Australia is a party, with New Zealand and the United States, to the Pacific Security Treaty, commonly known as the ANZUS Pact, which was signed in San Francisco on Sept. 1, 1951, and came into force on April 29, 1952. Article 4 of this treaty states that each party "recognizes that an armed attack in the Pacific area on any of the other parties would be dangerous to its own peace and safety, and declares that it would act to meet the common danger in accordance with its constitutional procedures". Whereas successive Australian governments, both conservative and Labor, have stressed their commitment to the ANZUS Pact, the Labor Government which took office in New Zealand in 1984 effectively suspended its full participation by banning US nuclear-armed or nuclear-powered warships from New Zealand waters (for further details see introductory section under New Zealand). Within the ANZUS framework, some 250 US military personnel man a number of "joint facilities" on Australian territory for military intelligence, communications, tracking and refuelling purposes. On Feb. 1, 1985, the Australian Goverment agreed to allow US aircraft monitoring test flights of MX missiles to be stationed in Australia, but maintained its refusal to permit the testing of nuclear devices or nuclear delivery systems on or over Australian territory.

Other Australian defence commitments include (i) the 1944 ANZAC agreement with New Zealand, which established a "regional zone of defence comprising the South-West and South Pacific areas" and also specified that "no change in the sovereignty . . . of any of the islands of the Pacific should be affected except as the result of an agreement to which [Australia and New Zealand] are parties"; (ii) the South-East Asia Collective Defence Treaty signed in Manila on Sept. 8, 1954, with France, New Zealand, Pakistan, the Philippines, Thailand, the United States and the United Kingdom, which remains in force despite the dissolution of the South-East Asia Treaty Organization (SEATO) in mid-1977 and the earlier withdrawal of France and Pakistan; and (iii) the 1971 five-power ANZUK agreements under which Australia, New Zealand and the United Kingdom established a joint force for the defence of Malaysia and Singapore (the British component being subsequently withdrawn in 1975–76). In addition, Australia participates in an advisory capacity in the defence forces of Papua New Guinea.

The consistent opposition of Australian governments to French nuclear weapons tests at the Mururoa Atoll site in the South Pacific was stepped up by the Labor administration which came to power in 1983, notably by the imposition of a ban on exports of Australian uranium to France. Moreover, at a meeting of the South Pacific Forum in Rarotonga (Cook Islands) in August 1985, Australia was a signatory of the South Pacific Nuclear-Free Zone Treaty, which committed its adherents not to acquire, manufacture, store, station or test nuclear weapons nor to permit or engage in the dumping of nuclear wastes in their territories. Principally at the insistence of Australia, however, the treaty placed no restrictions on access to the region by nuclear-armed or nuclear-powered ships and aircraft.

Nor has the Australian Government acceded to domestic pressure from anti-nuclear groups for a cessation of uranium mining and exports, maintaining that such exports are used for peaceful purposes only.

As at end-1985 the Australian armed forces (all volunteers) numbered some 70,000 personnel (army 32,000, air force 22,000 and navy 16,000) and reserves about 32,000. The defence budget for the 1985–86 financial year was $A6,676,000,000, representing about 9.5 per cent of total government expenditure.

Anti-Bases Campaign (ABC)—see entry for People for Nuclear Disarmament (PND)

Association for International Co-operation and Disarmament (AICD)—see entry for Australian Coalition for Disarmament and Peace (ACDP)

Australian Coalition for Disarmament and Peace (ACDP)

Address. P.O. Box A243, Sydney South, New South Wales 2000, Australia

Aims and objectives. The ACDP campaigns for disarmament, an end to the arms race, an independent non-aligned Australia, the removal of US bases from Australia, a complete ban on the mining and export of uranium, a nuclear-free and independent Pacific and a nuclear-free Indian Ocean.

Activities. The ACDP has organized conferences (including a "national disarmament conference" in Melbourne in 1985) as well as protest marches and rallies and the signing of petitions. It also participates in regional meetings and actions for a nuclear-free Pacific. The ACDP is closely linked with the Association for International Co-operation and Disarmament (AICD), formed in 1964 and operating from the same address.

Publications. *Anti-War Action* (quarterly). (The AICD publishes a monthly newsletter.)

Australian Quaker Peace Committee (AQPC)

Address. 631 Orrong Road, Toorak, Victoria 3142, Australia

Aims and objectives. The AQPC focuses on peace education and reconciliation work, with the aim of strengthening the "peace witness" of the Australian Society of Friends (Quakers).

Activities. In co-operation with churches and other pacifist groups, the AQPC organizes and participates in conferences and rallies on the theme of disarmament. It also holds workshops on pacifism and non-violent training and arranges lectures and meetings in schools and public halls. The Committee has made a number of submissions to the Australian Parliament on questions such as disarmament and arms control and Australian military aid. It also provided support for the voyage of the *Pacific Peacemaker*.

Future plans include a national meeting of Quakers to discuss peace issues, and the establishment of a central office in Canberra, the federal capital, so as to facilitate the lobbying of parliamentary and government officials.

Membership. The AQPC is composed of 10 members with a full-time field worker (funded by the Quakers). Responsibility for the AQPC is shared by regional Quaker meetings on a three-yearly basis. Responsibility currently rests with the Melbourne regional meeting.

Publications. AQPC started to publish a newsletter, aimed particularly at parliamentarians and at church leaders, during 1985. It is currently developing other resources, including a slide pack on the nuclear winter and a study guide on the film *The Day After*.

Affiliations. AQPC is affiliated to the following groups in Australia and elsewhere: People for Nuclear Disarmament; Australian Coalition for Disarmament and Peace; Coalition for a Nuclear-Free Australia; New Zealand Peace Committee; Canadian Friends Service Committee; American Friends Service Committee; Quaker Peace and Service; and the Quaker UN Office.

Campaign for International Co-operation and Disarmament (CICD)

Address. P.O. Box 114A, 4th floor, 252 Swanston Street, Melbourne 3001, Australia

Aims and objectives. The CICD supports mutual and balanced disarmament, to be achieved through negotiation, with the highest priority in this process being the prohibition of all testing, manufacture and deployment of nuclear and other weapons of mass destruction.

Formation. The CICD was formed in 1959.

Activities. The CICD's activities are concentrated in the state of Victoria. It is currently involved in campaigns for an independent foreign policy and is actively opposed to the stationing, testing or transit of nuclear missiles through Australian territory. It also works for the removal of all foreign military bases from Australia, and for the establishment of nuclear-free zones in the Pacific and in the Indian Ocean. During the 1960s and 1970s, it played an active part in campaigning against Australian involvement in the Vietnam war.

The CICD takes part in campaigns against the mining and export of uranium in Australia, and is in favour of reallocating military expenditure towards social, educational and health needs and of converting military-related industry towards "socially-useful production". The Campaign works for the abolition of conscription and of compulsory military training, and for the establishment of peace research institutes and peace-related curricula in schools.

The CICD's methods include seminars, conferences, public meetings and participation in mass rallies, including demonstrations in Melbourne in April 1984, and events to commemorate the end of the Second World War and the Hiroshima bombing. It has held a Youth Art Project for Peace and Disarmament and a "post-atomic postcard" competition.

The CICD runs a resource library which loans out information material and films to other organisations. It also broadcasts a regular weekly radio programme on Channel 3CR.

Membership. The CICD's membership includes over 60 trade unions, churches and community groups, as well as individuals.

Publications. A regular monthly newsletter is produced together with an information and discussion journal. Other publications appear occasionally.

Affiliations. A founding member of People for Nuclear Disarmament, CICD is also a member of the Australian Coalition for Disarmament and Peace.

Canberra Peacemakers

Address. P.O. Box 1875, Canberra, ACT 2601, Australia

Aims and objectives. Canberra Peacemakers work for peace and social change through non-violent action, focussing on (i) social defence, (ii) strategies against war, (iii) non-violent action training.

Formation. The group came into being in 1979.

Activities. Most work is focused on social defence, involving various grassroots initiatives to see how community organizing can be carried out and how people in Canberra can non-violently oppose an invasion or coup.

Membership. 10 to 12 people.

Publications. *Social Defence*, broadsheet, 1982; *War*, 1984; Social Defence broadsheet in Russia; *Social Defence*, slide show.

Catholic Commission for Justice and Peace

Address. 154 Elizabeth Street, 2nd floor, Sydney, New South Wales 2000, Australia

Aims and objectives. The Catholic Commission for Peace and Justice in Australia seeks to apply in local circumstances the precepts of the Pontifical Commission *Justitia et Pax* of the Vatican.

Catholics for Peace

Address. 255 Lonsdale Street, room 8, 1st floor, Melbourne, Victoria 3000, Australia

Aims and objectives. Catholics for Peace regards its particular task as being "to encourage Catholics in the search and action for peace", with special emphasis on "the nuclear threat under which we live".

Formation. The movement came formally into being in May 1983, on the basis of earlier meetings of Melbourne Catholics seeking to make a specifically Catholic response to the nuclear arms race.

Activities. Catholics for Peace holds monthly public meetings in Melbourne during which speakers "are invited to sharpen our knowledge and understanding of specific aspects of the work for peace".

Publications. *Catholic Peacemaker* (monthly).

Affiliations. Catholics for Peace sees itself as a part of the broader-based movement for peace and is affiliated to Pax Christi Australia and People for Nuclear Disarmament.

310

Disarmament and Peace Committee of the United Nations Association of Australia (Victoria Branch)

Address. 341 Collins Street, Melbourne, Victoria 3000, Australia

Aims and objectives. The Committee seeks to increase awareness in the community of the dangers of war, particularly nuclear war, and of the benefits of peace. It aims to exert national and international pressure on governments to take measures leading to mutual understanding and peace.

Activities. The Committee undertakes various publicity actions and also co-operates in arranging speaking tours for overseas peace activists. It co-operates with other peace groups in the major national Palm Sunday Disarmament Rally.

Membership. About 20 people.

Affiliations. People for Nuclear Disarmament.

Fellowship of Reconciliation

Address. P.O. Box 345, Wahroonga, New South Wales 2076, Australia

Aims and objectives. The Fellowship aims to provide a point of contact between local and international spiritually-based peace groups. It also feeds information about Pacific concerns into international groups. The main objective of the Fellowship is to provide a bridge between peace workers and religious bodies; giving a spiritual input to peacework and promoting peace in the church and religious organizations. Pacifist literature is promoted and the Fellowship tries to present a positive vision of the future.

Formation. The Fellowship was founded in the 1950s but was revitalized in 1983 by a small group of Quakers and others.

Activities. The Fellowship has organized some of its activities around religious events, such as making a banner for the annual Palm Sunday Disarmament Rally. It tries to involve children in its creative activities, which have included making segments for the "peace ribbon" for placing around British and American battleships, and sewing peace quilts for children's hospitals in Leningrad, Kampuchea and Baltimore.

It has also explored and developed conflict resolution for very young children, run a conflict resolution course at a local college and held workshops on a world without weapons.

Membership. The Fellowship has around 50 members who are mainly Quakers and other Christians, although the group includes some Buddhists, Jews and Moslems.

Publications. The Fellowship produces a bi-monthly newsletter and occasional papers.

Affiliations. The group is affiliated to the International Fellowship of Reconciliation.

Manly-Warringah Peace Movement (MWPM)

Address. Manly-Warringah Peace Centre, 14A/26–28 Oaks Avenue, Dee Why, New South Wales 2099, Australia

311

Aims and objectives. The MWPM aims (i) to stimulate concern for international co-operation, disarmament, peace and social justice; (ii) to work to abolish the arms race, prevent the "unthinkable" war and create a worthwhile peace; (iii) to secure the reallocation of resources presently used for military purposes to eliminate world poverty; and (iv) to develop deeper understanding of the issues through public meetings, films, drama, small group discussions and workshops etc. The Movement is not aligned with any political group.

Activities. The MWPM has mobilized support for the concept of an independent, non-aligned and non-nuclear foreign and defence policy for Australia, and has also opposed the presence of foreign military bases and facilities on Australian soil. It has also supported regional initiatives for a nuclear-free Pacific and for a zone of peace in the Indian Ocean, as well as nuclear-free zones at local, state and federal levels. In 1984 the Movement established a Peace Centre at its headquarters.

Membership. The MWPM represents a broad cross-section of persons from different walks of life.

Move for Peace

Address. 20 Cupania Street, Midjimba Beach, Queensland 4564, Australia

Aims and objectives. To work for inner harmony and create a world free from hunger, war and fear; and to call on all governments to create a nuclear-free Pacific and negotiate reductions in nuclear and chemical weapons, and the Australian government to end the mining, sale and export of uranium.

Formation. Move for Peace began 1983.

Activities. These have included establishing and running a local peace centre; organizing the exchange of letters between children from East and West, and helping to build an international "peace surfing" competition on the "sunshine coast" of Queensland.

Publications. A monthly newsletter.

Affiliations. Incorporated branch office for Women for World Disarmament (UK); United Nations Association of Australia; the Sunshine Coast Environment Council.

Nuclear Disarmament Party (NDP)

Address. c/o The Senate, Canberra, ACT 2600, Australia

Aims and objectives. The NDP seeks in particular (i) the closure of all foreign military bases in Australia, (ii) the prohibition of the stationing in or passage through Australia of nuclear weapons, and (iii) the immediate termination of all mining and export of uranium.

Formation. The NDP was formed in June 1984 mainly by Australian Labor Party members disillusioned by what they regarded as Labor's gravitation towards the centre under the premiership of Bob Hawke and away from its anti-nuclear policy commitments.

Activities. In the December 1984 general elections the NDP contested six House of Representatives seats and 14 in the Senate. It returned one member to the latter chamber, namely Jo Vallentine from Western Australia, who has become the party's principal spokesperson. Another prominent member is Peter Garrett, a lawyer and lead singer in the punk rock group Midnight Oil.

Publications. Senator Jo Vallentine's office issues regular briefings and background material on the party's aims and activities.

Nuclear-Free and Independent Pacific Co-ordinating Committee (NFIP Committee)

Address. P.O. Box A243, Sydney South, New South Wales 2000, Australia

Aims and objectives. NFIP supports the goal of an independent and nuclear-free Pacific Ocean, aiming to build and maintain links with groups working for similar aims in the Pacific islands and Pacific "rim" countries, as well as co-operating with peace and disarmament, anti-nuclear and aboriginal land rights groups throughout Australia.

NFIP also supports efforts to secure an independent and non-aligned foreign policy for Australia, including the closure of all US military bases and the prohibition of visits to Australian ports by nuclear-powered vessels or those carrying nuclear weapons. The group is also involved in the campaign against the mining and export of uranium.

Formation. The NFIP co-ordinating committee was formed in February 1981 in Sydney, by members of several organizations which had earlier participated in (i) conferences on a nuclear-free and independent Pacific which had taken place in Honolulu (USA) and Sydney during 1980, and (ii) activities staged to mark the celebration of a "Nuclear-Free and Independent Pacific Day" on March 1, 1981.

Activities. NFIP's main activities take the form of co-ordination work for the organizations which support the broad goals of the movement. It has organized public meetings, demonstrations and petition campaigns; arranged speaking engagements (including a four-week national tour by a Micronesian delegation in 1984); and in general sought to act as a resource centre to provide advice and information on nuclear issues related to the Pacific.

Activities during 1985 were concentrated on organizing opposition to the planned deployment of US Navy Tomahawk cruise missiles in the Pacific area, culminating in an international day of action on June 15. It plans to continue its campaign of support for the constitution of Belau (which has specific "nuclear-free" provisions) and for the independence from France of the Kanak islanders of New Caledonia.

Membership. NFIP's membership is organized on a sponsorship basis, with about 50 organizations and 60 individuals currently acting as sponsors. The former include churches, trade unions, peace and anti-nuclear groups and women's organizations.

Publications. *Pacific News*, NFIP's "educative" newsletter, is produced every two months.

Affiliations. Australian Coalition for Disarmament and Peace; various anti-nuclear and pro-independence Pacific groups in Australia, the Pacific and elsewhere. The Australian Committee is part of the Pacific-wide Nuclear-Free and Independent Pacific network (see entry under International Organizations).

Pax Christi Australia

Address. P.O. Box 31, Carlton South, Victoria 3053, Australia

Aims and objectives. Pax Christi Australia describes itself as an "ecumenical peace movement which sees its role as bridge-builder, making links with like-minded groups working to bring about a more just, sustainable, non-violent society". It strives to spread interest in disarmament issues within the churches and undertakes peace education. It seeks greater integration between peace and environmentalist movements.

Formation. Pax Christi Australia began as a small movement in 1973 in Melbourne.

Activities. Believing that it would be most effective by co-operating with the broader peace movement, Pax Christi Australia played a part in the establishment of People for Nuclear Disarmament in 1981, having formulated its own peace policy in November 1980. It also participates with other church groups in the Australia-wide annual Palm Sunday Disarmament Rally. The organization holds a variety of regular meetings, including an annual conference.

Membership. There are about 500 active members.

Publication. Disarming Times (five a year).

Affiliations. Pax Christi International; People for Nuclear Disarmament.

Peace Education Commission (PEC)

Address. c/o Dr Robin Burns, School of Education, La Trobe University, Bundoora, Victoria 3083, Australia

Aims and objectives. The PEC aims to facilitate international co-operation between educators, peace researchers and activists towards more effective and widespread peace education. It also engages in activities which promote education about the causes of war and injustices as well as conditions for peace and justice.

To achieve these objectives the PEC undertakes, supports and sponsors educational projects within schools as well as out-of-school through close co-operation between researchers and educators at all levels. Where appropriate the PEC co-ordinates activities with other peace organizations, especially research and education agencies.

Formation. The PEC was established in 1970 as a study group within the International Peace Research Association (see entry under International Organizations).

Activities. PEC members have played an active role in UNESCO's disarmament education and human rights work, including chairing the 1979 Paris conference on disarmament education. They have jointly sponsored meetings on women, militarism and disarmament, programmes at the Inter-University Centre in Dubrovnik (Yugoslavia) and worked with the World Council for Curriculum and Instruction and the University of Peace.

The PEC has also prepared a handbook on disarmament education and disseminates its ideas through special editions of the *Bulletin of Peace Proposals* and the *International Review of Education* and through conference reports.

A number of cross-national projects have also been promoted including: a study of children's attitudes to and experiences of peace, war and violence; analysis of textbook content dealing with nuclear issues since World War II;

evaluation and implementation of peace education; peace education in tertiary institutions and teacher education; peace education in the third world; analysis of sexism, sex-role socialization and militarism.

Membership. The PEC has 140 members in 40 countries. Members fall into four groups: teacher educators; school teachers; peace researchers and teachers of peace studies who explore the pedagogical as well as the content aspects of peace research; non-formal educators and community development personnel.

Publications. The PEC has produced the following publications: *Handbook on Peace Education* (ed. Christoph Wulf); *Education for Peace: Reflection and Action* (ed. Magnus Haavelsrud); *Approaching Disarmament Education* (ed. Magnus Haavelsrud); *Friedenshorizonte—Zu Friedensbewegung und Friedenserziehung in 5 Kontinente* (Horizons of Peace—Peace Movements and Peace Education in 5 Continents) (eds. Wolfgang Beer and Angelika Rimmek).

Affiliations. The PEC is a formally constituted study group of the International Peace Research Association. It has no formal affiliations, but works from time to time, either as a commission or through members or groups of members, with other groups sharing the PEC's concerns, such as the World Council for Curriculum and Instruction and the Universities of Peace in Namur (Belgium) and Costa Rica.

Peace Education Foundation (PEF)

Address. 219 Railway Parade, Maylands, Western Australia 6051, Australia

Aims and objectives. The PEF seeks to promote the non-violent resolution of conflicts from an interpersonal to an international level. It also works towards the elimination of all weapons of human destruction and a more just society in which all peoples would attain human rights.

Formation. The PEF was formed in 1983.

Activities. Since its formation the PEF has run teacher in-service forums, made educational videos and been involved in the formation of a "One World Education Centre" which provides resources for educators on development and peace education issues. The Foundation undertakes peace research and is active in community debate on peace issues.

Membership. The PEF has around 100 members.

Publications. The PEF produces a regular newsletter and a *Peace Education Handbook.*

Affiliations. People for Nuclear Disarmament.

Peace Education Project (PEP)

Address. P.O. Box 452, Fremantle, Western Australia 6160, Australia

Aims and objectives. The Peace Education Project works to achieve a just, participatory and sustainable society for all, serving the needs of teachers and students in schools. To this end the project fosters non-violence, trust and co-operation at all levels. It also aims to establish creative conflict resolution and an awareness of the interconnections of peace and justice. It aims to make people aware of the many forms of violence in society.

Formation. The PEP began in March 1984 with two resource centres and five staff funded under the Community Employment Programme for 12 months. In March 1985 the funding came to an end, but one of the sponsors of the project, the Fremantle Education Centre, allocated a portion of its recurrent grant from the Federal Government to employ one project officer part time.

Activities. In 1984 the PEP offered two in-service sessions to teachers and organized a multi-media and writing exhibition. This attracted entries from over 1,000 children.

Since 1985 the project has narrowed its focus in order to cope with the funding cut-back and in response to the types of requests that were most prevalent in 1984. The area of non-violent conflict resolution has been focused on, with workshops being offered to teachers, students and the community.

A teacher network is administered by the project and activities are regularly offered to teachers. The project responds to requests for resources, advice and information on the whole issue of educating for peace. Activities are designed and tried in schools by the project officer and these are then available for use by teachers.

Membership. As an educational project and service, the PEP does not have members as such but the associated teacher network (One World Education Network) has 110 teachers on its list.

Publications. The PEP produces a regular newsletter and a resource handbook for teachers entitled *Educating for Peace, Justice and Hope.*

People for Nuclear Disarmament (PND)

Address. P.O. Box 132, Carlton South, Victoria 3053, Australia; *other major branches:* PND (New South Wales), P.O. Box A243, Sydney House, NSW 2000; PND (Queensland), P.O. Box 244, West End, Brisbane, Queensland 4101; PND (South Australia), 155 Pirie Street, Adelaide, SA 5000; PND (Tasmania), 102 Bathurst Street, Hobart, Tasmania 7000; PND (Western Australia), 1167 May Street, West Perth, WA 6005

Aims and objectives. PND seeks the removal from Australia of any military base or other facility which contributes to the preparation for a nuclear war or which would qualify as a possible target in the event of such a war. It supports existing campaigns aimed at making Australia a nuclear-free country, and it is also in favour of the establishment of a Pacific-wide nuclear-free zone and of the recognition of the Indian Ocean as a "zone of peace". PND is opposed to the ANZUS military alliance (of Australia, New Zealand and the United States) and to visits to Australian waters of nuclear-armed and/or nuclear-powered vessels. The group also works for an end to the mining of uranium in Australia.

Formation. PND was established in 1981 as a coalition of three peace movements.

Activities. PND staged three major peace rallies in April 1982 (attracting 40,000 people), and in the same month in 1983, 1984 (involving 60,000 and 100,000 people respectively) and 1985. It has held several protest actions against the deployment of nuclear-powered warships or ships carrying nuclear armaments.

PND activists staged a rally outside the Watsonia SIGNIT/OSIS base in 1983, and the following year held a two-week peace camp at the base. The group also took part in the blockade actions at Roxby Downs uranium mines in 1983–84.

In 1984 PND representatives presented a "disarmament declaration campaign" petition, containing over 200,000 signatures, to the Australian government. The group is maintaining a series of campaigns aimed at persuading local authorities to declare themselves nuclear-free zones, and it is continuing its "public education" programmes. PND took part in a variety of actions coinciding with the 40th anniversary of the nuclear bombing of Hiroshima in August 1985.

In mid-1986 PND was prominent in the launching of an Anti-Bases Campaign (ABC) by the Australian peace movement, involving the mounting of demonstrations at the three major US bases (known as "joint facilities") at Pine Gap (near Alice Springs in central Australia), Nurrungar (South Australia) and North West Cape (Western Australia). Demands were made for the closure of these facilities, used by US personnel for communications and monitoring purposes.

Membership. PND has many thousands of members and supporters involved in local groups throughout the country. It claims to enjoy the support of over 200 affiliated organizations, including peace and anti-nuclear groups, church groups, women's groups, trade unions, student organizations and political parties. The group also claims the support of a number of professional organizations representing teachers, actors, artists, doctors, lawyers, scientists, welfare workers and psychologists.

Publications. PND (Victoria) publishes a regular newsletter and also a journal entitled *Flashpoint*; other material, including research documents, are produced when required for specific campaigns. Other branches also publish regular newsletters.

Affiliations. As an umbrella organization, PND tends to have groups affiliated to it rather than vice versa. Most state PND branches are affiliated to the Australian Coalition for Disarmament and Peace (ACDP).

People for Peace

Address. P.O. Box 1025, Adelaide, South Australia 5001, Australia

Aims and objectives. People for Peace has four main aims, with the achievement of nuclear disarmament as a first priority and also including the abolition of all weapons of mass destruction, the winding down of the arms race and the transfer of expenditure from military purposes to "life promoting enterprises". It also lobbies the Australian government on the questions of support for the resolutions of the UN second special session on disarmament (UNSSOD II) in 1982, for the declaration of nuclear-free zones in the Pacific and Indian Oceans, for the adoption of a non-aligned foreign policy and for the removal from Australia of "any facility or operation which contributes to preparation for war, especially nuclear war".

Formation. People for Peace was set up in October 1982.

Activities. The group organizes rallies and demonstrations, mainly in the South Australia area, where it has been involved in all the Adelaide rallies for disarmament and an end to uranium mining. It also took part in countrywide peace actions on Palm Sunday 1985.

The group organizes displays and talks in schools, and campaigns on behalf of candidates favourable to its aims during election times.

Future plans include an expansion of campaign work against US bases in Australia, notably the base at Nurrunger, in South Australia, and against visits by nuclear-armed US warships.

Membership. There are approximately 400 members, including other peace groups, churches and Christian organizations, environmental groups, trade unions, political parties, development and aid groups, professional and student organizations and women's groups.

Publications. Critical Times (a monthly newsletter) is produced jointly with the Campaign Against Nuclear Energy.

Affiliations. People for Peace is affiliated to the Australian Coalition for Disarmament and Peace.

Trinity Peace Research Institute

Address. 72 St George's Terrace, Perth, Western Australia 6000, Australia

Aims and objectives. The Trinity Peace Research Institute is a research and resource body to assist and advise the Christian churches, the Australian government and the mainstream peace movement. It aims to complement existing government and university peace studies centres in that it is also involved in practical community education.

Formation. The Institute was inaugurated on Jan. 1, 1986, to coincide with the start of the UN's International Year of Peace.

Activities. The Institute is a new activity of the Trinity Uniting Church of Perth and represents "the first time that a parish of the Uniting Church in Australia has seen the need to explore key issues of peace and social justice facing the world today and to take the results beyond the local community out into the national and international sphere".

The post of foundation-director of the Institute was taken by Dr Keith Suter, an international authority on disarmament and hitherto general secretary of the Uniting Church's commission on social responsibility.

Women for Survival

Address. P.O. Box 163, Clifton Hill, Victoria 3068, Australia

Aims and objectives. This network of feminists seeks to end violence in personal lives (rape, pornography, wife-beating etc.) and at a global level (war, militarism, the nuclear threat etc.). Some local groups prefer the title Womyn for Survival.

Formation. The Women for Survival network developed in the early 1980s, linking local feminist action groups involved in peace and other campaigning.

Activities. The network works to change the perception which women have of themselves and which the community has of women, as the starting-point for global change. In addition to being involved in the feminist cause, the network's groups have participated in numerous peace and anti-nuclear actions.

Women's International League for Peace and Freedom (WILPF)

Address. 156 Castlereagh Street, 3rd floor, Sydney, New South Wales 2000, Australia

Aims and objectives. As the Australian section of the world-wide organization, WILPF works for disarmament and peace and shares the broad aims of the main Australian peace movements. It places emphasis on educational work and also espouses human rights issues.

Activities. The Australian WILPF hosted the Pacific Women's Peace Conference in Sydney in June 1985, which was attended by women's representatives from Belau, Fiji, French Polynesia, Japan, Kiribati, New Caledonia, Papua New Guinea, the Philippines, the Solomon Islands, Tonga, Vanuata and West Papua, as well as by Aborigine and Torres Strait Island representatives (Australia) and by Maori women from New Zealand.

Membership. There are WILPF branches in six Australian states.

Publication. *Peace and Freedom* (quarterly).

Affiliations. Women's International League for Peace and Freedom.

Other Movements

Australian Nuclear Veterans' Association

Address. P.O. Box 180, Fortitude Valley, Queensland 4006, Australia

Australian Peace Committee

Address. P.O. Box 32, Trades Hall, Goulburn Street, Sydney, New South Wales 2000, Australia

Canberra Programme for Peace

Address. P.O. Box 1875, Canberra, ACT 2601, Australia

Coalition for a Nuclear-Free Australia (CNFA)

Address. 291 Morphett's Street, Adelaide, South Australia 5000, Australia

National Network for Non-Violent Training

Address. 38 Yackatoon Avenue, Aspendale, Victoria 3195, Australia

Peace Institute

Address. c/o UNA, 306 Murray Street, Perth, Western Australian 6008, Australia

Peace Tax Campaign

Address. 1 Boa Vista Road, New Town, Tasmania 7008, Australia

Prolifers for Survival

Address. P.O. Box 181, West Bend, Brisbane, Queensland 4101, Australia

War Resisters' League

Address. P.O. Box 223, Broadway, Queensland 4000, Australia

Women for World Disarmament

Address. 20 Cupiana Street, Mudjumba, Queensland 4564, Australia

Women's Action Against Global Violence

Address. 34 Liverpool Street, Sydney, New South Wales 2000, Australia

Women's Action for Nuclear Disarmament

Address. P.O. Box A243, Sydney South, New South Wales 2000, Australia

Belau

capital: Koror   **population: 13,500**

The Republic of Belau (a United Nations trust territory under the administration of the United States) obtained internal self-government on Jan. 1, 1981, on the basis of its July 1980 constitution, this document being noteworthy for the ban which it placed on the "use, testing, storage or disposal of harmful substances such as nuclear, chemical, gas or biological weapons, nuclear power plants or waste materials therefrom" in the Republic's territory. In a further move towards limited independence, a "compact of free association" was signed in Washington in August 1982 under which Belau was to obtain full control over its internal and external affairs, although responsibility for military and security policy would remain with the United States. In the latter context the compact incorporated a 50-year agreement under which, in return for substantial US financial aid, two airports on Belau were to be expanded to take heavy transport jets and the United States was to have exclusive use of (i) large parts of the country's principal harbour, (ii) a 30,000-acre jungle-warfare training base (occupying about one-third of the main island), and (iii) a 2,000-acre storage base in which not only conventional but also nuclear weapons could be deposited.

In a plebiscite held on Feb. 10, 1983, more than 60 per cent. of the Belau electorate supported ratification of the free-association compact, but an accompanying proposal to lift the 1980 constitutional ban on nuclear and other materials secured only 50 per cent support, whereas a 75 per cent majority was required for it to be adopted. In further plebiscites held on Sept. 4, 1984, and Feb. 21, 1986, a lifting of the constitutional ban again failed to secure 75 per cent support, although on the latter occasion the proportion in favour rose to 72 per cent following a vigorous "public education campaign" by the Belau Government on the potential benefits of the compact. After both plebiscites moves by the Government to deem the results as sufficient endorsement of its intentions were thwarted by rulings by the Belau Supreme Court in favour of retention of the constitutional ban, the resolution of which issue was seen as necessary before the free-association compact could be ratified by the US Senate.

Belau Pacific Centre

Address. P.O. Box 58, Koror, Belau, Western Caroline Islands

Aims and objectives. The Centre is part of the network of peace movements which oppose the testing, deployment and transit of nuclear weapons and nuclear-powered ships in the Pacific, and seek the creation of a totally nuclear-free zone in that ocean.

Activities. The Centre's recent activities have focused on the defence of Belau's non-nuclear constitution of 1980 in the face of moves by the local administration to overturn its provisions in order to enter into a "compact of free association" with the United States which would accommodate the military requirements of the latter. When the Belau Government decided to regard the September 1984 plebiscite result as sufficient endorsement of the compact (despite the absence of the required 75 per cent majority for repeal of the constitutional ban on nuclear weapons), the Centre's leading activist, Roman Bedor, filed a suit which led to the Belau Supreme Court upholding the constitutional ban. In the campaign for the further plebiscite in February 1986, Centre supporters accused the Belau Government of accepting large sums of US money for a "public education campaign" in support of the compact (and thus against the 1980 constitutional ban). They also attacked as "self-deceiving" President Salii's advocacy of a non-nuclear policy modelled on that of Japan, whereby the United States would have military access to Belau without being required to confirm or deny the presence of nuclear weapons.

Following the February 1986 plebiscite, the Centre again successfully applied for a Supreme Court ruling upholding the constitutional ban and also launched an international campaign in support of the 1980 constitution, directed in particular at members of the US Senate (where the proposed compact of free association requires ratification). It is also seeking to prevent UN ratification of any compact which undermines the provisions of the 1980 constitution.

Within the broader Pacific contest, the Centre participates in the Nuclear-Free and Independent Pacific (NFIP) network of movements. It gave a qualified welcome to the South Pacific Nuclear-Free Zone Treaty (adopted by members of the South Pacific Forum in August 1985), while criticizing that treaty's failure to ban access to the region by nuclear-armed or nuclear-powered ships and aircraft.

Affiliations. Nuclear-Free and Independent Pacific network.

Fiji

capital: Suva   population: 700,000

Independent since 1970, Fiji has taken a broadly pro-Western stance in international relations, while at the same time advocating that the Pacific region should be free of super-power rivalries. In the latter context, the Government in 1982 imposed a ban on the passage through Fijian ports and territorial waters of nuclear-armed or nuclear-powered ships, but lifted this prohibition in August 1983, describing the decision as an obligation arising from Fiji's adherence to the UN Law of the Sea Convention. The Government stressed that the change of policy did not imply the abandonment of the goal of creating a nuclear-free zone in the Pacific and that its opposition to French nuclear tests in the South Pacific and to the dumping of nuclear waste by any country would continue. In August 1985 Fiji was a signatory, together with most other members of the South Pacific Forum, of the South Pacific Nuclear-Free Zone Treaty, which committed its adherents not to acquire, manufacture, store station or test nuclear weapons nor to permit or engage in the dumping of nuclear waste in their territories (but which placed no restrictions on access to the region by nuclear-armed or nuclear-powered ships and aircraft).

As at end-1985 Fiji's armed forces consisted of a 2,500-strong army and a small navy of under 200 personnel, all serving on a voluntary basis. Nearly half of the total complement were currently serving with the UN Interim Force in Lebanon or with the Multinational Force and Observers in the Sinai. The defence budget for 1985 was 16,000,000 Fijian dollars, representing about 4 per cent of total government expenditure.

Fiji Anti-Nuclear Group (FANG)

Address. 101 Gordon Street, P.O. Box 853, Suva, Fiji

Aims and objectives. FANG seeks to explain nuclear dangers, to educate people about nuclear issues and to provide information about both regional and worldwide events. This broad approach to increase awareness includes other issues, such as human rights, terrorism, refugees and the escalation of the arms race.

Activities. FANG has organized opposition to visits of US warships and submarines and it has picketed various nuclear-powered vessels visiting Suva. The group has arranged all-night vigils outside the US, Australian, French and Japanese embassies. FANG gives full coverage of alleged police harassment in its numerous broadsheets.

Publications. Since 1983 FANG has produced a quarterly newsletter. The group has also been involved in the production of a anti-nuclear book called *A Call To a New Exodus,* by Suliana Siwatibau and David Williams (Sunrise Publications).

Japan

capital: Tokyo   **population: 120,000,000**

Following its defeat in the Second World War, Japan signed a peace treaty with the Western allied powers (but not with the Soviet Union and its allies) in San Francisco on Sept. 8, 1951, and on the same day entered into a defence pact with the United States. The latter pact was replaced by the US-Japanese Treaty of Mutual Co-operation and Security, signed in Washington on Jan. 19, 1960, and still in force, under which (i) each party recognized that an attack in the Pacific area on the other would be dangerous to its own peace and safety and undertook to "act to meet the common danger in accordance with its constitutional processes", and (ii) the United States was granted "the use by its land, air and naval forces of facilities and areas in Japan". The treaty was clarified by an exchange of notes in which the United States agreed to prior consultations with Japan over any envisaged increase in its forces in Japan, any essential change in its methods of arming and equipping forces and the use of Japanese bases for any action outside the treaty area (defined as the territory under Japanese rule at any time).

There are currently some 52,000 US troops in Japan, half of them marines stationed on Okinawa in the Ryukyu Islands (which reverted to Japanese sovereignty in May 1972 after having been under US administration since 1945). In April 1985 a detachment of US fighter-bomber aircraft arrived at the Misawa US airbase, these being the first US combat aircraft to be stationed permanently in Japan for 14 years; two complete squadrons were due to be in place by 1987.

Although Japan and the Soviet Union normalized their relations in 1956 (formally ending the state of war between the two countries and re-establishing full diplomatic relations), they have not concluded a post-1945 peace treaty. The major stumbling-block has been the continuing Japanese claim to sovereignty over a group of islands off north-east Hokkaido (the northern-most main Japanese island) which were occupied by Soviet troops in the closing stages of the Second World War and which are strategically important because their surrounding waters provide the Soviet navy with ice-free deep-water access from the Sea of Okhotsk to the Pacific Ocean.* On the other hand, Japan signed a treaty of peace and friendship with the People's Republic of China on Aug. 17, 1978, declaring inter alia that "neither of them should seek hegemony in the Asia-Pacific region or in any other region and that each is opposed to efforts by any other country or group of countries to establish such hegemony".

Japan's 1947 constitution (promulgated under the US military occupation) embodies the ideal of pacifism, specifically providing in Article 9 for the renunciation of war and of war potential and for rejection of the right of belligerency. However, these provisions are not seen as denying Japan the right of self-defence as a sovereign nation, to which end the Self-Defence Forces (SDF) are maintained to provide "the necessary minimum military strength". The SDF

---

* For the Japan-USSR territorial dispute, see Alan J. Day (ed.), *Border and Territorial Disputes* (Longman 1982), pp. 302-19.

operate on the basis of having an "exclusively defence-oriented posture", which is defined as meaning that they would be used only if Japan were subject to an armed attack by another country. In light of its experience as the only country in the world to have undergone a nuclear attack (in August 1945, when the United States dropped atomic bombs on Hiroshima and Nagasaki), Japan has, as a fundamental national policy, adhered to three "non-nuclear principles" enjoining the non-possession, non-manufacture and non-introduction of nuclear weapons in Japan. At the same time, US warships in Japanese ports and territorial waters are covered by the standard US policy that neither confirmation nor denial is given as to whether they are carrying nuclear weapons.

As at end-1985 the SDF totalled some 243,000, consisting of 155,000 army, 44,000 navy and 44,000 air force personnel; there were also 44,000 reservists and 20,000 in the para-military Coast Guard. The Japanese armed forces are recruited on a wholly voluntary basis. The defence budget for the 1985-86 financial year was 3,137,100 million yen (6.9 per cent higher than the previous year), representing 6 per cent of general-account government expenditure and 0.997 per cent of gross national product (GNP).

Despite annual increases in the defence budget of 5 to 8 per cent between 1982 and 1985, Japan's military expenditure had remained within a ceiling of 1 per cent of GNP prescribed by the Liberal Democratic (LDP) Government in 1976. However, a government White Paper published on Aug. 7, 1985, called for an acceleration in the build-up of the SDF to counter an increasing "potential military threat from the Soviet Union". Accordingly, Prime Minister Yasuhiro Nakasone sought the agreement of his cabinet and party colleagues for the abandonment of the 1 per cent ceiling, particularly with a view to expanding Japan's maritime and air defence capabilities. On Sept. 18, 1985, a five-year defence spending programme of 18,400,000 million yen was announced for the period 1986-90, representing average annual expenditure of 1.038 per cent of GNP; however, in the face of vigorous political and popular opposition the defence budget for the 1986-87 financial year was eventually set at 3,340,000 million yen, just within the 1 per cent of GNP ceiling.

The planned increase in Japanese defence spending was welcomed by the US Government as "a further indication of Japan's continuing commitment to acquire the capability of fulfilling its agreed defence roles". In early June 1986 eight Japanese surface ships and a submarine—a higher number than ever before—joined units from the United States, Canada, Australia and the United Kingdom in the Pacific Rim ("Rimpac") naval manoeuvres. A further government White Paper on defence published on Aug. 8, 1986, reiterated the need to increase military expenditure in response to the perceived "persistent" Soviet military build-up in the Pacific region.

Centre for Peace Studies

Address. Shikoku Gakuin University, Zentsuji-Shi, Kagawa-Ken 765, Japan

Aims and objectives. The Centre undertakes the collection and dissemination of information on peace and nuclear issues, the Third World and environmental pollution.

Formation. The Centre was established in 1972.

Activities. The Centre runs a university course on peace studies, and is researching into the relationship between peace studies and the peace movement.

Publications. Citizens' Forum, in Japanese, irregular.

Affiliations. International Peace Research Association: Consortium on Peace Research, Education and Development (COPRED) of the United States.

Japan Congress Against Atomic and Hydrogen Bombs (Gensuikin)

Address. 4th floor, Akimoto Building, 2-19 Kanda Tsukasa-cho, Chiyoda-ku, Tokyo, Japan

Aims and objectives. Gensuikin campaigns for a nuclear-free future; it is opposed to both nuclear weapons and nuclear power.

Formation. Gensuikin was formed in 1965 as the result of a split in the ranks of Gensuikyo, hitherto the main Japanese group campaigning against nuclear weapons (see next entry). Gensuikyo, under the influence of the Japan Communist Party, had decided on a policy of opposing only US and Western weapons, claiming that Soviet nuclear capability was necessary as a defence against Western aggression. Members of the organization who favoured campaigning against all nuclear weapons left to form Gensuikin.

Activities. The group organizes an annual "Atomic Bomb Disaster Anniversary Conference" in Hiroshima and Nagasaki, and was also involved in organizing the World Conference against Atomic and Hydrogen Bombs in the two cities. It has given practical assistance to the victims of the atom bombs, including Koreans and Chinese who were working as forced labourers in Japan at the time of the 1945 bombings.

Gensuikin has also been concerned with the effects of the US nuclear testing programme in the Pacific. It has sent scientists and doctors to the Marshall Islands and invited Marshallese victims of the testing to the Atomic Bomb Hospitals in Hiroshima and Nagasaki for check-ups and treatment. The group also organized a radiation survey around French Polynesia (where French nuclear tests are conducted at Mururoa Atoll).

Gensuikin has held meetings in Japan to inform the indigenous people of the Pacific, Australia and the USA of the dangers associated with nuclear-waste dumping and uranium mining. It also assisted in the presentation of petitions to the Japanese Diet (parliament) on the nuclear waste issue by several Pacific island governments in May 1981. Gensuikin is currently collecting signatures for a petition opposing all dumping of nuclear waste in the area.

The group is also actively opposed to the presence of US bases in Japan, to Japanese participation in US-led naval manoeuvres in the Pacific and to the visit to any Pacific port of submarines carrying Trident missiles.

Membership. Gensuikin has no individual members, but it is supported and funded by the General Council of Trade Unions of Japan (SOHYO), which has an affiliated membership of some 4,500,000. It also receives support from the Socialist Party of Japan, the Social Democratic League and the Komeito (a Buddhist party). It has local branches in each of Japan's 46 prefectures.

Publication. *Gensuikin News,* an English-language newsletter, which appears four or five times a year.

Affiliations. Gensuikin maintains close contact with other peace movements and also with ecological groups, including *Die Grünen* (the West German Green Party) and Friends of the Earth.

Japan Council Against Atomic and Hydrogen Bombs (Gensuikyo)

Address. 6-19-23, Shimbashi, Minato-ku, Tokyo 105, Japan

Aims and objectives. Gensuikyo works for (i) the prevention of nuclear war; (ii) a total ban on nuclear weapons; and (iii) to provide support and assistance for Japanese A-bomb survivors ("*Hibakusha*").

Formation. Gensuikyo was formed in 1955 by the organizations which in 1954 collected 32,000,000 signatures in Japan asking for a total ban on nuclear weapons following an incident in 1954 when an American hydrogen bomb test at Bikini Atoll resulted in contamination by radiation of Japanese fishermen. Closely identified with the Japan Communist Party, Gensuikyo underwent a split in 1965 when those opposed to what they regarded as its anti-US bias broke away to form the Gensuikin movement (see previous entry).

Activities. Gensuikyo organizes an annual "World Conference Against A & H Bombs" and has campaigned against the military alliance between Japan and the USA and for a nuclear-free and non-aligned Japan. It also conducts yearly fund-raising campaigns to help the 370,000 people still suffering from the effects of the atomic bombs dropped on Hiroshima and Nagasaki in 1945. In 1985 it launched the "Appeal from Hiroshima and Nagasaki", an international petition against nuclear weapons, and during 1985-86 sent *Hibakusha* delegations abroad to further the building of an international anti-nuclear united front.

Membership. Japan Gensuikyo is a co-ordinating body to which 47 prefectural Gensuikyos and 60 other federations of trade unions, women's, youth, student, religious and cultural groups are affiliated.

Publications. Gensuikyo Tushin, monthly bulletin; *No More Hiroshimas!,* quarterly bulletin in English; documents of the "World Conference Against A & H Bombs", in Japanese; various pamphlets, leaflets and books.

Affiliations. World Peace Council; UN Non-Governmental Organizations' Committee on Disarmament (associate member).

Japan Peace Museum Committee

Address. 1-4-9 Shiba, Minato-ku, Tokyo 105, Japan

Aims and objectives. The Committee aims to build a peace museum in Tokyo which will provide exhibitions, films, videos and books on the theme of world peace.

Formation. The present Committee originated in 1983 from the Committee of Japanese Citizens to Send Gift Copies of a Pictorial Record of the Atomic Destruction to the Children and Fellow Human Beings. This original committee began by publishing a book of photos of the destruction of Hiroshima and Nagasaki, which also included drawings by survivors.

Activities. In addition to making films on anti-war themes, the Committee has organized exhibitions on such subjects as Hiroshima-Nagasaki, War and Ginza, World Caricatures and Cartoons for Peace, and Peace Posters. The Committee sells "peace goods" such as T-shirts and calendars to raise funds and promote interest in their activities. It also runs a "Peace Tile Campaign", involving the payment of contributions into a peace fund to be used for building the museum.

Membership. The committee has roughly 7,350 members.

Publications. The Committee produces a newsletter *Heiwa Haku* which keeps members informed of the progress of the museum and *Hagaki News* which informs members of events and programmes.

National Movement for Non-Deployment of Tomahawk

Address. Pal Aoyama 502, 2-5-9 Shibuya, Shibuya-ku, Tokyo, Japan

Aims and objectives. This Movement opposes the deployment of US Tomahawk sea-launched cruise missiles in the Pacific region and specifically their entry into Japanese ports and waters on visiting US submarines.

Activities. To mark June 15, 1985, as an international day of action against US and Soviet sea-launched cruise missiles, the Japanese Movement staged a large rally to protest against the deployment of Tomahawk missiles in the Pacific region, in concert with similar actions by other peace movements around the world. In late 1985 activists of the Movement demonstrated against the visit of the *USS Houston* to the Yokosuka naval base, while on June 29, 1986, a series of actions for a worldwide "Disarm the Seas" weekend culminated in a mass rally at Yokosuka.

Nipponzan Myohoji

Address. 7-8 Shinsen, Shibuya-ku, Tokyo 150, Japan

Aims and objectives. As part of the War Resisters' International (WRI) network, this movement is opposed to all forms of militarism and advocates non-violent means of solving conflicts and conscientious objection from participation in military activity.

Publication. Tenku, monthly.

Affiliations. War Resisters' International (associated member).

Niwano Peace Foundation

Address. Akasaka Grand House 202, 8-6-17 Akasaka, Minato-ku, Tokyo 107, Japan

Aims and objectives. This Foundation seeks to apply Buddhist principles to the struggle for international peace and co-operation.

Formation. The Foundation was created in 1978 by the Rissho Kosei-kai Buddhist movement.

Activities. The Foundation conducts and promotes peace research and education, sponsors conferences and symposia on peace and religious themes, and also awards an annual peace prize to an individual or organization deemed to have made a significant contribution to the causes of peace and inter-religious co-operation.

Nuclear-Free Citizens' Declaration Movement (NFCDM) of Yokosuka

Address. c/o Yokosuka Citizens' Group, Yamamoto Building, 3-14 Hon-cho, Yokosuka, Kanagawa 238, Japan

Aims and objectives. The NFCDM aims to create an anti-war network in the city of Yokosuka. It is particularly opposed to the US Navy and JSDF (Japan Self-Defence Force) bases in the city, nuclear weapons and a nuclear fuel processing factory located in Yokosuka.

Formation. The NFCDM was founded in 1982 when concerned citizens in Yokosuka formulated a "Nuclear Free Citizens' Declaration".

Activities. Since the deployment of US Tomahawk missiles in the Pacific in June 1984, the NFCDM has concentrated on campaigning for the abolition of these weapons.

In 1984 it launched the "Anti-Tomahawk Signature Obtaining Campaign" and collected 60,000 signatures to a petition which was presented to the Mayor of Yokosuka. The group demanded that the Mayor should refuse to allow US Navy Tomahawk-capable submarines to visit the city's port; however, the request was rejected on the grounds that the mayor had no authority to check whether a US Navy submarine was deploying Tomahawks or not. On June 29, the Movement participated in a mass protest rally in Yokosuka to mark the culmination of a worldwide "Disarm the Seas" weekend.

Membership. The NFCDM Declaration has some 340 signatories, from all social classes.

Publications. The NFCDM publishes a monthly newsletter in Japanese and a quarterly newsletter in English.

Peace Office
Heiwa Jimusho

Address. Room 43, Sanyo Building, 1-5-17 Hongo, Bunkyo-ku, Tokyo 113, Japan

Aims and objectives. The Peace Office seeks to promote the peace and disarmament movement, independently of any political party.

Formation. The Office was established in September 1984.

Activities. The Peace Office has organized regular meetings, including a "Grassroots for Peace" conference held in Tokyo Aug. 3-4, 1985, and has sponsored tours to military bases and peace exhibitions. It works to co-ordinate local peace groups throughout Japan, and has organized a letter-writing campaign in support of New Zealand's nuclear-free policy. In 1985-86 the Office has been involved in the opposition to any Japanese involvement in the US Strategic Defence Initiative.

Membership. The Office has no formal membership, but about 1,000 contacts in Japan.

Publication. Peacepia, monthly newsletter.

Peace Studies Association of Japan (PSAJ)

Address. Dept. of General Education, Okayama University, Tsushima-naka, Okayama 700, Japan

Aims and objectives. The PSAJ seeks to carry out and promote scientifically grounded research into the causes of conflicts between nations and the conditions necessary for peace.

Formation. The Association was established in 1973.

Activities. The PSAJ publishes works on peace-related topics, and co-ordinates national and foreign academic societies involved in peace research.

Membership. The Association has over 600 members, mainly university lecturers. (Members are admitted by the board of directors on the recommendation of two members, including at least one board member, subject to the approval of the general assembly.)

Publications. The PSAJ publishes books and annuals in Japanese and an annual newsletter in English.

War Resisters' International Japan

Address. 2-12-2 Asahimachi, Abeno-ku, Osaka, Japan

Aims and objectives. As the Japanese section of War Resisters' International, this group opposes all forms of militarism, advocates non-violent methods of solving conflict and supports conscientious objection from military service.

Publication. Namazu.

Affiliations. War Resisters' International (full member).

Women's International League for Peace and Freedom (WILPF), Japan Section
Fujin Kokusai Heiwa Jiyu Renmei, Nihon Shibu

Address. c/o Japan Women's University, 2-8-1 Mejirodai, Bunkyo-ku, Tokyo 112, Japan

Aims and objectives. The WILPF works to bring women of different political and philosophical attitudes together to study and help abolish the causes of war and work for a constructive peace. The League sees as its ultimate goal the establishment of an international economic order founded on meeting the needs of all peoples and not on profit and privilege.

Formation. The Japan Women's Peace Society was formed in 1921 and was recognized as WILPF's Japanese section in 1924. Open activity was suspended during the war years, and the society was re-admitted to the WILPF in 1956. In 1963 it changed its name to WILPF, Japan Section.

Activities. These include discussion groups and conferences on the prohibition of nuclear weapons, fund-raising for African famine relief and the promotion of an international human rights law.

Membership. The Japan Section has about 500 members.

Publications. Women and Peace, three times a year.

Affiliations. Women's International League for Peace and Freedom.

YMCA International Institute for Peace

Address. 7-11 Hatchobori, Naka-ku, Hiroshima 730, Japan

Aims and objectives. In accordance with the objectives of the YMCA, the aim of the Institute is the realization of a world of "eternal peace", based on the idea of mutual sharing. It works for the prevention of nuclear war through the banning of nuclear weapons and the creation of a world without war. It also seeks the creation of a just society where all races can coexist without fear, regardless of their faith or denomination. The Institute seeks the establishment of a World YMCA Peace Network based on the lesson of Hiroshima.

Formation. The YMCA International Institute for Peace was established in March 1984.

Activities. In 1984 the Institute sponsored the National Council of YMCAs of Japan's participation in the YMCA Peace Rally in West Germany. It also hosted religious delegations from the USSR and the Republic of China in Hiroshima, organized an International Youth Forum with the National Council of YMCAs of Japan and directed panel discussions in Hiroshima on nuclear issues and war and peace.

In 1985 the institute held a two-day symposium on "The Role of Hiroshima and the International Year of Peace" marking the first anniversary of the Institute. It also organized a six-day symposium on "Palestinian-Jewish Co-existence" and arranged speakers on the New Zealand nuclear-free zone movement.

The Institute is currently involved in sponsoring monthly speakers in Hiroshima on international peace issues and displaying a peace photo exhibit and international collection of political satire at the Hiroshima Peace Memorial Hall. It co-organized the World Hiroshima Day Telephone Project on Aug. 6, 1986.

Membership. The Institute has a 25-member advisory council and board of directors, 10 financially supportive corporate members and 100 dues paying members. Around 400 people participate annually in seminars and symposia and 350 individuals and groups are on the Institute's mailing list.

Publications. The Institute produces a quarterly journal in Japanese and a semi-annual newsletter in English, entitled *Our Planet*.

Other Movements

Citizens' Committee for a Nuclear-Free Nagasaki

Address. 3-3 Tsuki Machi, room 401, Nagasaki 852, Japan

Hiroshima Council Against A and H Bombs

Address. 1-17 Kinya-cho, Minami-ku, Hiroshima, Japan

Hiroshima Peace Culture Foundation

Address. 1-2 Nakajima-cho, Naka-ku, Hiroshima 733, Japan

Hiroshima-Nagasaki Peace Foundation

Address. SY Building, 12-15 Hatchobori, Naka-ku, Hiroshima, Japan

Movement for Peace and Disarmament

Address. Tachibana Building, 3-1-7 Kojimachi, Chiyoda-ku, Tokyo, Japan

Service Civil International

Address. 2-31-16 Minami-urawa, Urawa-shi, Saitamaken 336, Japan

New Zealand

capital: Wellington   **population: 3,240,000**

New Zealand is a party, with Australia and the United States, to the Pacific Security Treaty, commonly known as the ANZUS Pact, which was signed in San Francisco on Sept. 1, 1951, and came into force on April 29, 1952. Article 4 of this treaty states that each party "recognizes that an armed attack in the Pacific area on any of the other parties would be dangerous to its own peace and safety, and declares that it would act to meet the common danger in accordance with its constitutional procedures". Under the ANZUS Pact New Zealand assumed certain security responsibilities in its area of the Pacific and has made communications and monitoring facilities available to the United States, while under a memorandum of understanding signed on Feb. 26, 1982, the scope of the Pact was expanded by the establishment of procedures for the provision to New Zealand of US logistical support in time of emergency.

In July 1984, however, a Labour Government came to power under David Lange committed to banning the entry of nuclear-armed or nuclear-powered ships into New Zealand ports and territorial waters (New Zealand having previously accepted the standard US policy of neither confirming nor denying whether any particular warship was carrying nuclear weapons). Although Lange reaffirmed his Government's basic commitment to the ANZUS Pact, its "non-negotiable" policy on the nuclear issue provoked a serious crisis within the alliance, with not only the United States but also Australia (under a Labor Government) insisting that unfettered access by ANZUS ships and aircraft to member states' ports and airports was essential to the continued effectiveness of the Pact. In February 1985 New Zealand refused a US request for port facilities for a warship with a potential nuclear capability and thereafter New Zealand's participation in ANZUS meetings and activities was effectively suspended.

In August 1986 the annual meeting of the Pacific Council (the main organ of the ANZUS Pact), held in San Francisco without the participation of New Zealand, concluded that New Zealand had in effect withdrawn from the Pacific Security Treaty but made it clear that a change of policy by New Zealand was still hoped for, in which event its participation in the Pact could be resumed. Lange responded by regretting the decision to expel New Zealand but stressed that his Government "remained determined to honour its election pledge and the wishes of the overwhelming majority of New Zealanders to keep nuclear weapons out of New Zealand"; he added that legislation to ban nuclear weapons would proceed through Parliament as planned. (In view of New Zealand's non-participation in the Pact, it was decided that Australian forces would take over a greater share in South Pacific surveillance and defence duties.)

Other New Zealand defence commitments include (i) the 1944 ANZAC agreement with Australia, which established a "regional zone of defence comprising the South-West and South Pacific areas" and also specified that "no change in the sovereignty . . . of any of the islands on the Pacific should be affected except as the result of an agreement to which Australia and New Zealand are parties"; (ii) the South-East Asia Collective Defence Treaty signed in Manila on Sept. 8, 1954, with Australia, France, Pakistan, the Philippines, Thailand, the United Kingdom and the United States, which remains in force despite the dissolution of the South-East Asia Treaty Organization (SEATO) in mid-1977 and the earlier withdrawal of France and Pakistan; and (iii) the 1971 five-power ANZUK agreements under which Australia, New Zealand and the United Kingdom established a joint force for the defence of Malaysia and Singapore (the British component being subsequently withdrawn in 1975-76).

At a meeting of the South Pacific Forum held in Rarotonga (Cook Islands) in August 1985, New Zealand was a signatory with most other member states of the South Pacific Nuclear-Free Zone Treaty, which committed its adherents not to acquire, manufacture, store, station or test nuclear weapons nor to permit or engage in the dumping of nuclear waste in their territories. Principally at the insistence of Australia, however, the treaty placed no restrictions on access to the region by nuclear-armed or nuclear-powered ships and aircraft. The Rarotonga meeting also received a New Zealand proposal for regional security co-operation (including a central maritime surveillance agency, anti-terrorist and other military training and the exchange of security operation), but no decision was taken on the proposal.

Successive New Zealand administrations, both Labour and Conservative, have strongly condemned French nuclear weapons tests at the Mururoa Atoll site in the South Pacific. In this context a major crisis in relations with France developed in July 1985 when the *Rainbow Warrior* (a ship of the environmentalist pressure group Greenpeace International) was sunk, and one crew member killed, by a bomb explosion in Auckland harbour shortly before sailing on a protest voyage into the area of the French testing site. The French Government eventually admitted that those responsible were members of the French security service and two such agents were arrested and subsequently convicted in New Zealand (although in August 1986 they were handed over to serve three years of detention on the French island of Hao in return for a formal apology from France and the payment of $7,000,000 in compensation).

As at end-1985 the New Zealand armed forces numbered 12,500, consisting of 5,500 army, 4,300 air force and 2,700 navy personnel; there were also some 9,500 reserves, including a Territorial Army of 6,500. Service in the armed forces is voluntary. The defence budget for the 1985-86 financial year was NZ$885,900,000, representing about 5.2 per cent of total government expenditure.

Anglican Pacifist Fellowship (AFP)

Address. P.O. Box 15106, Wellington 3, New Zealand

Aims and objectives. The New Zealand section of the AFP aims to persuade Anglican members that pacifism is inherent in the Christian faith, and thereby build up a body of opinion within the Church in order to influence its leaders to issue declarations that war is incompatible with Christianity. The AFP also concerns itself with "positive peacemaking", and as such is "opposed to much that we find in the present social, economic and political order".

Formation. The New Zealand section has its roots in individual membership of the British AFP by New Zealanders in the 1930s. When a significant number had joined, there was sufficient demand for New Zealand to have its own national Fellowship.

Activities. The AFP holds study days and meetings on biblical themes and on current topics, such as apartheid and opposition to visits to New Zealand by foreign warships. It has also made several radio programmes.

Membership. Membership is open to all who sign a declaration which reads: "We, communicant members of the Church of England, or of a Church in full communion with it, believing that our membership of the Christian Church involves the complete repudiation of modern war, pledge ourselves to renounce war and all preparation to wage war, and to work for the construction of Christian peace in the world."

There are currently about 80 members, both clergy and lay people, including some who were conscientious objectors in the Second World War. The vast majority of members are over 30.

Publication. The Fellowship organizes distribution in New Zealand of *Challenge,* the British AFP's journal.

Affiliations. Part of the world-wide APF network, the New Zealand section is affiliated to the International Fellowship of Reconciliation. Within New Zealand, it has informal links with the Christian Pacifist Society and the Society of Friends.

Campaign for Nuclear Disarmament (CND)

Address. P.O. Box 8558, Auckland, New Zealand

Aims and objectives. The Campaign seeks the abolition of all nuclear weapons.

Formation. CND was founded in the 1960s.

Activities. The group organizes protests against the deployment or testing of nuclear weapons in the southern Pacific, and in particular against the visit of nuclear-armed or nuclear-powered ships to New Zealand. It works for the establishment of a Pacific nuclear-free zone.

The New Zealand CND engages in parliamentary lobbying towards these ends, and has recently established a "Nuclear-Weapon-Free Register" of national and local politicians who are prepared to sign a statement declaring that they "totally oppose visits by nuclear-armed or nuclear-propelled warships to New Zealand ports and support the establishment of a nuclear weapons-free zone and a ban on the dumping of waste in the South Pacific".

CND supports the policies of the Labour Government of David Lange with regard to its opposition to nuclear testing and to the visit of nuclear ships to New Zealand.

Membership. There are approximately 700 paid-up members.

Publications. In addition to the Nuclear-Weapon-Free Register, CND produces a bi-monthly journal, *Boom Times,* and has published *A New Zealand Guide to the Nuclear Arms Race* by Marie Leadbeater.

Christian Pacifist Society of New Zealand

Address. 29 McGregors Road, Christchurch 6, New Zealand

Aims and objectives. The Society seeks to promote universal peace, human friendship and welfare, and to challenge the Christian Church to follow the spirit and teaching of Christ on these matters.

Formation. The Society was formed in 1936; some members were put in detention camps or prisons for refusing to serve in the Second World War.

Activities. The Society encourages church members and those in peace groups to adopt an explicitly pacifist stance; it supports the present New Zealand Government in its nuclear-free policy.

Membership. There are 400 members, many of whom are elderly.

Publication. CPS Bulletin, quarterly.

Affiliations. International Fellowship of Reconciliation; War Resisters' International.

Citizens for the Demilitarization of Harewood (CDH)

Address. P.O. Box 2258, Christchurch, New Zealand

Aims and objectives. CDH's central goal is the removal of the US military presence from Christchurch airport (Harewood), which it describes as "the only true foreign military base in New Zealand" despite its official purpose as an Antarctic support base known as "Operation Deep Freeze". The group has no objection to a wholly civilian US support base, but believes that "as long as there is an American military base operating under the guise of Operation Deep Freeze, Christchurch airport will find itself host to all sorts of totally extraneous military activity".

Formation. CDH was formed in mid-1983 as a coalition of peace groups concerned about the US military presence at Harewood.

Activities. The group has organized local and national demonstrations and in March 1984 set up a peace camp at Christchurch airport. It conducts detailed research, based on observation of US activities at Harewood, and has also sent a petition to the New Parliament. In its newsletters and other material, CDH has made a number of assertions, including (i) that Operation Deep Freeze" is a multipurpose US military base beyond New Zealand control and in breach of New Zealand sovereignty"; (ii) that the Antarctic research support operation "is heavily militarized, with major aspects having nothing to do with civilian research"; (iii) that Harewood would be a prime nuclear target, just like the US base at Australia's North West Cape; and (iv) that the military airlift command of the US Air force operates at Harewood "with annual blanket diplomatic clearance and could carry anything, including nuclear weapons, in its cargoes without the knowledge of the New Zealand Government."

Membership. There is a subscribing membership of 50 and a core steering committee of 10.

Publication. Off-Base, bi-monthly newsletter.

New Zealand Friends Peace Committee

Address. P.O. Box 657, Wellington, New Zealand

Aims and objectives. The Committee was established to serve the New Zealand Society of Friends in their peace testimony.

Activities. The Peace Committee is active in the field of peace education, and in monitoring the output of the media and of the New Zealand Parliament on disarmament issues. It issues press releases and submissions to public bodies on pacifist and other matters (including anti-racism). The Committee arranges accommodation and publicity for peace travellers, and offers support for the Quaker "peace caravan" in its travels in the country.

Membership. The Committe is composed of eight members of the Wellington monthly meeting of the Religious Society of Friends of New Zealand.

New Zealand Nuclear-Weapons-Free Zone Committee (NZNWFZC)

Address. P.O. Box 18541, Christchurch 9, New Zealand

Aims and objectives. This Committee has campaigned for New Zealand to be declared a nuclear-weapons-free zone and to adopt a policy of "positive neutrality", involving withdrawal from the Anzus Pact and other military commitments combined with active international peacemaking.

Activities. The NZNWFZC has undertaken various actions and campaigns to further its view that New Zealand is uniquely situated, because of its geographical isolation, its relative political stability and absence of direct causes of conflict with other states, to declare itself a nuclear-weapons-free zone. It has strongly supported the moves of the post-1984 Labour Government in this direction and has sought to maximize their international publicity potential for setting an example to other countries and movements.

Publication. Nuclear Free, journal.

Peace Movement Aotearoa (New Zealand)—PMA(NZ)

Address. P.O. Box 9314, Wellington, New Zealand

Aims and objectives. The PMA(NZ) works in Aotearoa (i.e. New Zealand), in the Pacific region and globally towards world peace, co-operation, justice and disarmament by (i) improving communications among groups and individuals; (ii) helping to co-ordinate peace campaigns; (iii) informing and educating people on peace issues and the peace movement; and (iv) encouraging analysis and research for the peace movement.

Formation. The PMA(NZ) began in 1981 at a National Peace Workshop where delegates put forward a proposal to establish a national co-ordinating organization.

Activities. The Movement's campaigning has concentrated on three main areas: (i) opposing the ANZUS Pact "and its many tentacles" such as the electronic signals intelligence station at Tangimoana; (ii) working for a stronger New Zealand role in the demilitarization and decolonization of the Pacific; and (iii) supporting the creation of nuclear-free zones in New Zealand and the Pacific generally. It supports the post-1984 Labour Government's decision to ban nuclear-armed and nuclear-powered ships from New Zealand waters, while urging it to act on the decision of the Labour Party conference of September 1984 in favour of withdrawal from military exercises and alliances with nuclear powers.

The Movement's actions have included concerted opposition to nuclear-armed ships entering New Zealand ports and territorial waters, to French nuclear testing in the South Pacific and to the French military presence on New Caledonia. It conducts research on peace and nuclear issues and also contributes to peace education through its mobile "peace van" (launched by Education Minister Russell Marshall on Oct. 1, 1984), which tours schools, youth groups and local communities to promote discussion and other activities on peace and disarmament themes.

In its publicity material the Movement has maintained (i) that "the New Zealand spy base discovered at Tangimoana supplies targeting data for US naval weapons systems"; (ii) that the Soviet Union "has 27 nuclear missile submarines based at Pacific ports"; (iii) that the United States is planning to have 42,000 nuclear weapons by 1990; (iv) that in the UN General Assembly New Zealand "has voted against resolutions calling for the prohibition of the neutron bomb, elimination of nuclear weapon stockpiles and cessation of the nuclear arms race"; and (v) that New Zealand's military expenditure "amounts to over $200 per year for each adult and child and about $1,000 per year for an average family".

Membership. The PMA(NZ) is an umbrella organization to which some 300 peace groups are affiliated.

Publications. Peacelink, monthly; *Beyond ANZUS,* proceedings of a conference held in Wellington in June 1984 to discusss alternatives to the Anzus Pact.

Affiliations. Nuclear-Free and Independent Pacific (NFIP) network.

Peace Tax Campaign (PTC)

Address. 38 McLeod Street, Upper Hutt, New Zealand

Aims and objectives. The Campaign aims to secure legislative provision for the diversion of a pro-rata proportion of taxes from military expenditure to a peace fund, which should be used exclusively for non-military, peacemaking purposes. The group works on behalf of all people who object to paying for war or military preparations on the grounds of conscience or profound conviction.

Formation. The PTC was launched in December 1983.

Activities. The Campaign publicizes its cause by providing information to the public and anyone interested. It is made up of voluntary workers who work to spread the message. Campaigners also meet MPs to put pressure on the Government to bring about reform. The group does not accept "direct action" on its behalf.

Membership. The PTC is not a membership organization, but has many supporters.

Publications. The Campaign produces newsletters and single-sheet pamphlets.

Other Movements

Auckland Peace Forum

Address. P.O. Box 5510, Auckland, New Zealand

Christchurch Peace Forum

Address. P.O. Box 2547, Christchurch, New Zealand

Group for Research and Action for Nuclear Disarmament

Address. P.O. Box 19683, Christchurch, New Zealand

Nuclear-Free and Independent Pacific Group

Address. P.O. Box 61086, Otara, New Zealand

Peace Action Dunedin

Address. P.O. Box 5507, Dunedin, New Zealand

Women's International League for Peace and Freedom (WILPF)

Address. 7A Queenstown Road, Auckland 6, New Zealand

Philippines

capital: Manila   **population: 55,500,000**

A mutual defence treaty between the Philippines and the United States, signed in August 1951 and in force a year later, specified that "an armed attack on the metropolitan territory of either of the parties, or on the island territories under its jurisdiction in the Pacific, or on its armed forces, public vessels or aircraft in the Pacific" would be deemed by the other to be "dangerous to its own peace and safety" and that both would "act to meet the common danger" in accordance with their constitutional processes. An earlier agreement of March 1947 had provided for the establishment for a 99-year period of 23 US military, naval and air bases in the Philippines, whose sovereignty over the base areas was formally recognized by the United States in July 1956. The military bases agreement was revised by a memorandum signed in October 1959 under which the US leases were shortened from 99 to 25 years and the US Government undertook to consult with the Philippines on the operational use of the bases and before deploying long-range missiles therein. A new Philippines-US agreement concluded on May 31, 1983, provided for unimpeded US access to the Subic Bay naval base and the Clark airbase for a five-year period from October 1984, in return for substantial US military and economic aid. There are currently some 15,360 US military personnel stationed in the Philippines.

The Philippines is also a party to the South-East Asia Collective Defence Treaty signed in Manila on Sept. 8, 1954, with Australia, France, New Zealand, Pakistan, Thailand, the United Kingdom and the United States. This treaty remains in force despite the dissolution of the South-East Asia Treaty Organization (SEATO) in mid-1977 and the earlier withdrawal of France and Pakistan. In January 1980 the Philippines Foreign Minister emphasized that the Manila treaty was "still alive" and that the US Government had repeatedly pledged to defend Thailand (not covered by a bilateral security pact with the United States) in case of aggression or invasion under the terms of the treaty.

As at end-1985 the Philippines armed forces (all volunteers) numbered some 115,000, consisting of 70,000 army, 28,000 navy and 17,000 air force personnel; there were also 40,000 para-militaries and 50,000 reserves. The defence budget for 1985 was 6,132 million pesos, representing 10.5 per cent of total government expenditure.

The issue of US influence over the regime of President Ferdinand Marcos (who came to power in November 1965) featured prominently in the run-up to the February 1986 presidential elections. Damaging allegations were made concerning the profligate and corrupt use of US military aid by the Marcos regime and widespread opposition was manifested to the US military presence in the Philippines. In its minimum election programme the opposition United Nationalist Democratic Organization (UNIDO) committed itself to respecting the current agreement on the US bases but said that it would "keep its options open" as regards the position after the expiry of the agreement. The UNIDO presidential candidate, Mrs Corazon Aquino, adhered to this line following her accession to power on Feb. 25 and also instituted a far-reaching programme of reform of the country's armed forces.

Anti-Bases Coalition (ABC)

Address. 53 3rd Street, New Manila, Philippines

Aims and objectives. The Coalition calls for the immediate and unconditional removal of US military bases and installations in the Philippines, claiming that they make the country "a magnet" for a Soviet nuclear attack.

Formation. The Coalition was launched in February 1983 under the chairmanship of Lorenzo Tanada (a former Liberal senator who had been elected chairman of the newly-formed Philippine Democratic Party in February 1982). It was formed within the framework of the (then opposition) United Nationalist Democratic Organization (UNIDO).

Activities. Following its formation, the Coalition mounted various campaigns and actions in opposition to the presence of US bases in the Philippines. It has claimed that these bases are "actual storage sites of nuclear weapons" and are "regularly visited by nuclear-armed ships and other craft"; it also asserted that the US military presence in the Philippines strengthened the "authoritarian" rule of President Marcos. In January 1986, in the run-up to the February presidential elections, the Coalition organized a major protest against a visit by the *USS Blue Ridge,* the flagship of the US seventh fleet.

Whereas the UNIDO election programme accepted that the current US bases agreement should be honoured, those associated with the Coalition called for its abrogation on the grounds that the bases made the Philippines a target for a Soviet nuclear attack and also that US nuclear weapons were being stockpiled at the bases.

Non-Violent Movement (AKKAPKA)

Address. Manila, Philippines

Aims and objectives. AKKAPKA propagates the application of non-violent principles to political life and to international relations.

Formation. The Movement was formed in July 1984 following a series of seminars for Catholic Church leaders, student leaders, trade unionists, social workers and intellectuals to study the possibility of a non-violent "third way" in opposing the regime of President Ferdinand Marcos.

Activities. From its foundation AKKAPKA was prominent in the development and study of non-violent strategies to overthrow the Marcos regime, holding a series of seminars to that end and also publishing literature in English and Tagalog. By the end of 1985 the Movement had five paid employees and 30 volunteers, as well as grassroots groups in 30 provinces. In the campaign for the February 1986 elections AKKAPKA participated in NAMFREL (the citizens' organization for supervising the election process) and also evolved scenarios for non-violent resistance in the event that Marcos tried to maintain his regime in power despite the popular verdict. It also set up "tent cities" for fasting, prayer and training in non-violent resistance in the heart of Manila's financial district and in 10 other locations, playing a major role in the "people power" movement which eventually obliged Marcos to surrender power and flee the country.

Nuclear-Free Philippines Coalition (NFPC)

Address. 2215 Pedro Gil Street, Santa Ana, Manila, Philippines

Aims and objectives. The NFPC seeks to make the Philippines a nuclear-free zone by (i) educating people on the dangers and ill-effects of nuclear power; (ii) building a broad and militant mass movement that will oppose the use of nuclear power in the Philippines, if necessary by direct militant action, and (iii) by generating strong international support through contacts with international and national peace movements abroad. It also demands an end to foreign intervention (i.e. principally US) in the country's affairs.

Formation. The Coalition formed in January 1981 as a response to the construction of Bataan nuclear power plant.

Activities. The NFPC has taken part in the campaign against the Bataan Nuclear power plant, including the organization of "people's strikes" in the Bataan peninsula in December 1984 and June 1985. It has also articulated opposition to arms proliferation and the presence of US military bases in the Philippines. In late 1985 and early 1986 it was prominent in the opposition movement which eventually achieved the downfall of the Marcos regime.

Membership. The NFPC is an umbrella body consisting of 83 member organizations, including organizations concerned with peace and human rights issues, movements opposed to nuclear power and nuclear weapons and environmentalist groups. It claims a support base of about 1,200,000 people.

Publication. Call for an Independent, Democratic and Nuclear-free Philippines, pamphlet.

Affiliations. The NFPC is part of the Nuclear-Free and Independent Pacific (NFIP) network and has close links with the Pacific Concerns Resource Center and the Pacific Campaign Against SLCMs, both based in the US Pacific state of Hawaii.

6. ASIA AND THE INDIAN OCEAN

China

capital: Beijing   **population: 1,060,000,000**

The treaty of friendship, alliance and mutual assistance signed between the newly-established People's Republic of China and the Soviet Union in February 1950 became a dead letter as a result of the sharp deterioration of Sino-Soviet relations from the late 1950s and was allowed to lapse on the expiry of its 30-year term in 1980. The only mutual defence agreement to which the People's Republic is currently party is that with the Democratic People's Republic of (North) Korea signed in July 1961, although China has friendship and co-operation treaties with a number of third-world countries, notably in Africa. In August 1978 a Sino-Japanese treaty of peace and friendship was concluded (China having taken no part in the signature of the post-war peace treaty between Japan and the majority of the allied powers in 1951) and at the end of 1978 the People's Republic normalized its relations with the United States.

The first Chinese nuclear weapon test took place in October 1964 and about 30 such explosions have been recorded since then. The People's Republic has equipped itself with inter-continental and medium-range nuclear missiles and the first Chinese nuclear submarine equipped with ballistic missiles was launched in mid-1983. China is a non-signatory of the Treaty on the Non-Proliferation of Nuclear Weapons which entered into force in March 1970.

As at end-1985 the Chinese People's Liberation Army (PLA), embracing all sections of the armed forces, was estimated to number about 4,000,000 (including 3,000,000 army, 500,000 air force and 350,000 navy personnel), reserves 5,000,000 and various categories of para-military forces a further 12,000,000. Over half the PLA were believed to be conscripts, there being selective conscription of three years for the army and four years for the air and naval services. The defence budget for 1985 was given as 19,148 million yuan, representing about 10 per cent of total state expenditure.

The ascendancy of the moderate wing of the ruling Communist Party from the late 1970s led to the introduction of far-reaching plans for the reform and modernization of the PLA, including a reduction in its manpower strength by 1,000,000 by the end of 1986 (as announced in April 1985). The programme was reported to include the equipping of the navy with five aircraft carriers and the modernization of two classes of surface warships to give greater range to Chinese missile-carrying destroyers in light of the perceived need to protect China's developing offshore oilfields in the South China Sea.

Chinese People's Association for Peace and Disarmament (CPAPD)

Address. 12-A Wanshou Road, P.O. Box 188, Beijing, China

Aims and objectives. The CPAPD describes itself as a non-governmental organization, which is sponsored by and composed of various people's organizations and prominent public figures from various nationalities and sectors in China. The Association's main objective is "to work together with the people of the world in a joint effort to safeguard world peace, strive for disarmament and realize the total prohibition and thorough elimination of nuclear weapons, oppose the arms race and prevent a new world war".

Formation. The Association was established in Beijing on June 1, 1985.

Activities. The CPAPD works to inform and educate on issues of peace and disarmament. It co-operates with other non-governmental organizations of all countries and organizes relevant activities to promote peace. It also organizes or participates in international activities which correspond with the objectives of the Association. In March 1986 the Association was represented at the Chinese People's Rally for World Peace held in Beijing and sponsored by the Chinese Organizing Committee of the International Year of Peace (of which the CPAPD president, Zhou Peiyuan, is a vice-chairman).

Membership. The Association is primarily composed of member organizations, which number 21; any people's organization in China devoted to the cause of peace may become a member of the Association, which also accepts a certain number of noted figures from various sectors as individual members. The following organizations are members of the Association: Chinese Association for International Understanding; All-China Federation of Trade Unions; All-China Federation of Youth; All-China Students' Federation; All-China Women's Federation; Chinese People's Association for Friendship with Foreign Countries; Chinese People's Institute of Foreign Affairs; China Association for Science and Technology; China Federation of Literary and Art Circles; Chinese Writers' Association; All-China Journalists' Association; China Medical Association; Chinese Red Cross Society; All-China Federation of Returned Overseas Chinese; Chinese People's National Committee for the Defence of Children; The Song Qingling Foundation; Chinese Buddhist Association; Chinese Taoist Association; Chinese Islamic Association; Chinese Patriotic Catholic Association; Chinese National Committee of Christian Three-self Patriotic Movement.

Publication. Peace, quarterly journal.

Committee of Uygurs for a Nuclear-Free Zone in Xinjiang

Address. n.a.

Aims and objectives. According to a Japanese radio report broadcast in May 1986, this Committee was set up by residents of the Uygur autonomous region of Xinjiang province to seek an end to Chinese nuclear testing and the dumping of radioactive waste in the region and also the removal of nuclear weapons from the Soviet border region. The report said that the Committee had sent an anti-nuclear declaration to foreign organizations in Beijing and had also supported street demonstrations by Uygur students in the capital and other cities the previous December.

India

capital: New Delhi   **population: 758,000,000**

India is a founder member of the Non-Aligned Movement but has gravitated towards close relations with the Soviet Union, against a background of persistent tensions in its relations with Pakistan and China. India has concluded a number of major arms supply agreements with the Soviet Union, but in recent years has also purchased increasing amounts of military items from France, the Federal Republic of Germany and the United Kingdom.

India tested a nuclear device in 1974 but since then has consistently denied that it has developed a nuclear weapons production programme. In December 1985 India concluded an agreement with Pakistan (which has also denied developing nuclear weapons) under which each side agreed not to attack the other's nuclear power facilities and also undertook to seek to improve their bilateral relations. Neither India nor Pakistan are parties to the Treaty on the Non-Proliferation of Nuclear Weapons which entered into force in March 1970. On the other hand, India has supported moves within the United Nations to designate the Indian Ocean as "a zone of peace" from which the great powers would be required to eliminate all bases and military installations, as well as all nuclear weapons and other weapons of mass destruction.

As at end-1985 the Indian armed forces numbered 1,260,000 (all volunteers), made up of 1,100,000 army, 115,000 air force and 45,000 navy personnel; there were also 250,000 reserves and equal number of para-militaries of various types. The defence budget for the 1985-86 financial year was 76,860 million rupees, representing 15 per cent of total government expenditure.

Anti-Nuclear Forum

Address. c/o Dr Dipankar Sengupta, B-23/2 Kalindi Housing Estate, Calcutta 700089, West Begal, India

Aims and objectives. The Forum exists to discuss the threats posed to the Indian environment, economy and society by civil and military uses of nuclear energy, and to educate and organize the public against nuclear power and nuclear war.

Activities. The Forum organizes meetings, seminars, workshops, debates and research on various aspects of nuclear power and the arms race. It publishes literature in English and Bengali, has a small library and documentation centre and tries to co-ordinate its work with that of other Indian anti-nuclear groups.

Membership. About 100, including scientists, teachers, students and political activists.

Publications. Bulletins in Bengali; pamphlets in English.

Committee for a Sane Nuclear Policy (Cosnup)

Address. M-120 Greater Kailash 1, New Delhi 110048, India

Aims and objectives. Cosnup opposes both military and civil use of nuclear power and seeks to inform people in India and other third-world countries of its dangers.

Formation. The Committee was established in 1981.

Activities. In addition to opposing India's civil nuclear-power programme, Cosnup has called for the creation of a nuclear-free zone in the Indian sub-continent.

Membership. The Committee is a non-partisan organization composed mainly of professional people and intellectuals.

Publication. Philosophy and Social Action, quarterly.

Documentation and Dissemination Centre for Disarmament Information

Address. 21 Railway Parallel Road, Nehru Nagar, Bangalore 560020, India

Aims and objectives. This Centre seeks "to create an awareness of the urgent task of disarmament" with particular reference to developmental needs.

Formation. The Centre was established in January 1984.

Activities. The Centre works to inform and educate people on the nuclear threat, emphasizing "the destructive and ever-growing arms trade" as well as violations of human rights and other issues, making information and documents available for study, research and reference. It supports and co-operates with small action groups around the country, providing speakers and resources for conferences and seminars and aiming to reach new audiences at the lowest possible cost. In its first 20 months the Centre was involved in co-ordinating over 160 programmes and was successful in persuading several institutions and non-governmental organizations to include peace and disarmament issues on their agendas. In January 1985 the Centre was invited by Jammu University to assist with the planning of a new peace studies course.

Membership. The Centre is an organization of volunteers in different parts of India.

Publications. In addition to its publicity and educational material, the Centre plans to publish a handbook on peace-oriented movements active in India.

Group for a Peaceful Indian Ocean (GPIO)

Address. c/o S.P. Udayakumar, 27 Esankai Mani Veethy, Nagerooil 629002, Tamil Nadu, India

Aims and objectives. The GPIO works for the realization of the UN resolution declaring the Indian Ocean to be a "zone of peace". It seeks to educate the public to the advantages of the proposal, and to keep them informed of the military build-up in the area.

Formation. The Group was set up in 1985.

Activities. Apart from activities pursuant to the objectives specified above, the Group's future plans include the construction of a "peace temple" at Cape

Comorin and the conducting of an essay competition for secondary school and college students on the problems facing countries on the Indian Ocean littoral.

Publications. A quarterly magazine is at the planning stage, with the possibility of other publications being launched subsequently.

Group for Nuclear Disarmament (GROUND)

Address. 4 Habib Court, Causeway, Bombay 40039, India

Aims and objectives. The fundamental aim of GROUND is to work for the establishment of a nuclear-free zone in South Asia and the Indian Ocean, as well as in other parts of the world. It strives for complete nuclear disarmament, the elimination of existing nuclear stockpiles, a complete ban on nuclear tests and a freeze on all types and numbers of nuclear weapons. GROUND seeks to build a strong, independent, popular movement to act as a pressure group in matters of public policy regarding nuclear issues and to oppose the nuclear arms race.

Formation. GROUND was formed in early 1984 in Bombay.

Activities. In its first year, GROUND commemorated the 39th anniversary of the atomic bombings of Hiroshima and Nagasaki. This involved a series of public meetings and discussions, including film shows on the bombings and their effects on the population, exhibitions and discussions. Such meetings were subsequently held at over 50 educational establishments in Bombay and in many other public organizations throughout India. Among the panel were scientists, professionals and journalists; a public demonstration was also held.

GROUND is currently involved in the organization of a seminar, which will be followed by a debate, on India's nuclear policy options. It is also mounting various other activities to increase public awareness through lectures, debates, slide shows and exhibitions.

Membership. The Group consists of about 50 people, coming from all walks of life.

Indian Campaign for Nuclear Disarmament (ICND)

Address. c/o Gandhi Memorial Committee, 59B Chowringhee Road, Calcutta 700020, India

Aims and objectives. The ICND aims to raise Indian public consciousness about the effects of nuclear weapons and to mobilize opinion against the manufacture, testing and threatened use of all nuclear, chemical and biological weapons. It is committed to total disarmament and to the resolution of all international conflict by non-violent means.

Formation. The Campaign was launched in October 1981.

Activities. The ICND holds a regular national convention and organizes national and zonal workshops as well as day schools and seminars. In 1983 it instituted an annual "Indian Peace Award", the first recipients of which were Mother Teresa of Calcutta and Shri R.R. Diwakar, former governor of Bihar and central minister. It is currently organizing a national poster competition and photographic exhibition.

Membership. As a national campaign, the ICND has members from all over India, including teachers, scientists and lawyers.

Publications. The Group has produced several pamphlets and mimeographed articles.

Indian Fellowship of Reconciliation—FOR(I)
Shanti Seva Samithi

Address. c/o Acharya K.K. Chandy, Christavashram, Manganam, Kottayam, Kerala 686018, India

Aims and objectives. FOR(I) is "a fellowship of those who commit themselves, in obedience to the will of God and the example of Jesus, to exercise a ministry of reconciliation among men, to overcome evil with good, and to meet enmity with love, forgiveness and service".

Formation. The FOR(I) was founded at a conference at Christavashram, Managam, in November 1950 by leading Gandhians and members of the Christian Ashram movement. Much of the impetus for establishing an Indian section of the IFOR had come from the Youth Christian Council of Action, which itself had been founded in 1938. Members of the international Fellowship had maintained considerable contact with Indian leaders, including Mahatma Gandhi, since its formation in 1919.

Activities. The FOR(I) has worked for the settlement of specific disputes, for disarmament and an end to conscription and for reforms of property and land ownership. Shortly after its formation, it was involved in efforts to reduce communal tension between Hindus, Moslems and Christians in Travancore state. During the same period, it helped resolve disputes between rival sections of several Christian churches in India. On the nuclear question, the Fellowship passed a resolution in 1954 condemning the manufacture of nuclear arms, and two years later conducted a petition campaign calling for India to remain nuclear-free. In the foreign sphere, the FOR(I) sent representatives to Vietnam, South Africa and the Middle East during the 1960s. It condemned the forceful nature of the recovery of Goa from the Portuguese in 1962, and urged a peaceful settlement of the border disputes with China, sending a delegation on a Delhi to Beijing peace march in 1964. It made representations to both the Indian and Pakistani governments with regard to the disputes over Kashmir in 1965 and over Bangladesh in 1971.

The FOR(I) campaigned against the introduction of compulsory military training for students (in the form of the National Cadet Corps) in 1964, with the result that such training ceased to be compulsory the following year.

Other areas covered by FOR(I) include campaigns against capital punishment and in favour of the introduction of peace education. It has also actively supported housing and land aid projects.

Membership. There are currently approximately 200 individual members, most of whom are grouped in cells centered on various ashrams.

Publication. Arunodayam served as the journal of the FOR(I) from 1953 until 1976, when its publication was suspended as a result of the national emergency; its function has been partly taken over by the *FOR(I) Bulletin.*

Affiliation. War Registers' International; International Fellowship of Reconciliation.

Institute for Total Revolution
Sampoorna Kranti Vidyalaya

Address. Vedchhi 394641, Surat, Gujarat, India

Aims and objectives. This Institute aims to enrich every aspect of human life through the transformation of the individual and society; its objective is to train people who want to participate in a movement to create a better world and a peaceful planet.

Formation. The Institute was started in January 1982 as a continuation of the youth movement led by the well-known Gandhian, Jayaprakash Narayan.

Activities. The Institute runs various training programmes in "total revolution" and self-reliance. It has organized a people's campaign to protest against a nuclear power station being constructed 30 kilometers from the Institute's headquarters, taking the form of meetings, publications, intellectual groups and group discussions.

The Institute hosted the War Resisters' International (WRI) 18th triennial conference and the annual council meeting of the Peace Brigades International in January 1986.

Membership. The Institute is open to all those who believe in non-violence and are interested in creating a fuller life; the number of participants on Institute courses varies between five and 125.

Publications. Books, reports, pamphlets and leaflets on various topics.

Affiliations. War Resisters' International; Peace Brigades International.

Other Movements

Gandhi Peace Foundation

Address. 221 Deen Dayal, Upadhyaya Marg, New Delhi 110002, India

Service Civil International (SCI)

Address. K5 Green Park, New Delhi 110016, India

Women's International League for Peace and Freedom (WILPF)

Address. Septa Farm, Gular Bhoj, Nainital, Punjab 262408, India

Mauritius

capital: Port Louis   **population: 1,000,000**

Having had a defence agreement with the United Kingdom for the first six years after attaining independence in 1968, Mauritius is now a member of the Non-Aligned Movement and maintains no regular defence forces of its own. Within the United Nations framework, Mauritius has strongly supported moves to designate the Indian Ocean as "a zone of peace" from which the great powers would be required to eliminate all bases and military installations, as well as all nuclear weapons and other weapons of mass destruction.

Since 1980 Mauritius has pursued a dispute with the United Kingdom and the United States over the island of Diego Garcia (part of the British Indian Ocean Territory and situated some 1,900 kilometres to the north-east of Mauritius), where since 1980 a substantial US military and naval base has been built up to counter the perceived Soviet threat in the Indian Ocean and Western Asia. Claiming that the island should be restored to Mauritius (of which it was a dependency when Mauritius was a British crown colony), successive Mauritian governments have contended that the United Kingdom has violated an undertaking (which Britain denies having given) that Diego Garcia would not be used as a base for military purposes.

In July 1982 Mauritius, Madagascar and the Seychelles established the Indian Ocean Commission (of which the Comoros became a member in 1985), the declared purpose of which was to examine all possibilities of co-operation between the states of the region. Mauritius also has a territorial dispute with France over the ownership of Tromelin Island (about 550 kilometres to the north of Mauritius and the French overseas department of Réunion).*

Campaign for the Demilitarization of the Indian Ocean (CDIO)

Address. 22 bis Trotter Street, Beau Bassin, Mauritius

Aims and objectives. This group campaigns for a nuclear-free Indian Ocean and for the non-proliferation of nuclear weapons by the coastal and hinterland states of the region. It demands the closure of US military installations on Diego Garcia and elsewhere in the Indian Ocean, and seeks the reversion of Diego Garcia to Mauritius. The group is the Mauritius section of the movement of the same name formed in Britain in 1982 (see entry under United Kingdom).

Other Movements

Mauritius Peace Council

Address. 44 Abbe de la Caille Street, Curepipe Road, Port Louis, Mauritius

* For the territorial disputes mentioned in this introduction, see Alan J. Day (ed.), *Border and Territorial Disputes* (Longman 1982), pp. 122-24 (France-Mauritius) and 146-50 (Mauritius-United Kingdom).

Voluntary Service International
Service Volontaire International

Address. Arcades Ramdour, Route Royale, Rose Hill, Mauritius

Women's International League for Peace and Freedom (WILPF)

Address. P.O. Box 545, Port Louis, Mauritius

Sri Lanka

capital: Colombo   **population: 16,000,000**

As a member of the Non-Aligned Movement, Sri Lanka has within the United Nations framework strongly supported moves to designate the Indian Ocean as "a zone of peace" from which the great powers would be required to eliminate all bases and military installations, as well as nuclear weapons and other weapons of mass destruction. In 1981-82 speculation that the US Navy was seeking to secure oil storage facilities at Trincomalee in Sri Lanka was firmly rebuffed by both the US and the Sri Lankan governments, the latter emphasizing the country's strict adherence to a non-aligned foreign policy and also denying that a secret military agreement had been concluded with the United States.

In recent years Sri Lanka's relations with neighbouring India have been overshadowed by the upsurge of ethnic strife, especially in northern Sri Lanka, between Hindu Tamils (the descendants of immigrants from India) and native Sinhalese and by the activities of extremist Tamils seeking the creation of a separate Tamil state. Among the measures taken by the Government to cope with the internal security situation was the introduction of powers of military conscription in 1985.

As at end-1985 Sri Lanka's armed forces numbered some 38,000, including 30,000 army, 4,000 air force and 4,000 navy personnel; there were also about 16,000 reservists and 20,000 para-military forces. The defence budget for 1985 was 3,600 million rupees, representing 8 per cent of total government expenditure.

Non-Violent Direct Action Group (NVDAG)

Address. Vale Cinema Road, Chavakachcheri, Jaffna, Sri Lanka

Aims and objectives. The NVDAG seeks to apply non-violent principles to internal and international conflicts, with particular reference to achieving a reconciliation of the ethnic strife within Sri Lanka between Tamils and Sinhalese.

Formation. The Group dates from 1979.

Activities. In the face of the renewed upsurge of Tamil-Sinhalese conflict since 1983, the NVDAG has mounted a major effort of reconciliation, involving rehabilitation of refugees, pre-school activities, community development projects, seminars, provision of library and exhibition resources and general peace education. The NVDAG has also opposed caste-based conflict and discrimination within the Hindu community through non-violent fasts and other actions in the Jaffna district. It appealed successfully for legislation to curb the Tamil practice of slaughtering animals in holy places and has campaigned for equal access to Hindu temples for the lower castes.

Membership. The Group has about 600 members.

Publication. NVDAG Report, quarterly.

Affiliations. War Resisters' International; International Fellowship of Reconciliation.

Other Movements

Service Civil International (SCI)

Address. Talawa Farm, Talawa NCP, Sri Lanka

Women's International League for Peace and Freedom (WILPF)

Address. 37/2 Pedris Road, Colombo 3, Sri Lanka

7. OTHER REGIONS

Middle East

Despite the high incidence of actual conflict in the Middle East region (where Iran and Iraq have been at war since 1980 and where Israel and its Arab neighbours have fought four major wars since the establishment of the Jewish state in May 1948), virtually no country manifests organized peace movements of the type with which this volume is concerned. The exception is Israel, where the open system of democratic government provides the conditions for various relevant groupings to make their existence and views felt.*

Israel

Committee for Israeli-Palestinian Dialogue

Address. P.O. Box 20373, Tel Aviv 61204, Israel

Aims and objectives. This group believes that oriental Jewish Israelis (i.e. those of North African and Sephardic background) can serve as a bridge between the Arabs and Israel; it seeks to promote Israeli-Palestinian dialogue and to disprove the generalization that Sephardic Jews have a particular hatred for the Arabs.

Formation. The Committee was set up in February 1986.

Down With the Occupation
Hal'ah Hakibush

Address. P.O. Box 4497, Tel Aviv, Israel

Aims and objectives. This group is a protest movement against the continued Israeli occupation of the West Bank and Gaza Strip.

Formation. The group dates from 1985.

East for Peace
Hamizrach El Hashalom

Address. 37 Meir Hanakar Street, Jerusalem 93803, Israel

Aims and objectives. Founded after the Lebanon war, this movement consists mainly of eastern Jews seeking the integration of Israel into the Middle East and also urging full social equality within Israel.

---

* The data on Israeli movements in this section is partly drawn from a survey published by the Israeli peace magazine *New Outlook* in mid-1986.

Interfaith Peace Academy

Address. P.O. Box 19556, Jerusalem 91194, Israel

Aims and objectives. The Academy seeks to provide a "ministry of support" for theologians, philosophers, clergy and lay people involved in the search for Arab-Israeli and universal peace.

International Centre for Peace in the Middle East (ICPME)

Address. 107 Hahashmonaim Street, Tel Aviv 67011, Israel

Aims and objectives. This independent body provides a focus for Israelis and those abroad who are actively involved in the quest for Arab-Israeli peace. It organizes research, public discussions and educational programmes (the last mainly through its Jewish-Arab Council for Peace Education).

International Movement of Conscientious War Objectors (IMCWR)

Address. P.O. Box 28058, Tel Aviv-Jaffa 61280, Israel

Aims and objectives. This Israeli affiliate of War Resisters' International is composed of pacifist and secular conscientious objectors working for a non-violent solution to the Arab-Israeli conflict. It is working to consolidate links with an emerging group of Palestinian pacifists in the occupied territories.

Interns for Peace
Nitzanei Shalom/Bar'am A'Salaam

Address. P.O. Box 16441, Tel Aviv 61163, Israel

Aims and objectives. This independent movement sets up co-operative programmes between Israel's Arab and Jewish communities and places "interns" in paired communities (e.g. villages and schools) with the aim of building understanding and mutual respect. It seeks to strengthen Israel's democratic character through improved majority-minority relations and to develop models of conflict resolution for other areas of the world.

Formation. The movement was initiated in 1976 by the US rabbi Bruce Cohen.

Israel Peace Committee
Va'ad Hashalom Hayisraeli

Address. P.O. Box 4232, Tel Aviv 61041, Israel

Aims and objectives. As the Israeli section of the World Peace Council (WPC), this Committee has a series of broad objectives including the fostering of détente and peaceful coexistence, an end to the nuclear arms race and agreement on mutual arms control and disarmament. In recent years it has taken part in campaigns against Israeli involvement in Lebanon, but acknowledges that its standing among Israelis has been damaged by the pro-Palestinian stance of the WPC.

Formation. The Committee was established shortly after the creation of Israel in 1948 and itself helped to set up the WPC.

Affiliations. World Peace Council.

Israeli Committee for the Prevention of Nuclear War

Address. P.O. Box 1171, Hod Hasharon 4511, Israel

Aims and objectives. This Committee opposes the production, acquisition and proliferation of nuclear weapons in general and the nuclearization of the Middle East in particular, seeking to raise Israeli consciousness on the dangers inherent in the latter course.

Israeli Council for Israeli-Palestinian Peace

Address. P.O. Box 956, Tel Aviv 61008

Aims and objectives. The Council campaigns for a resolution of the Arab-Israeli conflict on the basis of the creation of a Palestinian state in the West Bank and the Gaza Strip (both captured by Israel in the 1967 war).

Formation. The Council was formed in 1976 in response to the readiness of elements of the Palestine Liberation Organization (PLO) to enter into dialogue with Zionist Israelis.

Publication. The Other Israel, bi-monthly newsletter.

Oasis of Peace
Neve Shalom

Address. Doar Na Shimshon 90760, Israel

Aims and objectives. Neve Shalom is a community of Jews, Moslems and Christians basing itself on the principles of pluralism, equality and inter-dependence and thus seeking to provide a model for Arab-Jewish co-operation and understanding. It runs a "school of peace" for its children and also organizes weekend workships for Jewish and Arab high school students. The community is situated on 100 acres of land leased from a monastery.

Formation. Neve Shalom was founded in 1972 and the first family arrived in 1978 (there being now over 60 permanent residents).

Paths to Peace
Netivot Shalom

Address. P.O. Box 4433, Jerusalem 91043, Israel

Aims and objectives. Describing itself as a centrist, humanistic group with values stemming from traditional Jewish teaching, this group of religious Zionists has campaigned against aspects of Israel's intervention in Lebanon, concentrating its efforts in religious educational establishments.

Formation. The movement was founded in 1982.

Peace Now
Shalom Achshav

Address. P.O. Box 108, Jerusalem, Israel

Aims and objectives. Peace Now was formed in 1978 to raise support in Israel for a positive response to President Sadat's peace initiative and subsequently organized mass demonstrations against the Israeli intervention in Lebanon. It is currently concentrating on the search for a solution to the Israeli–Palestinian impasse.

There is a Limit
Yesh Gvul

Address. P.O. Box 4172, Tel Aviv, Israel

Aims and objectives. This movement was initiated in 1982 as a support group for soldiers refusing to serve in Lebanon and is concerned with the philosophical question of the limits of obedience to the state.

Africa

Consisting for the most part of non-aligned developing states whose priorities are economic and social, the African continent is remote from the influences which have spawned peace movements in the developed world. In many African countries the immediate threats to life are famine and disease, not inter-state conflict or the possibility of nuclear obliteration. Nevertheless, such movements have emerged in certain African countries, mostly as local sections of larger international peace organizations with a strong concomitant concern for development and social progress or as church groups. Moreover, the special internal circumstances of South Africa have produced several significant peace groups whose energies are concentrated on opposing the policies of the Pretoria Government.

Botswana

Kagisong Centre of the Society of Friends

Address. P.O. Box 20166, Gaborone, Botswana

Ghana

International Fellowship of Reconciliation (IFOR)

Address. P.O. Box 1443, Accra, Ghana

Aims and objectives. The IFOR group in Ghana is "trying to find ways to apply the ideas of Martin Luther King and Gandhi to the problems of our society, including arms trade and racial discrimination between whites and blacks". It also believes in the need for closer links between peace movements of the northern hemisphere and those of Africa, particularly in trying to stop the international trade in armaments.

Women's International League for Peace and Freedom (WILPF)

Address. P.O. Box 8365, Tema, Ghana

Kenya

Friends International Centre

Address. P.O. Box 41946, Nairobi, Kenya

Madagascar

Friends International Centre

Address. B.P. 3001, Tananarive, Madagascar

Nigeria

Nigerian Council for Peace

Address. 5A Thomas Street, Ebute Metto, Lagos, Nigeria

Aims and objectives. While seeking "to promote peaceful coexistence within communities, Africa and the world", this Council is in particular concerned with publicizing in Nigeria the dangers and likely effects of nuclear war and pointing out "that nuclear weapons will not differentiate between classes, good or evil, capitalists and communists".

Formation. The Council was set up in 1962 by P. A. Curtis Joseph, formerly a member of the presidential committee of the World Peace Council (1964-69).

Activities. After four years of work, largely consisting of information activities and building contacts with similar groups abroad, the Council was banned by order of the then military regime in May 1966, and this order has yet to be revoked.

Peace Research Institute of Nigeria

Address. c/o Dept. of Political Science, University of Nigeria, Nsukka, Nigeria

South Africa

Anglican Pacifist Fellowship (APF)

Address. P.O. Box 4849, Johannesburg, 2000 South Africa

Aims and objectives. The Fellowship attempts to provide a point of contact between Anglican pacifists and conscientious objectors in southern Africa.

Formation. The Fellowship was formed in 1982 by members of the (UK) Anglican Pacifist Fellowship who were resident in southern Africa.

Activities. The Fellowship's activities are largely confined to the distribution within southern Africa of material produced by the Anglican Pacifist Fellowship in the UK (i.e. the newsletter, *Challenge,* and other publications relating to Christian pacifism).

Membership. There are approximately 20 members, all of whom are members of either the Church of the Province of Southern Africa or the Church of the Province of Central Africa.

End Conscription Campaign (ECC)

Address. 227/9 Khotso House, 42 de Villiers Street, Johannesburg, 2000 South Africa

Aims and objectives. The ECC seeks (i) the withdrawal of the South African Defence Forces (SADF) from the African townships; (ii) the withdrawal of the SADF from Namibia; (iii) freedom for young men to choose not be part of this army; and (iv) a just society in South Africa. The Campaign is committed to non-violent methods of action.

Formation. The ECC was launched at the end of 1983 after Black Sash had called for an end to conscription.

Activities. In June 1985 the ECC held a major peace festival in Johannesburg under the slogan "Stop the Call-up", attended by over 1,000 people of all races (although one major intended speaker from Brazil was refused entry into the country and another, an ECC office-holder, was arrested). The festival heard that since October 1984 evasion of conscription had risen steeply, there being an estimated 7,000 "draft dodgers" by January 1985. On Sept. 9, 1985, the South African security forces carried out a major clamp-down on ECC activists, searching homes and offices, confiscating documents and detaining four people for questioning. Before the police action, a government minister had claimed that the ECC was being "used" by the banned African National Congress to achieve its "evil goals" by launching a "Troops Out of the Townships" campaign.

On March 21, 1986, an ECC representative presented a 226-page submission to the UN Special Committee Against Apartheid in New York. A section of the report analysed how the process of militarization had penetrated every level of South African society, enabling the SADF to mobilize 400,000 people in a war crisis and providing a constant standing force of 80,000. The report also noted that 95 per cent of SADF personnel were white and that some 800 companies were involved in military production. In April 1986 the ECC staged a further rally in Johannesburg to mark the conclusion of a three-week campaign under the slogan "Working for a Just Peace", which sought to demonstrate the alternatives to military conscription.

Membership. Over 40 organizations are affiliated to the ECC.

International Fellowship of Reconciliation (IFOR)

Address. Ecumenical Centre, 20 Andrews Street, Durban, 4001 South Africa

Aims and objectives. The Fellowship stands for non-violent social change in South Africa and seeks to support and inform local groups involved in non-violent direct action. It campaigns actively for the right of conscientious objection and the abolition of compulsory military service.

Phoenix Settlement Trust

Address. P.O. Box 331, Verulum, 4340 South Africa

Aims and objectives. The Phoenix Settlement, situated near Durban and founded by Gandhi in 1904, functioned as "a symbol of non-racialism, self-reliance and peace in South Africa", its past residents having included Steve Biko. (The Settlement was, however, largely destroyed in August 1985 when Zulu nationalists went on a rampage against Indian-owned property in the Durban area.)

Society of Friends

Address. P.O. Box 7205, Johannesburg, 2000 South Africa

Tanzania

Society of Friends

Address. P.O. Box 100, Chake-Chake, Pemba, Tanzania

Zimbabwe

Fellowship of Reconciliation

Address. 11 Ferguson Avenue, Greendale, Zimbabwe

Society of Friends

Address. 3 Vincent Avenue, Belvedere, Harare, Zimbabwe

Latin America and the Caribbean

The selection of Latin American and Caribbean groupings covered below attempts to make a distinction between peace movements as defined in this volume and the wide range of other movements active in the region in fields such as human rights, developmental problems and opposition to repressive regimes. This is often a difficult distinction to make, since the various movements frequently overlap and are usually inter-related in terms of their fundamental objectives. For example, the Latin American sections of the Peace and Justice Service (a general description of which is given in the entry under International Organizations) are as much concerned with economic and social issues as with "peace" in the sense in which the latter term applies to European and North American peace movements; nevertheless, they are listed below because of their belief that social justice can only be achieved in conditions of peace. On the other hand, political parties and movements are not covered, even though many—e.g. those opposing US interventionism in Central America—would see the achievement of their goals as contributing to the peace of the region.*

Argentina

Calling of the Hundred to Continue to Live
Llamamiento de los Cien para Seguir Viviendo

Address. Corrientes 1985, 3°E, 1045 Buenos Aires, Argentina

Aims and objectives. This group seeks to increase people's awareness of the danger of nuclear weapons, urges international agreement to reduce armaments to a minimum and to maintain nuclear-free zones, and calls for a freeze on the production of nuclear weapons.

Formation. The group was founded in late 1984 and within nine months had secured 15,000 signatures to a petition supporting its aims.

Freedom of Conscience Group
Grupo Libertad de Consciencia

Address. Av. J. F. Kennedy 33, 1778 Ciudad Guemes, Argentina

Aims and objectives. This pacifist movement upholds "the inalienable right to refuse military service that is improperly called obligatory" and campaigns for change in the laws providing for such service.

Formation. The Group came into being in March 1983; later that year it promoted the formation of the Family Movement for the Abolition of Military Service (*Movimiento de la Familia por la Abolición del Servicio Militar Obligatorio*).

* For data on the region's political parties and movements, see Ciarán Ó Maoláin, *Latin American Political Movements* (Longman 1985).

Front in Opposition to Obligatory Military Service
Frente Opositor al Servicio Militar Obligatorio (FOSMO)

Address. Hipolito Yrigoyen 1516, piso 5°, Buenos Aires, Argentina

Aims and objectives. FOSMO seeks the total abolition of military conscription arguing that the inculcation of the military mentality is contrary to peace and general welfare. It has attracted substantial support, including that of the Freedom of Conscience Group (see above).

International Movement of Reconciliation
Movimiento Internacional de la Reconciliacion

Address. c/o Methodist Church, Rivadavia 4044, Buenos Aires, Argentina

Movement for Life and Peace
Movimiento por la Vida y la Paz (MOVIP)

Address. Av. Bouchard 468, 4°G, 1106 Buenos Aires, Argentina

Aims and objectives. This pacifist grouping opposes militarism, especially nuclear weapons, and advocates the right of conscientious objection. It campaigns for peace, human rights, democracy and the alleviation of hunger, poverty and environmental pollution. It urges the demilitarization of the Falklands/Malvinas and seeks to promote awareness of the 1967 Treaty of Tlatelolco (on the prohibition of nuclear weapons in Latin America).

Formation. MOLIP was founded in 1983.

Activities. The Movement has organized round-table discussions on issues such as the Beagle Channel dispute with Chile and the Falklands/Malvinas dispute with Britain (being in favour of the peaceful resolution of both issues). In November 1985 MOVIP was co-organizer, with the Chilean Committee for the Demilitarization of the South Pacific, of the "First Conference for Disarmament and Reconciliation of the People" in Santiago in order to promote better Argentinian-Chilean relations at peace movement level.

Membership. There is a 10-member executive board and a further 20 members; one of the Movement's honorary presidents is Nobel Prize winner Adolfo Perez Esquivel.

Publication. The first MOLIP bulletin appeared in July 1986.

Affiliations. The Movement is part of the Science for Peace International (SPIN) network and has close links with the Bertrand Russell Peace Foundation in the United Kingdom.

Peace and Justice Service
Servicio Paz y Justicia (Serpaj)

Address. Av. Mexico 479, 1097 Buenos Aires, Argentina

Bolivia

Peace and Justice Service
Servicio Paz y Justicia

Address. Casilla 5039, La Paz, Bolivia

Brazil

Brazilian Movement for Disarmament and Peace
Movimento Brasileiro pelo Desarmamento e a Paz

Address. Rua Haddock Lobo 1307, conj. 22, CEP 01414, São Paulo, Brazil

Justice and Non-Violence National Service
Serviço Nacional Justiça e Não-Violência

Address. Av. Iparanga 1267, 1° andar, 01039 São Paulo, Brazil

Aims and objectives. Dating from 1978, this movement aims to unite people and groups who support non-violent action in order to build a society based on justice and fraternity.

Affiliations. International Fellowship of Reconciliation; Pax Christi International.

Peace and Justice Service
Servicio Paz y Justicia (Serpaj)

Address. Av. Ipiranga 1273, 01039 São Paulo, Brazil

Chile

Chilean Committee for the Demilitarization of the South Pacific
Comité Chileño de Desarmo del Pacífico Sur

Address. Casilla 16774, Correo 9, Santiago, Chile

Aims and objectives. In addition to campaigning for the demilitarization of the South Pacific, this group also advocates the resolution of traditional Chilean-Argentinian hostilities, to which end it co-organized, with the Movement for Life and Peace of Argentina, the "First Conference for Disarmament and Reconciliation of the People" in Santiago in November 1985.

Chilean Exiles for a Nuclear-Free Pacific

Address. P.O. Box 4032, Auckland 1, New Zealand

Aims and objectives. This exile group is particularly concerned about the decision by the Chilean regime to lease Easter Island to the United States (see next entry). It has launched a campaign of solidarity with the inhabitants of the island in their "struggle against imperialism and militarism".

Committee for the Defence of Peace and Easter Island

Address. n.a.

Aims and objectives. This campaign group was formed after the approval by President Pinochet on Aug. 2, 1985, of a plan to lease Easter Island (3,700 kilometres west of mainland Chile) to the United States for use as an emergency landing site for the US space shuttle. This project, to be founded by the US National Aeronautic and Space Administration (NASA), was understood to involve the extension of the island's airstrip and the installation of technological equipment, at a total estimated cost of $15,000,000. Noting the reluctance of the regime to inform public opinion about the proposed arrangement, the Committee argue that it will involve serious risks for Chile in that the island could become a target for nuclear attack if it is developed as a military base by the United States.

Peace and Justice Service
Servicio Paz y Justicia (Serpaj)

Address. Av. Pedro Leon Ugate 1164, Santiago, Chile

Colombia

Peace and Justice Service
Servicio Paz y Justicia (Serpaj)

Address. Apartado 54287, Bogotà DF, Colombia

Costa Rica

Christian Peace Movement
Movimiento Cristiano por la Paz

Address. Apartado 2053, 1000 San José, Costa Rica

Friends Peace Centre
Centro de los Amigos para la Paz

Address. Apartado 1507, 1000 San José, Costa Rica

Aims and objectives. The Friends (Quakers) in Costa Rica aim in particular to preserve and strengthen the country's tradition of peace and non-militarism and to form a "bridge of understanding" between the people of Costa Rica and the United States.

Formation. The Centre was established in November 1983.

Activities. In addition to oranizing a programme of public meetings, the Costa Rican Friends have participated in peace rallies, including a 40,000-strong peace march on May 15, 1984, a "continental march for peace and life" on July 13, 1984, and a "march for neutrality" on Nov. 16, 1984. The Centre also engages in educational and information work.

Publication. The Centre publishes a quarterly newsletter.

Peace and Solidarity Council
Consejo da Paz y Solidaridad

Address. Apartado 3916, San José, Costa Rica

Peace Movement
Movimiento por la Paz

Address. Apartado 112, San Pedro Montes de Oca, San José, Costa Rica

Women's International League for Peace and Freedom (WILPF)
Liga Internacional de Mujeres pro Paz y Libertad (LIMPAL)

Address. Apartado 1507, 1000 San José, Costa Rica

Aims and objectives. As the Costa Rican section of the WILPF, LIMPAL aims to unite women of different political and philosophical beliefs in the cause of peace and freedom, promoting disarmament and non-violent methods of resolving conflicts.

Formation. LIMPAL was founded in January 1981.

Activities. In November 1985 LIMPAL organized a peace seminar in San José attended by women representatives from all over Latin America. The League co-ordinates its efforts with local peace groups and opposes militarism and repression in Central America.

Cuba

Movement for Peace and Sovereignty of Peoples
Movimiento por la Paz y la Soberania de los Pueblos

Address. Linea 556, Vedada, Havana, Cuba

Society of Friends

Address. Libertad 114, entre Agramonte y Garayalde, Holguin, Cuba

Jamaica

Friends Centre

Address. 11 Caledonia Avenue, Cross Roads, Kingston 5, Jamaica

Women's International League for Peace and Freedom (WILPF)

Address. 1 Metcalf Road, Kingston 13, Jamaica

Mexico

Friends Centre
Casa de los Amigos

Address. Av. Ignacio Mariscal 132, 06030 Mexico DF, Mexico

Women's International League for Peace and Freedom (WILPF)
Liga Internacional de Mujeres pro Paz y Libertad (LIMPAL)

Address. Av. H. Frias 349/2, Mexico 12 DF, Mexico

Nicaragua

Peace and Justice Service
Servicio Paz y Justicia (Serpaj)

Address. Apartado 1806, Managua, Nicaragua

Panama

Peace and Justice Service
Servicio Paz y Justicia (Serpaj)

Address. Apartado 861, Panama City 1, Panama

Peru

Peace and Justice Service
Servicio Paz y Justicia (Serpaj)

Address. Apartado 5602, Lima 100, Peru

Puerto Rico

Caribbean Project for Justice and Peace
Proyecto Caribeno de Justicia y Paz

Address. P.O. Box 21226, Rio Pièdras, 00928 Puerto Rico

Aims and objectives. This church-based movement seeks to build peace and a more just social order in the Caribbean region.

Uruguay

International Movement of Reconciliation
Movimiento Internacional de la Reconciliación (MIR)

Address. Av. Lavalleja 1531, Montevideo, Uruguay

Aims and objectives. As the Uruguayan section of the International Fellowship of Reconciliation, this group, since its creation in 1940, has been particularly concerned to advance the cause of conscientious objectors, although the scope of its activities has been limited by the existence of military rule.

Peace and Justice Service
Servicio Paz y Justicia (Serpaj)

Address. Apartado 701, Plaza Independencia 723, Montevideo, Uruguay

INDEX OF MOVEMENTS

Page references in bold type indicate main entries.

INDEX OF PUBLICATIONS